THE POLITICAL ECONOMY OF EUROPEAN INTEGRATION

THE POLITICAL ECONOMY OF EUROPEAN INTEGRATION

States, Markets and Institutions

Edited by

Paolo Guerrieri
University of Rome

Pier Carlo Padoan
University of Urbino

BARNES & NOBLE BOOKS
Savage, Maryland

First published in the United States of America 1989 by
BARNES & NOBLE BOOKS
8057 Bollman Place, Savage, MD 20763

ISBN 0-389-20891-4

Library of Congress Cataloging-in-Publication Data

The Political economy of European integration: markets and
  institutions / edited by Paolo Guerrieri, Pier Carlo Padoan.
    p.   cm.
  Includes bibliographical references.
  ISBN 0-389-20891-4
  1. Europe—Economic integration.   2. Monetary policy—European
Economic Community countries.   3. European Monetary System
(Organization)   4. European Economic Community countries—Economic
policy. I. Guerrieri. Paolo, 1933–   . II. Padoan, Pier Carlo.
HC241.P58   1989
337.1'42—dc20   89-17759
                                                               CIP

Printed in Great Britain

1 2 3 4 5   93 92 91 90 89

CONTENTS

CONTRIBUTORS

Benjamin J. Cohen, Fletcher School of Law and Diplomacy, Tufts University, Medford, MA

Marcello De Cecco, University of Rome

John B. Goodman, Graduate School of Business Administration, Harvard University

Peter A. Gourevitch, University of San Diego

Paolo Guerrieri, University of Rome

Louka T. Katseli, University of Athens, NBER and the Centre for Economic Policy Research, London

Pier Carlo Padoan, University of Urbino

Jacques Pelkmans, European Institute of Public Administration, Maastricht

Pascal Petit, CEPREMAP, Paris

Elke Thiel, Stiftung Wissenschaft und Politik, Research Institute for International Affairs, Ebenhausen

Loukas Tsoukalis, St Antony's College, Oxford University and College of Europe, Bruges

FOREWORD

The essays contained in this volume are original contributions developed in a research project directed by Paolo Guerrieri and Pier Carlo Padoan at the Centro Europa Ricerche in Rome.

The topic of the project is on the process of co-operation and integration in Europe, which is presently undergoing a new and exciting phase. The approach follows the 'International Political Economy', a rising field which considers in a unified view political and economic determinants of the relations among markets, states and institutions in the international system. Each of the essays considers a particular aspect of the process of European integration. The overall product, we hope, provides a unified picture which is then reconsidered with respect to three national experiences: France, Germany and Italy.

The Centro Europa Ricerche wishes to thank the Commission of European Communities and the Istituto San Paolo di Torino for having made such an effort possible. A special thanks is due to Cristina Boitani and to Antonella Pirro for extremely patient and competent secretarial assistance.

INTRODUCTION

Over the past 15 years the international economic system has changed its hegemonic structure into an interdependent oligopoly, i.e. a system which is characterized by a small number of leading countries. The hegemonic (Bretton Woods) structure allowed for the supply of a particular public good, an international system. In the oligopolistic system, on the contrary, the supply of such a public good falls short of demand. This is due to the fact that in such a system each leading country is able to constrain the other's decision while not being able to impose its own solution to arising conflicts.

The state of unrest of international relations is a clear sign of such difficulties. Lack of a single leading country requires that leadership is to be provided by the interaction of several countries. The search for more co-operation has become the major problem in international relations as well as the pressing suggestion of scholars and experts. It remains, however, difficult to fulfil.

This volume presents the results of research on the process of co-operation in Europe. The European case is well suited to consider the issue of co-operation without hegemony. No single European country, not even Germany, is in the position to act as a hegemon, while it is crucially the interaction among a small number of medium-sized countries which makes Europe a typical example of oligopolistic interdependence. These countries must establish and enforce rules in financial, monetary and commercial relations.

In the essays contained in this volume the experience of three major countries in continental Europe – France, Germany and Italy – is examined with respect to both domestic and international aspects of policy formation. The studies presented are based on the 'international political economy' which aims to analyze the political base of economic choices.

The essay by Guerrieri and Padoan (Chapter 1) considers the paradox present in traditional integration theory. According to the traditional approach the benefits of integration are more easily obtainable by the unilateral adoption of free trade and financial policies on the part of individual countries. This implies that there are no incentives to implement integration policies; it is necessary, therefore, to explain the diffusion of integration processes. This is possible by jointly considering economic and political aspects in the production of the public goods involved in the process of integration.

This, however, gives rise to both co-operation and conflict among the countries involved. These elements clearly emerge if one takes into consideration the dynamic effects of integration, deriving from economies of scale and technological innovations. It also appears that governments play a central role in influencing the process of increasing specialization and in minimizing the costs of adjustment. In other words the benefits of the integration process are the result of competition both among market forces and among nation states.

Starting from this premiss the essay considers the interaction among governments in the integration process. The role of macroeconomic regimes is considered, i.e. the set of policies which determine the amount and distribution of effective demand which is a preliminary condition for the success of the integration process. The formation of a macroeconomic regime is hindered by the widespread mercantilistic tendencies in European countries and in the largest one in particular.

Taking regime theory into consideration one may exclude that the EMS is organized as a hegemonic regime since Germany cannot be considered a hegemonic country. It follows that co-operation in continental Europe must be analyzed with the help of the theory of co-operation without hegemony which requires the following conditions to be fulfilled: lengthening of the time horizon, minimization of the factors involved, alteration of national preferences.

This last point deserves particular attention. The essay suggests that there is a connection between national preferences, as they are revealed from macroeconomic policies, and the structure of economic systems. The process of integration brings about the goal of increased structural competitiveness defined as the ability of a country to reach high rates of growth in international markets. Structural competitiveness, in turn, depends on the interaction of the economic structure with the political and social structure. An improvement in national competitiveness requires the alteration of national preferences: inter-state and intra-state policies. This is analyzed in a simple conceptual framework.

Louka Katseli in Chapter 2 investigates the economic, political and institutional factors which determined macroeconomic policy in Europe during the 1980s. To explain these policies one must take into consideration first of all the development of international monetary and financial relations in the last few years. Growing world financial inter-dependence and the dominance of a few hard currencies in international transactions has had profound implications for the relative bargaining power of countries in dictating macroeconomic policy. A hierarchical and oligopolistic system of decision-making has in fact developed internationally. Key players in that system are the United States, West Germany and Japan. Market power in this bargaining game is more a function of portfolio holders' asset preferences across these currencies than a function of predominance over world trade. This system of decision-making has adopted a supervisory role in the functioning of the international monetary system. Bargaining over macro-policy in that set-up involves to a large extent the management of exchange rates internationally. Thus, at the same time that decision-making has been relegated to a few international actors, central bankers have increased their influence in dictating policy outcomes. *Ceteris paribus*, these two trends taken together exercise a deflationary bias on policy outcome. It is the asymmetries in financial interdependence across countries and the departure from a purely competitive system in international finance that introduces political factors into the analysis. The deflationary bias is made worse by the increasing costs of forming sustainable coalitions against the pursuit of such policies.

Within that framework, during the 1980s, both the policy stance in Europe and the choice of policy instruments were dictated by the net benefits derived by the key players in the system. In the early 1980s co-ordinated fiscal expansion was against West Germany's perceived interests which coincided with the interests of European central banks and domestic capital. Instead fiscal deflation, monetary contraction and tough wage policies were aggressively pursued. Today a unilateral fiscal expansion by West Germany is mildly acceptable. The way in which reflation or expansion takes place also depends to a large extent on political and institutional factors. The same can be said for deflation.

In conclusion, the unemployment problem in Europe today is as much an 'institutional' and 'political' problem as an 'economic' one. It highlights our failure as an international community to develop representative institutions that can cope effectively with the complexity of economic policy in a world of flexible exchange rates and financial interdependence.

The European Monetary System is analyzed by Loukas Tsoukalis and Marcello De Cecco in Chapters 3 and 4. In a world of generalized floating, characterized by high instability of exchange rates, the European Monetary System (EMS) has helped to curb overshooting and also avoid long periods of misalignment of participating currencies. The EMS has also served as an important instrument in the fight against inflation. The system of stable exchange rates and the pegging of national currencies to the D-Mark have created an external discipline which seems to have reinforced the determination of national authorities in the pursuit of anti-inflationary policies.

The EMS can be considered as a major step towards the creation of a regional currency bloc and a collective system of decision-making. Some progress has been made towards a closer co-ordination of monetary policies, with an institutional infrastructure ready to develop along federalist lines, once the political will exists. Exchange rate changes have become a matter of collective decisions.

The EMS has coincided with a long period of low growth and high unemployment in Western Europe. Therefore, the question which needs to be asked is whether there has been a simple coincidence or some form of correlation between the two.

Because of its economic weight and the combination of low inflation, high unemployment and large current account surpluses, the Federal Republic of Germany has been considered as the natural candidate for stimulating demand and growth in Western Europe. To the extent, therefore, that there has been, and still is, room for non-inflationary expansion of aggregate demand, the continuous refusal of Germany to move in this direction has acted as an important constraint for the other European countries.

The role of Germany in the EMS differs in many respects from previous historical examples of leading countries. The leading country in the EMS does not provide the financial centre for the region as a whole. Second, and more important, is that, unlike Britain and the United States in the past, the Federal Republic has not adopted a policy of 'benign neglect' towards its balance of payments. On the contrary, the German economy has very much relied on export-led growth, with some clear elements of mercantilism in the policies pursued. Finally Germany's dominant economic position is only partially supported by a similar position in the political sphere.

The general attitude towards the EMS appears to be positive in all participating countries. This is true of both political and business circles. There are, however, important national differences in the evaluation of the EMS experience.

France has always attached considerable importance to exchange rate stability. Participation in the EMS has also served as an anti-inflationary instrument and as a weapon against protectionist pressures inside the previous Socialist government, especially in 1982–3. Capital controls have been used, sometimes very effectively, as a shield protecting domestic economic agents from the large fluctuations – mainly upwards – of interest rates in offshore markets.

The external discipline function of the EMS has been more important in the case of Italy, where the Banca d'Italia has used the participation of the lira in the exchange rate mechanism (ERM) as an important anti-inflationary weapon *vis-à-vis* Italian industry, the trade unions and even the political establishment. The progressive overvaluation of the lira has been a deliberate choice. The wider margins of fluctuation may have given Italian authorities more room for manoeuvre in terms of monetary policy. At the same time, they may have also reduced Italy's influence over the development of the system.

The peculiar position of the German economy in Europe has dominated the evolution of the EMS in its first experience but it is also bound to influence its future development. The transition to the second phase of the EMS, which should have taken off two years after the implementation of exchange agreements, is still there to be started. Several proposals have been advanced but what seems to be lacking is the political agreement. On the other hand if one examines the political characteristics of the EMS the future of the agreements does not appear too favourable. If one accepts the view that Germany's low-growth strategy is dictated by structural factors which are also deeply rooted in its socio-economic framework the support that Germany will be able to provide to European monetary agreements cannot be very far off from the one that has prevailed so far, i.e. in a way which can hardly be considered as desirable by other major EMS members. The end of favourable external factors, such as the revaluing dollar and high US growth, will make internal problems more difficult and conflicting interests will come to the surface. What seems to lie ahead, in other words, is that the destiny of European integration will largely depend, as in the past, upon factors taking place outside Europe.

A question to be addressed is whether the possible 'deflationary bias' in the EMS, especially in the years since 1981, has prompted Member States to become more protectionist and hence undermining the common market. The short answer is given by Jacques Pelkmans in Chapter 5. He argues that there may have been some additional protectionist impact. If so, it is not of great importance and is overshadowed by other reasons for protection. These include the restrictive effects of the structure of (national and partly European Community (EC)) protection already in place; and new initiatives, going in exactly the opposite direction (namely, the completion of the Internal Market).

Certainly, some impact has taken place. Proof of the proposition, however, is technically impossible. One has to interpret. It is possible to trace some instances where the recent increase in protection may well be a response to the serious demand constraints (including an interest squeeze) having accompanied the consolidation of the EMS and the convergence at a low rate of inflation.

But the protectionist impact was not of great importance. Even if the proposition would account for all the increase in voluntary export restraints (VERs), public aid and export subsidies, it has clearly not threatened the common market as a whole – only some sectors. There are other reasons for protection. In particular, where there was a marked increase in protection it was almost always sectoral (except export subsidies).

As regards the national protection still in place, we could remark that:

protection in place became more 'visible' in the early 1980s, but was already there; the neo-protectionism frequently emerged in times of flexible rates (the 1970s), i.e. before the EMS; existing protection may be discretionary to some extent, and this may lead to complaints in difficult periods; the EC level – and not the effect of individual Member States against one another – increased protection externally; in steel and agriculture, output quotas were introduced, but certainly not for macroeconomic reasons.

About the new initiatives, the Cockfield initiative on the White Paper is now ratified via the Single Act. It is in full swing. There are problems but it is not justified to deny that it has only a marginal impact. Yet, it did and does coincide with the convergence issue in the EMS. To sum up, the implications of the possible 'deflationary bias' in the EMS for the internal market are at worst, modest and largely transitory. Other causes and pressures should be considered as more relevant.

Benjamin Cohen (Chapter 6) analyzes the political economy of financial integration in the EC. The 'politics' of EC financial integration can best be understood as a problem of collective action, a game involving two separate but interrelated levels of play – inter-state and intra-state. Financial integration itself is understood as a kind of public good in scarce supply, demanding direct and explicit co-operation among the Community's members to overcome inherent tendencies toward underproduction. In this context one faces the classic collective-action dilemma of how to avoid underproduction of a public good. At least one state individually must be willing to pay disproportionately for the collective goal of financial integration. Is there any such state in the EC today?

The obvious candidate is Germany, which is already the dominant financial power on the European continent. Indeed, were Germany to play this role it would be perfectly consistent with the 'theory of hegemonic stability'. But will the hegemon's incentive suffice to persuade Germany to play role of paymaster on behalf of financial integration? At this level the issue is whether or how, given established state preferences, systemic constraints or incentives for state behaviour might be manipulated to enhance prospects for co-operation. In addition to the strategic game played between states (international politics) is a game played within states (domestic politics) between supporters and opponents of a single banking market both inside and outside of government.

At this level of analysis, then, the practical challenge is to identify just which domestic forces are most influential on the specific issue of financial integration and to investigate just how their interaction in each EC member affects the determination of observed policy preferences over time. 'Governmental models', for example, point to the critical role that may be played by key bureaucratic entities whose institutional interests might seem threatened by the creation of a single banking market.

For central banks, the risk that financial integration poses for the auto-nomy of national monetary policy would inevitably translate into losses of power, prestige, and privileges within the apparatus of political authority. In parallel fashion, societal models point to the critical role that may be played by key actors outside the public sector, where individual incentives could also diverge sharply from collective incentrives.

At the level of domestic politics (unit-level analysis) the issue then is whether and how, given the broader system of inter-state relations, the domestic structures of states might be manipulated to enchance prospects for co-operation. As a final stage of analysis, we must also explore how and to what extent the internal processes of state may be constrained or influenced by their external environment. At this two-level analysis the issue is whether or how, given both the existing inter-state system and established state preferences, external interdependencies might be mani-pulated to alter international policy processes.

In Chapter 7 John Goodman analyzes the politics of monetary policy in France, Germany and Italy. The literature on the determinants of mone-tary policy tends to fall within two alternative perspectives. The first one is the economist's approach based on 'reaction-function' analysis. The second perspective, by contrast, is grounded in concepts of political science: par-ties, elections, and interest groups. Implicitly, it adopts the vantage point of a large country with a more closed economy.

Each of the two perspectives offers useful insights into the process of monetary policy-making, but neither alone provides an adequate basis for explaining monetary policy in medium-sized countries, such as France, Italy and Germany. These countries are neither so small that their mone-tary policies are determined by international economic pressures, nor are they so large that their policies primarily reflect domestic concerns. In medium-sized countries, monetary policy is more likely to reflect the tension between international economic factors and domestic political ones. The key to understanding the process of monetary policy-making in a medium-sized country, therefore, is to determine the logic of the inter-action between these two different kinds of factors. That logic turns upon the role of institutions.

The past diversity and current conformity of monetary policy in France, Italy and Germany may be explained by the reactions of national mone-tary authorities to the increasing pressure of financial integration. The ability of the monetary authorities in France, Italy and Germany to pursue monetary policies has been dramatically reduced by this increase in financial integration. Comparing the experiences of the three countries reveals that the effects of financial integration were more significant in France and Italy than in Germany. This difference is explained by the asymmetry of the adjustment process between countries that face down-ward pressure on their exchange rates and countries that face upward pressure, as well as the effects and opportunities of international regimes.

Domestic factors are not irrelevant to the degree of autonomy a country enjoys in the international financial system or to the process of adjustment to the external constraint. France, Italy and Germany did not all face the same burden of adjustment. The critical difference between the three countries was the degree of central bank independence from the government. Where the central bank is independent, as in Germany and post-1981 Italy, monetary policy is relatively free from partisan and other political influences and will be more anti-inflationary. Where it is dependent, as in France and pre-1981 Italy, monetary policy will be more sensitive to political influence.

The significance of the party control of government hinges on the degree of central bank independence. In Germany, changes in political parties had little effect on the conduct of monetary policy. Similar party changes were more important in France and Italy although they appeared to be overwhelmed in the early 1970s by other domestic factors – in particular the role of labour. The effects of party control declined over time as policymakers recognized the increasing power of the external constraint. Labour power and militancy help account for variations in monetary policy across both nations and time. Countries with less militant working classes are more able to conduct restrictive monetary policies than are countries with highly militant working classes. But even when labour is highly militant, the independent status of a central bank may permit monetary policy to be tightened. As labour power has declined, countries have become increasingly able to practise monetary restriction.

Chapters 8 and 9 contain two case studies on the domestic base of national economic policies in France and Germany, two key countries in the process of European integration. Elke Thiel states that since Germany has experienced two periods of extensive inflation after World War One and World War Two, price stability has always been the dominant political priority. Price stability is considered as an indispensable means to secure a social consensus regarding income distribution, to protect private savings and to prevent creditors from deprivation. This objective has always been strongly supported by all domestic groups, including the trade unions.

The German Bundesbank is committed to defending price stability by constitution and its status of autonomy provides the political independence to enforce this goal. All German governments have been very cautious to avoid any open conflict with the Bundesbank on monetary policy issues. Moreover, governments have been strongly aware that increasing inflation will erode confidence in the ruling coalitions and may thus endanger re-election.

More than any other country, in the Bretton Woods period Germany had been faced with the policy dilemma of achieving price stability and exchange-rate stability simultaneously. Exchange-market interventions to keep the D-Mark pegged to the dollar poured hot money into the country so that the Bundesbank lost control over money supply. D-Mark appreciation offered an escape, but decisions to adjust parities were always taken too late to prevent inflationary pressures. In view of a high specialization in modern production and comparatively small domestic markets, German firms have to rely on foreign markets to achieve economies of large scale. D-Mark overvaluation thus threatens domestic economic activities and employment. German domestic production would, however, come to a halt, if it were not fuelled by imports of energy, raw materials and semi-finished products. A decline in the external value of the D-Mark will therefore have an immediate effect on domestic inflation. This may help to explain recent remarks on the part of German economic officials that world economic growth is pre-eminently threatened by exchange-rate fluctuations and not by failures to achieve domestic expansion via macroeconomic policy co-ordination.

Under conditions of floating, the Bundesbank has frequently been faced with the policy problem of defending price stability and calming down exchange-rate fluctuations simultaneously. The strategy has been to keep both objectives in a delicate balance, but the dominant emphasis has been to prevent inflation.

At the international level, the ensuing debate on macroeconomic policy co-ordination focused on the locomotive approach, which was, and is, strongly opposed by most of the German economic research institutes and by economic authorities as well. Objections primarily focus on the demand-side approach of the locomotive strategy and the underlying assumptions concerning the international transmission of expansionary effects.

The European Monetary System is strongly supported by the German government and the Bundesbank as being complementary to the implementation of the internal market. Common market transactions, e.g. about 50 per cent of German trade, will benefit from monetary and price stability. It is doubted, however, whether German leadership can safeguard price stability, if this goal is not also strongly supported by other principal members of the EMS. German officials have, for instance, favoured a British participation within the system for this reason. The achievement of the Internal Market will link monetary policies more closely. If monetary autonomy is forgone, it is, however, most important to resist any pressures to compromise on inflation from a German point of view.

French foreign economic policy is analyzed by Pascal Petit in Chapter 9. He considers two starting points representing a somewhat different approach with respect to other papers included in this research. The first one is that the analysis of the external constraint on macroeconomic policies is considered in the broader context of the policies of the French state *vis-à-vis* the rest of the world over a very long time. The second one is the idea that the state is a multi-faceted entity which bears the signs of its history. In particular, the role of the state is considered in monetary relations, trade relations and power (military and strategic) relations.

A long (historical) perspective highlights certain aspects which crucially affect contemporary external policy-making in France. These elements may help to understand the different ways in which the French economy has adapted itself to a changing international environment. In the expansionary (hegemonic) period French foreign economic policy has been characterized: (a) in political and military relations by the dismantling of the colonial empire and by a drawback from strategic involvment in defence affairs; (b) in monetary relations by a policy of competitive devaluations, and (c) in trade relations by a participation in the extension of new markets by the support of liberal trade policies. This period witnesses a strong interaction of economic and political (power) relations.

During the 1970s the way in which the French economy was integrated into the world economy has changed completely primarily as a consequence of floating exchange rates and the slow-down in the process of growth. Within such an environment the margins for a policy of power have been curtailed. The strategy of 'grandeur' has tended to vanish as a consequence of trade problems. The favourable structure of trade which had developed in the previous period is threatened.

The fragility of the trade structure emerges through triangular trade and the dispersion of 'strong points' in foreign trade. Increasing trade integration within the European community reduced margins for an autonomous industrial policy within the country especially in the period 1981–3 and with respect to the less-concentrated sectors (textiles, machinery, wood).

As far as monetary policy is concerned the collapse of the Bretton Woods system and the integration of financial markets has put heavy pressure on a weak currency such as the French making the strategy of competitive devaluations pursued in the 1970s less and less attractive. In this perspective the entry into the European Monetary System has been considered primarily as a protection against the fluctuations of the dollar. The price for this was the (almost complete) inhibition to pursue competitive devaluations *vis-à-vis* the D-Mark. The perspectives for a larger degree of autonomy for French economic policy are seen as dependent on a set of conditions at international, European and national level.

The last chapter (10) is dedicated to the politics of economic policy choice of European and other major countries in the post-war era. To explore the politics of the post-war economic policy debate, Gourevitch uses two sets of analytic tools:

1. A typology of policy alternatives around which the debate took place.
2. A typology of political factors or explanations, the causal variables which shaped choices from among these policy alternatives.

All the countries in the decade after World War Two moved towards a social compromise. The political formulas have different labels but roughly the formula involves compromise on the hard positions of pre-war years. The left accepted the market and property rights. The capitalists accepted trade unions and collective bargaining in a constitutionalist political framework, and the welfare state. Both groups supported agricultural programmes while the agricultural sector accepted support of industrial goals. All groups supported relatively open access to the international economy. All groups accepted some measures of government intervention and regulation.

The very success of the post-war boom sowed the seeds of subsequent difficulties – we cannot say 'destruction' because the historical compromise has by no means been destroyed. It is none the less under considerable strain. That strain derives in large measure from changes in the international economy engendered by the post-war boom itself.

These changes meant new costs and new opportunities. Economic changes altered the pay-offs of various policy and political arrangements. In each country, stiff foreign constraints put pressure on costs. To be competitive, costs must be cut – but who will bear that cost? Each group seeks to shift the blame and the burden on another. The politics of accommodation shifts to the politics of blame.

The historical compromise of the post-war years was possible because recent experiences provided the framework for compromise; in the current situation the need for compromise seems less obvious – each group is tempted instead to make others pay costs. As the relationships among societal actors has changed over time, so has the relationship of the state to society in ways which shape policy outcomes.

When the crisis of the 1970s began, the political meaning of state action had changed. Activism was the incumbent philosophy, and the catch-all state had replaced the night-watchman state. With the shift in the ideological location of state action have come important changes in the relationship of intermediate associations and state institutions in mediating the relationship between social pressures and policy outputs.

As the state has become more active, more able to intervene, the mechanisms which link the state to society have grown in importance as well. The more active state is both more powerful and more constrained. Its interventions frequently require the complicity of forces it seeks to regulate or direct. State action is frequently corporatistic – state and groups borrow from each other the authority to do what they cannot do alone.

The broad changes previously analyzed – in cleavages around economic issues among social actors, in the institutions of intermediate associations, political parties and the state, in economic ideology, and in international factors – have altered the political context of economic policy debates in Western Europe and North America. The issues which defined the post-war settlement and the policy cleavages of the period of high Keynesianism have been altered. The specific manifestation, however, of these general points alters from country to country.

1 · INTEGRATION, CO-OPERATION AND ADJUSTMENT POLICIES

Paolo Guerrieri and Pier Carlo Padoan

INTRODUCTION

International integration has been long debated in economic analysis and it has recently acquired revived popularity thanks to new theoretical results and to relevant policy changes such as the start of the European Internal Market. As is well known, standard theory does not provide adequate justification, from an economic viewpoint, for national choices in favour of integration. It is, however, possible to explain the wide diffusion of integration agreements by following new research developments in the field which allow us to reinterpret costs and benefits of integration, with respect both to single countries and to the area as a whole.

The main point suggested by the new approach is that integration offers collective benefits for the whole of the participating countries and individual incentives for each of them to pursue adjustment policies. The latter, if generalized, may hinder the exploitation of collective benefits. In such a perspective economic integration may be interpreted as a classic problem of collective action which may be studied with the help of those analytical techniques developed by the 'international political economy' approach and often applied in the investigation of the processes of international co-operation. This chapter proposes a conceptual framework within which to investigate the process of integration as well as the problems met in such a process by the specific European countries whose experiences are analyzed in other chapters of this volume.

The discussion is structured as follows. The following two sections briefly review existing micro- and macro-integration theories. Section three uses the results offered by 'international political economy' in the analysis of international co-operation to investigate the costs and benefits of integration and the redistributive conflicts which arise in the process of integration and in the implementation of the adjustment policies which the process activates. Section four discusses the concept of structural competitiveness linking economic and political determinants. Section five discusses the domestic determinants of adjustment policies and tries to integrate elements concerning the economic structure with aspects of the political and institutional system following the lines of the 'political economy of growth'. Section six offers a conceptual framework which integrates domestic and international politico-economic determinants of the policy choices of states involved in the process of integration.

INTEGRATION IN TRADE AND INDUSTRY AND POTENTIAL INTRA-NATIONAL CONFLICTS

Analysis of integration investigates a wide range of topics, including the removal of trade barriers, the establishment of co-ordination rules and the implementation of processes of co-operation.[1] Traditional theory, as is well known, has taken into consideration the economic aspects of the formation of a custom union stressing the analysis of the so called 'static' effects of integration on trade flows determined by the new enlarged market, both on the union members and on third countries.[2] These include the well known 'trade creation' and 'trade diversion' effects (Johnson 1962), the former being the creation of trade flows among the members of the union which displace the more costly domestic production and the latter being the substitution of imports from non member countries with imports from member ones. Integration will increase output and hence welfare in member countries if the net result is the creation of new trade flows. Only in such a case the integration process will benefit the member countries as these will exploit the advantages of the greater efficiency which derives from the increased specialization.

This very elegant framework, however, raises serious analytical problems. As has been noticed (Johnson 1965; Robson 1984) if the results of the integration process are those claimed by the standard approach it is no longer possible to provide rational justifications for the choices of single countries in favour of the formation of custom unions or of other forms of integration. It can be shown, on traditional lines, that benefits accruing from the integration process (net trade creation) with the exception of terms-of-trade aspects,[3] are equally or even more efficiently obtained through the unilateral adoption by single countries of free trade policies aimed at the abolition of existing barriers to trade. Such a strategy allows avoidance of the undesirable 'trade diversion' effects produced by the integration process.

Now, if no pure economic justifications exist for the pursuit of integration processes by single countries, it remains an open question why integration processes at different levels are so widely undertaken. The traditional 'non-economic' explanations suggested by traditional theory

(Krauss 1972) which stress the role of non-economic targets (defence, national prestige, etc.) in integration processes cannot be considered as satisfactory. Non-economic factors do play an important role, and they will be considered below, but their consideration still leaves open the question of providing economic justifications for the formation of integrated areas.

A more satisfactory approach involves abandoning the traditional theoretical model in its more rigid formulation. A first solution–which permits retaining the traditional model–consists of the introduction of collective goals (such as the growth of employment and production, social stability, distributive justice) in the social welfare function of each country in addition to individual goods (Johnson; Cooper and Massel 1965; El-Agraa 1984). In such a case one takes into account the role of the state in the production of public goods. The hypothesis that is implicit in such an approach is that, on the one hand the optimal solution to the problem of the integration of national productive systems is the formation of the largest possible unified market; on the other hand the economic justifications of the role of nation states lies in the existence, and in the necessity, of production of collective goods for which single states may have different preferences (Cooper 1977; Kindleberger 1978). In such a case it can be shown that the formation of a custom union allows for the production of public and private goods by national governments in a more efficient way than in the case of unilateral adoption of free-trade policies.

In such a case a policy of preferential agreements is economically efficient in the production of a number of public goods as it decreases the supply costs measured in terms of private goods (Johnson 1965; Cooper-Massel 1965). In such a case, in addition, the participation of single countries in an integrated area is coherent with the assumption of rationality insofar as it is aimed at an efficient production of public goods which satisfy collective preferences. It also minimizes the difference between private and public costs (and benefits). These results are invariant with respect to the kind of public good involved and may be extended to a wide range of cases where externalities are present.

An important implication of the above analysis is that the pursuit of national efficiency goals, which imply different combinations of private and public goods, influences in different ways the processes and strategies of the single countries participating in the agreement. This leads to the appearance of both co-operation and conflict opportunities in the distribution of benefits accruing from the integration process, both among and within countries (Johnson 1965).

Opportunities of conflict and co-operation emerge more neatly, however, if the so-called dynamic effects of integration are taken into account. Dynamic effects are felt, in the first place, on the internal organization of industries and subsequently on the behaviour of firms under competitive conditions, on the existence of dynamic returns to scale, on the change in production processes deriving from the enlargement of the market and from the creation of a single economic space.

These effects, as is well known, cannot be studied within a traditional approach due, in particular, to the rigidity of its underlying assumptions.[4] New ideas in this field have been advanced by the recent, and less-recent, developments in trade and trade-policy theory. The abandonment of the more restrictive assumptions of the traditional factor scarcity model – in particular the assumption of perfect competition among and within countries – has led to identifying the foundations of international exchange in elements different from factor scarcity such as returns-to-scale, product differentiation, and technology (Helpman and Krugman 1985).

Gains from integration may be reconsidered within this new theoretical framework. Its results challenge much of the conventional wisdom and offer new perspectives in the understanding of national policy choices. Let us first consider the advantages of integration accruing from returns to scale. Increasing returns in production deriving from static (dimensions of productive units) and especially dynamic (learning by doing) economies of scale allow firms to exploit the larger market dimensions in terms of more efficient productive organizations. This is more relevant in the European case if one considers that the largest part of intra-European trade is made up of the simultaneous import and export of goods belonging to the same production sector or branch – intra-industry trade – and which represent different varieties of the same product (because of differences in quality, design, brand) and whose production is greatly affected by economies of scale.[5]

Secondly the advantages of technological innovation must be considered. This phenomenon, as is well known, can produce relevant fall-outs outside the single firm or industry which, in some cases, may be of such a magnitude as to influence the productive system of the country as a whole (Dasgupta 1987). The production of such externalities, however, requires R&D investments and markets whose dimensions are larger than the domestic ones and which may be obtained only through a process of integration (Jacquemin and Sapir 1987).

Finally one must consider the positive effects which descend from increased competition deriving from the process of integration. These effects are particularly important if the starting scenario at the national level implies imperfect competition rather than atomistic competition as assumed by traditional analysis.

The recognition, which has been made possible by the consideration of new trade theories, of the fact that benefits from integration may derive from factors such as economies of scale and technological innovations brings in also the recognition of the fact that there exist potential conflicts among countries in the distribution of such benefits.

An important element in this respect is the fact that, in a world of monopolistic and oligopolistic competition, market forces may lead to an increase in the geographical concentration of the benefits and in the production of goods thus leading to a deepening of existing disparities. At the same time it must be understood that government policies, targeted at influencing specialization strategies of the single countries and at minimizing the adjustment costs brought by the integration process represent, at least in principle, instruments which may significantly affect the results brought about by market forces.[6]

It can be shown that each member of the integrated area, while sustaining its own firms in international competition through a 'strategic adjustment policy' in industry and trade, can try to increase its share of integration benefits even if at the expense of the remaining countries.[7] In such a context what is most relevant are the dangers of the potential conflicts which may arise among the Member States on the distribution of net benefits deriving from the process of integration. These conflicts may give rise to different outcomes according to the policies which are adopted, including those which would lead to a complete arrest of the integration process, in spite of the benefits which this could produce (Krugman 1987).

To sum up. It is certainly true that it is convenient for a group of countries to foster a process of integration as this permits exploiting each national resource to the full, in terms of productive capacity and the production of public goods, given the dynamic effects which were recalled above. It is also true, however, that the benefits from integration may be unequally distributed among member countries and that such a distribution depends on the kind and the effectiveness of national adjustment policies. Nationalistic policies of the 'beggar-thy-neighbour' kind may be fully justified from an economic viewpoint if they are aimed at improving the nation's share of the benefits from the integration process. Such policies, however, decrease the net benefits of the other participants in the integration process and tend to set up reactions that may lead to an arrest of the process itself.

ECONOMIC INTEGRATION AND THE MACROECONOMIC REGIME

At the industrial and commercial level market integration processes determine both overall benefits for member economies and incentives for each single country to implement policies which are unilaterally remunerative but highly harmful when they are generalized. The other dimensions of economic integration, such as monetary and financial ones, display similar distinctive features. Other chapters in this volume deal at length with these different aspects of integration so there is no need to dwell upon them here. However it is important to focus on the link among the various areas of integration (industry, trade and finance), which is often neglected in the analysis. This requires taking into consideration the macroeconomic environment of integration.

A suitable starting point is the assumption that a high and stable rate of growth improves the benefits stemming from the different dimensions of the integration process. It has been shown, for example, that the benefits of productive and commercial integration increase with the rate of growth of member countries' trade flows and, hence, with the rate of growth of integrated areas' overall production (Easton-Grubel 1982). It may also be added that while trade liberalization influences the allocation of trade flows among member countries, macroeconomic regimes determine the overall size of trade. Most of the empirical tests of the benefits of protection have so far failed to produce convincing evidence in favour of market integration processes because they have concentrated on static benefits (El-Agraa 1987), overlooking the dynamic benefits connected with the overall expansion of an integrated area.

As far as financial relations are concerned it is well known that a market's integration reinforces the macroeconomic interdependence of member countries whatever exchange rates regime is adopted (Gandolfo 1986). Macroeconomic adjustment to external imbalances is less costly in a growing integrated system as weak (deficit) member countries are less pressed by mercantilistic policies of strong (surplus) ones. At the same time, in a growing context less pressure is put on exchange rates for adjustment processes and, hence, monetary arrangements and capital mobility are easier to sustain.

In a stagnant or deflationary environment opposite results are obtained. Nationalistic 'strategic trade policies' spread rapidly, especially in deficit countries, which also ask for derogations and exemptions in the financial area to limit the effects of capital mobility; payment imbalances call for large devaluations which impose increasing strains on monetary relations. In all these cases the role of domestic interest groups in shaping foreign economic policies increases (Katzenstein 1978) as do the conflicts among member countries in the integrated area. Consequently, the governments' capacity to formulate and implement coherent and stable economic policies decreases.

To sum up, the consideration of the role played by the rate of growth makes the links among different dimensions of integration such as trade, money and finance clearer, which – as noted above – are often neglected in the analysis of economic integration. There are two implications of this. The first one is that a stable and high rate of growth, by increasing the effects of integration in different areas, creates positive issue linkages and, hence, sustains favourable supply conditions in product and factor markets. These are in terms of higher specialization, flexibility and competition, which interact positively with demand conditions. On the contrary, an unstable and stagnant macroeconomic environment may decrease and even cut out the benefits of integration, the microeconomic ones too.

The second implication enlightens a sort of hierarchy among different dimensions of integration. As has been shown by the post-war period, different integration regimes display different degrees of resistance to macroeconomic crises. In general it is hardly questionable that the exchange rates regime is the weakest one, since it has to bear the first brunt of the crisis and, hence, it will be rapidly changed. The finance regime follows in terms of resistance, especially if it is based mostly on market forces, as the experience of the last decade has shown. Finally we place the trade regime which until now has shown remarkable resistance to turbulence in macro–monetary relations. If it is true that macroeconomic environment plays a relevant role in the development of integration process, it is also true that a high and stable rate of growth is difficult to achieve insofar as the degree of interdependence is very high among member countries (Buiter-Marston 1985; Cooper 1985). Demand and supply factors, as is well known, both contribute to the economy's expansion. In the European case, in particular, many agree that improving growth prospects requires an expansionary policy of domestic effective demand of the EC area, in addition to supply policies to increase factor-markets' flexibility.

However, while supply factors depend more closely on domestic structures and policies of single member countries (such as labour market behaviour), in a highly interdependent system, such as the European community, the expansion of effective demand is more closely dependent on the co-ordination of domestic macroeconomic policies (Cooper 1985). All the more so since what is more important to growth is the expectation of effective demand that policy makers convey to market agents.

It follows that a stable growth environment in an integrated area depends both on the co-ordination of member countries' macroeconomic policies, especially of the larger countries, and on the institutional mechanisms which determine the diffusion and stability of expectations. It is highly doubtful that independent and autonomous economic policies implemented by member economies should be able to determine a high and stable rate of growth of the integrated area as a whole. On the contrary, it has been shown that in an oligopolistic interdependent system, which is characterized by a strategic and uncertain confrontation among countries – as in the case of European ones – unilateral and independent national policies are rational and remunerative for each single country insofar as they produce negative effects for the countries as a whole (Oudiz 1985). In an oligopolistic system high and stable growth paths (both current and expected) can be considered as a public good (Wallace, 1983; Colander-Koford 1985), in the sense that macroeconomic co-operation is not only desirable, but is a necessary condition to produce such a good and to avoid serious imbalances in the system, which may hinder the development of the integration process in itself.

Macroeconomic co-operation requires above all that rules of the game for growth be established (Guerrieri-Padoan 1988). This difficult task is related to the problem of asymmetric adjustment between surplus and deficit countries, which, in turn, is rooted in the mercantilistic attitudes of key industrial countries (Guerrieri-Padoan 1986). In an integrated area characterized by oligopolistic relations among member countries and without a leader (hegemon) country, neo-mercantilism induces a deflationary 'bias' on the system which is enhanced by differences in national preferences with respect to growth (Johansen 1982; Van der Broucke 1985).

It may be added that no fully satisfactory solution to this problem may come from strengthening institutions and co-operation in related areas of integration. Monetary agreements can impose indirect constraints on macro-economic policies insofar as these must follow courses which are coherent with exchange-rate agreements. However a monetary system may be quite stable and still produce a deflationary bias on member economies. The EMS is a classical example in this direction (Padoan 1988). Moreover, trade liberalization may promote growth by opening market opportunities and improving supply conditions. However (expected) growth is a precondition for liberalization rather than vice versa. To sum up, a growing environment is a prerequisite for the positive development of the economic integration process and it implies co-operative agreements at macroeconomic level among countries involved.

INTEGRATION AND SYSTEMIC ANALYSES

As we have seen, the main problem with new integration theories is the presence of collective benefits for the whole of the countries taking part in the integration process, but also the existence of incentives for each of them to implement unilateral policies which may make it impossible to reach such collective goals. Unilateral adjustment policies will lead, in the majority of cases, to widespread conflicts and to a stop in the process of integration.

Integration, therefore, poses a problem of collective action with all of its well-known aspects, first of all the distribution of costs and benefits of collective action among and within the participating countries (Olson 1965). The solution of collective-action problems requires 'ad hoc' mechanisms (cooperation) which may reconcile national policies. Relevant contributions have been produced, over the last few years, both by economists and by students of international relations in this area. An analysis of co-operative mechanisms and of their difficulties has been produced thanks to the joint utilization of conceptual frameworks and techniques stemming from both economics and political science. We will now recall them briefly and stress their implications for the analysis of integration, both in general and with respect to the European dimension.

Game theory, which analyzes the formation of choices under conditions of interdependence (Oye 1985) and the theory of collective action, which analyzes the problems associated with the production of public goods, represent the two main tools for investigating the characteristics of a system of decentralized decisions, such as in the case of independent national policies, which does not guarantee optimal results for the whole of the countries involved. The formation of collective choices, in turn, is influenced by the regime within which such choices are made. By regime we mean the set of rules, norms, and institutions which govern the behaviour of the participants to the system (Krasner 1983). The role of institutions is crucial in an interdependent system as they determine the distribution to each participant of information about the behaviour of the remaining participants. The formation of collective choices, finally, is dependent on the distribution of power among the countries involved. For a long period of time it has been assumed that a co-operative agreement (integration) could be established and implemented only if a marked asymmetry in the distribution of power prevailed; more precisely in the presence of a single country (hegemon) significantly larger than the others and therefore able to sustain a more than proportionate share of the costs of supply of the public goods of international co-operation (Kindleberger 1973; Krasner 1976). Such a condition was considered essential to overcome the free-riding behaviour of the countries involved.

Hegemonic stability theory, correctly stated, should hold that the hegemon is the most powerful country. The problem then arises of giving an empirical content to power. The issue is difficult and controversial, yet it cannot be ignored if power is to remain an operational concept. One suggestion can be advanced. Power cannot be associated with only one dimension (such as size). A larger country need not be a more powerful country. Power is associated with a number of variables which interact among themselves.

Keohane (1984) defines four conditions which, in his view, the hegemonic economy must meet in order to fulfill its role in the international economy. The hegemon must exert control over: (a) raw materials; (b) capital; (c) markets; and must hold a competitive advantage in the production of highly valued goods. Strange (1982) suggests a definition of financial power directly associated with the role of a country's currency as an international vehicle of exchange, as well as with the capacity of that country to act as a financial centre in the international system. According to this approach the power of a country derives from the necessity that others have to obtain credit from it. This view may be, partially, associated with the one expressed by Fratianni and De Grauwe (1984) who (implicitly) suggest that a measure of the international financial power of a country is associated (inversely) with the cost of supplying lender-of-last-resort support to commercial as well as central banks of other countries. Lake (1984) provides an interpretation of the transformations of the international system based on long-run productivity changes. His definition emphasizes real aspects of economic power while Strange's approach centres on financial aspects. Keohane's approach is more comprehensive but it does not provide a full definition of the links between the elements of what could be called a 'power vector'.

A related point has been raised by Padoa-Schioppa and Papadia (1984). They discuss a classification of national currencies which are ranked according to their relative quality. The quality of a currency, in turn, is directly related to its purchasing power stability (i.e. inversely correlated to the rate of inflation). The determination of the relative quality of a currency is discussed in an oligopolistic setting. The central banks of each country are considered as oligopolistic firms which are faced with a trade-off between short-term and long-term strategies. Quality is achieved only if a long-term strategy is pursued.

The approach followed by Padoa-Schioppa and Papadia rests on Hayek's (1976) model of currency competition. In an international setting, deterioration of the quality of a currency (inflation) leads to devaluation. Inflation, in turn, depends only on monetary policy. Market forces will punish central banks which choose short-term strategies allowing inflation to depreciate their currencies. Low-quality currencies will be substituted for high-quality ones.

To sum up, the financial power of a country may be taken to be an increasing function of three variables:

1. The extent to which the national currency is used in the international system (quantity).
2. The quality of the currency.
3. The country's ability to adjust to changes in the external environment.

Another link is associated with finance and industry. National financial systems and national industrial systems have developed together and expanded in international markets mutually sustaining each other, although not necessarily having one lead the other (Kindleberger 1983). Success in international trade, in turn, is associated much more with dynamic industrial sectors, technological innovations and hence with the overall behaviour of the growth process.

It follows that financial power and commercial power are closely connected. Commercial power, in turn, is directly connected to the international dimension of the economy (in terms of national product, for instance). Financial power and commercial power, in turn, provide the support for macroeconomic power, i.e. the ability to fulfil the role of 'engine of growth'. In this respect the power of an economy is inversely connected to its degree of openness, both in trade and finance, as the increase in openness increases the vulnerability to external shocks. As we have seen, the overall productivity of a nation can well be taken as a measure of the country's position in the international economy (Lake 1984). However, to associate changes in the country's relative position in the international economy with changes in relative productivity is only a first step.

We have discussed elsewhere (Guerrieri and Padoan 1988a) the criticisms that may be advanced of the theory of hegemonic stability. We must stress here that such a theory cannot be applied to the process of European integration. The European Monetary System (EMS), for instance, which represents the most recent example of a process of integration in Europe, cannot be considered a hegemonic system because it is hard to assume that Germany, the largest country in the EMS and in Europe, has enough economic power to act as a hegemon.

As we have seen above, economic power is a difficult concept to translate in operational terms. Here we will consider only some of the variables which are usually taken into account: economic dimension, degree of openness and international financial position.

As far as the economic dimension (GDP: Gross Domestic Product) and the degree of openness are concerned the German economy is not really different from those of the other major EMS members, France and Italy. Germany would be unable, therefore, to carry on a role similar to that of the United States in the post-war period. It must also be added that unlike the US economy, Germany does not represent the 'engine of growth' of the European economy.

A different argument can be advanced with respect to monetary and financial aspects. Germany's financial position differs from that of the other major European countries both in its role and for the behaviour of its monetary authorities. The D-Mark is the only international currency among those adhering to the exchange rate agreements while the reputation that the Bundesbank has acquired thanks to its conduct ranks high above any other among the industrialized countries. In this respect Germany is in the position to provide partial leadership associated with the supply of the public good of monetary stability. It is hard to consider such a role as a sign of hegemony, however, for at least two reasons. Such a public good ranks high in the preferences of the smaller members of the EMS which have taken up the 'strong currency option' (Thygesen 1979; Moon 1982; Padoan 1988) but not necessarily in the same degree for the larger members of the exchange agreements for which a satisfactory rate of growth is also quite important (Tsoukalis; De Cecco, this volume). In the second place Germany's power in the monetary field depends on relations *vis-à-vis* the

United States while London is still the most important financial centre in Europe. Germany, therefore, does not hold absolute power as in the case of a pure hegemonic system, both because its power is limited to some aspects of monetary relations and because it ultimately depends on the ability to take care of the external policy of the EMS, on behalf of the other member countries *vis-à-vis* the United States, i.e. with respect to a country with which Germany enjoys only a 'relative' monetary power.

The power relations among European countries in the 1980s suggest that the European Community may be defined as a system of oligopolistic interdependence. In such a case integration will be possible only to the extent that it will be the outcome of a joint (co-operative) effort. In this respect, rather than a hegemon, Germany can be defined an oligopolist leader, albeit the most influential, which may unilaterally stop any integration process undertaken by the other European countries. This defines the terms of the integration problem in Europe today. How is it possible to develop an integration process when the leading country intends to define the public good of integration in terms (such as monetary stability) which may contrast with others (such as growth) considered just as urgent by the other members?

It then becomes necessary to investigate the determinants of the 'propensity to co-operate' of oligopolistic countries. Recent developments in the analysis of international relations have shown, in the case in which nation states are considered as unitary actors, that in the absence of hegemony (i.e. under oligopoly) co-operation (integration) is difficult but not impossible to achieve if a number of conditions are fulfilled (Axelrod and Keohane 1985, Oye 1985). The first condition is the adoption by the governments involved of a 'long shadow of the future', i.e. a time horizon long enough for repeated games to be implemented which allow for a repeated exchange of information and, therefore, a decrease in the propensity to defect from the agreements. In this respect is shown the expedience of adopting 'tit-for-tat' policies based on reciprocity.[8] The second condition is that one or more nations should be willing to alter the structure of their policy preferences. This question is strictly connected to that of the implementation of the national adjustment policies.

A third condition is the minimization of the number of actors involved. This condition should not be taken at its face value, i.e. the minimization of the actors involved in the co-operative process, but in the sense of the minimization of the number of the different positions. In other words, the achievement of co-operative agreements is helped by the aggregation of different national positions around common policy strategies. A final condition is the strengthening of institutions considered as mechanisms of production and diffusion of information about the behaviour of each nation involved in the process.[9]

To sum up, systemic analyses offered by the political economy of international co-operation suggest that national policies which follow a reciprocity approach and are linked to a vast and solid institutional framework which is able to enforce behavioural rules on national governments may lead to successful co-operatives outcome. This has immediate consequences for national policies. The pay-off matrix which identifies the strategic interplay among countries belonging to an integrated area is built upon the structure and the policy preference orderings in different countries. Some structures are more conducive to co-operation than others (Jervis 1978; Hardin 1982). It follows that when countries adopt policy strategies targeted at changing the pay-off matrix they may directly influence the probabilities of achieving the integration targets in the medium term. Different considerations hold when there persist significant differences in national preferences.[10]

All this calls for an analysis of the nature and of the determinants of national adjustment policies which respond to the integration process. It is well known that domestic factors, such as internal interest groups and the socio-economic structure exert a decisive influence on national policy strategies (Katzenstein 1978; Gourevitch 1986 and this volume). It follows that determinants of national policy choices are much more complex than those assumed by systemic analyses.

INTERNATIONAL COMPETITIVENESS, ADJUSTMENT POLICIES AND THE POLITICO-ECONOMIC SYSTEM

We will develop, in what follows, a conceptual framework to investigate the determinants of national-policy choices when confronted with an integration process. We will proceed in two steps. The first step defines the long-term policy goals of a country in a highly interdependent environment as the improvement of international competitiveness which may be defined, along non-traditional lines, as the capacity of a country to adapt its structure to a changing international system. This capacity, in turn, involves both economic and political features as suggested by 'the political economy growth approach'. The second step considers the motivations underlying the strategies of the policy authorities which are linked both to the socio-economic structure and to the interaction between the government and the leading interest groups. In this respect an adjustment policy may be considered as the result of a policy optimization problem under the constraint of the socio-economic system.

The international competitiveness of a country may be defined as its ability to maintain high rates of growth in the long term. This may be achieved through the adaptation of its national characteristics, in terms of economic, technological and institutional structure, to changes in world demand and production patterns. National differences in growth rates may be explained in terms of the different adjustment capabilities of national economies.

The ability to adapt depends in the first place on economic factors, such as investment, technological and production capabilities. But these economic factors must be integrated with social and political factors which are usually considered exogenous by economic analysis although they deeply influence the overall international competitiveness of the economy.

Economic analysis considers international competitiveness as a crucial variable both in the evaluation of the performance of an economy and as a policy target. However a rigorous definition of international competitiveness is still lacking. Traditional definitions stemming from the orthodox approach consider price (and hence cost and exchange rate) factors as the main determinants of competitiveness. Price competitiveness, however, has been able to explain with decreasing success differences in national trade performances and the growing payment imbalances which these differentials have produced. Empirical studies of relations between price–cost competitiveness and medium-term trade performances have shown poor results and sometimes even 'perverse' ones (Fagerber 1985).

Investigations at the micro level, on the other hand, have shown that the international competitiveness of single firms and industries is strongly affected by a large and heterogeneous set of non-price factors which affect differences in input productivity and product quality (Freeman 1981). If the analysis is extended to the macro level of the economic system the role of the non-price factors increases and their interaction determines what is known as the 'structural competitiveness' of an economy, which is reflected in the ability of a country to sustain relatively high rates of growth. Such a result, in turn, depends on the ability of a country to combine efficiently its own national characteristics, in terms of industrial, technological and institutional structure, in order to adapt to world demand and production patterns (Mistral 1983).

The extended definition of international competitiveness set forward requires that a wide range of economic, political and institutional indicators be considered. A suitable starting point is post-Keynesian growth theory which assumes that the rate of growth of an open economy is dependent above all on two factors: the rate of growth of world demand (and world trade) and the ability of national producers to compete successfully with other countries' producers (Kaldor 1981; Thirlwall 1983). The ability to compete may be measured by the income (world and domestic) elasticities of export and import (Thirlwall 1979).[11] Differences in growth rates depend on different import and export elasticities. These parameters, on the other hand, must be considered as proxies of a large number of structural factors, such as the organization and flexibility of the industrial sector, the rate of growth and composition of fixed capital, the technological infrastructure endowment, etc., which influence the economy's ability to adjust in terms of its trade and potential growth performances (Chesnais 1986).

A number of authors, who follow a post-Keynesian approach, have investigated the economic determinants of long-period competitiveness. These authors have emphasized the relationship between the innovative capacity and competitiveness of a country (Cornwall 1977; Pavitt and Soete 1982; Fagerber 1985). According to these analyses, which share a schumpeterian view of technical progress and a neo-technology approach to international trade,[12] the sources of comparative (and absolute) advantage and the long-term determinants of a country's growth depend on the technological progress dynamic (both in processes and products innovations) which should be considered as endogenously determined by the economic system.

At the same time the international distribution of technological capabilities determines the distribution of absolute–comparative advantage among countries and produces a hierarchy among national systems which influences national specialization and policies as well as national preferences. Empirical tests have provided only partial support of these neo-technology analyses. Ambiguous results concern, in particular, the relation between international specialization and competitiveness of a country (Tharakan 1985).[13]

It is hardly questionable, however, that the new research avenues stress the dynamic aspect of international trade and comparative (absolute) advantages much better than the orthodox approach. Such advantages, rather than deriving from exogenous factor endowments, are mostly acquired by different countries according to their different abilities to exploit technological innovations. In such a framework, government economic policies – industrial, trade and macroeconomic – aimed at influencing the productive structure and specialization of different countries play a much more relevant role than the one usually assigned to them in the traditional approach. The relative position of a national economy in the world market – as determined by its structure and development stage – restricts its choices in the short run but does not suppress its ability to improve (or diminish) its performance according to the effectiveness of its adjustment policies in the long term. These will ultimately affect the dynamic efficiency of a country's overall growth path and, hence, its international competitiveness.

The international competitiveness of a country, however, as mentioned above, depends not only on economic factors but also on social and political factors which are usually left exogenous in economic analysis. This attitude is justified on the grounds that it is not possible to produce satisfactory quantitative indicators of the influence of social and political factors on economic adjustment strategies, other than introducing political dummy variables which rarely if at all improve the empirical results (Pavitt-

Soete 1982). The integration between economic, social and political elements in the determination of the competitiveness and growth capability of a country is possible along the methodological lines suggested by the political economy of growth, a recent outspring of 'modern political economy', the emerging discipline which aims at providing an interpretation of political processes in economics according to a rational model of choice (Frey 1978; Alt and Chrystal 1983).

Research in quantitative political economy has so far concentrated on the interaction between the political system and macroeconomic management, such as the political business cycle (see Alt and Chrystal 1983; Padoan 1985). This kind of analysis, which is oriented mostly towards short-run objectives, is not of much interest to the issues dealt with here. Our interest focuses on a different area, recently considered within the so-called political economy of growth approach (Olson 1965, 1982), which has produced a number of empirical tests (see the essays in Mueller 1983; Whiteley 1983; Garrett and Lange 1985, 1986; Maitland 1985; Rotschild 1986). Research has concentrated on testing Olson's hypothesis that the long-run propensity to grow of national economies depends on the degree of social cohesion among domestic interest groups. One of the implications of this approach is that it is possible to explain some of the crucial parameters which are generally left unexplained in standard economic models, such as the propensity to invest, the rate of growth of productivity, etc. The political-economy approach maintains that these crucial parameters are dependent on the social and political interactions in the economic system, which may be translated in quantitative terms by defining an appropriate set of variables and indicators.

Following the political-economy approach a general framework for the analysis of the interaction between structural competitiveness and political and social factors may be the following. Structural competitiveness, defined as the ability of a country to adapt itself to change in the international system, generally depends on the interaction of the business sector with, at least, three other sectors: the financial system; the system of industrial relations; the state and the 'welfare system' (Zysman 1984; Dauderstat 1987). It is convenient to consider these three aspects one by one.

Two general models of financial systems may be examined (Nardozzi 1983; Zysman 1984; Dauderstadt 1987). One model, which is prevailing in the United States and the United Kingdom, is 'market-oriented' in the sense that firms collect their funds, in addition to profits, directly from savers through the stock market. A second model, prevailing in continental Europe and Japan, is based on a strong reliance on bank credit to finance the accumulation process. This second model is more closely controlled, directly and indirectly, by the state as a consequence of the more extended links of the latter with the banking system.[14]

The two financial systems allow, *ceteris paribus*, different abilities to adapt, since in the second model, for example, the state will in general be more supportive of the system during a crisis. An additional element to consider is the degree of autonomy of monetary authorities from the government. A high degree of autonomy is expected to produce adjustment policies which are more supportive of banking interests rather than business interests *ceteris paribus*.

As to the second aspect, the degree of conflict in industrial relations covers a very broad area of concern for economic adjustment, ranging from wage and distributional policies to the ability to introduce technological innovations which have to be 'accepted' by workers. A view shared by several studies (Black 1982, Garret and Lange 1985, 1986) is that structural adjustment is easier if the degree of cohesion in industrial relations is high. The degree of cohesion may be considered differently. In some cases it is defined by the degree of 'corporatism' in industrial relations, which is itself a function of the degree of concentration of unions (Black 1982) but also of the action of 'encompassing' interest groups (Olson 1982). Other authors (Garret and Lange 1985, 1986) consider also the degree of 'coherence' of the socio-political structure. A socio-political structure is 'coherent' if workers are 'strong' (weak) both in the society and in the government, i.e. if the ruling coalition is leftist (conservative). A coherent structure will favour the ability of a country to adapt to changes in the international system and, hence, its growth capacity as this will produce macroeconomic policies which are coherent with the state of industrial relations.[15] This analysis may be extended to consider the interaction among unions, entrepreneurs and the banking community (Epstein and Schor 1985).

Finally, one must consider the interaction of the business sector with the state. The degree of involvement of the state in the economy influences significantly, but not necessarily in a positive way, the structural competitiveness of a country. Some authors (Cameron 1978) note that highly open economies display a high share in government expenditure as the government implements policies to sustain the competitiveness of the industrial system in world markets. This will take different forms. In some cases government subsidies will take the place of more protectionist policies (not only tariff policies but more often non-tariff and normative ones).

But the support of the state is not limited to this kind of intervention. In addition, the role of the state in supporting structural adjustment is linked to the provision of 'social buffers'. This notion is directly related to the previous issue of the degree of conflict in industrial relations. An efficient system of public support may reduce social costs of adjustment policies whenever their implementation leads to widespread social unrest.

To sum up, international competitiveness of a national system is a global phenomenon which may be defined as the ability to grow in and to adjust to a changing international market. This in turn depends not only on the behaviour of the productive system but also on the interaction with the political and social system. Each of the elements we have mentioned above presents two distinct components. One component, which may defined as 'structural', is associated with the 'objective' characteristics of the system (such as the financial structure, industrial relations, the welfare system, etc.). The second component is associated with the politico-economic relations among different interest groups which are influenced by the structural element.

The next step is to identify the long-run determinants of adjustment policies. Suggestions coming from the 'modern political economy' literature look promising but they need more elaboration. The literature on the political manipulation of the economic system, including the political business cycle approach, has largely ignored, with a few exceptions (Thompson and Zuk 1983) international aspects. More promising seem to be the investigations on the structural bases of foreign economic policies (Katzenstein 1978) which aim at identifying the long-run determinants of economic policies (the policy-makers' revealed preferences) and to link them to the structure of interest groups (business, finance, trade unions) and to their interactions.

The success of the ruling coalition in influencing the foreign economic policy of a country may be said to depend on two elements. In the first place leading interest groups will be more effective in shaping state policy in 'weak' – as opposed to 'strong' – states (to use Katzenstein's distinction) (Katzenstein 1978), i.e. situations in which national governments are highly sensitive to domestic pressures, and state bureaucracies and political elites do not enjoy enough independence to pursue their own goals. In the second place the ruling coalition will be more effective in pursuing its goals in situations in which the number of interest groups is low and/or where an 'encompassing' interest group exists which will be able to establish – much like a hegemon – the interests of the society at large (Olson 1982).

Examples of this kind of analysis deal with the relation between the industrial structure and the political economy of protection (Brock and Magee 1978). A few studies have been produced on the long term determinants of monetary policy including both macroeconomic policy and regulation of the financial system (Dean 1984; Epstein and Schor 1985). These studies show that the propensity to pursue restrictive monetary policies depends on the degree of independence of the central bank from the government (Frey and Schneider 1982) and on the relation between the central bank and the financial community as well as on the degree of internationalization of the latter.

The connections of these studies with the topics discussed above seem evident, yet they await further investigation in spite of some initially interesting results (Black 1982). In addition, they limit themselves to the determinants of macroeconomic policies while our interest lies in the determinants of adjustment policies. What is still lacking, in other words, is a more general approach which links the policy process and the structure of the economy. The direction of research to analyze the structural adjustment policies of a country may be designed along the following lines (Breton 1981). The political (adjustment) process is the outcome of a demand and supply of policies. Policies are demanded by interest groups and supplied by the government (which is to be kept separate from the bureaucracy). Interest groups demand policies to improve their position in the domestic as well as in the international economy. Governments supply policies in exchange for political consensus (power) which may also be considered in terms of 'popularity' (Frey 1978).

The demand for policies is a function of the kind and number of interest groups and of their degree of cohesion. In a corporatist setting, for example, the alliance between trade unions and entrepreneurs will produce a demand for industrial support policies. A strong banking community will demand policies in support of financial interests. The relative pressure of demand for policies will depend also on the relative power of the different interest groups.

The supply of policies will be determined by the policy-maker in relation to its 'power deficit' (Breton 1981) or its 'popularity deficit' (Frey and Schneider 1978). A higher popularity deficit will increase the propensity to supply adjustment policies.

The supply of policies will be increasing in the power deficit (i.e. the difference between the existing popularity level and the minimum level required for re-election) the government is suffering. Policies will be directed in favour of those groups which will provide the maximum popularity. A coherent political and social structure (as defined above) will increase the efficacy of policies.

This general framework may be applied to the problem of structural competitiveness (Ikenberry 1986). A government will select an adjustment policy taking into account its costs in terms of loss of power (popularity). It is thus possible to build a preference function of the government with respect to adjustment policies given a trade-off between popularity costs and increase in competitiveness. Adjustment policies may also be distinguished between those aimed at modifying the international environment (outward-looking) and those aimed at modifying the domestic environment (inward-looking). The first have lower popularity costs but are also hardly exploitable by smaller countries which must resort to the latter thus bearing a higher popularity cost. Both outward- and inward- looking strategies may be offensive (i.e. they attempt to change the domestic and/or international environment) or defensive (they attempt to 'muddle through' the existing environment). Defensive strategies are less costly and less effective than offensive ones.

Table 1.1 gives some examples of each of the policies involved. The

Table 1.1 Patterns of adjustment policies

Strategy	Effect on competiton	Political cost	Example
Offensive outward 1.	high	low	New internal regime
Defensive outward 1.	low	low	Changes in existing regime
Offensive inward 1.	high	high	Internal structure adjustment
Defensive inward 1.	low	low	Protection of existing structure

elements discussed in Table 1.1 should be included in a general framework explaining adjustment strategies along the following lines. The policies of adjustment to a changing international environment (integration) which will be implemented are the result of choices the government makes according to its own utility function taking into account the constraints represented by the politico-economic system and its position in the international system. The construction of such a model is a complex task which will need further research as it requires a full specification of the connections between the economic system and the political and social structure. No such model exists today to our knowledge in spite of growing interest in this area of research.

ECONOMIC INTEGRATION AND NATIONAL POLICIES: THE INTERACTION OF SYSTEMIC AND DOMESTIC FACTORS

The success of the process of economic integration according to regime or systemic theories of international co-operation depends on a particular set of events which should characterize the interaction among member countries. But systemic theories assume that nation states are unitary actors and, hence, disregard the role of political and economic interactions at the national level.

On the other hand, domestic analyses of economic adjustment policies assume international regimes as exogenous variables which can be modified at the margin by unilateral action. A more satisfactory analysis, and indeed the most demanding research path in international political economy (Haggard and Simmons 1987) requires a full integration of these two levels of analysis.

The literature on this topic is at a very early stage of development and it is definitely too soon to provide a survey. This paragraph will be devoted, therefore, to a simple illustration of an approach to the interaction of international politics (i.e. relationships among the states) and domestic politics (i.e. relationships within the states) in the process of international co-operation and integration. Putnam (1986) assumes that this process may be described as a two-level game. At level one, national governments play a game among themselves for the definition of rules for the international system as well as for the implementation of specific policy actions. At level two, each national government (or leader) plays a game with the interest groups acting within its own country in order to have the policies agreed upon at level one accepted. The success of international co-operation – and in our case of international integration – depends on the definition, at level-one politics, of policies which can be ratified at level-two politics. Considering a bargaining model which was originally developed for the analysis of industrial relations Putnam maintains that the probability of the success of international co-operation increases with the dimension of the 'win set', i.e. the set of all policies agreed upon at level-one politics which will obtain a ratification at level-two politics. Although the framework discussed by Putnam is described as a game it is not formalized in game-theoretic terms. We shall not attempt to produce such a formalization, rather to present a very simple graphical illustration. The purpose of such an illustration is not only to present Putnam's argument but also to apply it to the problems of economic integration, in the light of the issues which have been surveyed in the previous paragraphs.

LEVEL-ONE POLITICS

We may assume that at the international level national negotiators (or heads of governments) will try to maximize their reputation and they will use both the power of the country and the conduct of domestic economic policy to do so. National power will be used to alter the international environment – that is, the integration framework or regime – within which national policies are implemented. For simplicity's sake we may assume that each national government controls one policy variable X which increases when expansionary policies are implemented (so that X may be thought of as the size of the public deficit). Given an international regime, a set of rules, which in turn requires a given power distribution in the international system, reputation will be an inverse function of the size of the policy variable X if we assume that reputation increases with the ability of a country to resist expansionary pressures. This point may be expressed graphically in Fig. 1.1: reputation (R) decreases with X. However the position of the R function in the diagram depends on the nature of the international regime, i.e. on the internationally agreed rules of the game. A more expansionary regime (i.e. one in which all countries agree to pursue expansionary policies) will shift the R function to the right as the national government enjoys the same reputation *vis-à-vis* the other governments with a higher expansionary policy.

A different way to state this is the following. In order to participate in an international agreement each national government must obtain a minimum

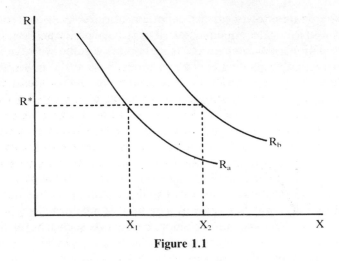

Figure 1.1

level of reputation R* *vis-à-vis* the other national governments; i.e. the implementation of its macroeconomic policies is constrained by the attainment of a minimum level of reputation. The nature of the international regime determines the position of the 'reputation function' and therefore the maximum value which may be obtained in order to satisfy the constraint $R \geq R^*$ for participation in the international regime. Such a constraint may be interpreted alternatively in the following way. If participation in the international regime requires, for example, that an external constraint on the national economy be respected then the domestic policy variable cannot exceed a given value. The more expansionary the international regime the higher will be the maximum value of X (respectively X_1, or X_2) which will allow participation in the regime.

LEVEL-TWO POLITICS

At the domestic level the national government will try to maximize its popularity (in order to maximize re-election probabilities as well as to pursue its own ideological targets) and, in order to do so, it will implement macroeconomic policies according to a popularity function such as the one presented in Fig. 1.2. As the figure shows government popularity increases with the level of the policy variable X. However, the position and the shape of the popularity function P depends on the political and economic characteristics of the country. In the first place we may assume that the higher the degree of 'social sclerosis', in Olson's sense, the flatter will be the P-function. In a country in which there is a large number of interest groups and no true 'encompassing group', then in order to increase its

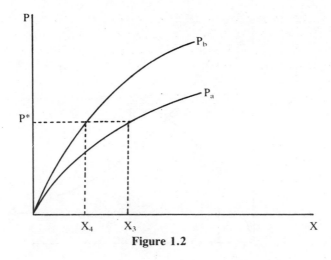

Figure 1.2

popularity the government will have to increase the level of X proportionally more as it will have to meet the demands of a larger number of groups, i.e. its constituency will be, *ceteris paribus*, less efficiently organized.

The position of the P-function will depend on the nature of the constituency of the ruling coalition as well as on its ideological preferences. A more conservative-oriented coalition will produce a P-function shifted leftwards (such as P_b) as the relative weight of disinflation (i.e. restrictive) policies in determining the government's popularity will be larger. We may assume, as it is generally done in the literature, that there is a minimum level of popularity P^* which the government must obtain in order to assure re-election. The nature of the coalition and its ideological orientation will determine the level of X (X_3 and X_4 respectively) which will assure re-election.

THE DETERMINATION OF THE WIN SET

With these very simple tools it is possible to see how the win set is determined. The determination of the win set may be described as the interaction of the two levels of policy action in which the solution to one game is subject to the solution of the other game. At level-one politics reputation will be maximized subject to a popularity constraint. At level-two politics popularity will be maximized subject to a reputation constraint. This is shown in Fig. 1.3. At level-one politics the government wishes to maximize its reputation R subject to the popularity constraint $P \geq P^*$. It will therefore choose a policy X, which yields a level R_1 of

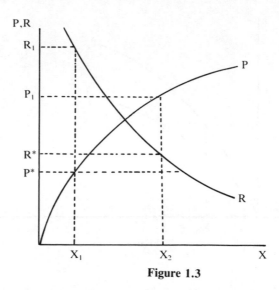

Figure 1.3

reputation. At level-two politics the government wishes to maximize popularity subject to reputation constraint $R > R^*$. It will therefore choose policy X_2 which yields a level of P_1 of popularity. The segment $X_1 - X_2$ determines the set of feasible policies, the win set, i.e. the set of policies which will simultaneously satisfy the constraints of both level-one and level-two politics.

Figure 1.3 is built in such a way as to admit the existence of a win set. However one may consider the case in which the win set does not exist. Such a case is presented in Fig. 1.4. Level-one politics requires that the policy variable is not pushed above the value of X_2 in order to satisfy the reputation constraint R^*. However, this produces a popularity level P_2 which is below the minimum level P^*. Conversely, level-two politics produces a policy level X_1 which produces a reputation level of R_1 which is below the minimum level R^*. In such a case level-one and level-two poiitics are mutually incompatible.

Clearly the existence and the dimension of the win set depend on the relative position of the P and R functions. In the case presented in Fig. 1.4 implementing integration is impossible both because the international regime – which determines the position of the R function – is too restrictive and because the degree of social sclerosis in the country under consideration is so large that it requires an over-expansionary policy.

The question then arises of what can be done in order to increase international integration, i.e. to generate a positive win set. This can be done in two, not mutually exclusive ways. One is to adopt an outward-looking strategy aiming at a modification of the existing regime. Such a

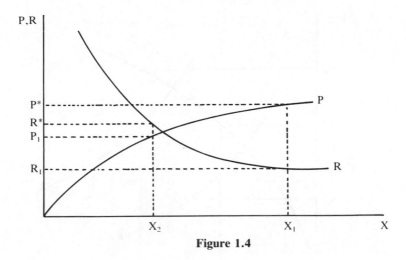

Figure 1.4

strategy would allow the R-function to be shifted to the right, i.e. to allow for a more expansionary international environment which would, at the same time, maintain the minimum level of reputation necessary to participate in international agreements.

The second alternative is to adopt an inward-looking strategy aimed at modifying the domestic politico-economic environment. Such a strategy would allow the P-function to be shifted upwards, i.e. to allow for a more restrictive policy and to achieve the minimum level of popularity to assure re-election.

The first strategy requires a government which is strong internationally, i.e. a country with sufficient international power to force a change in the international regime. The second strategy requires a government which is strong domestically since it is equivalent to engineering a change in the structure of preferences within the country. However the two levels of politics may influence each other. As Putnam suggests, a domestically weak government may obtain substantial concessions at the international level as other government leaders wish to avoid a political crisis in the country. In such a case, a domestically weak government may become quite powerful at the international level (level-one politics). Alternatively a weak government may wish to use the existing international regime as a political leverage to impose a change in the domestic policy stance. This is the case in which the domestic government does not have the necessary popularity surplus to impose its own ideological goals on the economy. In such a situation it may be in the interests of a domestically weak government to adhere to an international regime in order to enforce a change in the domestic-policy stance.

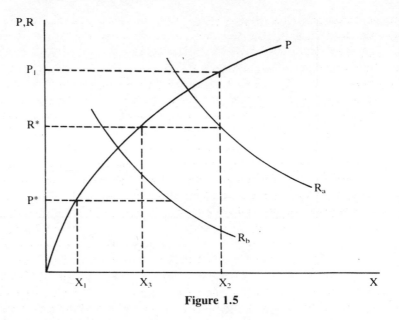

Figure 1.5

This simple framework allows discussion of a different but rather interesting case. Consider a situation in which a country enjoys a rather large popularity surplus given the international regime. This is described in Fig. 1.5. The international regime determines an R-function R_a requiring a minimum level of reputation R^* and a maximum policy level of X_2. Such a level of X is quite larger than the one-X_1 necessary for the government to obtain the minimum popularity level P^*. In such a case the government enjoys a popularity surplus X_2-X_1. If the government is ideologically oriented towards anti-inflationary policies and it has enough international power it will try to change the international regime towards a more restrictive configuration shifting the R-function to the right.

IMPLICATIONS FOR THE PROCESS OF INTEGRATION

The simple discussion we have presented above illustrates two cases in which integration may be implemented. An integration regime will be implemented as long as there exists, in each country, a win set. Two cases which were discussed in the previous paragraphs to investigate international co-operation and integration may be illustrated here. One is the hegemonic case. A hegemon will be able, by definition, to produce a change in the international regime to allow for a shift of the R-function to the right in other countries as well as in its own so as to produce a large enough win set for the new regime to be implemented. In terms of our graphic representation this means that the action of the hegemon will increase the popularity surplus (i.e. the difference between the maximum level of P attainable and the value of P*) of other governments irrespective of what the latter do. This may be considered as an example of the public-good nature of an integration regime. The smaller the beneficiary country the larger will be the benefits, in terms of the popularity surplus generated by the policy of the hegemon. Our discussion also shows that the probabilities of building international regimes (integration) increases if the hegemon pursues expansionary policies, i.e. it favours an expansion-oriented regime. If it is true that government expenditure follows a secular trend towards expansion (Mueller 1987) and if we assume that the variable X considered in our illustration is positively correlated with governments' expenditure, the possibility of establishing restrictive international regimes depends on two events. One is the existence of a large popularity surplus in a country whose government is at the same time ideologically oriented towards restriction and powerful enough to force such a preference onto other countries. The second one is that some less powerful and weaker country finds it convenient to adhere to such a regime in order to impose a shift in domestic preferences which would otherwise be impossible. In such a case the international regime supplied by the larger country is a public good (monetary stability), even if it is a different one with respect to the case discussed above.

Another case which we have discussed in this section fits in well with the issue of co-operation–integration without hegemony. One of the conditions for the international regime in these cases is the possibility that the domestic preferences be altered. We have seen that, in so far as this is reflected in a shift of the popularity function, this increases the win set and hence the chances of establishing international regimes. But the achievement of an international regime without hegemony is not an easy task. Something else may be discussed with the aid of our graphical device; that is the sequence of different foreign economic policies which a government is likely to follow in the interaction with other governments in an oligopolistic system. What follows reconsiders some contributions (Bergsten 1986; Randall Henning 1987) which discuss the foreign economic strategy of the United States in the post-hegemony period and which contain some general elements which may be extended to other countries, especially to large to medium-sized ones, i.e. those most likely to be involved in the process of integration.

Let us consider this process from the point of view of a single country, assuming that its foreign economic policy moves across three distinct phases which may be illustrated with the help of Fig. 1.6. In the first phase ('nationalism') the country will try to ignore international relations and it will set domestic policies disregarding their international consequences. In phase one the government will aim at maximizing popularity, setting

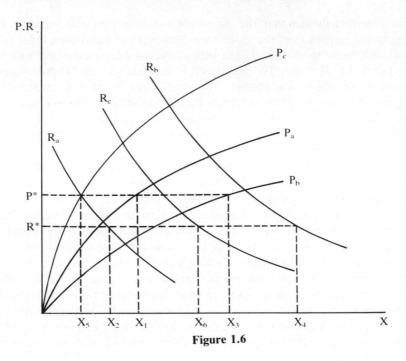

Figure 1.6

policies well to the right of X_1, even if the prevailing regime would require policies not larger than X_2. If the country is powerful enough it may disregard its international reputation for a rather long time. However this process may not go on indefinitely both because of external reasons (such as the erosion of power) and because of internal reasons (prolonged expansionary policies will, *ceteris paribus*, diminish the popularity function by shifting it to the right, e.g. to P_b requiring a policy X_3 and therefore aggravating the international position of the government).

This will eventually induce a change in foreign policy ('active unilateralism'). The country will try to use its international power to induce a change in the international regime, i.e. to try to shift the R-function to the left (e.g. to R_b) which would allow e.g. a policy X_4. However the diminished international position of the country is unlikely to allow for such a change and so the government will eventually shift to a third strategy ('co-operation') by which it will try both to alter its level-one and its level-two politics and therefore engineer a shift in both the P-function and in the R-function so as to produce a win set. In Fig. 1.6 this is the case obtained by functions P_c and R_c, which determine a win set X_5–X_6.

Such a case offers a useful illustration of the process of integration without hegemony, which, as we have seen, characterizes countries' relations in Europe. In the case of hegemony the interaction between level I and level II politics is limited. The win set depends, for a non-hegemon, either on the position of the R-function which is exogenous to the policy of the country itself or, given the R-function, on the possibility of shifting the P-function, but only to a limited extent on the interaction of the two policy levels. As the international power distribution becomes less asymmetric (i.e. the power lead of the hegemon fades away) the achievement of the international regime increasingly depends on the simultaneous shift of the two functions and, hence, on both external and domestic policies.

NOTES

1. These phenomena are the outcome of the various forms that can be taken up by international integration: free-trade areas, custom unions, common markets, economic unions up to full political integration (Balassa 1962; Robson 1984).
2. Literature in the field is immense. The post-war debate has been started by a seminal work by Viner (1950) followed by major contributions by Meade, Lipsey and Johnson which are all based on neo-classical trade theory. For a survey see Robson (1984).
3. See Johnson (1965) for the modest terms-of-trade gains stemming from a custom union.
4. The most binding assumption is perfect competition on all markets (of factors and goods).
5. All contributions relating to the completion of the internal market in 1992 stress the role of economies of scale in production and exchange as the most relevant benefit accruing to European firms. See 'The economics of 1992', *European Economy* no. 35, March 1988.
6. The now numerous contributions on trade policies are relevant here. They have been stimulated by the seminal contributions by Brander and Spencer (1981), (1983), (1984). For a survey see Guerrieri and Padoan (1988b).
7. Brander and Richardson in Krugman (1986) offer a definition and an analysis of 'strategic trade policies'.
8. The efficacy of these policies in promoting co-operation is enhanced by an institutional structure which increases transparency and mitigates negative side effects. See Axelrod (1984) and Axelrod and Keohane (1985).
9. The EMS is an important example of an institution which has strengthened co-operative mechanisms in Europe (Padoan 1988).
10. These differences are still present in the positions of the major European countries. Germany's main trade-off involves growth and monetary stability, while France's and Italy's involve growth and external equilibrium (Oudiz 1985; Padoan 1988; Petit and Thiel in this volume).
11. In the long run less-competitive economies will produce lower-than-average growth rates as they will have to adjust their growth rates to the balance of payments constraint. This, in turn, is made stringent both by a low-income elasticity of exports and by a high-income elasticity of imports. More competitive countries will show an opposite behaviour. Such a mechanism will be reinforced by the fact that productivity gains derived by structural changes, transfers of resources to more dynamic sectors, static and dynamic economies

of scale depend on the rate of growth of demand and, therefore, on net exports (Kaldor 1981).

12. Sources of inspiration are the technology gap theories by Posner (1961) and product-cycle theories (Vernon 1966, 1979).

13. A key problem is the measurement of the propensity to innovate. Different approaches have been followed. One approach uses intensity of R&D expenditures as a proxy for the rate of innovating products and processes. Expenditure intensity may be measured in two different ways; one is the ratio between R&D expenditure and total sales. Another indicator is the ratio between the amount of workers employed in research activities over total employees. Industrial sectors are then ranked according to the value of these ratios. However these indicators have failed to produce significant evidence of the correlation between technological capacity and competitiveness. Critics of the use of R&D expenditures as indicators of technological efforts have pointed out that there is not a one-to-one correspondence between sectors in which research is carried out and sectors which benefit from it; channels of technological innovations are not limited to R&D expenditures; expenditure and employment in R&D are inputs of the research process while one should look at the output of the process.

This problem has stimulated new research in the field. Soete (1981) has proposed an indicator of technological output defined as the number of patents deposited by a country in order to protect its products. The most important results are that, when using a coefficient of 'technological elasticity' derived from patenting for different sectors, high-technology sectors include not only the traditional research-intensive sectors but also several sectors of electrical and non-electrical machinery as well as transport equipment. All other sectors are under-represented in classifications using R&D indicators. These more recent studies, however, present some ambiguities. The link between technological success, specialization and competitiveness has so far found poor empirical support and calls therefore for better theoretical specifications.

14. This depends on the fact that in financially developed economies the government usually exerts a strong control over financial institutions in order to keep the financial system between the two extremes of excess regulation, which depresses competitiveness, and excess deregulation, which may lead to financial distress.

15. An expansionary macroeconomic policy will minimize inflationary tensions if workers and employers agree on some form of incomes policy. It is easy to understand that the same policy would produce far different results in the case of a non-coherent structure (e.g. the coexistence of a conservative government and strong unions).

2 · THE POLITICAL ECONOMY OF MACROECONOMIC POLICY IN EUROPE[1]

Louka T. Katseli

INTRODUCTION

High unemployment, low inflation, current-account surpluses and since 1985 appreciating currencies: these are the main economic characteristics of Europe's major industrialized countries today. These developments can be easily explained in terms of relatively standard economic analysis.

The announced tax cuts and the restrictive monetary policy pursued by the US government since 1981 raised US nominal and real interest rates, induced a foreign capital inflow and prompted the substantial appreciation of the dollar. As was expected, the foreign capital inflow was matched by a mounting current account deficit (Branson 1985).

Already by mid-1983 there was speculation that the US current account would eventually become unsustainable, and scenarios were worked out for the optimal response of the European countries in the event of 'a dollar crash' or of 'smooth landing'. Faced with the increase of US interest rates and the ensuing capital outflow, the major European countries in 1983 had the following options:

1. Erect some form of capital controls that would prevent capital flight while maintaining a wedge between domestic and foreign interest rates.
2. Resist the increase in interest rates and let instead the exchange rate bear the main burden of adjustment; this would have implied an increase in export demand and hence aggregate demand but also an increase in import prices with possible negative terms-of-trade effects on the supply side of the economy.
3. Match the increase in US interest rates through restrictive monetary policy that would reduce internal demand and would dampen pressures on the foreign exchange market.

These policy options were discussed extensively in the relevant committees of the EC (Emerson 1985). The first option was discarded on the grounds of undesirable market intervention. The second option, known as 'the decoupling option', was supported more vigorously by France and those countries that faced at the time severe balance-of-payments constraints. The third option, 'the coupling option' was mostly favoured by West Germany and the D-Mark area countries. The outcome of these negotiations, which took place during the spring of 1983, was a compromise. Long-term real interest rates were raised in all major EC countries: in West Germany from 4.2 per cent in 1982 to 5.3 per cent in 1984; in France from 4.8 per cent to 6.1 per cent; in the United Kingdom from 4 per cent to 5.9 per cent. Only in Italy did long-term real interest rates stay roughly constant during this period. Money supply growth decreased. For the Community as a whole the annual growth of the broad money supply was reduced from 11.6 per cent in 1982 to 8.7 per cent in 1984. At the same time the ECU followed the D-Mark in its downward trend against the dollar. The price of the dollar relative to the D-Mark rose by roughly 30 per cent between 1981 and 1985.

The ensuing boost in export demand, however, was not sufficient to offset the contractionary effects of monetary policy that were aggravated by severe fiscal restriction. For the EC as a whole, cyclically- and inflation-adjusted deficits were reduced by close to 2 per cent of GDP from 1981 to 1984. Germany and the UK recorded fiscal surpluses in 1984. It is thus not surprising that output remained practically stagnant during the period 1981–3. It rose moderately in 1984 and 1985 by 2.0 per cent and 2.4 per cent respectively, largely as a result of high export growth (almost 8 per cent in 1984 and 5.7 per cent in 1985) and a very gradual resumption of private consumption. By 1986, the average unemployment rate for the Community countries hovered around 11 per cent up from 4.7 per cent during the second half of the 1970s. Inflation was lowered to 3.7 per cent down from 12 per cent during the years 1974–80. By 1986, West Germany's inflation rate was practically zero. At the same time its current account surplus exceeded 3 per cent of GDP.

Most analysts would thus agree with the general conclusion of a group of noted international economists who in a recent study wrote:

> It is our opinion that a sharp decrease in aggregate demand is indeed the proximate cause of the rise in unemployment in the EC since 1980. The use of monetary policy to fight inflation and the major shift in fiscal policy towards budgetary consolidation, however justified, seem to explain much of the poor growth performance of the 1980s.
>
> (Blanchard *et al.* 1985)

To most economists the correct policy prescription for a case of high unemployment, low inflation and current account surplus is 'expansion'. Indeed there is by now a growing consensus that expansion is necessary if the situation is not going to be substantially aggravated on the employment

and investment fronts with harmful long-term economic and social consequences (Layard *et al.* 1984; Emerson 1985; Oudiz and Sachs 1984;
Frankel 1986). What is, in fact, surprising is the resistance which proposals
of this kind have met among government officials and EC bureaucrats.

Despite the call for a 'co-operative growth strategy for more employment'
endorsed by Community countries in subsequent Annual Economic Reports (1985–6 and 1986–7), the thrust of macro-policy prescriptions coming out of Brussels is still largely cautious if not overtly restrictive. 'Public
finance policy', according to the 1986 Annual Report, should aim at the
'medium-term consolidation of public finances' (EC 1986, p. 12) calling for
'judicious balance-of-budget positions' (ibid., p. 50), dismantling of subsidies and some selective lowering of taxes and social security contributions in few countries (ibid., p. 12). Monetary policy should be exercised
cautiously 'to ensure that there is no new build-up of inflationary potential'
(ibid., p. 12). Finally, continuous moderation of real wages and improvement in 'market adaptability' and the 'business environment' are perceived
to be major policy instruments for employment-creating investment and
employment generation.

'Consolidation' appears to be the key word in most European policymaking circles today. Its meaning is rarely explained analytically, or in
terms of concrete policy goals, yet it can be loosely interpreted as the
continuation of deflationary policies especially with regard to finances and
incomes policy. It is based on a strong preference for private as opposed to
public spending and the conviction that redistribution of income towards
profits is a sufficient condition for private investment and future employment generation.

The prevailing uniformity of views as to the conduct of macroeconomic
policy across major European countries and national institutions, including
central banks, cannot be justified simply on economic grounds as the next
section of this paper shows. The present policy stance can only be understood if one adopts a dynamic political-economy framework which focuses
on the interaction between economics and politics in an open-economy
set-up.

Institutional factors or 'structural politics' can affect critically both the
direction of policy and the choice of policy instruments. Institutions in turn
are themselves affected by economic developments. It will be argued that
increased interdependence through trade and integration of financial markets has determined over time not only the internal distribution of power
between governmental institutions and non-governmental groups but also
the degree of national autonomy in the conduct of policy. International
financial integration in other words has given rise to institutional developments that in turn have influenced the conduct of national policy and the
prospects for macroeconomic policy co-ordination.

A rudimentary framework that highlights these interconnections is developed later in this paper. It is used in the following section to analyze the economics and politics behind the new 'consolidation doctrine' prevalent among policy-makers today. The deflationary bias in Europe is attributed not only to national policy choices but to the gradual development of a 'supra-national monetary club' that has over-represented the interests and points of view of central banks, especially those of hard-currency countries.

THE ECONOMICS PUZZLE OF THE 1980s

Autonomous expansion of output and employment in an economy requires either an increase in aggregate demand through expansionary policy or an increase in aggregate supply, mostly as a result of productivity increases.

In the early 1980s, 'supply-side economics' with its exclusive emphasis on tax cuts as an incentive for rapid capital accumulation, was discredited in Europe largely as a result of its budgetary and inflationary repercussions. In Europe, 'supply-side' measures were linked instead with policy that aimed at greater 'flexibility' and 'adaptability' of labour markets. This in turn implied greater real-wage flexibility, mostly in a downwards direction, the abolition of wage indexation schemes, the relaxation of work rules, the introduction of part-time employment and of flexible hours and the reduction of labour unions' market power.

This view was supported by a sizeable literature in economics that presented evidence of relative real-wage rigidity in Europe at least during the 1970s (Bruno and Sachs 1985; Branson and Rotemberg 1980).

The implication of real wage rigidity for policy was two-fold:

1. That expansionary demand policy was inflationary as opposed to having favourable output effects, since any potential expansion of labour demand was thwarted by offsetting increases in nominal wages.
2. That expansion of output and employment could only be achieved through appropriate policy that ensured greater flexibility in the functioning of the labour markets.

It should be noted that adherence to this strict 'real-wage rigidity' view that characterized informed opinion also implied, at least indirectly, that better US growth prospects that would stimulate exports from Europe would only have inflationary consequences as opposed to favourable output and employment effects. It thus justified policy inactivism both on the part of any single European country, e.g. Germany or France, as well as on the part of the Community as a whole. So long as labour markets in Europe were characterized by real-wage rigidity, there was no room for either unilateral or co-ordinated expansion.

Whatever the merits of the argument in the 1970s, it is clear that by the second half of the 1980s conditions in the labour markets have changed. Real unit labour costs (real per capita labour costs to productivity) have declined considerably in all major European countries (EC Annual Report). A number of recent studies (Bruno 1985; Sachs 1986) show that the 'wage gap', i.e. the excess of the real-wage level above the marginal product of labour at full employment, has declined. Even though there is still room for greater flexibility, it is clear that the 'classical thesis' is becoming less relevant today than it was five to ten years ago.

High real wages have also been mentioned as a principal factor behind the investment slow-down in Europe through their negative effect on profits. In a recent study on the determinants of investment behaviour, Bruno shows that the real-wage performance had in fact a small direct role in the slow-down of capital accumulation. Instead, he argues that 'the output contraction (from the demand side) played the dominant role in the profit squeeze and the resulting contraction in investment' (Bruno 1985, p. 14).[2] In the case of France and Italy in particular, aggregate demand seemed to be the major explanatory variable behind the reduction in profitability and investment in the manufacturing sector. Real wages do not appear to have played a significant role in the fall of the real profit rate.

Despite the growing evidence that 'real-wage rigidity' has been reduced and that private investment is hampered by low aggregate demand and slow expected growth of sales, European policy-makers still appear unwilling to undertake expansionary demand-side policy to alleviate the unemployment problem.

There seem to be at least two additional economic considerations that would work against an active use of demand-side policy on the part of any single European country. These should therefore be properly evaluated under present conditions.

The first point is that in a world of floating exchange rates, expansionary fiscal policy on the part of countries whose financial markets are closely integrated into the world financial system, is expected to put upward pressure on domestic interest rates and thus to induce a financial capital inflow with an incipient appreciation of the domestic exchange rate. As a result, the current-account situation will worsen and the expansion of domestic demand will be offset by the reduction of net foreign demand. This is a well-known result largely associated with the name of Mundell (1962). It emphasizes the inability of unilateral fiscal policy to affect aggregate demand and output in a world of high capital mobility and financial integration.

It should be noted, however, that the actual effect of expansionary fiscal policy on bilateral exchange rates remains an open empirical question. The net result is determined in practice not only by the degree of substitutability between domestic and foreign assets but also by institutional factors regarding the degree of interest-rate flexibility and the cost of operation in world financial markets. Thus the Mundell results can be easily overturned if there is limited substitutability between assets and/or if the incipient capital inflow is curtailed for institutional reasons. Furthermore it can be shown that if world demand for domestic bonds is limited, a fiscal expansion is likely to result in currency depreciation (Oudiz and Sachs 1984). This is because, in that case, fiscal expansion will cause a larger increase in the excess supply of home bonds that would necessitate a large increase in the interest-rate differential for equilibrium to be maintained in financial markets. Thus, whereas a US fiscal expansion is more likely to strengthen the dollar, the effect on the D-Mark–dollar rate of a German fiscal expansion is not as clear. Applying the same line of reasoning to intra-European exchange rate parities, a German fiscal expansion will probably appreciate the D-Mark *vis-à-vis* the other European currencies, whereas expansionary policy on the part of France or Italy is likely to bring about a depreciation of the relevant currencies *vis-à-vis* all major trading partners.

The second point is that the cross-effects of unilateral expansion are determined not only by the degree of capital mobility but also by the extent of wage indexation of the trading partner's labour market as well as by its use of imported inputs in production. Thus whereas an appreciation of the D-Mark *vis-à-vis* the pound and the dollar will most likely increase output and prices in the United Kingdom and the United States, it might have stagflationary effects in Italy or in other countries whose economies are relatively indexed. This is because the increase in imported prices as a result of the Italian currency's depreciation will raise the consumer price index relative to producer prices and will put upward pressure on real wages in many sectors of the economy.

This might explain why German fiscal inactivism was virtually unchallenged by its major European partners in the first half of the decade. Beset by what was considered a high inflation record and relative labour market inflexibility, France, Italy and less so the UK feared the internal effects of a currency depreciation *vis-à-vis* the D-Mark that would have lowered further their effective exchange rates. Germany itself opposed demand expansion on the grounds of expected inflation. The underlying hypothesis regarding the expected exchange-rate movement was not altogether clear. Europe was thus united in its acceptance of fiscal inertia and opposed tacitly US mild pressures towards expansion.

It is clear today that co-ordinated fiscal expansion at that time would have lessened substantially the risk of higher inflation coming from intra-European exchange rate movements and would have slowed the rise of the US dollar. In view of the fact that the post-1981 US expansion did contribute significantly to European growth, the justification of fiscal inertia on the grounds of European real-wage rigidity seems today unfounded. Thus, the opportunity for joint reflation was lost with important consequences for employment and new investment in Europe. When the possibility of a co-ordinated reduction in the value-added tax, small enough so as not to offset the expected and desirable depreciation of the EC currencies *vis-à-vis* the dollar, was in fact discussed in the pertinent EC committees in 1983, it was readily discarded.[3]

Currently, when labour-market conditions in Europe are favourable enough that no one seriously argues against expansion on internal grounds, external conditions make the option of co-ordinated fiscal expansion less attractive. From a US point of view, a co-ordinated European fiscal expansion would increase downward pressure on the dollar even more than is actually desired. From a European perspective it would reduce export competitiveness further and worsen the prospective balance-of-payment position. The likely drop in external demand would thus mitigate the positive effects of domestic expansion on employment while it is unlikely that real wages would fall substantially more. A co-ordinated fiscal expansion would finally threaten the consolidation of budgetary gains in France and Italy. Thus it is highly unlikely that it is today a viable option. On the other hand, a unilateral fiscal expansion by Germany is welcomed by almost all its European partners and is probably acceptable to the United States.

Trade with Germany accounts for a large percentage of total trade for most European countries. Imports from Germany exceed 17 per cent of the total imports of the rest of the EC countries and exports to Germany account roughly for 18 per cent of total exports. The likely appreciation of the D-Mark relative to the currencies of its European partners, requiring perhaps a more substantial EMS realignment, will tend to offset the consequences of the dollar's recent decline, increase export demand and improve growth prospects with negligible effects on inflation. For the United States, a German mild fiscal expansion, hopefully complemented by Japanese fiscal expansion, will sustain a slow further decline of the dollar and overall world demand as the United States reverses its domestic expansionary policy stance. It is thus not surprising that there is growing momentum for unilateral fiscal reflation by Germany. Having reviewed fiscal policy considerations, we now turn to monetary policy.

A co-ordinated policy to lower interest rates in the major European countries either directly or through expansion of the money supply would put downward pressure on the D-Mark and the ECU relative to the dollar both as a result of the current-account effects of expansion as well as of the incipient capital outflow. Such policy would thus mitigate the undesired effects of the dollar's recent slide and work towards stabilizing the foreign-exchange market. At the same time it would lower capital costs and thus lower the cost of investment. The usual reservation about monetary expansion is its effect on prices and inflation. Yet in a time of excess capacity and zero inflation such considerations seem less important. Moreover, as capital costs and the cost of credit are important components of marginal costs in most countries, a reduction in the price of capital is likely to have supply-expansionary effects.

Unilateral monetary expansion in Germany as opposed to co-ordinated expansion would probably have asymmetric effects across European countries once again depending on bilateral exchange-rate effects and the structural characteristics of the economies. For the United Kingdom, which is more integrated in world financial markets and less indexed domestically, a reduction in German interest rates would probably bring about an appreciation of the pound with a deflationary impact on the economy. In that case, we have the traditional beggar-thy-neighbour policy effects associated with flexible exchange rates. For France and Italy, with higher degrees of wage indexation and greater sensitivity of domestic prices to imported prices, the currency appreciation will tend to produce a wage and price disinflation diminishing those countries' loss in competitiveness due to the exchange rate movement. The larger this supply-side effect, the more expansionary the outcome. Thus, France and Italy have more to gain from a German monetary expansion than the United Kingdom.

Unilateral and even more so co-ordinated monetary expansion in Europe will tend to mitigate the dollar's decline at the cost of output and employment. In light of the harmful effects of the protracted rise of the dollar between 1983 and 1985 especially for US export industries, the United States will be cautious in pushing actively for monetary expansion in Europe. Furthermore, given the accumulated international debt of the US, which has risen to $600 billion and $900 billion at the end of the decade[4], and the need to service that debt, it is highly unlikely that the United States would support policies that would tend to reverse substantially the downward trend of the dollar.

This highlights the delicate balance that the United States has to strike between the dollar's position as an international reserve currency and domestic output and employment considerations.

Appendix 2.1 gives the simulation results of a permanent 1-point cut in German short-term interest rates on output (Y), unemployment (UN), the inflation rate (IN) and the effective exchange rate (EER) in the major OECD countries. These seem to support the analysis of the likely effects of German monetary expansion. The model used for these simulation results is GEM, the quarterly econometric model of the UK's National Institute of Economic and Social Research. Over a two-year horizon, a 1-point cut in German interest rates which brings about a small devaluation of the D-Mark would increase output growth in Germany, and reduce the unemployment rate. The results would be mildly expansionary in France and Italy but contractionary in the United States. The brunt of adjustment seems to be borne by the United Kingdom with a rising deflationary effect on output growth, an increase in unemployment and a substantial appreciation of the pound. It is thus not surprising that there is no unanimous support for German monetary expansion within Europe and a preference for fiscal measures on the part of the United States.

The preceding analysis of benefits and costs to various countries from unilateral expansion in Germany or from co-ordinated expansion in Europe over the two periods is summarized in Table 2.1. The first period coincides with the precipitous rise of the dollar (i.e. spans the period 1981–5 I) and is a period of relative high inflation and real-wage rigidity especially in France and Italy. The second period is characterized by the fall of the dollar (1985 I to the present) and by low inflation and more flexible labour-market conditions in almost all European countries. A positive or negative sign indicates support for or opposition to the relevant policy action based on each country's perceived pay-off. This is determined by initial structural conditions in financial and labour markets, by the degree of openness of the economy and by expectations about bilateral and effective exchange rate movements.

From Table 2.1, one gains some insights as to the policy outcome(s) that would be expected purely on economic grounds:

1. A unilateral fiscal expansion by West Germany alone is more likely today than it was in the early 1980s as support for such action is more uniform across Germany's major trading partners.
2. A co-ordinated fiscal expansion today is probably to no one's interest as it will exacerbate the appreciation of the European currencies *vis-à-vis* the dollar and worsen further export competitiveness.
3. Co-ordinated monetary expansion on the part of European countries is probably discouraged by the United States as it will slow down considerably the downward trend of the dollar which is still desirable on external balance grounds.

Given the above, it is easy to understand why the European Commission's economic services, while revising downwards their forecast of the 12-nation growth rate for 1987 to only 2.3 per cent, urged Bonn to 'bring forward its proposed tax reforms, in an effort to counteract the flagging economic growth rate of the EEC' (*Financial Times* 27 Feb. 1987, p. 2).

Table 2.1 also highlights the questions that are still open regarding macroeconomic policy in Europe over the 1980s:

1. If the 'real-wage rigidity' thesis is discarded on empirical grounds, it is not easy to explain why EC countries did not chose the 'Decoupling II option' in 1983, namely to pursue a co-ordinated fiscal expansion that would have cushioned but not offset the falling ECU relative to the dollar; instead they chose to contract aggregate demand through fiscal and monetary means.
2. Why is 'consolidation' of public finances, which implies further monetary tightening and reduction in public expenditures, a preferable

Table 2.1 Expected pay-off for unilateral or co-ordinated expansion in Europe

	Period A 1981–5 I (dollar rising)				Period B 1985 – Present I (dollar falling)			
	Fiscal expansion		Monetary expansion		Fiscal expansion		Monetary expansion	
	Unilateral[1]	Co-ordinated	Unilateral	Co-ordinated	Unilateral[1]	Co-ordinated	Unilateral	Co-ordinated
G[2]	−(?)[3]	−(?)	−	−	+(?)	−	+	+
US	+	+	−	−	+(?)	−	−(?)	−
UK	−	+	−	−	+	−	−	+
FR, I	−	+(?)	−	−	+	−	+	+

High degree of wage indexation especially in France and Italy. Low degree of wage indexation in all European countries.

Notes
[1] Only by Germany.
[2] G = Germany, US = United States, UK = United Kingdom, FR = France and I = Italy.
[3] A question mark indicates an uncertain pay-off.

policy option today as opposed to a co-ordinated monetary expansion on the part of European countries?

3. Given that a unilateral German fiscal expansion is a desirable policy outcome for most major countries, what determines the choice of appropriate instrument, i.e. the stated preference for tax reduction as opposed to expenditure increases?

4. What are the reasons behind the EC Commission's advice for cautious if not overtly restrictive policies in most European countries and its persistent call for further moderation of real wages and improvement in market adaptability?

These considerations bring to the fore some of the major political determinants of macroeconomic policy outcomes. They relate (a) to the role of individual governments in international economic decision-making, especially to their respective degree of power in international negotiations; (b) to the internal political process that dictates target preferences and the choice of specific policy instruments, and finally, (c) to the role of international institutions such as the EC in European macro-policy determination.

A DYNAMIC POLITICAL ECONOMY ADJUSTMENT SYSTEM

An article by Woolley (1983) proposes a rudimentary typology of political factors that affect the conduct of macroeconomic policy. He develops a 2 × 2 matrix whose rows consist of either 'variable' or 'structural' factors and whose columns pertain to 'governmental' and 'non-governmental' ones. The first distinction relates to the time involved in the process of political change and the latter to the familiar distinction between state and society. Table 2.2 presents a revised version of Woolley's framework that incorporates some additional structural characteristics regarding the country's international position and the structure of domestic product markets.

Subsets of the factors mentioned in Table 2.2 also appear in the work of other authors. Epstein and Schor (1985) for example, focus on four variables which they view as important determinants of macro-policy. These are the relative power of labour and capital, the relation between financial and industrial capital, the degree of central bank independence and the position of the country in the world economy. Black (1982) on the other hand, develops a 'political game' model of the factors influencing the design of policy that is based on distributional preferences. Within the framework of that model, Black argues that differences in institutional structure in both labour and capital markets influence policy choices and the outcomes observed in different countries.

Most of the literature on the political economy of macroeconomic policy

Table 2.2 A typology of political factors that influence macroeconomic policy

	Governmental Type I	Non-governmental Type II
Variable	Election contests Dynamics of public opinion Legislative politics Bureaucratic politics Interest group politics	Wage bargaining Strike behaviour Business confidence
	Type IV	Type III
Structural	Division of Power between executive and legislature Structure and control of public bureaucracy	Degree of unionionization Links of parties and unions Organization of business sector Financial structure/relation with industrial capital National preferences for inflation/unemployment
	Central bank independence Trade structure Position of national currency	Structure of domestic markets Degree of international capital mobility

treats certain economic variables, such as the interest rate, as endogenous variables and political factors, such as the degree of unionization, government popularity or proximity to elections, as exogenous.

The hypothesis that is put forward in this section is that economic and political outcomes are jointly determined over time in relevant interconnected markets. One can then study not only the short-run responses of the system to exogenous disturbances but also the path of dynamic adjustment to a long-run economic and political steady state. As will be shown in the next section increased financial interdependence has influenced not only the direction of policy but variable and structural political factors such as wage bargaining, the degree of unionization and/or the relative power position of industrial versus financial capital.

An overview of this adjustment mechanism that incorporates both political and economic variables is presented in Fig. 2.1. It is an effort to extend analytically the stock-flow model that has become common in the international economics literature so as to include the political factors mentioned in Table 2.2. According to the stock-flow model, financial variables such as the exchange rate and the interest rate behave like asset prices and are determined by the short-run requirements of asset-market equilibrium. The values of these variables feed with a lag into trade and investment decisions, and thus over time feed back onto themselves through lagged effects on the accumulation of asset stocks, both abroad and at home (Branson 1979). Thus in an open-economy framework, the initial values of the domestic money supply, M, domestic bonds, B, net foreign assets, F, and domestic capital, K, determine a value for the exchange rate, e, and the domestic interest rate, r. Given other parameters of the system, such as the level of government purchases, G, and the tax structure, T, income, y, and prices, P, are simultaneously determined by equilibrium in the 'real' sector of the economy, that is by demand and supply conditions in commodity, real-capital and labour markets. Wages, W, and employment, N, are implicitly determined as well. The values for e, r, y, P, W and N, determine the accumulation equations for all assets, i.e. the rate of growth of domestic money and bonds $\dot{M} + \dot{B}$, which has to equal the budget deficit, $G - T$, the rate of growth of the capital stock in the economy, K, which is equal to investment, I, and the rate of growth of net foreign assets, $\dot{F}$, which is equal to the current account in the balance of payments, $X + r^*F$ where X is the value for net exports.

Thus, in this stock adjustment system, the stocks and other parameters determine, through the short-run equilibrium system, their own rates of change, which then feed back to move the stocks and the short-run equilibrium through time. If the entire system is stable, it will move the economy from an arbitrarily given set of initial stocks towards the steady state which is associated with balanced growth paths.

In Fig. 2.1 the institutional or political factors that are usually mentioned in the literature are embedded in this stock-flow adjustment system in a way that highlights the functional interconnections between economic and political variables.

The organization of labour markets or national preferences for inflation and unemployment are no longer parameters of the system but endogenous variables in the steady state. The experience of the 1980s offers a good example of this process: the protracted deflationary bias in economic policy has created structural unemployment and has marginalized important segments of the labour force such as young workers or residents of specific regions. Under such conditions, not only the degree but also the effectiveness of unionization has been radically altered. The experience or even the fear of protracted unemployment has also affected political behaviour as well as the nature of interest-group politics and national preferences regarding the inflation – unemployment trade-off. These feed-back effects from economic to political variables are easily captured within the framework of Fig. 2.1.

Similarly, in the context of the political-economy adjustment system proposed, the government's popularity surplus or deficit is considered an endogenous variable jointly determined with investment, the balance of payments deficit and the budget deficit. It is affected by a number of institutional factors and structural economic characteristics.

Finally, in this context, the conduct of monetary policy is determined not only by initial economic conditions but by a whole vector of institutional

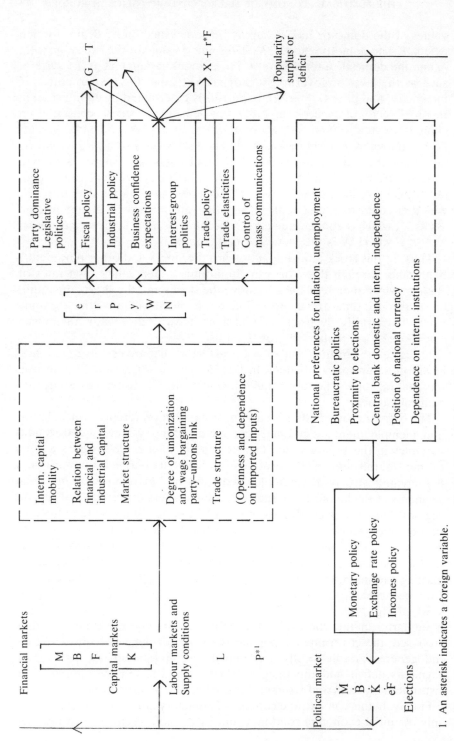

Figure 2.1 Political-economy adjustment system

1. An asterisk indicates a foreign variable.

factors including proximity to elections, the degree of central bank independence and business confidence as Lindblom (1977) suggested.

The causal relationship between any one factor and the policy outcome critically depends on the time horizon of the analysis and the specific country in question. Thus whether or not governments take action to lower interest rates as a result of a business confidence deficit, as Woolley (1983) stipulates, would also depend on balance of payments criteria and the degree of independence of the central bank of the country in question. It is not surprising, therefore, that the empirical support for hypotheses which are based on simplistic general theorizing is often extremely weak.

Within this political-economy adjustment framework, the conduct of exchange-rate policy is determined not only by variable or structural economic considerations but by institutional and political factors as well. Proximity to elections, national expressed preferences for inflation as opposed to unemployment, the degree of central bank independence relative to other domestic or international institutions and finally the relative degree of power of financial versus industrial capital, are important determinants of the desired role of the exchange rate in economic adjustment and the magnitude of central bank intervention in the exchange market. The differences in policy stance between German and French authorities during the early 1980s can be largely attributed to these factors.

It is by now well documented that the Bundesbank in West Germany is more independent than the Banque de France relative to the Treasury or the central authorities and that German banks in general exercise greater control over industry than do their counterparts in France (Francke and Hudson 1984). It is thus not surprising that in discussions or international negotiations over exchange-rate policy, financial and industrial interests are more unified in West Germany than in France, enhancing the former's negotiating position. This was evident in 1983 when the Bundesbank was able to dictate its policy preference for tight money and relatively strong currency not only to the German government but to its other European partners. It was able to do so because of the lack of strong domestic opposition from its export-oriented industrial sector and the fragmentation of domestic interests in France which weakened considerably the French government's negotiating position.

The dynamic interplay between domestic, political and economic variables determines not only the outcome of policy at home but the degree of policy co-ordination achieved at the international level. It also affects the development of international institutions which in turn exert an independent influence on national policy preferences and outcomes. These issues are discussed in the following section of the paper in relation to the analysis of the deflationary bias of macroeconomic policy in Europe during the 1980s.

THE POLITICS OF THE CONSOLIDATION DOCTRINE

The rise of monetarism from a local sect to worldwide eminence had been preceded by a shift of power from industry to the banks.

(Bhaduri and Steindl 1985, p. 60)

The 'economics puzzle of the 1980s' which was summarized earlier in this paper can now be re-examined in light of the political and institutional variables introduced in the previous section. The main argument presented in this section is that the uniform deflationary bias in macroeconomic policy at the international level is the result of a gradual shift of power from domestic capital and/or labour to financial capital and of the concomitant institutionalization of a supranational system of decision making which legitimizes this shift of power by over-representing the interests of financial capital in important areas of economic policy.

Even before the advent of floating exchange rates, the phenomenal growth of the Eurodollar market altered the balance of power away from the traditional domestic actors towards the international commercial banking system. The Eurodollar market developed quickly into an international commercial money market, comprising not only dollars but all other major convertible currencies, all of which were detached from their national monetary base (Bhaduri and Steindl 1985). The total value of such expatriate currencies held in the commercial banking system was estimated in November 1981 at 1.35 trillion US dollars. Even as early as 1973, the volume of the commercial bank's transactions in such expatriate foreign currency exceeded the total value of foreign exchange transactions by all central banks and monetary autorities taken together. Thus:

like multinational corporations in their field, international commercial banks emerged as a main focus of financial power, largely independent of the control of national monetary authorities.

(ibid., p. 66)

As Bhaduri and Steindl correctly note, the deposit base of the international commercial banks expanded dramatically following the first oil crisis in 1973 as petromoney was deposited in short-maturing accounts. The commercial banks thus enhanced their institutional role further by managing not only the provision of liquidity at the international level but by monitoring the required speed of adjustment of the borrowing countries. They were able to do so largely detached from the control of domestic governments, industry or national monetary authorities.

The development of Euromarkets and the power of commercial banks to operate extensively in foreign currencies created a new international environment for the central banks of key-currency countries. As capital mobility increased and international financial flows became substantial, central banks had to manage, mostly through monetary policy, substantial unexpected inflows or outflows of capital. Thus, the policy of high interest rates that the Bundesbank and other European Central Banks favoured in the early 1980s has to be explained largely as an attempt to slow down the capital outflow towards the United States rather than as a policy dictated by internal profit considerations (ibid, p. 58). In other words, the increased financial integration at the international level not only limited the effectiveness of monetary control but imposed new requirements for the conduct of policy and built up pressures for a new institutional set-up for macro-policy co-ordination. This trend was reinforced by the collapse of the Bretton Woods system.

The advent of floating exchange rates was supposed to increase the effectiveness of domestic monetary policy as a macro-policy instrument. Under floating rates, expansionary monetary policy was expected to give rise to an incipient currency devaluation that would increase aggregate demand and output whereas, under a system of fixed exchange rates, the loss in foreign exchange reserves would offset the planned increase in the domestic monetary base.

Experience during the 1970s showed that governments were not indifferent to the range of exchange-rate movements. A devaluation of the currency had implications not only for output but more importantly for internal income distribution as it affected differently the interests of specific groups in the society. Thus a devaluation was supported by the export sector of the economy and by industrial capital but was opposed by importers and the financial sector especially in countries where the latter was attempting to maintain a dominant international role (Epstein and Schor 1985). Furthermore, depending on the degree of wage indexation, a devaluation lowered real wages and raised the cost of production especially in the presence of imported inputs. Finally, exchange-rate movements produced important regional effects as they affected specific industries that were located in different areas. Since the exchange rate is the relative price of national currencies, the conduct of monetary policy abroad also influenced in a similar manner the internal income distribution.

The advent of floating exchange rates thus 'politicized' the conduct of monetary policy both at home and abroad. If this trend was allowed to continue, then the independence of central banks would have been eroded further as domestic actors would have interfered more systematically in the design of monetary policy. Central banks in the 1970s faced, therefore, the dual challenge to adjust to international capital flows and control international commercial bank operations as well as to safeguard their relative independence *vis-à-vis* domestic actors (the national government, domestic industrial capital, labour etc.). The management of exchange rates which were determined in highly volatile financial markets became not only increasingly difficult but threatened to undermine the autonomous institutional role of central banks. The development of the European Monetary System (EMS) within Europe and the strengthening of the role of the Group of Five, can be seen as natural responses of monetary authorities and governments of reserve-currency countries to retain control on key policy issues.

Within Europe, domestic monetary authorities chose eventually to lose some of the 'economic effectiveness' of domestic monetary policy and accept the leadership of the Bundesbank rather than face the erosion of their political autonomy by international commercial banks, by national governments or by other domestic actors. The acceptance of the Bundesbank hegemony by other Central Banks is not surprising given the institutional objective that they share, namely 'to defend the internal and external value of the currency' (Frey and Schneider 1981)[5]. The creation of an enlarged currency area with greater control over reserves enabled central banks to enhance their relative power vis-à-vis private financial capital. At the same time, the recall of external institutional commitments derived from the working of the EMS gave the domestic monetary authorities greater degrees of freedom in the conduct of policy vis-à-vis domestic government, labour and industry.

The delegation of authority over important macro-policy decisions to the West German monetary authorities had, in turn, important domestic repercussions in all countries. It enhanced the relative power not only of the central bank but also of domestic financial capital, of traders, and less so of industrial capital, i.e. the traditional supporters of conservative parties. Given West Germany's consistent preferences towards low inflation and a balance-of-payments surplus, acceptance of its leadership position implied domestic monetary discipline and maintenance of a slightly overvalued currency that would decrease the authorities' incentives to create inflationary surprises (Giavazzi and Pagano 1986). In other words, choosing to be the follower on an international scale, lowered the political capital required domestically to lobby for and maintain an anti-expansionary policy stance. According to Fischer (1987), 'the EMS was an arrangement for France and Italy to purchase a commitment to low inflation by accepting German monetary policy'. According to *The Economist*:

> If sterling does join the EMS the biggest change will be the transfer of responsibility for Britain's monetary policy from the Bank of England to Germany's Bundesbank which, as the central bank keenest on sound money, sets the pace for others to follow. This would be a blessing: Tory governments may like appointing City gents as governors of the Bank, but Mr Karl Otto Poehl would do a better job.
>
> (*The Economist*, 21 September 1985)

Wage earners and unions were apt to be the losers from the internationalization of the policy game. The functioning of the EMS raised significantly the costs of lobbying for a more expansionary policy stance while the complexity of the issues involved made it difficult for national unions to organize effectively on a European scale. The structural asymmetries across the European countries made the formation of cross-country alliances by labour and other groups even more difficult to attain.

Already by the late 1970s what, in fact, developed internationally was a hierarchical system of decision making that delegated increased power to the central banks of hard-currency countries. This development was the outcome not only of financial integration and the high degree of substitutability of international assets in domestic portfolios, but of the growing desire of Central Banks to circumvent domestic political pressures in the exercise of policy. This trend was supported by the corresponding governments as it allowed them to maintain their traditional hegemonic lead in the international economy despite the profound changes that had occurred in the 1970s in the international division of labour. Thus, even though the United States had lost its hegemonic power in world trade, it retained its lead position in macro-policy determination as a result of the role of the dollar as a reserve currency. The same can be said for Germany and the United Kingdom.

The informal institutional set-up that emerged for the co-ordination of macroeconomic policy, that is, the Group of Five, strengthened even further the negotiating position of these countries. Thus the political market for macro-policy determination evolved quickly into an effective oligopoly with market power positively related to the weight of each currency in private holders' portfolios. In this light, Japan's efforts to expand its position in world financial markets can thus be linked directly to its effort to increase its negotiating power within the group.

The central banks' primary concern for financial profitability and their traditional adherence to the pursuit of restrictive policies to meet their targets for low inflation and 'sound' balance of payments positions have tilted policy especially in Europe in a deflationary direction. Even so-called 'socialist' governments have sooner or later streamlined themselves to pursue overall deflationary policies that have been condoned by Bonn and the 'supranational monetary club' of the Group of Five.[6]

The uniform deflationary bias in macroeconomic policy during the 1980s can be explained only with reference to the institutionalization of this hierarchical and supranational system of decision-making which over-represents specific domestic interests in the negotiated outcome. Through this system, not only have central banks of reserve-currency countries increased their power relative to economic or sectoral ministries but domestic groups that traditionally oppose central bank positions have found themselves under-represented if not marginalized in the formulation of policy.

The other set of actors that has derived implicit benefits from the working of the present system consists of conservative parties.

In the domestic macro-economic policy sphere, parties have traditionally differentiated themselves at least over three aspects of policy: (a) on their desired position on the Phillips curve; (b) on income distributional grounds, and (c) on the choice of instruments in attaining these positions. Party platforms are determined primarily by the strength of preferences of party members and by the probability of being elected. Both of these factors and their respective effect on policy stance change over the business cycle (Brock and Magee 1978).

Conservatives tend to attach a larger weight on low inflation as opposed to low unemployment. They also favour a greater profit share in total income distribution. This is associated, in their view, with a larger share of savings[7] and private investment and greater overall competitiveness.[8] Thus on inflation grounds, conservative parties have traditionally promoted deflationary policies on the demand side and restrictive incomes policies on the supply-side. The preferred instrument to pursue deflationary policies from a conservative perspective is fiscal-expenditures contraction. This is because an income-tax increase will tend to hurt primarily conservative supporters while a monetary policy squeeze will raise interest rates and thus increase the cost of capital. A cut in fiscal expenditures on the other hand will hurt primarily the sector which is not likely to vote conservative.[9]

Given these preferences over targets and instruments shared by conservative parties, and central banks, it is not surprising that in the early 1980s deflation in Europe took mainly the form of fiscal expenditure contraction and 'greater labour-market flexibility', especially in West Germany and the United Kingdom. Other countries were explicitly or implicitly pushed in that direction. This was made easier, as we explained, by the system of hierarchical decision-making that has evolved over time and the asymmetric representation of players in that system. Thus even though co-ordinated fiscal expansion might have been a feasible economic option in the early 1980s, it was not a feasible political option for the leading countries in the European bloc.

Today, when inflation is very low and the cost of prolonged recession has raised the political costs of maintaining the past policy stance, tax cuts and mild monetary expansion are the only instruments that conservative governments will most likely consider. The tax-cut option will be marginally preferred over monetary instruments as it probably has a smaller impact on price performance and confers more direct benefits to specific targeted groups. At the same time, the supply expansionary effects of continued real-wage reductions favour the continuation of present incomes policies and the pursuit of even greater 'labour-market flexibility'. The combination of these two sets of policies will considerably worsen income distribution in Europe and might have important consequences for social cohesion.

The choice of policy instruments over the business cycle is thus largely affected by political considerations. For conservatives, deflation is largely pursued through fiscal-expenditures contraction. For labour or progressive parties tax increases are usually preferable fiscal policy tools. A monetary contraction affects borrowers across the political spectrum and can thus be considered a more 'politics-neutral' policy instrument. Thus, a different configuration of governments in Europe and primarily in West Germany and the United Kingdom could have produced a different configuration of policies. This however would have been increasingly more difficult under the present system of international macro-policy co-ordination which has managed to institutionalize a deflationary and conservative bias in policy outcomes. For these reasons, today, when reflation is contemplated, the most likely outcome is going to be tax reductions as opposed to increased government expenditures.

The creation of this informal but dominant institutional set-up at the international level has not only affected the direction of policy and the choice of policy instruments in participating countries but has changed the role of other international institutions such as the European Commission. This can be seen more clearly if one analyzes the prescriptions of the EC Annual Economic Reports over the past years.

The central objective of the 'co-operative strategy for more employment' in the 1986 Annual Economic Report is to 'create a more dynamic growth environment in the Community', chiefly by 'improving the business environment through appropriate adjustment policies that are the responsibility of national and regional authorities' (ECAR 1986–7, p. 34). To further fresh investment, 'authorities should pursue policies aimed at creating an enterprise-friendly economic and political environment' (ibid, p. 33). The main policy instruments for employment generation include 'raising the profitability of more employment-creating investment through maintaining moderate increases in real wages and the adaptability of labour market, holding demand at appropriate levels and the strengthening of competitive forces' (ibid, p. 36). 'Monetary policy should be conducted with a view towards price stability' while 'differing degrees of success in pruning public sector deficits may threaten the consolidation of the convergence towards monetary stability' (ibid., p. 30). West Germany alone should consider 'decisive' action:

> The public deficit has been reduced to such an extent that an easing of income tax in two stages – in 1986 and 1988 – is possible without endangering the success of consolidation. If the associated necessary expenditure cuts were set out at the same time, it would be easier for the repeatedly announced selective dismantling of subsidies to take place.
>
> (ibid., p. 79)

What is striking in the excerpts quoted is the conservative trust of macroeconomic policy direction and the political nature of the prescribed intervention.

According to many authors (Frey 1984; Messerlin 1981) bureaucracies tend to advocate policies that further their own interest, most notably their desire to cater to their own clients' interests. Thus, with minor exceptions, the EC Commission's policy prescriptions tend to provide semi-technical justification for the 'dominant' strategy. What is interesting to analyze is whether the key positions of an international organization such as the EC over policy issues are dictated more by national politics or by supranational institutional considerations. Under the first hypothesis, EC positions reflect mostly the political power-play between the key actors. Thus, if there are strong but divergent views across Community countries, Commission reports and policy prescriptions will reflect a minimum consensus view without strong policy recommendations. Under the latter hypothesis, an organization such as the EC Commission plays in fact the role of secretariat not to Community governments but to the European members of the Group of Five and more importantly to their central banks. West Germany is the designated leader in that set-up.

During the first part of the 1980s, the political and institutional interests of key players largely coincided. As a result we have had an exceptionally strong dose of 'conservatism' coming out of Brussels. The only notable exception that would support the institutional view, was the handling of the French case under the early Mitterrand government. In that case the cost of streamlining for the French government was partly reduced through the extension of an EC loan. The same happened a few years later in the case of a much weaker player, Greece.

It would take a few years before the political map of Europe is sufficiently changed, especially in key countries, so that one can assemble enough evidence in favour of the first or second hypothesis. However one can predict that the more national governments lose their autonomy in making key decisions over macro-policy, and the more they delegate authority to other decision-making units in the international arena, the more likely it is that the international system will become more oligopolistic and more conservative. In that case, international institutions such as the EC will increasingly further the interest of specific members and domestic institutions, such as the central banks, and will eventually have their credibility and authority questioned. This brings us to a more general point.

The Bretton Woods institutions and the EC are not properly designed to handle questions of macro-policy co-ordination. The compartmentalization of issues across institutions in a world of increased financial interdependence does not favour the development of a consistent view about international macro-policy and about the costs and benefits of specific policy actions. Exchange-rate policy and balance-of-payments adjustment are under IMF supervision, trade under GATT, development under the World Bank and UNCTAD, European policy under the EC. The inadequacy of existing institutions to deal effectively with present-day international economic problems has prompted the creation of more or less informal groups for policy discussion and co-ordination. This process of 'selective decision-making' has favoured the stronger countries who can now exclude not only other players from entering the policy game but also specific topics from the policy agenda. It has also made it difficult for many smaller actors to voice their concern and to form powerful coalitions. It has finally narrowed the domestic base of political support for the workings of international institutions.

Thus, in contrast to the 1960s when a premium was put on effective representation and the opening up of the international system, the 1980s is characterized mainly by retrenchment and the consolidation of existing power positions.

In a recent article Padoa-Schioppa made a similar point, emphasizing the distinction between 'ad hoc co-operation' and 'institutionalized co-operation'. Whereas the first type of co-operation is based on discussions among interested parties which lead to joint action only if agreement is reached, the latter type ensures that actions are taken at the multi-country level even when the parties fail to agree. He concludes that:

> as the scope for discretionary decisions in the government of multi-country economies will have to be greater than in the 1950s and 1960s, international institutions will have to be strengthened if such decisions are to be taken at the appropriate level.
>
> (Padoa-Schioppa 1985, p. 336)

CONCLUSIONS

Macroeconomic policy in Europe over the 1980s has been determined largely through the interplay of economic, political and institutional factors.

Growing world financial interdependence, floating exchange rates, and the dominance of a few hard currencies in international transactions has had profound implications for the relative bargaining power of countries in dictating macroeconomic policy. A hierarchical and oligopolistic system of decision-making has in fact developed internationally. Key players in that system are the reserve-currency countries, most notably the United States, West Germany and less so the United Kingdom, Japan and France. Market power in this bargaining game is more a function of portfolio holders' asset preferences across these currencies than a function of pre-dominance over world trade. This system of decision-making has evolved outside the traditional system of UN institutions or of the European Community and has, in fact, adopted a supervisory role in the functioning of the international monetary system. Bargaining over macro-policy in that

set-up involves to a large extent the management of exchange rates internationally. Thus, at the same time that decision-making has been relegated
to a few international actors, central bankers have increased their influence
in dictating policy outcomes. *Ceteris paribus*, these two trends taken
together exercise a deflationary bias on policy outcomes.

The development of this 'supra-national monetary club' in response to
the growing role of international financial investors and the politicization
of exchange-rate management strengthens the evidence in favour of a
'world politics paradigm' that transcends an exclusive 'state-centric' view of
international relations (Keohane and Nye 1971). It is the asymmetries in
financial interdependence across countries and the departure from a purely
competitive system in international finance that introduces political factors
into the analysis. Since a few agents (especially the central banks of key
reserve currencies) can exercise control over the world environment, problems of bargaining, strategy, influence and leadership immediately arise.
It is this factor that gives the club the potential to affect outcomes, i.e.
gives it 'power' (Keohane and Nye 1977).

The deflationary bias is made worse by the increasing costs of forming
sustainable coalitions against the pursuit of such policies. The complexity
of the issues involved in macroeconomic management and the structural
asymmetries across countries in their response to external shocks and/or
policies prevent the formation of an alliance among those groups which are
adversely affected. The internationalization of macroeconomic policy thus
worsens the misrepresentation of weaker groups in society in decision-
making.

Within that framework, over the 1980s, both the policy stance in Europe
and the choice of policy instruments were dictated by the net benefits
derived by the key players in the system. In the early 1980s co-ordinated
fiscal expansion was against West Germany's perceived interests which
coincided with the interests of European Central Banks and financial
capital. Instead fiscal deflation, monetary contraction and tough wage
policies were aggressively pursued. Today a unilateral fiscal expansion by
West Germany is mildly acceptable.

The way in which reflation or expansion takes place also depends to a
large extent on these political and institutional factors. The same can be
said for deflation. Conservative governments will show a clear preference
for tax cuts in expanding and for retrenchment of government programmes
and services in contracting. Progressive governments will have opposite
preferences. As conservative policies are institutionalized internationally
through the workings of the 'supranational monetary club', there is likely
to be a persistent conservative bias in policies even if domestic governments
change.

Finally, the outcome from the policy game will tend to be supported
rather than questioned by existing official institutions as these derive

credibility from their relative role *vis-à-vis* this 'dominant' international institution.

In conclusion, the unemployment problem in Europe today is as much an 'institutional' and 'political' problem as an 'economic' one. It highlights our failure as an international community to develop representative institutions that can cope effectively with the complexity of economic policy in a world of flexible exchange rates and financial interdependence. It also highlights the failure of democratic societies to create appropriate institutions that would serve the interests of their weaker members. As a result of these two failures we have managed to consolidate unemployment.

APPENDIX 2.1

In this appendix a graphical representation is offered of the interactions between the macroeconomy and the politico-economic system.

NOTES

1. I would like to thank Dr Simon Wren-Lewis of the National Institute for simulation experiments with the Institutes' GEM model.
2. The equation for investment in manufacturing that was estimated for eight countries during the period 1965–82 was of the following form:

$$\ln k = b_o + b_1 r + b_2 ir \quad \text{where}$$
$$r = a_o + a_1 r\,(w_v - \lambda_t) - a_2 d$$
i.e. $\ln k = b_o + b_1 a_o - b_1 a_1 w + b_1 a_2 d - b_2 ir$

where r is the logarithm of the real rate of profit, ir, the real rate of interest, w, the real product wage and d, a measure of demand pressure. In estimating this equation, Bruno finds that the elasticity of investment with respect to w is 2.4. Thus a permanent increase in w of 5 per cent over its equilibrium level would imply a fall in k of 12 per cent. The total elasticity of the d variable on the other hand amounts to 4.5. Given that the relative fall in its level over the period was of the order of 20 per cent, changes in d can explain drops of up to 90 per cent in k.
3. It became known as the 'Decoupling II' option.
4. Estimates by A. Meltzer for the Senate Banking Committee, quoted in *Financial Times*, 26 Feb. 1987.
5. The decision to join the EMS on the part of the French and Italian governments can also be viewed as a 'hedging strategy' in light of the expected victory of the socialists in the upcoming election.
6. In that light, it would be interesting to analyze the sharp reversal of macro-policy in France in 1982 as the outcome of a bargaining game between the French government on the one hand and the French and German Central Banks on the other with the German government throwing its weight behind the latter two.
7. The marginal propensity to save out of profits is assumed to be higher than it is out of labour income.

Table 2.3 Simulations of a 1-point cut in German short-term interest rates (% change)

	Germany				France				United Kingdom				Italy				United States			
	Y	UN[1]	IN[2]	EER[3]	Y	UN	IN	EER	Y	UN	IN	EER	Y	UN	IN	EER	Y	UN	IN	EER
83 01	0.1	-0.1	0.087	-1.9	0.1	-0.1	0.084	-1.1	-0.1	0.0	-0.080	1.2	0.1	0.0	0.209	-1.4	0.0	0.0	-0.013	0.9
02	0.2	-0.4	0.202	-2.9	0.1	-0.3	0.170	-1.6	-0.2	0.1	-0.222	1.8	0.2	-0.1	0.251	-1.3	0.0	-0.1	-0.041	1.6
03	0.3	-0.9	0.344	-4.0	0.2	-0.4	0.296	-2.3	-0.3	0.2	-0.446	2.8	0.2	-0.3	0.502	-1.3	0.0	-0.1	-0.079	2.5
04	0.5	-1.6	0.545	-5.5	0.2	-0.6	0.471	-3.3	-0.4	0.4	-0.772	3.8	0.2	-0.3	0.697	-1.5	0.0	-0.1	-0.129	3.5
84 01	0.7	-2.5	0.737	-7.4	0.3	-0.8	0.616	-4.8	-0.6	0.6	-1.071	5.2	0.3	-0.4	0.810	-2.0	0.1	-0.3	-0.187	4.9
02	1.0	-3.5	0.966	-9.7	0.5	-1.1	0.827	-6.6	-0.9	0.9	-1.447	7.1	0.3	-0.4	1.146	-2.5	0.1	-0.4	-0.250	6.5
03	1.3	-4.6	1.218	-11.6	0.6	-1.4	1.052	-8.1	-1.1	1.2	-1.890	8.6	0.2	-0.5	1.349	-2.9	0.1	-0.4	-0.324	7.9
04	1.5	-5.9	1.434	-12.8	0.7	-1.7	1.239	-8.9	-1.4	1.5	-2.300	9.6	0.2	-0.5	1.376	-3.2	0.0	-0.3	-0.395	8.8
85 01	1.8	-6.8	1.555	-12.8	0.8	-1.8	1.313	-8.4	-1.6	1.7	-2.605	9.2	0.0	-0.3	1.578	-2.5	0.0	-0.2	-0.441	8.7
02	2.0	-7.7	1.644	-14.5	0.9	-2.1	1.378	-9.8	-1.8	1.8	-2.662	10.1	-0.1	-0.2	1.652	-2.8	0.0	0.0	-0.471	10.0
03	2.2	-8.7	1.730	-17.4	1.0	-2.5	1.416	-11.2	-2.0	2.1	-2.610	12.1	-0.2	0.0	1.526	-2.6	0.0	0.1	-0.520	11.9
04	2.5	-10.1	1.821	-20.6	1.4	-3.3	1.470	-12.6	-2.3	2.3	-2.636	14.5	0.0	0.0	1.466	-2.3	-0.1	0.4	-0.608	13.9

Notes
[1] % change from simulation run.
[2] Difference between original % change and simulation % change.
[3] A '+' indicates an appreciation.

8. The larger the profit share, the smaller the labour share. Since this can be written as:

$$S_L = \frac{WN}{P_y} = W\frac{P_y}{N}$$

lowering the labour share implies lower real-wage growth relative to productivity and hence lower unit labour costs.

9. The reduction in fiscal expenditures has also been advocated on 'direct' or 'indirect' crowding-out grounds implying that a reduction in government consumption or investment will tend to increase private expenditures. This is usually complemented by an argument that private investment is more efficient than public investment and thus that there are net efficiency gains to the economy as a whole.

3 · THE POLITICAL ECONOMY OF THE EUROPEAN MONETARY SYSTEM[1]

Loukas Tsoukalis

After a difficult and rather unexpected birth, which was greeted with considerable scepticism, if not sheer cynicism, by the majority of bankers and professional economists, the European Monetary System (EMS) celebrated its ninth birthday in March 1988. The scepticism has been gradually replaced by a growing consensus about the practical achievements and shortcomings of the new system. Meanwhile, interest in the EMS has been constantly growing, as witnessed by the large number of plans put forward and the lively discussions taking place in both official and academic circles. The EMS is likely to remain high on the European political agenda for many years, although there are as yet few signs of an agreement being formed on its future shape and evolution.

The large bulk of the work done until now on the EMS falls broadly into two categories: a technical assessment of the effects of the EMS on various economic variables and a constantly growing set of proposals regarding possible developments in the future. With few exceptions, the work is characterized by a narrow economic approach.

This paper starts with two basic assumptions. The first is that monetary and financial affairs do not take place in a political vacuum. The second, closely following from the first, is that any economic arrangement – or policy regime, if one is to use the current jargon – entails costs and benefits which are not equally distributed among participants. In other words, there are winners and losers or, at least, in positive sum game situations, some who gain more than others. The survival of any particular economic arrangement, or alternatively the shift from situation A to situation B, should largely depend on the existing balance of power, both internal and external, and the actual or expected distribution of gains and losses.

In this paper, we propose to introduce the above considerations in the study of the EMS, in the hope of gaining a better insight into its wider economic and political significance as well as its possible development in the future. Our main objective is not to offer a new interpretation of the broad economic effects on the EMS during its first nine years of life. There

are already numerous works done in this area. Instead, we propose to concentrate mainly on the nature of policy co-operation which has gradually
emerged and which sustains the operation of the system. This should
enable us to identify better the role and interests of the main actors and
their expectations in terms of its future evolution.

We will start with an overview of the broad economic effects of the EMS
until now, drawing mainly from the results of econometric studies already
available. This will lead to an analysis of the implicit framework of policy
co-operation on which the everyday functioning of the EMS relies; and the
wider economic and political implications, both as regards the European
Community in general and individual member countries in particular. This
is intended to be in a sense the political economy balance sheet of the
EMS. It will be followed by some general conclusions and a discussion of
future prospects, always concentrating on the relation between the intrinsic
merits of specific proposals and the feasibility of political coalitions which
will be needed for their implementation.

EXCHANGE RATE VARIABILITY AND GENERAL
MACROECONOMIC PERFORMANCE

Undoubtedly, the most important achievement of the EMS has been the
increased stability which has characterized bilateral exchange rates between participating currencies. In an IMF study,[2] which contains the most
systematic analysis so far of available data, all measures used indicate a significant decline in nominal exchange rate variability between participating
currencies in the period 1979–85, when compared with the pre-EMS experience of those currencies. Since the same is not also true of a control group
of major non-EMS currencies, this decline in nominal exchange rate variability cannot be attributed to exogenous events. On the other hand, the
variability between EMS and non-EMS currencies has increased during
this period.

Real exchange rate variability among participating currencies also declined between 1979 and 1985. This, therefore, suggests that the reduction
in nominal variability has been accompanied by a convergence of national
inflation rates.

Indeed, the EMS period has been characterized by a reduction of inflation differentials.[3] After an early peri6d,'which saw an opening of the gap
following the second large increase in oil prices in 1979, inflation rates in
EMS countries have been dropping steadily, and the divergence between
those rates has been rapidly reduced. A similar trend can be observed in
terms of unit labour costs.[4]

Admittedly, inflation rates have been declining virtually everywhere else
in the industrialized world, and it is impossible to isolate the EMS effect on

participating countries. However, it seems plausible to argue that the determination of countries such as France and Italy to pursue an anti-inflation policy has been much strengthened by their participation in the system. In the case of Italy in particular, the exchange rate has been consciously used as an anti-inflationary instrument.

Despite the convergence downwards of national inflation rates, the operation of the EMS has been accompanied by some changes in the international competitiveness of individual countries.[5] This means that exchange-rate movements have not fully compensated for differences in national cost and price developments. When measuring competitiveness in terms of consumer prices adjusted for exchange-rate changes among EMS currencies, it appears that Ireland and Italy have suffered a significant loss, while Belgium and the Federal Republic have been the main beneficiaries. When unit labour costs are used as a yardstick, then the changes in competitiveness among the EMS countries appear to be much smaller, with the exception of two, namely Belgium and the Netherlands, which have gained significantly. Measured against a larger sample of trading partners, broadly similar conclusions apply regarding the development of international competitiveness of EMS countries.[6]

Can the relative exchange-rate stability achieved by the EMS countries be attributed to a closer convergence of economic policies? Here, the picture becomes more complicated. In terms of monetary aggregates, the EMS period is characterized by a significant reduction in growth rates and a narrowing of intra-EMS differences. Absolute differences in terms of nominal domestic credit expansion also decline during the same period. Short- and long-term interest rates rise and differentials widen until 1984, when the process starts being reversed. In terms of interest rates, the correlation is much stronger between the Federal Republic and the smaller members of the system which have clearly adopted a D-Mark exchange-rate target.[7]

Contrary to developments in the monetary field, there are no clear signs of convergence in terms of fiscal policies. This seems to suggest that national authorities have relied mainly on monetary instruments in order to achieve the convergence of inflation rates and exchange-rate stability.

The next question is whether the reduction in exchange-rate variability has had any discernible effects on real economic variables. The EMS has coincided with a considerable slowing down of real growth rates, a reduction of investment and low rates of expansion of intra-EMS trade.[8] The general macroeconomic performance of EMS countries during this period, and especially in more recent years, does not compare favourably with that of major countries outside the system, such as the USA, Japan and the UK. Has the positive welfare effect, if any, of the EMS not been able to compensate for the influence of other factors operating simultaneously? Or, perhaps, is there anything inherent in the system, like a deflationary bias, which may partly account for the unfavourable development of real economic variables in recent years?

A NEW FRAMEWORK FOR POLICY CO-OPERATION

The everyday functioning of the EMS requires a certain degree of co-operation among the monetary and political authorities of participating countries. The pattern of co-operation which has gradually developed differs, in some respects substantially, from the original intentions of the architects of the system, as translated into the specific rules contained in the EMS agreement of 1979.[9] Some rules have been changed in the meantime. It is too early to judge whether the latest changes introduced as a result of the Nyborg-Basle agreement in September 1987 will have any substantial effect on this pattern of co-operation which has so far been characterized more by discretion and informal understandings than the strict application of existing rules.

The EMS has developed into an asymmetrical system, with the Federal Republic performing the role of an informal leader.[10] The source of this asymmetry is essentially dual: the German low propensity to inflate and the international role of the D-Mark. The former, combined with the economic weight of the country and the priority attached until recently in the other EC partners to the fight against inflation, has enabled Germany to set the monetary standard for the other countries. On the other hand, the increasingly important role of the D-Mark as an international reserve currency places the German central bank in a key position with respect to the external monetary policy of the EMS as a whole. These two factors seem to suggest that, irrespective of the specific rules agreed at the time of the creation of the EMS, some degree of asymmetry was inherent in the system.

The margin of manoeuvre of the other countries *vis-à-vis* Germany has depended essentially on their willingness to have recourse to foreign-exchange interventions, capital controls and, in the last resort, to currency realignments.[11] In this respect, they can be divided into three different groups: the Netherlands, a country which has chosen free capital markets, a *de facto* pegging of its currency to the D-Mark and close alignment with German monetary policy; the other small countries (with Ireland being perhaps an odd case) which, although tying their monetary policy closely to that of Germany, have looked for some flexibility through capital controls and limited exchange-rate adjustments; and France and Italy, which, in their search for a greater degree of monetary independence, have had to rely more heavily on the use of the other instruments.

The above-mentioned asymmetry manifests itself in a concrete form during periods of tension, when the commitment of central banks to the existing bilateral rates is tested through speculation in the exchange markets. The source of tension can be either internal – bilateral trade or financial imbalance – or external. The former is straightforward, while the latter is essentially a function of the disproportionate effect of dollar fluctuations on the D-Mark, which in turn acts as a centrifugal force inside the EMS.[12]

Especially after the March 1983 realignment, most central bank interventions have taken place inside the permitted margins of fluctuation. The aim of intra-marginal interventions has been to strengthen market confidence in the stability of existing bilateral rates and thus avoid the development of crisis situations. At least until the Basle-Nyborg agreement, these interventions were made exclusively by the authorities of the weaker currencies; there was hardly any evidence, for example, of the Bundesbank being involved in intra-marginal interventions. However, in a few instances, the central banks of the other countries had deliberately let their currency hit the floor of the permitted band of fluctuation, in order to bring into operation the intervention and credit mechanisms of the EMS and thus force the Bundesbank to play an active role.

The increasing reliance on intra-marginal interventions has had a number of important consequences. First of all, the burden of supporting the exchange-rate system has rested disproportionately on the shoulders of the countries with the weaker currencies. Furthermore, the very short-term credit facility, which, until the September 1987 agreement, could be triggered off automatically only as a result of marginal interventions, fell increasingly into disuse; and this had a negative effect on the use of the ECU in the credit mechanism.

A growing share of intra-marginal interventions has been carried out in EC currencies.[13] This has also led to an increase in the share of official reserves held in those currencies. However, in view of the many restrictions still imposed by EC central banks, and most notably the Deutsche Bundesbank, in the use of their currencies by each other as well as of the ECU, the US dollar has remained an important intervention instrument even for purely intra-EMS operations. Thus, little progress has been made in terms of reducing Europe's dependence on the dollar.

Recourse to the EMS credit mechanism has been very limited. Largely because of increasing intra-marginal interventions, the use of the very short-term credit facility was until September 1987 drastically reduced. The short-term monetary support and the medium-term financing facility have been never used until now. In times of difficulty, EC countries have preferred to borrow directly from the Eurocurrency markets. Recourse has only been made to a second type of medium-term financing facility, which involved EC borrowing in capital markets on behalf of a particular country. This was used for the benefit of France in 1983, and for Greece, which does not participate in the exchange-rate mechanism (ERM), in 1985. As regards the ECU, it has remained essentially a credit instrument despite the original intentions of the architects of the system and some modest attempts in the meantime to improve its attractiveness as an official reserve asset.

The increasing reliance on intra-marginal interventions has also meant that the threshold of the divergence indicator was rarely reached, thus contributing to what had already appeared as the inoperational nature of this new mechanism. Perhaps, the 'presumption to act', mentioned in the 1979 EMS agreement, was, in any case, a very difficult concept to translate into concrete policy measures in an intergovernmental context. It may be only a curious coincidence that Belgium, the country which had invented the divergence indicator, has persistently ignored it as a sign for policy action. The important conclusion is, however, that the attempt made with the EMS to design rules which would guarantee a certain degree of symmetry between strong and weak currencies has proved almost totally ineffective.

Another concrete manifestation of the asymmetry in the system is the way in which short-term interest rates have been used as part of the exchange-rate policy of participating countries. The evidence suggests that the burden of adjustment has been borne almost entirely by France, Italy and the smaller countries, while changes in German interest rates have been mainly in response to international monetary developments.[14] Capital controls, the effectiveness of which seems to be limited to short periods, have enabled a country such as France to insulate partly domestic interest rates from developments in the offshore markets, where short-term rates have been used frequently as a weapon in defence of the exchange rate of the franc.[15]

Exchange rate stability has not been interpreted as rigidity. During its first nine years of life, the EMS experienced eleven realignments, five of which can be considered as major ones involving most EMS currencies.[16] Changes in bilateral exchange rates have become, after some early attempts at unilateralism, a matter of collective decision. This is in itself a revolutionary development, as it touches at the very heart of monetary sovereignty. Furthermore, realignments have often been accompanied by changes in domestic economic policies.

On the other hand, collective decisions have not always been either easy or smooth, especially when taken under market pressure. In some instances, negotiations have turned into major political confrontations between individual countries. Currency realignments are not governed by any specific rules. Discussions among EC Finance Ministers, leading to an agreement on a new set of bilateral rates, can be initiated by any country participating in the exchange rate arrangement. The final agreement is, however, subject to certain practical constraints which derive mainly from a desire, shared by all members, to guarantee the survival of the system. As realignments take place during weekends, a final agreement has to be reached before Monday morning when exchange markets open again. Furthermore, the new set of bilateral rates needs to be credible to market operators.

On the basis of the experience accumulated until now, a few general observations can be made regarding realignment decisions in the EMS. Although some degree of negotiation has almost invariably accompanied each realignment, concerning mainly the size of bilateral exchange-rate changes, the only occasions in which the negotiation has turned into a serious political confrontation between participating countries have involved the French franc and, by implication, the D-Mark. Two characteristic examples of such confrontations are the realignments of March 1983 and January 1987, which took place in an atmosphere of crisis, with accusations and threats being exchanged between the two sides of the Rhine.

On the occasion of those currency realignments, France directly challenged the leading position of the Federal Republic inside the EMS. The discussions leading to the final agreement took place in two distinct phases: the first one involving a negotiation between France and Germany regarding the bilateral exchange rate between the franc and the D-Mark, and a second one in which all the other countries took part. This does not mean that Franco-German decisions were imposed on the other members of the system. On the contrary, in the case of both realignments mentioned above, the other countries seemed to enjoy a considerable margin of manoeuvre. However, it was abundantly clear that a Franco-German agreement was a precondition and also the basis on which the general EMS realignment would have to be built. After all, this pattern of negotiation has frequently appeared in other areas of EC activity.

Conflicts with respect to currency realignments have been as much about substance as about appearance. National positions have been a reflection of different, and sometimes opposing, considerations. Domestic interest groups, mainly industrialists and farmers, have played an active role in trying to influence the formulation of those positions. Mercantilist interests – the desire to secure a competitive edge for one's producers and satisfy domestic political pressures – have often clashed with anti-inflationary objectives. The resulting dilemma, in terms of government policy, has sometimes taken an acute form in Germany, where ministers usually show greater sensitivity to the former interests, while the central bank sees itself as the defender of the latter. Internal political divisions have often been apparent during intergovernmental negotiations taking place in the context of the EMS.

Divisions among countries have centred on different economic philosophies, the distribution of the burden of adjustment between surplus and deficit countries, and the effect of EMS realignments on national farmers, resulting from the denomination of common agricultural prices in ECUs.

However, much of the conflict which has accompanied EMS currency realignments can only be explained in terms of disagreements regarding their presentation to national public opinion. No government wants to be seen as devaluing the national currency, which is still considered as a blow to national virility. Thus, it is always far preferable for Germany to revalue its currency than for any other country to have to devalue its own. Much of the crisis, which surrounded the March 1983 and January 1987 realignments, was not about the size of bilateral exchange-rate changes, which was agreed upon at some stage of the negotiation; it was more about the form in which this change would be presented. It is interesting that national public opinion is still considered to be virtually illiterate even in simple financial matters.

The EMS is certainly not a self-contained system. International monetary developments, and especially shifts in market sentiment towards the US dollar, have a considerable effect on EMS currencies collectively as well as on intra-EMS exchange rates. The early period of the system was marked by the strength of the US currency, while in more recent years the continuous depreciation of the dollar has contributed significantly to increased tension between strong and weak EMS currencies.

Co-ordination of national monetary policies *vis-à-vis* the dollar is still in an infant stage, although a few attempts have been made in this direction as evidenced, for example, by the Gleneagles agreement in September 1986. On most occasions, the Bundesbank has *de facto* assumed the responsibility for conducting the external monetary policy of the EMS. While German monetary authorities have been mainly preoccupied with the D-Mark–dollar relationship, thus also dragging the whole EMS along with them, the monetary authorities of the other countries of the system have, grudgingly, concentrated their efforts on keeping the bilateral rate between their currencies and the D-Mark within the permitted margins of fluctuation. This has meant an implicit division of labour in terms of exchange-rate interventions between the different central banks.

The gradual emergence of the Group of Five (or Six or Seven, depending on how insistent Italy and Canada have been in their demands for inclusion) as an important, informal body for the collective management of the world economy, means that the majority of EMS countries are completely excluded from major decisions which may affect the internal workings of the system. Even within this group, Germany occupies, in view of its economic weight and the international role of the D-Mark, a much stronger position than France, Britain or Italy.

In institutional terms, the management of the EMS has remained in the hands of national central banks and monetary authorities. The Council of Economic and Finance Ministers (ECOFIN), meeting at least once a month, is the highest political body in which all important economic and financial matters are discussed. Decisions on periodic EMS realignments and the granting of loans to individual member countries are taken by ECOFIN. In the field of budgetary policies, co-ordination at the EC level is supposed to take place in the context of the so-called 1974 Convergence Decision.

However, the concrete effects of this co-ordination effort are rather difficult to discern, and recently the whole approach has been criticized as
flawed for both political and economic reasons.[17]

Needless to say, economic and financial issues also regularly appear on
the agenda of meetings of the European Council. Important initiatives
have been taken at summit meetings, including the one which led to the
launching of the EMS. However, under normal circumstances, ECOFIN
acts as the highest decision-making body pertaining to economic policy co-
ordination and the general operation of the EMS.

Day-to-day management is left to the central banks of individual countries, which keep a close and regular contact with each other. There are also
two important EC committees which have played a significant role in laying
the foundations for European monetary co-operation, and later managing
the 'snake' and the EMS, and negotiating changes with respect to the rules
governing the operation of the latter. The Monetary Committee consists
of senior officials from the finance ministries and central banks. It meets
monthly in Brussels and is responsible for all matters of monetary relevance,
including the preparatory work for currency realignments. The Committee
of Governors of Central Banks meets monthly in Basle. Its responsibility is
more immediate, in the sense that it is directly in charge of the ERM and
the application of the EMS agreement.

The European Monetary Co-operation Fund (EMCF) is still nothing
more than a brass plate on a door in Luxembourg. The Bank for International Settlements (BIS) acts as its agent regarding all operations arising
from the credit and monetary mechanisms. In fact, this amounts to an accounting task. The BIS has also become the first 'other holder' of ECUs,
following the agreement of central bank governors of June 1985. It will also
act as the final clearing institution in MESA (Mutual ECU Settlement
Account), a clearing house for private ECUs.

According to the agreement reached at the European Council in Brussels
in December 1978, the EMS was due to enter its institutional phase at the
latest in March 1981. The consolidation of the EMS into a permanent structure would have involved the transformation of the EMCF into a European
Monetary Fund as well as 'the full utilization of the ECU as a reserve asset
and a means of settlement'. But this consolidation has not happened as yet,
and the role of the EMCF can therefore only be measured in terms of
potential.

The role of the EC Commission has been essentially supportive. The
Commission is represented in all Council meetings, and participates in the
work of specialized committees. It also provides some of the administrative
and analytical backup. However, its input in the everyday management of
the EMS is marginal, and the same has been so far true of its impact on the
more long-term development of the system. The Commission's influence in
the field of co-ordination of macroeconomic policies has also been very

limited indeed. Its annual economic report, containing an extensive analysis of the macroeconomic situation in the Community and policy guidelines, has had little effect on the actual policies pursued by member countries.

The ERM, added to the ever-present reality of trade interdependence, acts as the only real binding constraint on the formulation of national macroeconomic policies. Its effect is, predictably, more evident in terms of monetary than fiscal instruments. The Community interest and policy are still defined mainly through intergovernmental procedures at best or as the sum of unco-ordinated national interests and policies at worst. And in this respect, some have clearly more influence than others.

POLITICAL ECONOMY BALANCE SHEET

The EMS is certainly the most important manifestation of the macroeconomic dimension of the EC, which, until the adoption of the Single European Act, remained at the margin of Community activity.

In a world of generalized floating, characterized by high instability of exchange rates, the EMS has helped to curb over-shooting and also to avoid long periods of misalignment of participating currencies. Its positive effect on intra-EMS trade and economic growth is difficult to determine, although generally assumed, sometimes almost as an act of faith, to be considerable.

The EMS has also served as an important instrument in the fight against inflation. The system of stable exchange rates and the pegging of national currencies to the D-Mark have created an external discipline which seems to have reinforced the determination of national authorities in the pursuit of anti-inflationary policies. In this respect, the operation of the EMS until now can be seen partly as a function of a particular economic conjuncture in which the fight against inflation constituted the first priority of Western European governments.

For the European federalist, the EMS can be considered as a major step towards the creation of a regional currency bloc and a collective system of decision-making. Some progress has been made towards a closer co-ordination of monetary policies, with an institutional infrastructure ready to develop along federalist lines, once the political will exists. Exchange-rate changes have become a matter of collective decisions, although the negotiations leading to currency realignments have sometimes taken the form of dangerous poker games in which the players continued to bluff until the last minute, while the survival of the whole system was at stake.

The EMS has also laid the foundations for the development of a truly European currency. While the official ECU remained underdeveloped and underutilized, the private ECU market has developed rapidly.[18] The ECU quickly reached the fifth rank in terms of assets and liabilities of commercial banks, after the US dollar, the D-Mark, the Swiss franc and the yen. A similar development has occurred with respect to the ECU bond market. The ECU exchange market has also expanded significantly, and the new currency has had some limited use in the foreign trade of individual EC countries. Although linked by a common definition, the official and the private ECU remain, however, completely separate.

The main factors behind the rapid growth of the ECU in private markets are its quality as a basket of currencies which, unlike the SDR, is backed by a collective agreement in terms of policy co-ordination, the role of EC institutions in familiarizing the banking sector in the use of this basket unit, and the general process of financial innovation.

There is, however, also some truth in the somewhat cynical argument, namely that the growth of the private ECU is mainly a reflection of the still insufficient convergence among participating economies. Interest-rate differentials have been a determining factor behind the issuing of ECU-denominated loans. Most of the borrowers have come from countries with high nominal and real interest rates, such as France and Italy, while investment has been generated mainly from the Benelux countries, where low interest rates have prevailed. The deceleration of the growth of the ECU market in 1986 was largely attributed to the reduction in the interest-rate differential between the ECU and the D-Mark.[19]

The EMS has coincided with a long period of low growth and high unemployment in Western Europe. Therefore, the obvious, albeit somewhat unexpected, question which needs to be asked is whether there has been a simple coincidence or some form of correlation between the two.

The unfavourable macroeconomic performance of the EMS countries has usually been attributed either to supply-side factors, which form part of the notorious 'Eurosclerosis', or to the restrictive policies pursued by European governments during this period.[20] This is a highly controversial question which has divided not only economists but also governments. In more recent years, it has entered into the domain of high politics as a result of the growing pressure from the United States, addressed mainly to Germany and Japan, to shift their policies to a more reflationary gear and thus act as mini-locomotives for the world economy.

As regards the members of the EMS and the EC more generally, virtually every proposal made in recent years in the direction of co-ordinated reflationary action, with a strong emphasis on fiscal measures, has been pointed mainly towards Germany.[21] Because of its economic weight and the combination of low inflation, high unemployment and large current-account surpluses, the Federal Republic has been considered as the natural candidate for stimulating demand and growth in Western Europe. To the extent, therefore, that there has been and still is room for non-inflationary expansion of aggregate demand, the continuous refusal of Germany to move in this direction has acted as a major constraint for the other European countries.

Assuming that the above argument is correct, then the next question is whether the EMS as such has significantly strengthened the deflationary impact on other countries of German policy priorities, which are, in turn, a function of national perceptions and the domestic distribution of power. The EMS has meant that the Federal Republic sets the monetary standard for the other members, although some degree of flexibility has been retained through capital controls and periodic currency realignments. Convergence of fiscal policies is still very limited. Would member countries have enjoyed a much greater freedom in their fiscal policies, if they had allowed themselves greater use of the exchange rate instrument?

To put it differently, assuming that German economic policies have been too restrictive in recent years and that German influence on policies pursued by other EC countries has been decisive, to what extent is the acceptance of this situation by the other countries, as an exogenous constraint, the result of their participation in the EMS and to what extent is it simply the result of the dominant position of the German economy in the regional system?

It is not at all easy to provide clear-cut answers to the above questions. The combination of a system of relatively fixed exchange rates based on a D-Mark standard and the lack of a real and symmetrical co-ordination of fiscal policies may have produced a deflationary bias, thus further reducing the margin of manoeuvre of the weaker economies. There is, however, an alternative and not altogether implausible thesis, namely that the countries with weak currencies have purchased extra credibility in their fight against inflation by linking their currencies to the D-Mark. If this is true, then they need to decide whether they are happy with the price attached to this credibility.

In discussing the leading role of Germany in the EMS, some writers have argued[22] that this asymmetry was inevitable either because of the particular economic conjuncture – anti-inflation priority – or because of the very nature of a fixed exchange-rate system and the n-1 problem. Comparisons have been drawn with the role of Britain in the Gold Standard and that of the United States in the Bretton Woods system, often in the context of the so-called hegemonic-stability theory.

Leaving aside the many problems which arise in trying to apply the theory of public goods to international or regional monetary systems and in identifying the nature and source of instability, which in turn leads to the need for a hegemon, the role of Germany in the EMS differs in many respects from previous historical examples.

First of all, the leading country in the EMS does not provide the financial centre for the region as a whole. Second, and more important, is that, unlike Britain and the United States in the past, the Federal Republic has not adopted a policy of 'benign neglect' towards its balance of payments. On the contrary, the German economy has very much relied on export-led growth, with some clear elements of mercantilism in the policies pursued. Germany's bilateral trade surpluses with the other members of the EMS (with the exception of the Netherlands and Ireland) have been growing rapidly since 1979,[23] thus adding to the deflationary pressure in the other countries. The EMS in itself must have played some role in this development. Last but not least, the leading position of Germany in the economic and monetary sphere is neither consistent with the political balance of power in the region nor with the general Community model of decision-making.

Some general observations can also be made regarding the role of the EMS inside the Community system. The EMS operates essentially on the basis of intergovernmental co-operation. It has been and continues to be the most important manifestation of variable geometry or the two-tier Community model. Britain and Greece do not participate in the ERM, which is after all the cornerstone of the whole system, while the two Iberian members are still in their transitional period following accession, with only Spain being a candidate for full membership in the foreseeable future. Other countries, such as Austria and Switzerland, have been *de facto* associated with the ERM through the close link between their currencies and the D-Mark. More recently, Britain has also tried, although not very consistently, to pursue an exchange-rate policy with a clear D-Mark target.

The general attitude towards the EMS appears to be positive in all participating countries. This is true of both political and business circles. There are, however, important national differences in the evaluation of the EMS experience.

As far as the Federal Republic is concerned, the EMS has undoubtedly developed more favourably than expected or feared, especially by the central bank, back in 1978. It has created an area of exchange-rate stability which represents approximately two-thirds of German trade, if non-member countries which have linked their currencies closely to the D-Mark are also included. It has also enabled Germany to gain a competitive advantage against some countries, since currency readjustments have not until now fully compensated for inflation differentials. This is partly reflected in the growing bilateral trade surpluses of recent years.

At the same time, there is little evidence of the EMS imposing a serious constraint on German monetary and, even less so, fiscal policy. Thus, because of its leading position, Germany may have been able to achieve what is sometimes considered to be an impossible combination, namely stable exchange rates, free capital movements and an independent monetary policy. This conclusion may, however, need to be slightly modified in view of the 1986–7 experience, when the over-shooting of German monetary targets could be partly attributed to EMS interventions and, perhaps, to some currency substitution.

France has always attached considerable importance to exchange-rate stability. Participation in the EMS has also served as an anti-inflationary instrument and as a weapon against protectionist pressures inside the previous Socialist government, especially in 1982–3. Capital controls have been used, sometimes very effectively, as a shield to protect domestic economic agents from the large fluctuations – mainly upwards – of interest rates in offshore markets. Successive effective devaluations of the national currency have been the result of an agonizing process of trying to catch up with the loss in international competitiveness arising from higher French inflation rates.

The French have been disappointed with the lack of symmetry in the system, both in terms of domestic and external policies. 'Les dirigeants allemands ne conçoivent les progrès de l'Europe que dans l'alignement des politiques des autres pays sur leurs propres priorités'.[24] 'The German authorities consider progress in Europe only insofar as this means the alignment of other countries' policies to their own priorities.' This aptly summarizes the feelings of French policy-makers.

The external discipline function of the EMS has been more important in the case of Italy, where the Banca d'Italia has used the participation of the lira in the ERM as an important anti-inflationary weapon vis-à-vis Italian industry, the trade unions and even the political class. This may be the clearest case of a central bank trying through the EMS to strengthen its position in the domestic process of economic policy-making. The progressive over-valuation of the lira appears to be a deliberate choice. The wider margins of fluctuation have given Italian authorities a greater margin of manoeuvre in terms of monetary policy. At the same time, they have also reduced Italy's influence over the development of the system, an influence which certainly does not match the intellectual contribution of Italian central bankers and academics to the EMS debate.

As regards the smaller countries,[25] the range of choice in terms of economic policy is limited, almost irrespective of the existence of the EMS. The operation of the system has, perhaps, led to an even closer alignment of their monetary policies with that pursued by Germany. This is mainly true of Belgium and Denmark, since the Netherlands had already, at an earlier stage, adopted a D-Mark standard. The Benelux countries and Denmark have succeeded in substantially improving their competitive position against the other members of the EMS by gradually moving towards an effective under-valuation of their currencies in comparison to the situation back in 1979. Exactly the opposite has happened with Ireland, where the economic benefits of its participation in the ERM are still not abundantly clear.

CONSOLIDATION AND INSTITUTIONAL REFORM

The transition to the second stage, associated with major institutional changes, was originally planned to take place at the most two years after the launching of the EMS in March 1979. However, no important reforms have been introduced until now, and the system still operates on the basis of transitional structures and arrangements.

The more far-reaching proposals, involving major institutional reforms, have usually come from the EC commission, Italy and the Benelux countries, although, more recently, the initiative in this area has been taken by France. There has also been a plethora of ideas and proposals from the academic community. Interestingly enough, the architects of the EMS, Messrs Giscard d'Estaing and Schmidt, have been consistent advocates of a more rapid evolution of the system involving eventually the creation of new European institutions.

The discussion has revolved around the development of the ECU into a parallel currency,[26] circulating alongside national currencies and also acting as an international reserve asset, and the role of a European Monetary Fund, replacing the largely fictitious EMCF and progressively performing, with respect to the ECU, some of the functions presently entrusted to national central banks. This could be the precursor of a European central bank.

The creation of a truly European monetary identity needs to be discussed in a wider context of economic and political objectives. One such objective, which has been for long a recurrent theme in the intra-European debate, is to reduce Europe's dependence on the dollar,[27] thus partly insulating the region from the effects of economic policies pursued on the other side of the Atlantic and also reducing the intra-EC divergence arising from dollar fluctuations. A second objective, closely related to the first, is to increase Europe's bargaining power in international negotiations through collective action. Thus, the EC would repeat in the monetary sphere the successful example of the common commercial policy.

Monetary and financial integration, an end in itself, could also act as a catalyst for regional economic integration in general. Last but not least, the emergence of a European central bank, managing a new common currency, would obviously have major political implications. Money has for long been considered by many in Europe as 'la voie royale vers l'union politique'.

In view of their far-reaching implications, it should not be at all surprising that ambitious proposals for the further development of the EMS have usually met with strong scepticism from deeply conservative central bankers and the majority of national politicians, still strongly attached to the principle of national sovereignty. The Federal Republic in particular, as the leading country, remains a staunch defender of the *status quo* and strongly opposed to the further institutionalization of the system.

The Single European Act makes it clear that institutional changes in the area of economic and monetary policy would require an amendment of the Treaty of Rome, and hence a unanimous decision by the Council of Ministers and ratification by all national parliaments. Therefore, any serious initiative which involves such changes may have to wait for a more favourable political conjuncture. It is understandable that much of the debate about the future of the ECU has centred on possible extensions of its role which would not necessitate any institutional reform.

Official discussions have concentrated mainly on proposals which aim at the consolidation of the system or at specific changes within the existing institutional framework.[28] An important issue in terms of the consolidation of the system is, undoubtedly, the participation of sterling in the ERM. This has been the subject of a long debate in Britain, under the continuous encouragement of the EC Commission and the other members of the system, among whom German bankers and politicians have been the most prominent.

The traditional arguments against participation have been the need to preserve policy autonomy, especially when the government operated on the basis of a strict monetary target, the petrocurrency status of the pound and the role of London as a financial centre, which means that the UK currency would be vulnerable, without a possible recourse to administrative controls, to big shifts in international capital movements. On the other hand, advocates of full membership have pointed to the significant economic convergence of recent years between Britain and the other members of the system. They have also argued that, since the abandonment of a clear monetary target, membership of the ERM could provide a solid anchor for monetary policy and a strong weapon in the fight against inflation. As for the petrocurrency role of sterling, it seems to have been greatly exaggerated.[29]

City and industry views have gradually shifted in favour of full membership of the EMS, while the Conservative government has been continuously postponing the decision to join, allegedly always in search of the right time. The problem seems to be mainly a political one: the British Prime Minister is neither keen on tying her hands nor particularly enthralled by the idea of European co-operation. The prospect of foreign governments having a say on the exchange rate of sterling must be highly unattractive to Mrs Thatcher. As for the economic arguments used by the British Prime Minister against membership of the ERM, they have not been exactly models of consistency. As a result, sterling has usually followed closely the movements of the EMS currencies, and the D-Mark in particular, while the government has retained a greater flexibility of action. The price paid for this flexibility is surely a greater variability of the exchange rate and perhaps also a risk premium in terms of interest rates.

Although the full participation of the UK in the EMS would be an important event in itself and also for the process of European monetary integration in general, the further development of the system does not crucially depend on it. The strong German insistence on the integration of sterling in the ERM may be somewhat puzzling, since the introduction of another international currency would certainly increase the amount of intervention needed and might also create a further challenge to the leading role enjoyed by the Bundesbank; unless the burden of intervention and adjustment is expected to fall mainly on the Bank of England.

As regards the new southern European members of the EC, inflation rates in Greece and Portugal, coupled with fragile payments situations, make the participation of the drachma and the escudo in the ERM unlikely for the immediate future. In this respect, the prospects for the peseta are much better. The wider margins of fluctuation of the lira, although not necessarily a permanent feature of the system, could eventually serve as a possible example for those countries to follow.

Naturally, a great deal of the discussion inside the EC, and especially inside the Committee of Governors and the Monetary Committee, has been about the rules governing the operation of the ERM. This discussion, although usually in a sterilized and technical form, has been largely about the distribution of costs of intervention and the burden of adjustment between strong and weak currencies. The contrasting positions taken by France and Germany in this respect, with the other members of the system usually siding with one or the other, have been in fact a continuation of an old debate between 'monetarists' and 'economists' dating back to 1970, when the first plans for an economic and monetary union were discussed among the Six.[30] Although mainly a reflection of an objective divergence of interests among countries, those contrasting positions were also the result of different perceptions and ideologies, which sometimes extend beyond the purely economic sphere.

One recent example is the negotiations which were originally sparked off by a French memorandum in February 1987 and which have continued in a second round despite the Nyborg-Basle agreement reached in September of the same year. The so-called Balladur proposals included the extension of joint responsibility and the use of the EMS credit facilities to intra-marginal interventions; the further mobilization of ECU reserves for the settlement of inter-bank debts and a greater use of EC currencies for intervention purposes; a joint surveillance of national economic policies based on a small number of economic indicators, following similar attempts made at the international level; and a closer co-ordination of central bank interventions with respect to the dollar and the yen within the framework of informal target zones.[31] Some of those proposals were also supported by the EC Commission and other member countries.

The French proposals were clearly an attempt to introduce rules which would lead to greater symmetry within the EMS, both as regards the internal distribution of the burden of adjustment and the formulation of the external policy of the group as a whole. After the failure of the divergence indicator to guarantee such a symmetry, France was making another attempt in this direction.

The German response was far from enthusiastic. The Bundesbank was obviously not at all keen on extending its responsibilities regarding market interventions and the provision of credit facilities. The fear of massive interventions in D-Mark, which would undermine domestic monetary stability, and the danger of unlimited financing of the payments deficits of other countries have always been present in the mind of German central bankers. Partners were also reminded of the international role of the D-Mark and hence the special responsibilities which fall on German shoulders regarding intervention in the exchange markets.

German priorities about the consolidation of the EMS were very different. The Federal Republic put the emphasis on further economic convergence, implying, naturally, convergence towards the German standards, at least as regards inflation. Germany also insisted on the participation of all EC currencies in the ERM under the same conditions, which meant the inclusion of sterling and the reduction of the margins of fluctuation for the lira to 2.25 per cent. Last but not least, Germany stressed the need for a complete liberalization of capital movements.

The changes introduced in September 1987 can be seen as a compromise but also as the first important German concession towards the establishment of a more symmetrical system. They included an extension of the very short-term credit facility and the doubling of the amounts of credit which would be automatically renewed under this facility. Furthermore, the existing limit on settlement in ECUs was lifted for a trial period of two years.

The most important part of the agreement was, however, the 'multilateralization' of intra-marginal interventions. But, unlike interventions at the margin, there would be no automaticity; instead, the agreement referred to a 'presumption' that loans of EC currencies would be available through the EMCF for the financing of intra-marginal interventions. This 'presumption' would depend on the domestic monetary conditions of the potential creditor country which, therefore, would have the last word in determining its own obligations under the new agreement. Loans of EC currencies for intra-marginal interventions would also be subject to certain specified limits.

The governors of central banks undertook to monitor more closely the development of intra-EMS exchange rates and also implicitly accepted the need for closer co-ordination of interest rates as a means of influencing those developments. The Monetary Committee would complement this role by monitoring the economies of member countries on the basis of certain indicators which were to be defined. The objective was again a more effective co-ordination of national economic policies.

The Nyborg-Basle agreement is the first modest step towards recognizing the reality and importance of intra-marginal interventions in the functioning of the ERM. At the same time, it is also a reflection of the changing economic and political environment within which the whole system operates. This changing environment should have a decisive influence on the actual application of the new agreement, especially since the latter relies much more on discretion rather than formal rules. In the early stages of the application of this agreement, there are already signs pointing to a closer co-ordination of intra-marginal interventions and interest-rate changes.

A number of developments, both internal and external to the system, have already influenced the operation of the EMS and could also act as catalysts for further change in the future. One such development is the process of capital liberalization, which forms part of the overall objective of establishing an internal market in the EC by 1992. Some capital controls have already been lifted, most notably in France and Italy. The willingness of national governments to move in this direction is essentially a response to the rapid process of internationalization of financial markets, the more liberal economic ideologies prevailing in Western Europe and, last but not least, the perceived need to strengthen national financial markets. It was largely in response to the liberalization moves in partner countries that the Bundesbank has finally lifted the ban on ECU-denominated deposits with German banks, which had been previously justified with reference to the German currency law prohibiting indexation.

The Commission has stressed the need for a further strengthening of the co-ordination mechanisms for monetary policies resulting from the process of liberalization. The argument is simple and straightforward: in a world of fixed exchange rates and free capital movements, the scope for independent monetary policies is drastically reduced. The counterargument is, however, that with further convergence of national inflation rates and with a move towards periodic and small currency realignments, such as the one which took place in January 1987, the possibility of destabilizing capital movements is strongly reduced.[32] Nevertheless, even in a pre-federal stage of economic policy integration, a high degree of capital mobility would put a system of fixed but periodically adjustable exchange rates under severe test. It would be interesting then to wait and see which one gives way first.

The success of the EMS until recently was very much based on the convergence of macroeconomic policy priorities, with the emphasis on the fight against inflation. At this fight was progressively won, some of the more 'disobedient' members of the system[33] started adopting a less benign view of the kind of economic leadership exercised by Germany. Hence, the growing stress on the alleged deflationary bias of the system. This has been the source of new tensions and also seems to be, at least partly, behind the new agreement reached in September 1987.

An important catalyst for change could again, as it has happened so frequently in the past, come from outside the system. Interest in European monetary integration has always been closely correlated with perceptions of instability in the international system and European vulnerability to outside shocks. A renewed decline of the dollar, or even the gradual approach to a saturation point as regards the direct financing of the US payments deficit by European (and Japanese) central banks, could lead to a resurgence of interest in the further strengthening of the EMS. The realignment of January 1987 and the subsequent pressures on Germany to accept some change in the rules governing the operation of the ERM were closely related to the state of the dollar in exchange markets. It is also arguable that the strength of the US currency in the early 1980s was an important factor then behind the lack of interest of some members in moving to the second stage of the EMS, a move which would have led to the gradual development of the ECU as a European reserve currency.

In view of its economic weight and its leading position inside the system, Germany will have a crucial role to play in the future development of the EMS. *Status quo* attitudes have so far prevailed, and any proposals for reform have been treated as concessions to partner countries which should, if possible, be avoided. The German political leadership could eventually adopt a more far-sighted approach to national and European interests, gradually realizing the limitations and risks, both economic and political, inherent in the present state of the EMs and the implicit framework of policy co-operation which has developed. Economic leadership could then be translated into a major political inititative for the relaunching of European monetary integration.

APPENDIX 3.1

The following appendix presents, in graphical form, the performance of EMS currencies *vis-à-vis* the ECU, of the ECU *vis-à-vis* the dollar, and of the ECU *vis-à-vis* the pound sterling. (See Figs 3.1–3.3.)

APPENDIX 3.2

The following appendix provides, in tabular form, information about the competitiveness of the EMS member countries, measured according to different methods, the EMS realignments, and the bilateral trade balances of the EMS member countries. (See Tables 3.1–3.6.)

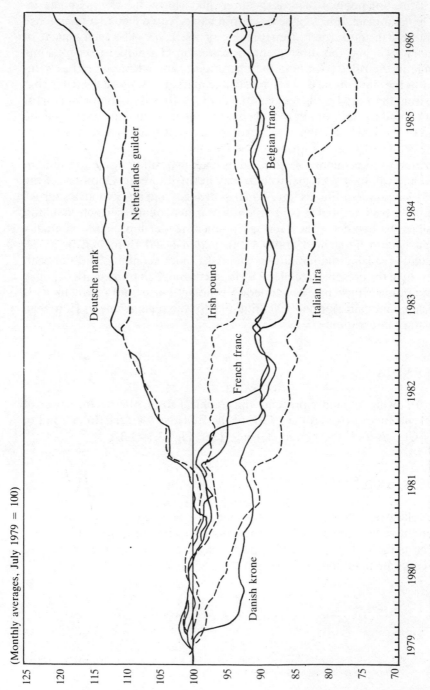

(Monthly averages, July 1979 = 100)

Figure 3.1 Movement of EMS currency exchange rates against the ECU. *Source*: Ungerer (1986).

Figure 3.2 Movement of the ECU against the US dollar (US dollar per ECU, monthly averages). *Source:* Eurostat.

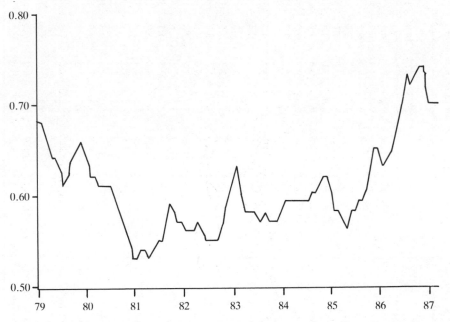

Figure 3.3 Movement of the ECU against sterling (ECU per sterling, monthly averages). *Source:* Eurostat.

Table 3.1 Consumer price indices 1974–85 (annual % change)

	1974	1975	1976	1977	1978	Average 1974–8	1979	1980	1981	1982	1983	1984	1985	Average 1979–85
Belgium	12.7	12.8	9.2	7.1	4.5	9.2	4.5	6.6	7.6	8.7	7.7	6.3	4.9	6.6
Denmark	15.2	9.6	9.0	11.1	10.1	11.0	9.6	12.3	11.7	10.1	6.9	6.3	4.7	8.8
France	13.7	11.8	9.6	9.4	9.1	10.7	10.7	13.8	13.4	11.8	9.6	7.4	5.8	10.3
Germany	7.0	5.9	4.3	3.7	2.7	4.7	4.1	5.4	6.3	5.3	3.3	2.4	2.2	4.1
Ireland	17.0	20.9	18.0	13.6	7.6	15.3	13.2	18.2	20.4	17.1	10.5	8.6	5.4	13.2
Italy	19.1	17.0	16.8	17.0	12.1	16.4	14.8	21.2	17.8	16.5	14.7	10.8	9.2	14.9
Netherlands	9.6	10.5	9.0	6.5	4.2	7.9	4.2	6.5	6.7	5.9	2.8	3.3	2.2	4.5
Arithmetic average ERM	13.5	12.6	10.8	9.8	7.2	10.7	8.7	12.0	12.0	10.8	7.9	6.4	4.9	8.9
Standard deviation	3.9	4.6	4.5	4.2	3.2	3.8	4.2	5.7	5.2	4.3	3.9	2.7	2.2	3.9
Difference between highest and lowest value	12.2	14.9	13.7	13.3	9.5	11.7	10.7	15.8	14.1	11.8	11.9	8.4	7.0	10.8
Coefficient of variation	0.29	0.36	0.41	0.43	0.45	0.35	0.48	0.48	0.43	0.40	0.49	0.42	0.45	0.43
Weighted average	11.7	10.4	8.7	8.1	6.5	…	8.0	11.1	10.9	9.7	7.6	5.9	4.9	…
Australia	15.1	15.1	13.5	12.3	7.9	12.8	9.1	10.1	9.7	11.1	10.1	4.0	6.7	8.7
Austria	9.5	8.4	7.3	5.5	3.6	6.9	3.7	6.4	6.8	5.4	3.3	5.7	3.2	4.9
Canada	10.9	10.8	7.5	8.0	9.0	9.2	9.1	10.2	12.4	10.8	5.8	4.3	4.0	8.1
Finland	16.7	17.8	14.4	12.7	7.8	13.8	7.5	11.6	12.0	9.3	8.4	7.1	5.9	8.8
Greece	26.9	13.4	13.3	12.1	12.6	15.5	19.0	24.9	24.5	21.0	20.2	18.4	19.3	21.0
Iceland	43.0	49.0	32.2	30.5	44.1	39.5	45.5	58.5	50.6	49.1	86.1	30.8	32.0	49.4
Japan	24.4	11.8	9.3	8.0	3.8	11.3	3.6	8.0	4.9	2.6	1.8	2.3	2.0	3.6
New Zealand	11.2	14.5	17.1	14.4	11.9	13.8	13.6	17.2	15.3	16.2	7.3	6.2	15.4	13.0
Norway	9.4	11.6	9.2	9.1	8.0	9.5	4.8	10.8	13.7	11.4	8.4	6.3	5.7	8.7
Portugal	28.0	20.4	18.2	27.1	22.7	23.2	23.6	16.6	20.0	22.7	25.1	28.9	19.6	22.3
Spain	15.7	17.0	15.0	24.5	19.8	18.3	15.7	15.6	14.6	14.4	12.2	11.3	8.8	13.2
Sweden	9.9	9.8	10.3	11.5	9.9	10.3	7.2	13.7	12.1	8.6	8.9	8.0	7.4	9.4
Switzerland	9.8	6.7	1.7	1.3	1.1	4.1	3.6	4.0	6.5	5.7	3.0	2.9	3.4	4.1
United Kingdom	15.9	24.3	16.6	15.8	8.3	16.1	13.4	18.0	11.9	8.6	4.6	5.0	6.1	9.6
United States	11.0	9.1	5.8	6.5	7.6	8.0	11.3	13.5	10.4	6.2	3.2	4.3	3.6	7.4
Arithmetic average non-ERM	17.2	16.0	12.8	13.3	11.9	14.1	12.7	15.9	15.0	13.5	13.9	9.7	7.9	12.8
Standard deviation	9.2	9.9	6.9	8.0	10.2	8.2	10.4	12.4	10.7	11.0	20.3	8.8	8.4	11.1
Coefficient of variation	0.54	0.62	0.54	0.60	0.86	0.58	0.82	0.78	0.71	0.81	1.46	0.91	1.06	0.87

Source: Ungerer (1986).

Table 3.2 Unit labour costs 1974–85 (annual % change)

	1974	1975	1976	1977	1978	Average 1974–78	1979	1980	1981	1982	1983	1984	1985	Average 1979–85
Belgium	15.7	15.2	2.6	5.9	1.3	8.0	3.4	4.0	5.0	3.3	1.8	2.0	2.6	3.1
Denmark	17.2	7.1	7.6	8.4	7.6	9.5	5.7	4.5	8.4	11.3	1.3	-3.2	4.4	4.5
France	14.6	18.8	7.9	6.7	7.2	10.9	9.3	12.4	11.9	11.1	7.6	1.9	1.4	7.9
Germany, Fed. Rep. of	9.0	10.3	0.6	5.3	5.1	6.0	2.3	7.3	5.1	4.1	-0.5	-0.3	0.1	2.5
Italy	18.8	32.8	10.4	17.5	11.1	17.9	9.6	12.3	19.0	18.2	14.0	3.9	4.5	11.5
Netherlands	10.1	15.6	0.1	4.7	1.7	6.3	2.5	4.0	0.8	4.3	-1.5	-6.7	-1.0	0.3
Arithmetic average ERM	14.2	16.6	4.9	8.1	5.6	9.8	5.5	7.4	8.4	8.7	3.8	-0.4	2.0	5.0
Standard deviation	3.6	8.2	4.0	4.4	3.4	4.0	3.0	3.6	5.8	5.3	5.4	3.6	2.1	3.7
Coefficient of variation	0.25	0.49	0.81	0.54	0.61	0.41	0.56	0.49	0.70	0.61	1.43	-8.88	1.06	0.74
Austria	10.6	16.6	0.1	5.4	2.7	6.9	-1.2	4.9	5.7	2.5	-0.2	-1.7	2.0	1.7
Canada	13.4	16.1	8.7	7.0	5.3	10.0	7.8	12.9	13.8	13.4	0.4	-4.6	2.3	6.4
Japan	28.5	14.7	-2.4	2.3	-1.8	7.7	-2.1	-2.0	1.8	-1.8	-1.6	-3.7	0.2	-1.3
Norway	13.1	22.4	11.6	12.4	8.0	13.4	0.2	10.8	11.1	6.5	5.1	7.3	5.5	6.6
Sweden	12.9	19.9	16.6	11.2	8.4	13.7	-0.1	9.6	10.2	4.2	0.6	4.0	4.6	4.7
Switzerland	9.6	12.9	-3.9	-2.5	1.6	3.3	-0.8	1.2	7.1	5.3	-1.6	-5.9	1.8	0.9
United Kingdom	18.2	34.4	11.0	14.9	14.8	18.4	17.3	21.6	6.8	4.5	0.2	3.0	5.4	8.2
United States	13.5	8.7	3.3	5.8	7.4	7.7	9.7	11.7	7.3	6.1	-2.8	-1.2	1.7	4.5
Arithmetic average non-ERM	15.0	18.2	5.6	7.1	5.8	10.1	3.9	8.8	8.0	5.1	-0.0	-0.3	2.9	3.9
Standard deviation	5.6	7.3	6.9	5.3	4.7	4.5	6.5	6.9	3.4	4.0	2.2	4.3	1.8	3.0
Coefficient of variation	0.38	0.40	1.23	0.75	0.82	0.44	1.70	0.78	0.43	0.79	-1.38	-12.47	0.63	0.77

Source: Ungerer (1986).

Table 3.3 Indicators of competitiveness as measured by consumer prices adjusted for exchange-rate changes in relation to EMS partner countries (1979: I = 100)

	Belgium	Denmark	France	Germany	Ireland	Italy	Netherlands
1979	97.8	99.4	101.1	98.8	103.2	103.4	98.2
1980	94.9	95.5	105.1	93.4	111.7	111.2	96.5
1981	92.6	97.8	107.3	91.2	121.5	114.3	95
1982	85.1	95.3	103.1	94.5	130.8	117.3	98.5
1983	84.1	95	98.3	95.4	129.8	124.2	97.2
1984	85.1	95.9	98.7	93.1	131.8	128.2	95.8
1985	86.5	98.2	101.8	90.7	135.2	127.7	94.2
1986 I	86.1	96.6	102.7	90.8	135	126.7	94.2

Source: Ungerer (1986).

Table 3.4 Indicators of competitiveness in manufacturing as measured by unit labour costs adjusted for exchange-rate changes in relation to EMS partner countries (1979: I = 100)

	Belgium	Denmark	France	Germany	Ireland	Italy	Netherlands
1979	97.8	97	101.2	99	106.4	104.3	95.9
1980	93.1	86.8	106.3	98.9	121.6	103.5	92.4
1981	89.6	87.7	107.8	97.2	127.2	109.7	87.4
1982	77.3	85.6	104.4	100	134.3	116.3	91
1983	74	86.1	100.9	99.8	122.6	125.9	88.9
1984	74.4	83.7	103	100.5	115.8	125.6	82.8
1985	77	87.8	105.4	99.2	117.4	123	81.1
1986 I	77.6	91.3	105.4	103.9	115.3	115.4	78.4

Source: Ungerer (1986).

Table 3.6 Germany's bilateral trade balances with other members of the ERM (in million ECUs)

	Belgium	Denmark	France	Ireland	Italy	Netherlands
1979	109	836	1,065	72	−537	−3,035
1980	190	318	1,166	−113	1,216	−3,928
1981	342	604	2,289	−35	1,904	−5,837
1982	596	773	2,968	−59	2,068	−6,105
1983	−436	626	1,553	−187	536	−7,293
1984	62	1,238	2,044	−317	1,910	−9,782
1985	1,376	1,623	2,229	−362	3,322	−11,073
1986	1,436	2,092	4,710	−355	3,074	−5,215
1987	2,177	1,326[1]	4,885	−640	3,452[2]	−3,489

Source: Eurostat.
Notes
[1] January–October 1987.
[2] January–November 1987.

Table 3.5 EMS realignments: % changes in bilateral central rates

	24 Sept. 1979	30 Nov. 1979	23 Mar. 1981	5 Oct. 1981	22 Feb. 1982	14 June 1982	21 Mar. 1983	22 July 1985	7 April 1986	4 Aug. 1986	12 Jan. 1987
Belgian & Luxembourg francs	−2.9				−8.5		+1.5	+2.0	+1.0		+2.0
Danish krone		−4.8			−3.0		+2.5	+2.0	+1.0		
D-Mark	+2.0			+5.5		+4.25	+5.5	+2.0	+3.0		+3.0
French franc				−3.0		−5.75	−2.5	+2.0	−3.0		
Italian lira			−6.0			−2.75	−2.5	−6.2			
Irish pound				−3.0			−3.5	+2.0		−8.0	
Netherlands guilder				+5.5		+4.25	+3.5	+2.0	+3.0		+3.0

Source: Commission of the European Communities.

NOTES

1. I am grateful to D. Israelachwili and M. Méndez Alonso for their valuable research assistance.
2. Ungerer (1986). See especially Tables 16–30. For the development of exchange rates with respect to the ECU, see also Figs. 3.1–3.3 in Appendix 3.1.
3. See Table 3.1 in Appendix 3.2. Inflation differentials were further reduced in 1986 and 1987. The range in 1986 was between −0.3 per cent in Germany and 5.9 per cent in Italy, and in 1987 between −0.2 per cent in the Netherlands and 4.8 per cent in Italy.
4. See Table 3.2 (Appendix 3.2).
5. See Tables 3.3 and 3.4 (Appendix 3.2). The situation has, if anything, slightly worsened in the last two years.
6. See Ungerer (1986), Tables 12 and 14.
7. Ungerer (1986).
8. See Table in Ungerer (1986). The relation between the EMS and economic growth is also discussed in De Grauwe (1987).
9. For a detailed analysis of EMS rules, see van Ypersele and Koeune (1984).
10. The concept of asymmetry is a familiar one in the EMS literature. See for example Sarcinelli (1986), Masera (1987b), Giavazzi and Giovannini (1987), Padoan (1988), and Thygesen and Gros (1987).
11. A similar argument is made in Commission (1987).
12. For an attempt to correlate dollar fluctuations with bilateral EMS exchange rates, see Giavazzi and Giovannini (1986).
13. See also Micossi (1985) and Masera (1987b).
14. Giavazzi and Giovannini (1987).
15. Gros (1986).
16. See Table 3.5 in Appendix 3.2.
17. See Commission (1987).
18. See for example Masera (1987b) and Lefevre (1985).
19. See BIS (1987), p. 122.
20. See also de Grauwe (1987).
21. Representative examples are the Annual Economic Reports (1985 and 1986) of the EC Commission and Blanchard (1986).
22. See Giavazzi and Giovannini (1987), Thygesen and Gros (1987). See also Padoan (1988).
23. See Table 3.6 in Appendix 3.2.
24. Aglietta (1986), p. 14.
25. For an earlier discussion of the role of smaller countries in the EMS, see De Cecco (1983).
26. There is a rapidly growing literature on the possible role of the ECU as a parallel currency. See, for example, Masera (1987a), Aglietta (1986) and Steinherr (1987).
27. This argument has been put forward by Professor Triffin. See, for example, Triffin (1984).
28. In the early months of 1988, a new public debate was started, as a result of a French initiative, about the eventual creation of a European central bank.
29. See Holtham (1987), Russo (1986), Federal Trust (1984) and Scott (1986).
30. See Tsoukalis (1977).
31. Balladur (1987). See also Holtham (1987).
32. See Commission (1987) and Thygesen and Gros (1987).
33. This term is used by Padoan (1988).

4 · THE EUROPEAN MONETARY SYSTEM AND NATIONAL INTERESTS

Marcello De Cecco

INTRODUCTION

After almost nine years since it was born, the European Monetary System (EMS) can be submitted to scrutiny. It has enjoyed, since it first appeared, a high degree of popularity with economists. Some of its salient features have been exalted or criticized, according to the convictions or disposition of the reviewing agent, but the economists' attention has unwaveringly remained focused on it. It has been decidedly 'adopted' by the EC (European Community) as one of its most important mechanisms, second perhaps only to the Common Agricultural Policy (CAP).

Because of its popularity with economists it is possible to analyze the EMS starting from a vantage position. The groundwork for analysis has been almost completely done, and an assessment of the EMS can therefore rely almost exclusively on the wealth of secondary sources that has hitherto accumulated.[1] I therefore propose to analyze the experience of the EMS from the point of view of the member countries, concentrating on what the member countries wanted from the EMS and on what they, individually, got from it.

This may be a peculiar and almost illegitimate way of studying a system which, from its start, could be considered as destined to reach exclusively collective targets. There is a plurality of people who think that the making of a united 'Europe' is an independent policy objective, since a united Europe would be superior to national states. These are the federalists who have acclaimed the EMS, and in particular the ECU, as an important achievement on the road to the United States of Europe. Vocal and well represented as they are, the federalists by no means represent the majority of European people. Regrettable as this may seem, it is a fact that the peoples of Europe and the political class that represents them are still reasoning in terms of nation states and of national interest. This justifies the slant of my analysis.[2] Pro-European altruism can rarely be seen to motivate the actions of politicans assembled in Brussels or Strasbourg.

National egoism seems to be still the principal rule of conduct, and not even a trend towards a more pro-European stance can be detected, especially since the United Kingdom joined the Community and made national interest in EC matters fashionable again.

It seems justified to take as a starting point that member countries will agree and stick to European arrangements that suit their perceived national interest. We can stretch this concept a bit in a Pareto-like fashion, and say that member countries will concur in policies which, while not penalizing their national interest, may enhance the construction of Europe. Only if this restriction is accepted, the notion of a positive sum game can be slipped in. If it is assumed, however, that one particular member country derives an 'exhorbitant privilege' from the workings of an EC policy or EC mechanism, this will be enough to convince the others that the advantage of that single country is to their disadvantage, even if no direct harm comes to any other of them from the operation of the measure or the working of the mechanism. We are back in a classic zero-sum power game. The EC, and even more the EMS, is an oligopoly, a system run by four large countries of similar size. Some respect for the smaller members' opinions is guaranteed, but it can be said that policies will be adopted or discarded only if they do not change in any way the power relations in which the four major countries stand to one another. There have been exceptions to this rule but they have not been many, and some of them can be explained as mistaken perceptions of the national interest on the part of some of the major players.

An analysis of the working of the EMS, therefore, has to concentrate on studying whether the EMS has furthered the cause of a United Europe without endangering the relative positions of the major member countries. Only if this is the case, can the EMS be called a stable state of the world, and the benefits to Europe be considered permanent. If one of the major members has temporarily over-gained from its working, this gain will be considered by the others to have been achieved at their own expense. The static arithmetic of a classic power game will apply, and the countries which have not gained will try to undo the benefits achieved by the favoured country, in order to re-establish the *status quo ante*. No hierarchical structure is, in fact, possible in the European Community, among the major member countries.

THE ORIGINS OF THE EMS

The European Monetary System was the outcome of a decade of turmoil in the international exchanges, which followed the US decision to abandon the Bretton Woods system in August 1971, and the policy of benign neglect which followed that decision. The formation of a stable currency area had been studied by academic economists for a long time before the US left the Bretton Woods system. It had, moreover, long been seen by pro-European political elites as the natural crowning of the process of European economic integration which had taken place in the 1960s.

The crisis of the international monetary system had been a long one. It had dragged on since the Kennedy administration had been sworn in, with a decade-long history of patching up operations which had delayed the day of reckoning. A school of academic economists had urged a return to floating exchange rates as a solution preferable to indefinite patching up. Their advice was to be followed by the US administration in August 1971.

Another school of economists had tried to solve the problems of the international monetary system by breaking it up into sub-systems. They argued that the world had been turned by the Bretton Woods agreement into one huge currency area, and that the strains which had developed in it signalled that this was not an optimal arrangement. It would have been preferable to re-draw the map of the monetary world and to design several currency areas, by identifying some criterion of homogeneity which would allow the countries of each area to maintain fixed exchange rates with one another.

Which criterion should be adopted to redesign the monetary map of the world, to break the Bretton Woods system into a few large sub-systems? Opinions differed and a lively debate opened up. Most of the solutions offered were open to serious criticism. This is not the place to review that debate, which was anyway far from conclusive.[3] Whatever the merits of the criteria offered to identify optimum currency areas it was clear, however, that academic opinion was split into two camps, one favouring floating rates and the other a plurality of currency areas, which would maximize the total area subjected to fixed exchange rates and reduce the number of currencies floating against one another. A fixed exchange rate system was seen by the latter faction as a framework for the conduct of orderly financial and commercial relations among states. It was some sort of public good, which had been supplied, for a few decades, by the United States and which, owing to the relative decline of that country, had to be preserved by the clever invention of a plurality of currency areas. Although most of the literature on currency areas, and on floating rates, was North American, European central banks and political authorities, by and large, identified with the fixed rates positions, while the floating rates position was adopted by American policy-makers (there were, however, quite a number of German economists, like Egon Sohmen and Herbert Giersch, who advocated flexible exchange rates).

Apart from the scientific considerations of academic economists, educated public opinion in Europe had begun to ask whether it was, in fact, possible for the countries of the European Common Market to sustain a situation of floating exchange rates for very long, without endangering the results hitherto obtained by the process of economic integration which had successfully taken place for more than 15 years. At the end of the 1960s the European Common Market countries had reached a level of trade integration higher than at any previous time. They had also built up a very expensive, and very rigid, price support system for European agriculture which had quickly turned the EEC into an agriculturally self-sufficient area, which even enjoyed a large surplus with the rest of the world in farm products.

The Common Market had been the creature of political parties, in the main countries of Europe, which relied more than proportionately on rural constituencies to win elections. Making a European Common Market had meant demolishing trade barriers for industrial goods, and allowing southern European workers (who were, in their overwhelming majority, former peasants) freedom of circulation in the northern states of the Community. But the creative part of the European Community was undoubtedly the Common Agricultural Policy. Here resources had been pooled and administered by the Eurocrats, to construct the largest price-support scheme ever designed outside the United States of America. The CAP relied on fixed exchange rates in a fundamental way. In the years when American 'benign neglect' had imposed floating rates, the administrators of the CAP had been compelled to devise all sorts of extremely complex measures to maintain their price-support scheme in operation. The most infamous of those were the so-called 'montants compensatifs', which tried to remedy the penalization inflicted on the farmers of re-valuing countries by the rising exchange rates, vis-à-vis their competitors in the EC countries which devalued their exchange rates. The perverse functioning of this device had given an unexpected new lease of life to German farmers, and turned, for instance, the Länder of Bavaria into a major agricultural exporter.[4]

It was obvious, from the very beginning of the floating-rate experience, that its application to the European Community would have been destructive of the level of integration hitherto achieved, which had come to be considered as permanent.

A 'European solution' to the exchange-rate turmoil had thus been sought, and tried with the 'snake' experiment. But it had not been a success at the European level. The three major countries had soon left Germany to be the core of a strong currency D-Mark bloc, formed by a host of small northern European countries whose trade integration with Germany was too high to allow them to float their currencies against the D-Mark.

The launching of the EMS was precipitated by the free fall of the dollar vis-à-vis the European currencies in 1978, and by the interest-rate war unleashed by the United States against Germany. It was a Franco-German venture, which saw other European countries on the side-lines, uncertain about what stand to adopt.[5]

THE COST–BENEFIT CALCULUS IN
INDIVIDUAL COUNTRIES

Germany

As is known, the German authorities were not a united bloc. The Bundesbank did not consider a European Monetary System with great favour, as it would diminish – it was feared – their monetary sovereignty, i.e. the independence of Germany's monetary policy. They thought the anti-inflationary stance of the Bundesbank would be watered down by a flood of lire and francs. But this was exactly one of the reasons why Chancellor Schmidt wanted the EMS to shield the German exchange rate from excessive revaluation with French and Italian monetary laxitude. Schmidt had the interests of German industry at heart, and German industry feared the loss of competitiveness, which derived from an excessively strong D-Mark, on European markets and external markets, against European and US competitors. The chemical industry and the steel industry stood in particular danger of losing market shares to US competitors and to Europeans whose currencies had shown a tendency to follow the dollar rather than the D-Mark. But the machine-tool industry and the automobile industry were not entirely free from danger, either. Together, these four sectors represented a very large share of industrial employment in Germany. An even bleaker fate confronted German light industry, textile and clothing and light engineering products. The creation of the EMS thus represented, in Germany, a victory of industry over the monetary authorities. It was seen as a truce in the struggle for market shares, where Germany was being heavily penalized by the strong currency option adopted in isolation. The supremacy of German industry over its European and American competitors was not so complete as to withstand a protracted policy of competitive devaluations.

A look at Italian trade statistics will give confirmation of the realism of German fears. The comfortable German surplus of the early 1970s had been transformed, by the radical devaluation of the Italian lira in 1976, into a deficit. The same had happened to countries which had followed Germany in the strong currency stance, Austria, Switzerland, the UK. Towards all of them Italy had transformed a trade deficit into a surplus in a matter of one or two years. A similar tale was told by German–American trade figures.

France

If Chancellor Schmidt's motives were clear, President Giscard's were less evident. One reason for returning to a stable currency area in Europe stood out in the French calculus of costs and benefits. As noted above, if Germany was traditionally the industrial core of the EC, France was its agricultural power-house. The floating-rate system in Europe wrought havoc with the CAP, of which France was the main beneficiary. A depreciating dollar also meant a direct threat to French agricultural exports. Altogether, a return to a stable currency area in Europe was highly advisable for French agriculture, still an over-represented sector after the Gaullist redesign of electoral constituencies.

Italy

What did Italy have to gain from an area of currency stability in Europe? It is now fashionable to say that Italy and France traded off growth against the greater price stability afforded by an exchange-rate system anchored to the D-Mark. But this was not clearly expressed in the Italian debates which preceded the launching of the EMS. The Bank of Italy was far from enthusiastic about the proposed system, especially after it became clear that the UK was not going to be part of it. When a political decision was taken in favour of membership, the Bank of Italy insisted on a wider band for Italy and on a low exchange rate for the lira as a starting floor – two provisions which would allow the central bank to economize on reserves.

The Italian monetary authorities had in the three years before the start of the EMS been piloting the lira close to the wind, with the aim of gaining on the dollar and losing on the D-Mark. This policy had been crowned by remarkable success. Italian exports, which had previously moved towards the American market, had invaded the northern European markets. Reserves had been rebuilt in a very short time and an attack was being launched on public debt and inflation.

In this context, however, the terrorist emergency exploded with incredible virulence, precipitating on institutional crisis of unprecedented gravity. The EMS decision had to be taken right in the middle of it. It became one of those *scelte di civilta* which have often been made in post-war Italy. To be in favour of the EMS meant to be in favour of freedom and of Western civilization. Economic considerations soon receded into the background. It became a purely political affair, where domestic-policy reasons were altogether more important than foreign-policy ones.[6]

The logic of individual country calculus

What emerged from the debate in the three major European countries, was a commitment to preserving economic sovereignty in the shape of an independent national monetary policy. Nobody wanted to be swamped by German monetary policy. The emphasis was thus on making really sure that the EMS would be a 'symmetrical' system, where no country (read

'Germany') would have the 'exhorbitant privilege' which the US had enjoyed in the Bretton Woods system. The actual EMS arrangements bear abundant witness to these European fears. They envisage a mechanism which safeguards symmetry and which has met in reality with the same fate as the 'scarce currency clause' of the IMF charter, i.e. total non-application. The bilateral exchange system of the 'snake' was considered faulty and an attempt was made to transform it into a multilateral system, by putting the ECU at the centre of the stage. This has also been disregarded by EMS practice.

The institution-building phase of the EMS – whatever subsequent practical experience may have been – shows that the major European countries were preoccupied with the maintenance of existing power relations. We cannot detect, in the whole EMS debate, many instances where European national authorities were seen to be building either a supra-national system or a new pattern of power relations in Europe. They were all making sure that perceived national interest would not be endangered. At most, we can see the EMS being used as an instrument for the achievement of domestic political aims by certain sectors of the national political spectrum.

ACHIEVEMENTS OF THE EMS

What has the EMS achieved, at the European level, and in particular, for the countries which founded it? Here the debate has been particularly lively throughout the existence of the system. And the sweep of opinion has changed from the early years of the EMS to the most recent period of its existence.

The second oil shock and the new monetarism

The early years were marked by the generalized turbulence which followed the second oil shock. As it became clear that the major countries had decided to react to it not by accommodation and inflation but by restriction and deflation, some EMS members were slower than others to align themselves to the new macroeconomic trend. Italy and France, in particular, lingered on inflating and growing, until they had to stop before the new reality. The result was a series of realignments which went on as long as the United States maintained its weak currency stance. When the Volcker Fed made its new policy targets known and the US slammed on the interest-rate brakes, with the ensuing revaluation of the dollar, the EMS came into a new era marked by a gradual convergence of monetary and real macroeconomic variables among its members. Under the umbrella of the strong dollar, the EMS currencies could avoid taking embarrassingly divergent courses and could happily agree on a joint downward float against the dollar. The US market was again available to imports and everybody in Europe could be wise and fat, exporting to the United States.

Those relatively happy years, however, were the ones which saw the undervaluation of the D-Mark, the Dutch guilder (and of the two honorary members of the EMS, the Austrian schilling and the Swiss franc) grow apace *vis-à-vis* other EMS members. The availability of the American market and the overvaluation of the dollar allowed Italy and France to buy cheap from Germany and to sell dear in the United States. Large deficits were developed by Italy and France with Germany, while the small members of the EMS followed the same course. The dollar over-valuation thus meant that Germany could reacquire market shares in Europe and in the US, while Italy and France, Belgium, Holland, Denmark and Ireland used the strong-currency option with the D-Mark to fight the inflation still present in their economies.[7] It is not clear whether it was the strong currency option *vis-à-vis* Germany coupled with the over-valuation of the dollar that permitted those countries their re-entry from inflation, or whether the oil price slump intervened as a giant *deus ex machina* to rescue them. EMS countries have not shown a better record than other OECD countries as far as inflation fighting is concerned. Convergence of other economic indicators, however, increased among EMS countries and realignments became relatively infrequent. In these years the EMS can be said to have coincided with exchange and monetary stability in Europe. It would be hard to conclude that the EMS induced monetary and exchange-rate stability, as the same exchange-rate mechanism coincided with monetary and exchange-rate instability in the previous years and could be said to have induced them. 'Teething troubles', 'learning by doing' and other similar arguments can be used to explain the change of results induced by the EMS, but the two phases are too radically different to permit that.

It will be very interesting to see whether the new international stance of the dollar will again bring turmoil among EMS exchange rates. If it does, the non-essential character of the EMS will have been proved. If monetary and exchange-rate stability in the EMS countries persist in spite of dollar devaluation, the EMS can be said to have caused them.

STRUCTURAL PROBLEMS OF TRADE DEBT AND PAYMENTS IN THE EMS

In whichever direction the causality chain may run, the EMS has certainly induced conditions of semi-structural trade imbalance among European countries, exactly as one would expect of a largely fixed-exchange-rate system with heterogeneous national economic policies. France and Italy (and the smaller countries of Europe, both members and non-members of the EMS) have provided Germany with a very large trade surplus, which is bound to increase as long as the conditions of monetary and exchange-rate stability in Europe are maintained. This has happened, because in spite of monetary, price, and exchange-rate convergence, the accumulation of public debt through fiscal deficits has been very rapid in every country of the EMS except Germany and Denmark, and has kept demand higher than it has been in Germany. Foreign-exchange controls have remained strict and pervasive in France and Italy for most of the period. This is considered a further complication, as they are now rapidly coming down.

Both foreign-exchange controls and public debt accumulation can be considered as signals of a fundamental disequilibrium, which may explode at a certain point, especially in the new context of dollar devaluation which makes internal European trade once again essential to European countries. The gradual narrowing of the American outlet will make macroeconomic consistency once again very precarious among EMS countries.[8]

It is already apparent that the strong currency option has been stuck to, in EMS countries, only by de-monetizing public expenditure, and by building up public debt instead. The accumulation of public debt has been as dramatic as the shrinking of monetary base growth rates.[9] What are the consequences of this policy choice in the EMS countries which have made it? The share of interest in public deficit, or as a percentage of GDP, has increased considerably, and stands to grow every time there is a rise in interest rates. The existence of a large public debt means that a rentier class has been created again, which is interested in monetary stability and will consider inflation with much greater alarm. A large creditor class has, however, to keep growing if the present level of public expenditure has to remain unchanged in EMS countries. The paradox appears quite glaringly of a state which borrows from the people at a high interest rate in order to give the same people subsidised public services and price stability. Thus far, the EMS countries have been allowed by the leeway that was given by their relatively small public debts to have their cake and eat it, and by the US import rise to allow Germany to make inroads in their home markets, without creating unsustainable external deficits. It will be interesting from now on to see how these contradictions can be reconciled.

As we noted above, the strong currency option has been possible for France and Italy also because they have maintained foreign-exchange restrictions. At the repeated urge of Germany, these restrictions have been now largely removed. Nothing except interest-rate differentials will in future separate the money markets of the EMS countries. If public debt accumulation continues to replace monetary base creation to finance the public deficit in some of these countries, there will be a strong urge to maintain 'real' interest rates (inclusive of a premium that reflects the likelihood of devaluation in the weaker currency countries) aligned to German ones to induce savers to hold government bonds. This will, *per se*, tend to align the level of economic activity in these countries to that of Germany. A continuation of convergence within the EMS will be reinforced by the very accumulation of public debt. But the fiscal imbalance may persist, on the assumption that state expenditure is interest-inelastic. In this case the problem arises of who is going to finance the trade deficits with Germany that these countries will still accumulate. On the assumption that a sale of French and Italian assets to Germany will finance these deficits, a situation not very different from the one that characterizes Japanese-US relations today will arise in Europe in the not-too-distant future. German savings will finance French and Italian consumption. Can such an arrangement be taken to be an equal one, even among distant relatives, as the EC countries can be considered with respect to the rest of the world?

This is highly improbable. And it must be considered as such if we look at the way the German authorities have managed to their own advantage the working of the European Monetary System. We have already noted the total disregard into which the 'divergence indicator' fell from the very beginning of the EMS. Bilateral rates became once again the actual indicators, and the German authorities did not go out of their way to do intra-marginal intervention, leaving the chore for the weak currencies' authorities to perform. The Bundesbank has been able to sterilize, without delay, most of its interventions, thus preventing the fixed exchange rate system from working, according to the 'rules of the game'. All this bears witness to a profound distrust of other countries on the part of the German authorities, and of an unwillingness to operate in the spirit of 'European unity'. The German authorities have shown an ability to free ride on the EMS which is quite remarkable under the circumstances. It is quite rare, in fact, that a country which is the *de facto* centre of a system manages to exercise power without responsibility. A remarkable coincidence of favourable circumstances has allowed Germany to use the EMS to achieve its targets, both in real and nominal terms, both domestically and abroad, without having to shoulder the burden of responsibility.

This set of favourable circumstances has now disappeared, and the mercantilistic features of German policy show up quite starkly. The problem now seems to be how to reconcile the needs of a monetary area with those of its centre, whose authorities firmly believe that their country's surplus is a structural one. Historical tradition wants Germany to be in surplus with the European countries. How is this going to be reconciled with the liquidity needs other EMS countries have to keep a satisfactory rate of factor utilization, if liquidity supply depends on a centre country which is in structural trade surplus?

We have always read that both the pre-1914 gold standard and the early Bretton Woods system worked well because the centre countries, Britain and the US, were in structural deficit and thus generated liquidity for the whole system. Moreover, their banking systems lent to the whole world at long term what they borrowed from the whole world at short term.

This is not the case with the EMS, as we have already said. It thus appears that the EMS is, really, only a sub-system, which rotates around the United States, which can be still considered the real core of the system, the *primum mobile*. As a sub-system, the EMS cannot lead an independent existence of its own. It came into being as a joint float against the dollar and as a way of stopping competitive devaluations in Europe, which would have isolated the D-Mark from the other major members of the European Community. But its peculiar feature, that of having a structurally surplus country as its centre, prevents it from being capable of self-sustained growth. It must derive aggregate demand from outside sources in order to function without excessive external friction.

If the necessary feature of a structural deficit centre country is missing, so is the other, a financial system in the centre country which is capable of maturity transformation, i.e. of borrowing at short term from foreigners to lend back to them at long term. The German financial system has proved to be incapable of and unwilling to perform this function. The almost complete sterilization of short-term capital inflows by the German monetary authorities has meant just that: a refusal to perform the function of financial intermediary to other European countries. In fact, the German banking system, which owns a considerable part of German industry, must, in order not to fall prey to instability, be regarded so strictly as not to allow it to successfully perform the function of financial intermediary for other European countries.

In the inter-war period we had an international monetary system centred on a structurally surplus country, the United States. It was not a very successful and happy period, to put it mildly. But the Germany of today cannot be compared to the US of the inter-war years. The US did not depend on its trade surplus as crucially as Germany does. American manufacturing industry never derived a large part of its demand from abroad. The Americans refused the strong currency option to maintain their role as agricultural exporters. Whatever the reasons, a structurally surplus country does not seem to be capable of sustaining the role of centre of a payments system, especially if it does not even have an outwardly oriented financial system. The lack of the latter is crucial. Without an outwardly oriented financial system, divorced from the manufacturing interests of the country, the chances that the centre country's monetary authorities will be able to impose the strong currency option for a reasonably long period are very small. The vital link which exists in Germany between banks and industry makes the welfare of the former directly dependent on that of the latter. The banking system is thus not the natural ally of the monetary authorities in promoting the strong currency option, as it has been in the UK and the

US. The fact that what is good for Mercedes is immediately good for the Deutsche Bank prevents the German banking system from playing the role which is expected of the banking system of a country which is the centre of a currency area.

This is a strong reason to be sceptical of the financial integration advocated by the Single European Act. The core country's financial system will probably not be able to play the part of catalyst of other European financial systems. This role is wanted by others, in particular by the British, much more than by the Germans. It remains to be seen whether a currency area can have its heart in one place, and its other vital organs in another, if total monetary unification does not come about.

THE FUTURE OF THE EMS

What, then, will be the future of the EMS? This is a hard question to answer. What the immediate future portends is probably clearer. A wider agreement to recycle funds from Germany back to the countries where they came from originally, under the form of medium-term ECU loans, is to be expected, because this is the direction which the EMS countries meeting at Nyborg have shown they want to take. As we saw above, it is also an uneven solution, as it does not face the structural surplus problem of the German economy and it creates asymmetry, by making other EMS countries dependent on German loans.

The original EMS architecture had foreseen a divergence indicator and a frequent use of realignments. We saw earlier how this device was never used. The Single European Act anticipates an active role for a central bank's governors directorate, the monetary committee of the EEC. It is a somewhat bureaucratic solution to an eminently political problem, because it is hard to imagine European governments delegating economic policy making to the central banks in such a fundamental way. Another traditional Bretton Woods-like solution contained in the original EMS agreements is the European Monetary Fund, which has never been given a role to play. It could be important if, like the Keynes Plan, it allowed deficit countries unlimited credit in ECUs, which should also be unconditional. This cannot be expected to come true, however, because it should have become clear by now that the EMS contains two philosophies of economic policy, represented by Germany and the small northern states on one side and by France and Italy on the other. These policies have not collided in the last four years because of the lucky coincidence of factors mentioned above.

Essentially, Germany has been allowed, all these years, to 'be herself', as her behaviour was seen by others as virtuous *per se* or instrumental to their own virtue. This is now finished. By continuing to be herself Germany endangers the new policy objectives of other EMS countries, who are convinced that inflation fighting has gone far enough and want to go for higher growth rates.

But Germany has not been asked to change her policy stance, as a compromise to achieve the result of European unification, for a good number of years. She has never acquired the habit, as her policy stance was considered a model and a standard for inflation-ridden EMS countries, of agreeing on compromise solutions which may trade more inflation for a higher rate of growth of output and a lower rate of unemployment. If the German policy stance can be considered not based on deep structural reasons there is hope for the future of the EMS. There is increasing awareness in Europe, however, that deep structural reasons motivate the German stance, that it is not just a gut dislike of inflation based on two traumatic experiences of high inflation in German history. This psychological theory is frankly insufficient to explain the German stance, even if it has been very popular with non-German economists and politicians.

An alternative explanation might start from considering German demographic trends, which are extremely negative and clearly point to a declining population and workforce in Germany. To this statistical certainty one must add the clear indication that Germany has no desire to see another massive inflow of foreign workers, which it is perceived would be necessary if a higher growth rate was attempted for the German economy.

To those who remind them of the very large pool of German unemployed workers now available, many German economists are quick to reply that a good part of German unemployment must be considered structural, not Keynesian. Structural unemployment is seen either as technological or as classical. Neither type would appreciably decrease – it is argued – if German demand was to be bolstered. The German economy is thus constrained to stick to its present snail-like pace for the foreseeable future by the state of its labour market.

To this we must add that the close interpenetration of banks and industry discourages German policy-makers from adopting stop-go policies, simply because the stop phases which would follow faster growth would be extremely dangerous for a banking system which is so heavily involved in the direct ownership of German industrial companies. Stabilization following inflation is bad for countries where industry is separated from banking, but it becomes destructive where they are closely linked. Numerous historical precedents, in Germany and elsewhere, that confirm this assertion come readily to mind.

At the same time, the German banking system, as discussed above, is not equipped to oversee and promote a massive emigration of industrial production from German soil, and a transformation of Germany into a rentier country.[10] The whole EMS experiment shows, on the contrary, that German bankers and policy-makers want to see a perpetuation of the present socio-economic structure of their country. The EMS has been used to undo many of the moves towards a different international division of labour in Europe which the German economy had made before the inception of the EMS. Agriculture was given a boost and labour-intensive light industrial sectors were called back into existence. Had it not been for pressure from the Asian countries, German industry would have had even more of a field day against other European and American industry.

CONCLUSIONS

It we take these structural considerations as seriously as they seem to deserve, we are led to conclude that the future of the EMS is even more in jeopardy than ostensibly appears. If the German low-growth policy is dictated by profound structural imperatives – and the German socio-political situation does not allow a transformation of the German economic and industrial structure similar to that which was attempted before the EMS was called in to stop and largely reverse it – the EMS can continue with German approval in its present form only, which is not in the best perceived national interests of the other large member countries.

A fundamental conflict of objectives has now been revealed by the disappearance of the favourable events, exogenous to the European economy, which have hitherto prevented the conflict from becoming explosive. People who value European integration as a good in itself must therefore pray for the appearance of some other *deus ex machina*. It may take the form of a democratic president in the United States, who may be bold enough to bear with a 7 to 10 per cent rate of inflation in the US to keep the American economy moving at a fast rate, and still liberal enough not to fall prey to protectionist pressures.

It may also take the form of an acceleration of East–West detente, which will allow the German economy to become the plant and machinery supplier of the Soviet bloc – as was its historical role for a very long time. In both cases, the fate of Europe would be determined outside Europe. In spite of what convinced Europeans say, there does not seem to be a European solution to the European impasse. The very fabric of the European Community needs to be fundamentally transformed to allow for a European solution and we fail to see the sign of a European resolve to do that.

NOTES

1. I am grateful to Meghnad Desai and Francesco Giavazzi who read an earlier draft of the present paper and commented on it. Usual disclaimers, however, apply. For a thorough review of the literture on the EMS see Padoan (1988).

Ungerer, Evans, *et al.* (1986) provide the best review to date of the EMS experience; see also Masera (1987).
2. The 'straightforward national approach' is also adopted by Jaques Melitz (1987).
3. The most recent review of the debate on optimum currency areas is Niels Thygesen (1987). On the monetary turmoil of the 1970s and the origins of the EMS, see also Thygesen (1979).
4. The most recent and best review of CAP is contained in Banca d'Italia (1987).
5. Peter Ludlow (1982) has written a blow-by-blow account of the inception of the EMS.
6. Luigi Spaventa has given a very lucid account of the Italian debate, quoted in Ludlow (1982).
7. A complete analysis of the development of intra-European trade and of European trade with the rest of the world is contained in Bini-Smaghi and Vona (1987). Their paper contains the statistical analysis on which I have based my assertions on European trade. On the consequences of the strong and weak dollar on the EMS, see Giavazzi and Giovannini (1986).
8. On the role of foreign exchange controls in the EMS see Basevi (1987).
9. The accumulation of public debt by EC countries is analyzed with great concern in the Annual Economic Report for 1987–8 submitted by the European Commission to Community Institutions.
10. It is instructive to compare the percentage of the labour force still employed in industry in Germany with the equivalent percentage in other developed countries, like the UK, France or the US. It appears that the German percentage is much higher, and does not seem to want to go much lower than 40 per cent as years go by, while it has declined steeply in the other countries mentioned.

5 · IS CONVERGENCE PROMPTING FRAGMENTATION?

The EMS and national protection in Germany, France and Italy

Jacques Pelkmans

INTRODUCTION

The record of the European Monetary System should be measured first of all against its major objective, that is, to be a 'zone of monetary stability'. The first three years after 1979 brought some improvement of exchange-rate stability, but there was no sign that macroeconomic policies in general were affected. Since 1982, however, a convergence of macroeconomic policies has taken place, especially in terms of bringing inflation rates down to a low of less than 3 per cent on average for 1987. This success has been criticized in two ways. First, it has not led to a strengthening of EMS membership (the UK still does not participate in the exchange-rate mechanism) and of the institutional set-up, hence the convergence is reversible. The present chapter will not deal with this issue. Second, convergence in the EMS is said to impart a deflationary bias and to hamper European growth, which is so badly needed for European and global purposes alike.

The second criticism is extremely serious. The European Community has had high unemployment and low growth rates ever since the second oil shock of 1979–80. Unemployment is high historically but also compared with the US, Japan, Sweden or Switzerland, for example. A higher growth rate would reduce unemployment and indirectly lower budget deficits which are high in about half of the Member States. Worldwide payment imbalances may also be lowered, given the export opportunities the US would find in a growing European economy as well as in third markets where higher growth might be transmitted to. But in fact, EC-12 growth rates between 1982–7 amounting to 2.2 per cent hardly compare with those of the US (nearly 4 per cent) and Japan (some 3.5 per cent); also in 1988 projected rates are 2.3 per cent compared to 2.7 per cent and 3.5 per cent respectively.

Other contributors to this volume deal with various macroeconomic aspects of the criticism. The present chapter investigates its corollaries for policies in the microeconomic sphere. It is frequently suggested that the demand for protection and shelter in the economy increases because secularly low growth rates render microeconomic adjustment processes much more difficult. From the supply side, politicians might be expected to respond positively to such demands, as a substitute for expansionary policies. The probability of protectionist responses increases in those cases where social hardship might lead to adverse voting behaviour. The implied proposition thus is that exchange rate co-operation in the EMS, in being too unambitious with respect to overall macroeconomic policy, reproduced the 'asymmetry' and deflationary bias problems of the adjustable peg system. In doing so, it induced EMS members to become more protectionist, hence threatening the common market, and adding to protectionism worldwide. While few economists would dispute the potential *gains* of macroeconomic convergence at low inflation rates amongst highly interdependent EC countries, some of the *costs* may not just be transitory but structural. For some countries, the deflationary effects of convergence would be drawn out over such a long period, that domestic sectoral pressures seeking relief would become irresistible. When the transitory costs of convergence would be over, the Community (and to some extent the world trade system) would be stuck with costly protection which would be difficult to remove. This proposition has recently been suggested in a context of neomercantilistic policies (Guerrieri and Padoan 1986) and it will be investigated with respect to recent variations in national protection of Member States, with special emphasis on the Federal Republic of Germany (FRG), France and Italy, the three big Member States having joined the EMS exchange rate mechanism.

To derive the answers needed to confirm or reject the hypothesis, the analysis requires a number of steps. First, the macroeconomic determinants of protection have to be studied. This should help us to understand the driving forces of protection prompted by macroeconomic convergence. It will appear that linkages do exist, so that the proposition cannot be rejected on this count. As a complement, the microeconomic determinants (usually grouped under the name of 'adjustment pressures') of protection will be addressed. These explanations may support the proposition in so far as adjustment can be shown to become distinctly more difficult under conditions of low economic growth. Third, the potential trade policy autonomy (in a wide sense of the word) of Member States has to be established so that it becomes clear what the true options for national protectionist responses are. An extensive discussion of 13 instruments (see Appendix 5.1) leads to the selection of a few tools, possibly relevant for the proposition. Three selection criteria are derived from the nature of the proposition (see Appendix). An instrument is carried over to the next section for further scrutiny of its application in France, Italy and Germany if the first criterion is met and one of the other two criteria. Fourth, for these selected tools a look at the facts in the three countries is needed. This is far from easy as protection in Europe is not always transparent and policy-relevant data for the FRG, France and Italy are often unavailable. Finally, the fact-finding is interpreted in order to support or reject the proposition. Since the EMS is only one element of a broader policy spectrum with some relevance for protection, the conclusions will be placed in a wider EC economic policy context.

MACROECONOMIC DETERMINANTS OF PROTECTION

Macroeconomic policy failure might influence protection in two ways (Pelkmans 1986a; Dornbusch and Frankel 1987; McCulloch 1983). First, policy-makers may respond by imposing across-the-board protection over the trade account, the capital account or both. The objective is to prevent the currency from depreciating (too quickly) or to improve the trade or current-account balance. Capital and exchange controls may be expected to prevent undesirable hikes in interest rates that the policy failure would otherwise have induced so as to stop capital from seeking a higher revenue net of exchange risks. Apart from the many problems with the efficiency of capital and exchange controls as an instrument, its effectiveness may be seriously questioned as it may loosen the pressure on governments to modify macroeconomic policy into the proper direction. Across-the-board tariffs or surcharges will shift demand towards non-tradeables while temporarily improving the trade balance. This will boost employment and growth in the short term. Even when ignoring the possibility of retaliation, it is almost certain that such a surcharge will work like a tax on exports, if not via wage drift led by booming import-competing sectors, then at least via a (*ceteris paribus*) rise in the exchange rate. In theory this could be tempered by export subsidies: an across-the-board surcharge plus non-specific export subsidies amount to a *de facto* devaluation. But retaliation cannot be excluded for big countries in an interdependent world economy, and is even harder to avoid in the highly integrated European Community. Thus across-the-board protection is unattractive.

Across-the-board protection in a flexible exchange-rate system is much more difficult to rationalize. Since appreciation and depreciation are essentially market decisions there is no obvious reason to substitute them by highly cumbersome administrative systems. Even if one would argue that it is asset markets rather than the supply and demand of currencies arising from trade that determine exchange rates, it takes rather extreme assumptions to maintain that 'the fundamentals' will not be reflected except in the short term. The motives for introducing the protection may well be political, however. In domestic politics the social or political costs of correcting erroneous or unsustainable macroeconomic policies may be considered too high and hence the external impact is dampened by increasing restrictions. Examples include: the (political) impossibility of stopping inflation without stopping the depreciation first; the socio-economic costs of a severe disinflationary policy; the political refusal to reduce a budget deficit, especially if it is financed by capital inflows rather than by domestic savings.

The second way protection may be prompted by macroeconomic policy failure is via sectoral pressures, claiming 'urgent' measures to offset the inimical effects of macroeconomic developments. A number of possibilities present themselves. First, sectoral pressures may result from generally adverse conditions in the economy. If macro-policies do not help (sufficiently) or if policy-makers resist the pursuit of an accommodating macro-policy, individual sectors will seek some kind of special treatment. In the case of tradeables it is plausible to expect a demand for protection. Suppose the level of economic activity has fallen; import-competing sectors will benefit from the demand switching induced by protection, quite irrespective of whether import competition was the (main) cause of stagnation. Similarly, a fiscal–monetary policy mix keeping real interest rates very high may hamper growth (for example, outlets of durable goods are restricted); reducing import competition may, in such a case, provide some room for growth or prevent the losses otherwise incurred; growth of exports would have similar effects and hence one can expect pressures to augment export subsidies or at least reduce the 'interest burden' of export credits.

Moreover, macroeconomic policy may exacerbate import competition through the exchange rate. One variant of this line is that exchange-rate flexibility itself negatively affects the level of trade. A survey by the IMF (1984) shows that short-run volatilities have no demonstrably negative effects on trade. Apparently, hedging, intra-firm denominations in one currency and long-term supply contracts suffice to cope with short-run fluctuations. The picture changes radically if we move from short-run volatility to much longer-run currency misalignments. The longer a certain over/undervalued spot rate can persist the more it will begin to erode/augment the competitiveness of all export sectors. The politically worrying scenario is, of course, overvaluation. Import competing sectors with small profit margins as well as traditional export sectors (especially those with relatively homogenous products) will be severely hit. In a climate of prevailing unemployment this is bound to lead to a build-up of protectionist pressure. The disquieting contribution by Bergsten and Williamson (1983) sets out a ratchet effect of higher protection as the left-over of each round of temporary but prolonged dollar over-valuation in the past. But it would be mistaken to think that this is a typical US phenomenon.

In the EMS exchange-rate mechanism eight countries are co-operating with different degrees of freedom in currency markets and with respect to transactions over the balance of payments. Yet, the EMS is clearly not a fixed exchange-rate regime. Therefore countries like France, Italy, Ireland and (up to 1983) Denmark could vary their exchange controls in order to prevent their currency depreciating or falling further than desired in the EMS. Such manipulation does not remove the need for convergence, it merely permits a slower pace, probably also at lower real-interest rates.

During exchange-rate crises, however, very stringent controls of trade credits (for example, by reducing the terms of financial settlement and imposing compulsory financing in foreign currency, especially for imports), zero-interest deposit schemes for imports and the taxation of buying foreign currency negatively affected intra-EC and international trade in a direct way. Hence, the first macroeconomic determinant of protection may well have been relevant in the EMS in that continuous variation in across-the-board exchange controls has accompanied the process of achieving macroeconomic convergence. Whether the degree of protection was (*ceteris paribus*) higher because of the 'deflationary' bias in the EMS, requires specific investigation (if this can be established at all).

The second macro-determinant may also have played a role in the EMS. To the extent the D-Mark was undervalued as a mirror-image of the dollar over-valuation up to 1985, the relative stability of EMS currencies might have exposed tradeables in weaker currency countries to more price competition. This might have led some EC countries to be more protectionist *vis-à-vis* third countries and, where possible, even EC partners. To the extent the appreciation of the ECU against the dollar (since 1985) was not accompanied either by more expansion in Germany or realignments appreciating the D-Mark, similar protectionist pressures might arise. Such pressures will be exacerbated by exchange controls, in as far as they keep the exchange rate above the free-market level. The highly specific manifestations of such protectionism are difficult to discover and even more difficult to attribute to 'the' convergence.

MICROECONOMIC DETERMINANTS OF PROTECTION

In the tradeables sector the retention of international competitiveness is essential for the health of the firm. On the export side the competitive position of a given sector will be strengthened by export subsidies or targeted domestic subsidies (say, for R&D) having similar effects on competitiveness in the longer run.[1] In a mercantilist perspective a closer look at the promotion of exports is warranted, especially since import restrictions run up against domestic and international constraints. However, direct export subsidies in non-agricultural products are outlawed by the GATT (General Agreement on Tariffs and Trade), so that indirect subsidization is the only option. Inside the EC, market integration is so advanced that indirect export subsidies are also excluded. This leaves indirect subsidies on exports to third countries. As we shall see, activities in this field have indeed grown tremendously. The empirical question is whether this indirect subsidization is a response to macroeconomic or sector-specific developments (hence, could possibly support the proposition), or merely a retaliatory response to export subsidies by non-European competitors in third markets.

On the import side, the complexity of sectoral competitiveness may be reduced to two key issues. First, for *inter*-industry trade comparative advantages may shift over time due to productivity increases in newly industrializing countries (NICs) or developing countries. Assuming a given technology, homogeneous products and a given international wage differential at initially given exchange rates, a catch-up process in NICs can rapidly erode competitiveness in developed countries. This will tend to squeeze profits and subsequently employment. Demanding protection is attractive because inter-industry trade is highly sensitive to price competition. In other words, the required adjustments are bound to be drastic before price competitiveness can be restored.

It is plausible to expect a preference for quantity protection in inter-industry trade since (a) tariffs are bound in GATT, and (b) even if they were not, tariffs effectively restricting imports may well have to be so conspicuously high as to become suspect in domestic politics. Quantity protection has the double political advantage of keeping the high tariffs implicit (indeed, the implicit tariff will 'invisibly' rise with an increase in domestic demand) while discouraging export-oriented investments in the NICs. Moreover, the uncertainty about future import competition reduces considerably: the nature of the effects is much the same as market sharing in a closed economy. A constraint is that quotas are prohibited by GATT and those which are 'grandfathered' are just as bound as tariffs. As is well-known, the voluntary export restraints have provided a way out.

Second, for *intra*-industry trade, products are imperfect substitutes and price is not the only determinant. So, competitive pressures may arise from a better exploitation of economies of scale, better marketing or a more suitable product design. Moreover, technology need not be given as learning-by-doing effects or new technological applications may reduce costs or raise quality. As a result, relative unit labour costs may diverge or demand may shift to imported varieties of the product (also in third markets!), leading to lower total profits (even if the profit as a mark-up over unit labour cost is kept constant) and falling employment. This development may prompt a stronger demand for protection.

The distinction between macro and microeconomic determinants of protection is analytically useful. A too rigid delineation between the two is not justified, however. For instance, the stubborn high unemployment in Europe is frequently ascribed to high unit labour costs, due to a combination of wage rigidities, high social charges, high taxes and high labour exit costs. Compared to the US, European firms cannot vary the workforce very easily; compared to Japan, unit labour costs in Europe cannot vary (via bonuses) with the profitability and performance of the firm. The upshot is that firms hold back before demanding labour. In practice, this argument is hard to separate from comparative advantages issues in inter-industry trade or from unit labour cost questions in intra-industy trade. If labour costs are out of line, the tradeables are clearly vulnerable because, in addition to a lower demand for labour caused by capital/labour substitution, they will suffer from losses of market shares (and lower profit), causing much more acute employment problems.

The micro and macro determinants intertwine in other instances too. This is rather obvious in the case of over-valuation, causing imports to increase rapidly at prices that may generate losses for domestic firms. Clearly, in sectors where competitiveness is already a problem, the survival of many firms will be at stake. If the over-valuation cannot somehow be undone, pressures for protection will become irresistible precisely in these sectors.

Export subsidies are related to the proposition because the process of convergence led in some countries to high real interest rates, making export credits unattractive, in turn negatively affecting export competitiveness. Export credit interest subsidies of one kind or another may take forms causing a direct link between convergence and national protection.

Quantity protection with voluntary export restraints (VERs) is virtually always prompted by several interacting factors, like sectoral demand decline, capital/labour substitution, comparative disadvantage and indeed sometimes a containment of domestic demand. The attribution to convergence is next to impossible although a coincidence might form an indication. Given the very wide scope of this chapter, it will not be feasible to pursue attempts at attribution with any rigour. Also, one seriously has to consider the arguments that certain sectors receive protection because of size (votes), geographical concentration (district system, etc.), seller concentration (effective lobbying) and number of workers (danger of unemployment). Convergence is then only one out of several causes of difficulty for the sector: it contributes to making the political case for relief and in this restricted sense promotes sectoral protection.

A special mixture of micro and macro is found in agriculture because exchange-rate realignments are not automatically effective for agricultural trade. Monetary compensatory amounts insulate this trade wholly or partly from changes of the central rates in the EMS grid. Convergence must have the effect of reducing this problem in the longer run, short of specific obstructive policy action by a Member State.

THE OPTIONS FOR NATIONAL PROTECTION IN THE EC

Before having a closer look at the facts of protection in the FRG, France and Italy, it is useful to establish in some detail what autonomy EC countries still have to engage in protection for their domestic producers. This autonomy is restricted in a formal and in a practical way. First, a most formidable set of constraints consists in the negative and positive integration of the European Community. This includes, as well, the obligations accepted under GATT rules, codes and tariff bindings. The second one is less straightforward. European Community countries clearly differ in their observable propensities to protect and intervene. Hence, they use the formal autonomy permitted by the EC and GATT with different degrees of intensity.

The meaning of national protection

The European Community is a customs union with a common commercial policy, a common competition policy and a great deal of joint economic regulation or harmonized national regulation. Therefore it seems puzzling to address the issue of 'national' protection of Member States. How can there be such an issue if commercial policy is a common one, and 'measures with equivalent effects' to tariffs (Art. 12) and quantitative restrictions (Art. 30) are outlawed?

Understanding the nature of the issue requires first an answer to two preliminary questions:

1. How (encompassing) is protection defined for purposes of the present analysis?
2. How encompassing are the relevant rules and policies at the EC level of government?

For present purposes *protection* comprises any non-monetary government measure influencing actual or potential competition between domestic and foreign-produced products. Inhibiting actual or potential competition from abroad can be accomplished through border measures and/or through domestic interventions of various types. A grey zone is formed by domestic interventions that do not affect all products in a relevant market: they will lead to distortions both among domestically produced goods and between affected domestic goods and foreign goods. The competitivity of domestic products can also be artificially influenced by various measures related to exports.

It is clear that this definition of protection reduces tariff setting to only one instrument on a broad spectrum of policy tools. The fixing of the common customs tariffs of the Community has traditionally been regarded as the cornerstone of EC trade policy. However, this seems inappropriate now that the level of EC tariffs is low and so many other instruments are available. The issue of protection as posed here goes much further. What counts is how encompassing the relevant measures are at the EC level of government. Omissions at the EC level will provide scope for 'national' protection.

Article 113, EEC, states that 'the common commercial policy shall be based on uniform principles' and that the implementation is a Community matter. The Community has exclusive powers for the common commercial policy. In other words, the Member States have effectively transferred them and cannot claim concurrent competences.[2] It would seem therefore that the simple logic of a customs union – the substitution of intra-group tariffs by union tariffs – has been extended consistently to other commercial policy instruments.

However, this inference is incorrect. The extension from tariffs to other instruments has not been pursued consistently. Although powers with respect to EC trade policy are exclusive, the Treaty does not exhaustively specify *what powers* actually have to be transferred. Article 113.1, EEC, lists changes in tariff rates, the conclusion of tariff and trade agreements, the achievements of uniformity in measures of liberalization, export policy and anti-dumping or countervailing duties as falling under uniform principles. This Article has two drawbacks:

1. It remains 'open-ended' with respect to other border measures unless one is to interpret 'uniformity in measures of liberalization' strictly (this has not yet been done).
2. It does not refer at all to domestic interventions.

The first drawback is exacerbated by the conjunction of Arts. 111, 113 and 115, EEC. The dividing line between Art. 111, EEC (allowing some omissions in the uniformity, during the transitional period up to 1970) and Art. 113, EEC (applying after the transitional period) is not watertight. This is also evident from the safeguards in Art. 115, EEC: their application is not explicitly confined to the transition period.

Therefore, the limits for national trade policy autonomy with respect to border measures will be determined by the Court's interpretation of Art. 115, EEC (on safeguards), given the failure of the Council to 'complete', that is, to fully unify, the border measures of the Community *vis-à-vis* third countries.[3]

The second drawback of Art. 113, EEC, is that it does not refer to domestic interventionism. Roughly similar economic effects for protectionist lobbies can be achieved by means of various instruments, be it that their incidence for other economic agents differ and overall costs for society (and indeed for politicians!) vary. Domestic instruments such as preferential public procurement, public aid to sectors or enterprises, certain kinds of technical barriers or exemptions to restrictive business practices may be construed such that they give rise to similar private economic gains as protective border measures would. Even if the ways of capturing these benefits for the protected would be distinct, an important common characteristic would remain: many domestic interventions can influence the actual or potential competition among foreign and domestic goods.

The Community would not have to regard the limitation of Art. 113, EEC, as a drawback if other Treaty Articles would effectively preclude the use of domestic instruments for affecting the competition between foreign and domestic goods. Despite the substantial accomplishments of the EEC (Pelkmans 1986b), particularly with respect to its internal market, it remains, nevertheless, an incomplete construct with a number of serious omissions. The scope for national authorities and existing national laws to affect the competition between foreign and domestic goods is greatly diminished but – with ingenuity and skill – a kind of truncated autonomy can still be enjoyed. Margins of manoeuvre would shrink to little, however, if the ambitious Cockfield White Paper (EC 1985) were implemented by 1993.

The scope for national protection

The constraints of the *acquis communautaire* are forceful and intricate. The scope for national protection of Member States is basically a residual after the *acquis* is considered. One should not lose sight of the fact that Member States strongly support the common market and generally adhere to the obligations it implies. National policy-makers tend to take the EC accomplishments as given. Assuming that the marginal use of an autonomous instrument will not affect the given state of integration, or at worst, only 'temporarily', Member States exploit national policy autonomy at the margin. Therefore it is useful for the purpose of this chapter to present the Community regime as a *set of constraints* for national protection.

Constraints are greatest if decisions are taken at EC level. But even then one has to inspect carefully whether the relevant EC decision excludes the possibility of using a similar national instrument as well. This two-tier system of policy varies greatly when comparing one instrument with another. There are instruments at EC level pre-empting the use at national level (e.g. tariffs); there are some at national level, although the same instrument is commonly used as well (e.g. VERs); there are some at national level while, in different product markets, the instrument applies at EC level (e.g. technical barriers), and there are several instruments at national level that are constrained by EC rules but have no counterpart at Council or Commission level (e.g. public procurement).

Were a Member State to consider whether to protect or help domestic producers, it would first of all have to inspect whether or not the decision will be taken at EC level. If so, the government may attempt to exert influence within the EC institutions. If not or not exclusively, the room for autonomous protection can be established and an assessment of the

Table 5.1 EC constraints for national trade policy

Policy instruments	EC level			Member-state level						
	Powers COM	Shared powers COM-Council	Powers Council	Execution EC policies		Implemention of EC law	EC authorization	Erosion Acquis	Omission Acquis	Outside EC realm
				Non-discret	Discretionary					
admin. frontier formalities	some	some	some	most	some	some		poss.	some	some
tariffs	most	some		all					some	
variable levies	most	some	some	all	some			some	some	
MCAs	some	some	some	most	some				some	
anti-dumping		all	most	all				some	some	
VERs	some	all						some	some	
agric. quotas	most	some	some	some				some	some	
quotas	most	some		most	some		some	poss.	some	
surveillance	some	some	some		some	most	some	some	some	
techn. barriers	some	some	some			most		some	some	some
public procur.	some	some			some			some	some	
public aid (agr.)	some	some				some	some	some	some	
public aid (ind.)	most	some				some		some	some	
indirect taxes	some		most		some	most			some	
cartels	all			all				poss.		
export aid	most	some		all	most	some		poss.		
agr. exp. subsid.	most	some	some	all				some	some	
min. prices	some	some	some	some	some	some		some	some	
exch. controls for trade	some	most		most	most	some	some	some	some	

measures made. Table 5.1 provides an attempt to define the Community constraints for national protection for 19 instruments related to product trade. The first three columns refer to the EC level of decision-making and indicate the scope for influence of Member States at that level. The column 'Powers Commission' may only exceptionally offer opportunities for national action, perhaps via advisory committees (where Member States are represented) or, seldomly, via political pressure at Ministers' level when a particular initiative or infringement procedure may be considered too costly for a weak coalition at home. The column 'shared powers' provides greater scope for national influence and this holds even more for the third EC column. In a Community of 12 Member States, coalition building is a necessity. Moreover, the EC is so closely knit together that continuous attempts to enjoy 'free riding' will not be accepted. Hence, even for the bigger Member States, the institutional, legal and political constraints at the EC level greatly circumscribe policy autonomy for the instruments listed.

The remaining seven columns indicate what opportunities could conceivably be exploited at home to influence actual or potential competition between domestic and foreign-produced products. The first five columns are subject to Community law, ranging from non-discretionary execution of EC policies, to Community authorizations of national measures and even to national measures that undermine the *acquis*. The Commission and the Court of Justice of the EC dispose of infringement procedures to prevent erosion from taking place or spreading. The Court may also help to stop erosion via prejudiciary rulings. If the Court were defied or the Commission ignored, only the Council could stop erosion. But the negotiations and bargaining strategies in the Council make this organ ill-suited to play measures made. Table 5.1 provides an attempt to define the Community the role of the 'guardian of the Treaty'. If one assumes that, following Cournot-type behaviour, other Member States follow the rules and hence assume integration as given, every country may pretend not to affect the common market with measures taken autonomously. But such an assumption is only valid if the Court is *not* defied and the Commission's role is duly respected. Failing to meet these conditions, the Council would find itself in a permanent bargaining session to prevent retaliatory escalation of national measures.

The last two columns of Table 5.1 point to the 'incompleteness' of market integration. The 'omissions' refer to the refusal of Member States to transfer sufficient surveillance power or common policy competences to the EC level so as to eliminate national autonomy. The difference between the 'erosion' and the 'omission' columns is legal, not economic. Domestic political pressures for protection may prompt national governments to lose sight of this difference. The substance of the omissions is not constant over time. There are permanent attempts by the Commission to reduce the number and the scope of omissions; at the same time the ingenuity of national administrations leads to regular additions to the stock of 'available' measures.

When considering the Member State level in Table 5.1 (especially column 4), certain severe constraints of national protection can be identified immediately. For six instruments (tariffs, variable levies, anti-dumping duties, agricultural quotas, cartels and agricultural export subsidies) there is no national discretion: Member States merely act as delegated authorities for a higher tier of government. These six types of measures can be excluded for the purposes of this chapter. The thirteen other instruments are all subject to some kind of EC involvement ranging from preponderant influence to a moderate one.

WHAT INSTRUMENTS ARE RELEVANT FOR THE PROPOSITION?

A brief discussion of the 13 instruments for which Member States have at least some discretion (see Appendix) should determine their possible relevance for the proposition outlined in the first section. This leads to the selection of five instruments for which a closer study of the conduct of the FRG, France and Italy would seem to be justified: monetary compensatory amounts, voluntary export restraints, public aid to industry, export credit and insurance subsidies and exchange controls. The selection has been based on three criteria which have been derived from the nature of the proposition. Before setting out these criteria, it is useful to remember what the chapter does not aim for. The following will neither analyze the extent of common EC protection nor the *level* of national protection. The proposition requires an analysis of national protection induced by macroeconomic convergence in the framework of the EMS. So it focuses on *new* or *additional* protection by Member States in the nine years of EMS existence.

THE CRITERIA FOR SELECTION

This restriction, imposed by the proposition, immediately leads to the first criterion for selection:

1. An instrument is only potentially relevant if it was newly introduced after 1978 (when EMS negotiations were completed) or if its use was intensified after 1978.

This criterion must be satisfied in every case.

A further reduction of the number of instruments might be achieved if the application of instruments cannot reasonably be attributed to the impact of exchange rate or macro-convergence policies. Later sections (pp. 113–28) show how difficult attribution is because of the simultaneity of causes for protection and because protection may be granted to offset indirect effects of convergence. Some narrowing down of choices may still be attainable, however, if we exclude intervention that neither mitigates direct effects of exchange-rate stability, sustained by macroeconomic policy convergence, nor supports sectoral employment and/or market shares.

2. An instrument can be relevant if it is used to mitigate or offset the direct effects of exchange-rate or macro-convergence policies.

Examples include the insulation from exchange-rate changes (e.g. for farmers) and from rising real interest rates (e.g. interest subsidies on export credits).

3. An instrument can be relevant if it is used to support current employment or current market shares for domestic sectors.

Criterion 3 leaves the door wide open for protection that is sought in response to a declining comparative advantage or for other reasons, which may be completely independent from the convergence issue in the EMS. But at this level of generality there is no easy way of distinguishing them empirically from cases where convergence has undermined the competitivity of a given sector. This distinction has to be established case by case. Criterion 3 is nevertheless useful because certain forms of protection do not affect *current* employment or *current* market shares and can therefore not reasonably be attributed to the impact of convergence. An example is R&D subsidies (unless the subsidy would fully substitute the sector's financing of projects that would have been undertaken anyway). Another example is a rise in taxation of products subject to inelastic demand (unless the rise would be so substantial that the indirect tax structure would be altered enough to induce substitution effects with similar products). Whereas criterion 1 must be met, either 2 or 3 must be met as well before further investigation of the instruments for Germany, France and Italy will be pursued in the next section.

ATTRIBUTING PROTECTION TO 'CONVERGENCE': THE CASES OF GERMANY, FRANCE AND ITALY

For the FRG, France and Italy, a qualitative and, where possible, quantitative description of recent protectionist trends will be provided for the five instruments selected (see Appendix): monetary compensatory amounts, voluntary export restraints, public aid to industry, export credit and insurance subsidies and exchange controls. With due regard to the caveats mentioned before, especially the informal approach and a lack of adequate data, the problem of attributing new or additional national protection to 'convergence' in the EMS will be addressed. This method should identify the cases for which the proposition in the first section can be substantiated.

The Federal Republic of Germany

Monetary compensatory amounts (MCAs)
Germany has enjoyed positive MCAs since 1969. Thus, it can afford a higher price level for farm products (at least, in terms of intervention prices) because exports are subsidized with MCAs and imports taxed. Every D-Mark revaluation *vis-à-vis* the ECU will either enlarge these MCAs or (in so far as they are gradually dismantled) reintroduce them. The internal agricultural market is thereby fragmented. The MCAs hinder reallocation as well as specialization by the more efficient suppliers in the EC of similar products. The stubbornness of the MCAs in Germany is a direct consequence of the powerful political swing vote of the farmers and their position in some Länder. It may also be explained by the implicit 'welfare' function of EC countries that a fall in income provides a prima facie case for shelter: abolition of positive MCAs implies an income reduction for farmers.

Since the beginning of the EMS, however, MCAs are *lower* than under the greater exchange-rate instability preceding it. MCAs result from nominal exchange variability and there is general agreement that, in this sense, the EMS reduced exchange-rate instability (Ungerer *et al.* 1986). In addition, since (real) interest-rate differentials are largely responsible for this stability, it is reasonable to argue that, without EMS, the D-Mark would have appreciated more. In a neo-mercantilist perspective, convergence and exchange rate stability reduce the degree of protection provided to German farmers. Therefore, the proposition of the first section cannot be supported. German appreciations *vis à vis* the French franc and the Italian lira have remained modest, unlike the pre-EMS period when MCAs were also larger.

German MCAs went down from 10.8 per cent on 17 April 1979 to 3.2 per cent on 10 April 1981. A series of realignments in the EMS pushed MCAs to a high of 13 per cent on 25 April 1983, falling to 9.8 per cent one year later. In 1984 a complex new system was accepted, forcing Germany to give up its positive MCAs but permitting full compensation through fiscal relief and aid for farmers. Therefore, the method of protection changed, not the income effects. But this does not affect the proposition.

Voluntary export restraints (VERs)
Germany sticks to its policy of condemning VERs as an erosion of GATT. An exception (vehemently denied by the German government) was the 'consultation' on a 10 per cent market share for Japanese cars by the then Economics Minister, Lambsdorf, in 1981. There seems to be a South Korean VER on 'simple cutlery' as well. Despite reservations, the FRG has also agreed to the ten VERs the EC 'concluded' with Japan in February 1983.

This leaves the border case of the Multi-Fibre Agreement (MFA), where quotas per Member State as well as EC quotas are used, but only after negotiations with exporting countries about the MFA framework and bilaterally about the volumes. Germany assumes a *relatively* liberal stance with respect to national quotas compared to Italy and France. Apart from the different starting positions of the three countries, this relative liberalism can be explained by the achievement of far-reaching adjustment, both by reducing the production of 'very sensitive' textile and clothing products and by achieving competitivity in up-market and speciality products. Currently the FRG is a net exporter in textiles.

The intentions of a government with respect to MFA-protection cannot wholly be derived from current 'quotas' in the MFA, since there are several safeguards for EC countries and, of course, the MFA is renegotiated every four or five years. The sensitivity can be read with more confidence from the intensity of surveillance of MFA-related trade flows. Counting at the six-digit NIMEXE-product level for 1985, Germany exercised surveillance for 'only' 65 out of 159 most-sensitive products (as against all products for France and Italy), 17 out of 192 sensitive products and none for less-sensitive products (Pelkmans 1987b, Table 2.4).

The indications are that the FRG has, if anything, loosened its protectionist stance in the MFA since the early 1980s and has not (bilaterally) engaged itself in seeking reliefs with VERs.

Public aid to industry

Germany being a federal country, federal subsidies do not reveal the entire picture. An internal Commission study shows that German federal aid remained at some 1.4 per cent of GDP between 1979 and 1983, this being far from marginal. In absolute amounts federal aid reached ECU 10 billion in 1983 (compared to ECU 11 billion for France, for instance, according to the same source). In terms of the public budget, Germany is in the lower-shares ranks of EC Member States but by no means is it exceptionally modest: in 1981 transfers to enterprises as a percentage of public current and capital expenditure amounted to 6.8 per cent (EC-average: 7.3 per cent). However, these figures – while surely being indicative – suffer from incomparability problems, particularly given the information gap on Länder aid and the lack of adequate information on fiscal aids.

In a probably unique paper, Juettemeier (1987) has scrutinized German public aid beyond the 300 federal programmes of subsidies and tax relief, also including the Länder and semi-state organs instrumental in subsidization. He claims that roughly 10,000 budgetary items related to public aid could be traced coming to a total of DM 103 billion for 1980 (which is 50 per cent higher than the federal government's report for that year). If one takes only financial grants (i.e. not fiscal relief) and excludes the CAP subsidies, federal and Länder/local grants both equal roughly DM 32 billion for 1984. The Juettemeier analysis attempts to be exhaustive and is not

Table 5.2 Sectoral subsidies to non-service sectors in Germany (DM million)

	1973	1980	1984	index ('73 = 100)
agriculture, fish	˙10,408	17,078	20,216	194
coal mining	1,602	6,023	5,528	345
(all manufact.)	(6,061)	(9,414)	(13,482)	(222)
nuclear fuel[1]	577	1,036	1,081	187
steel	95	336	2,009	2,115
mech. engineer.	779	1,247	1,819	234
aerospace	592	783	727	123
electric. engine.	1,116	1,538	1,971	177
textile/cloth.	190	235	312	164
food & bever.	547	712	962	176

Source: Juettemeier, 1987 (adapted).
[1] Includes aid to the chemical sector.

exclusively geared to public aids distorting competition in the common market. More than half of the totals found have little or no impact on intra-EC trade (subsidies to services, housing and non-profit institutions amounted in 1984 to DM 78.8 billion).

The subsidy per industrial worker employed in 1984 was DM 2000 (only in the sectors protected).

With respect to sectoral concentration in non-service sectors Table 5.2 provides selective data. First, all subsidies except aerospace to non-service sectors have increased more than inflation (± 60 per cent). Second, the absolute amounts of aid did not start from a very low base, except for steel. Table 5.2 reveals that Germany has disbursed fairly substantial amounts of public aid for a long time. Third, subsidization to industry has rapidly increased – more than doubling in eleven years. Fourth, aid to steel has exploded, especially in the 1980s. Fifth, sectors that have to compete in the common market at relatively undistorted conditions (food and beverages; mechanical engineering; electrical engineering) got substantial aid totals as well as increases over the 11 years considered.

However, although in real terms German public aid has increased significantly, since 1980 only two industrial sectors – steel and mechanical engineering – have shown conspicuous upwards jumps. In the case of mechanical engineering, a strong export sector for Germany, this may be explained by the recessionary climate in the Euromarket following disinflationary policies. But it surely does not apply to steel, where serious problems of overcapacity and modernization have plagued the EC steel industry since 1975. It is well-known that EC demand expansion cannot solve the permanent under-utilization of steel capacity. Capacity-reduction plans, agreed in 1983 at EC level, have not been sufficient and, in 1987, the Industry Council was confronted with Commission proposals for further capacity cuts. The rise in German steel subsidies can therefore be explained by sectoral rationalization, loss coverage (of the Saar steel works, for instance) and probably to a degree by 'matching' other EC countries.

Export credit and insurance subsidies
The bulk of export credits is financed by commercial activities of the Kreditanstalt für Wiederaufbau (KfW) and a private banks syndicate called AKA (Ausfuhrkredit-Gesellschaft). The KfW has some non-commercial export financing as well, the estimated maximum long-term credit capacity being approximately DM 800 million a year (OECD 1987, p. 62). These non-commercial activities are largely concentrated on the delivery of capital goods to developing countries, with eligibility requiring at least a seven-year repayment period (four years, if the exporting firm is small). KfW attracts capital market funds and blends them with subsidized export credits (from two public funds, one being the European Recovery Programme Fund) in a ratio of 3 to 1; the blended interest rate is therefore lower than commercial rates but, in actual fact, has always been at or above the OECD arrangement rates.

The AKA-banks maintain three lines of export credits, the so-called B-loans being subject to discounts. The B-loans relate to supplier credits (the KfW mostly dealing with buyer credits) to developing countries with a repayment term between one year and four years. Rediscounting at the Bundesbank yields a subsidy: the loans carry a rate equal to the official discount rate plus $1\frac{1}{2}$ per cent. The B-loans cannot cover more than 70 per cent of the contract. Depending on the spread between short- and long-term capital interest rates in the market, the subsidy may vary from less than 1 per cent to several per cent. However, rediscounted AKA-B-loans carry annual tax-cum-fees of 0.7 per cent. In 1985 the total of B-credits was DM 2,075 million, although DM 5 billion is available (OECD 1987).

Special cases such as ships and aircraft financing also have interest-rate subsidies; for ships, there are other OECD rules which leave more room for subsidies and matching; for aircraft, the OECD arrangement does not apply. Interest subsidies for the special cases are not published although there are data on outstanding credits: on ships they increased from DM 438 million in 1980 via a high of DM 1,941 million in 1982 to a low of DM 137 million in 1986; for aircraft, fluctuations are characteristic: the peak is 1981 with DM 1,216 million, with the other years being in the DM 460–840 million range, except 1986 (only DM 8 million) (BMWI 1987, p. 20).

Exchange-risk guarantees are not provided, except (by Hermes, the federal insurance agency for export credits) for aircraft sales (in US dollars). Hermes offers exchange-risk cover for other contracts in US dollars, sterling and Swiss francs (but no EMS currencies!), for losses of more than 3 per cent. The first 3 per cent are not covered and the loss is only covered if it occurs in the third year or later (given the problem of forward markets providing no cover).

Exchange controls
Germany does not normally apply exchange controls and has not applied the safeguards, Art. 108, EEC.

France

MCAs
As an agricultural exporter and as a country with a currency that is depreciating in the EMS *vis-à-vis* its major (green) export markets' currencies, France dislikes the system of MCAs more and more. In 1969 it was France which insisted on (temporary) MCAs for the first time. For a few years, however, France has insisted that the MCA system be abolished, or, at the very least, that its effects automatically phase out within a short adjustment period after a realignment. Since the Council decisions (of 1984) to phase out negative MCAs (i.e. those applying inter alia to France and Italy) and to automatically subject new negative MCAs to fixed phasing-out procedures, France has become extremely critical of Germany in the light of the latter's refusal to give up positive MCAs. (Even during the Brussels summit of June 1987 the head-on conflict was only solved half-heartedly). The effect of this strong public stance has been that France is in no position anymore to seek or claim new MCAs. At the moment it does not maintain any. It started out with a negative MCA of approximately 15 per cent when the EMS began in the spring of 1979. However, in April of the following three years France had zero MCAs. A surge to -8.1 per cent in April 1983 was the result of three realignments but reduction soon followed.

VERs
France believes in VERs as a possibly effective means to maintain the GATT order while dealing with its 'imperfections' bilaterally so as to minimize 'external effects' for other GATT parties. France advocates a common EC Japan-policy which almost inevitably will mean more numerous and stricter VERs at EC level. The Poitiers video tape recorder controls of late 1982 did have the effect of shifting positions in the EC Trade Council sufficiently to lay the basis for such a common Japan policy. In February 1983 ten VERs were concluded at EC level, two of which were rather strict and have been monitored since. France has also been active in negotiating VERs with Taiwan and South Korea on non-rubber footwear (in 1981) and with Japan for cars (3 per cent share of the French market, since February 1981) and, informally at industry level, for robotics and numerically controlled machines (from 1978 onwards).

For an informed judgement of French volume protection, however, it is crucial to study VERs in conjunction with the remaining 'national' quotas. On page 109 it is emphasized that these quotas show almost complete rigidity. To put it differently, France only 'needed' to use the VER alternative in product markets where national quotas were no longer authorized. Since France still has a considerable number of quotas, directed against imports from Japan and sometimes one or more NICs in products such as measuring equipment, consumer electronics and a few special cases, the demand for national protection will be lower. Thus, France never had a VER on the imports of black and white TV sets because there was a quota already, *not* because France was allowing free access. Conversely, France has no quota on footwear and felt compelled to negotiate a VER in 1981. A precise assessment is made very difficult, however, by the discretion in the French quotas: the EC has permitted a 'zone' system with many more countries in a 'zone' than countries against which quotas are actually enforced. Despite the gradual tightening of EC surveillance on quota systems, the Community has failed to explain, hitherto, the actual application.

The border case between VERs and quotas is the MFA where France led the Trade Council into distinctly more protectionist positions in the negotiations for MFA II (1977) and III (1982). Of all Member States France utilizes the surveillance system most intensively in these products. Counting at the six-digit NIMEXE product level for 1985, France exercised surveillance for all 159 most-sensitive products, for 189 out of 192 sensitive products and a staggering 229 out of 400 less-sensitive products (Pelkmans, 1987b). The country moderated its negotiation position only marginally for MFA IV (1986). The French textiles and clothing industry has undoubtedly adjusted during the last decade and a half, by shedding labour, rationalizing production and altering product composition. Whether it suffices to expect a more liberal stance by the government remains doubtful. In this respect, it should be realized that volume protection was combined with substantial public aid to the industry, causing endless disputes with the EC Commission and convictions by the EC Court.

Public aid to industry
In current francs total public aid to enterprises increased from FF 30 billion in 1979 to FF 82.5 billion in 1984 (= ± ECU 12 billion). In real terms this amounts to a quite high growth rate of nearly 13 per cent annually. Both the pattern of growth over the years and the composition of the aid are consistent with the proposition that public aid has served to substitute in part for exchange-rate changes and has helped to soften considerably the process of industrial adjustment, including attempts to prevent lay-offs. Consider the following indications:

1. General interventions, especially credits for industrial policy purposes, increased extremely rapidly as of 1981, having reached in 1984 FF 2,400 million, the ten-fold of the amount for the year 1981 when this provision was first altered by the Mauroy government but not yet provided under the new procedures. These credits comprise restructuring aids of various kinds, starting subsidies, etc.

2. Among the public-aid categories with 'horizontal objectives' (investment promotion; employment; exports; R&D plus innovation; energy saving), big upward jumps could be noted for investment aid (up some 160 per cent from 1981 to 1982; thereafter falling a little), employment (up 55 per cent from 1981 to 1982; up some 65 per cent to 1983 and another 25 per cent to 1984, reaching FF 8,384 million; however, the growth rate during 1979–81 was also high, nearly 50 per cent annually!), but above all for export aid (see below).

Conspicuous in the French case is that the country's reputation to increasingly favour specific aids to sectors is *not* borne out by the facts. Aid to shipbuilding did not increase, not even nominally between 1979 and 1984 (implying a real aid *decrease*); in real terms, aids to coal and the agro-industry barely increased, and for the energy sector some real increase could be registered. For textiles and clothing, a *pacte textile* was concluded that led to the exemption of social charges for this sector over the years 1983 and 1984. For steel a one-time jump in 1981 amounted to an addition of some 260 per cent, yielding FF 19 billion (!). This one-time jump included capital donations, themselves comprising a capitalization of the debt of steel firms. In 1982 the total for steel aid fell back to 'only' FF 7,900 million; the same for 1983 and 1984.

Capital participation to reduce debt burdens has also been used in other industries, especially in the early 1980s. According to the Haute Conseil du Secteur Public (1984, pp. 250–51), the largely non-tradeables sectors of public transport and energy have been aided by subsidies on current operations whereas public enterprises in industry were aided by capital donations (in shares). Over 1978–80 the average capital donation to industry was FF 1.3 billion; this increased to FF 5.5 billion in 1981; 10.4 in 1982; FF 12.7 billion in 1983, and FF 15.2 billion in 1984. This participation essentially covered losses, but was formally presented as a shareholder operation. Regional aid did increase, in the framework of devolution, initiated by the Mauroy government, but with a real growth rate of roughly 10 per cent or so since 1981 this is hardly of special interest. According to the EC Commission, total aid to French enterprises amounted to 2 per cent of GNP in 1981 and still 2 per cent in 1984. As a percentage of value-added, the EC includes industrial services, and finds 3.9 per cent in 1981 and 1983.

A special case of public aid is the 1974 commitment of the French Government to cover the losses from exchange-rate changes of loans (including bonds) in foreign currency. Until 1984 the state had shifted this burden to users or shareholders (also itself but not via transfers 'foregone'). The Court of Auditors reminded the state in 1984 that it violated commitments. According to the Haute Conseil (1984, pp. 252–3) these long-run debts are large.

Export credit and insurance subsidies

The disinflationary policies followed by France since mid-1982 rendered the tradeables sector exposed, because the exchange rate was kept high essentially with high real-interest rates. Import-competing sectors suffered from the high exchange rate and exporters both from the latter and, in theory, from the high interest rates, given the need to finance export credit. Export credit interest subsidies can provide relief to the extent that (European or global) real interest rate differentials, caused by a restrictive fiscal–monetary mix in the home country, are bridged for home exporters. As Melitz and Messerlin (1987) formulate what they call the 'optimal' rule, it suffices to provide exporters with the entitlement that export subsidies rise when interest rates rise. The authors claim that, whether by accident or design, French policy has captured this essential characteristic, mainly because fixed-rate rules were already designed in the early 1970s.

There are several estimates of French export credit subsidies available. The Melitz/Messerlin ones would seem to be economically the most satisfactory estimates. Furthermore, there are official estimates reported by the Banque de France, an estimate by Jean-Claude Dutailly (1984) and one by the EC Commission. Table 5.3 provides the data, which however are not fully comparable with respect to method of calculation.

The Dutailly estimates are probably too low because, unlike the other estimates, they do not include the treasury account on which the Banque de France rediscounting is based. The EC estimates are apparently based on official French estimates; in any event they hardly differ from them. The Melitz/Messerlin estimates are higher because, inter alia, they incorporated the fact that exporters encounter a higher market interest rate than public agencies, thus the opportunity costs (of these export subsidies) for the government are lower than for the economy at large.

Melitz and Messerlin also calculate the effective average subsidized rate (weighted average of old, very low rates on outstanding credit stock and new contracts). The comparison with the OECD minimum rates for new contracts shows that the real subsidy was indeed highest in 1981–3. The reasons lay in the effects of disinflationary policies on French interest rates and the considerable pre-1977 credit stock outstanding. In Messerlin (1986) a comparative calculation is also provided for rates of subsidization over total exports to non-EC countries and over export of equipment only to non-EC countries. This calculation does not cover the *préfinancements* on large scale operations, especially construction. It is really the equipment industry, and in fact a few major firms in a few subsectors, that benefit most from the other export credit interest subsidies. Subsectoral export subsidy rates may go up as high as 27 per cent (foundries) for 1979–83 on average; shipbuilding (22 per cent), aerospace (17 per cent) and even steel (10 per cent) benefited disproportionately. Although this sectoral concentration can be

Table 5.3 Export credit subsidies in France 1979–84 (various estimates, million FF)

	Melitz/Messerlin	Banque de Fr.	Dutailly	EC Commission
1979	5,374	3,300	(±) 1,660	3,384
1980	9,898	6,600	(±) 4,140	6,175
1981	14,916	11,500	(±) 6,435	11,545
1982	16,508	13,000	(±) 8,040	13,273
1983	13,691	12,600	n.a.	
1984	13,096	11,200	n.a.	

explained by typical public-choice determinants (and historically as a sub-stitute for colonial outlets) Messerlin shows that the rate of subsidization increases in every subsector from 1979 onwards.

The other major component of export subsidies consists of subsidized insurance for exports. The COFACE provides short-term credit insurances, longer-term credit insurance and insurance against cost escalation during the production process. According to Melitz/Messerlin, insurance for esca-lation above 6.5 per cent was so cheap as to amount to a pure subsidy. Data for 1981–4 are shown in Table 5.4 (in current francs).

For various technical reasons the Melitz/Messerlin estimates may be less reliable in this case. The EC Commission finds the following: FF 2,910 million in 1981; FF 2,946 million in 1982; FF 1,632 million in 1983; FF 3,639 million in 1984, consisting of the insurance of the export credits as well as political risk guarantees. It is difficult to deduce clear conclusions from these data. Presumably, the *ex ante* value of the premium is a key determinant and this has more to do with insolvency problems of importers in third countries, debt-servicing problems in developing countries (which increased dramatically in the first half of the present decade) and political risks. Nonetheless, it is equally clear that French exporters have received considerable protection so as to keep up their volumes of exports, especi-ally to areas with a problematic credit-standing.

The COFACE figures do not clearly show the problems emerging with the exchange-risk cover which is also provided. In fact (Messerlin 1986, p. 399) the 1981–4 results are favourable largely because of windfall profits caused by the appreciation of the US dollar.

Exchange controls
France has a long tradition of exchange controls. Although in the 1960s a gradual liberalization took place under pegged exchange rates, they were tightened in the early period of flexible rates. They varied during the 1970s, with a tightening before entering the EMS. When the D-Mark was weak (mid-1980 until mid-1981) they were immediately relaxed. From May 1981 until 1984 they were very strict, without however unduly affecting product

Table 5.4 Insurance against cost escalation in France

1981	FF 1887 million (official) (M/M: 1055)
1982	FF 3567 million (official) (M/M: 1709)
1983	FF 5485 million (official) (M/M: 3134)
1984	FF 4754 million (official) (M/M: 4369)

trade, apart from blocking manipulations with leads and lags and forward transactions (except for raw materials). Since 1985 a gradual relaxation of exchange controls has been realized, although largely as a unilateral measure. Close consultation and co-ordination with the EC Commission and the EC Monetary Committee has taken place, the Monetary Committee resumed its surveillance of exchange controls in December 1984. One ought not to forget that France received an EC loan in 1983, formally not under the EMS procedures but *de facto* conditional.

For relatively high inflation countries like France (as it used to be), membership of the EMS implies a costly transition period in order to capture the gains of the 'zone of monetary stability'. The *form* these costs take and on whom they fall depend on whether one opts for exchange controls with a little interest-rate variation or interest-rate variation with few or no exchange controls. France has shifted from the first to the second method as inflation rates came down in the middle of the decade. Giavazzi and Pagano (1985) show that the French exchange controls were effective in severing the link between interest rates on Euro-deposits and domestic interest rates in the years 1982–4.

In 1985 exchange controls began to be relaxed for trade financing (this chapter ignores the pure capital controls without an impact on trade). In March 1985 forward transactions in ECUs for imports were authorized up to six months. In October 1985, non-insured export credits in FF (crucial for intra-EC trade) for foreign buyers were permitted and payments deferrals for non-insured export controls were relaxed. In 1986 foreign currency accounts rules were relaxed and forward cover for imports was permitted up to six months. In 1987 liberalization was continued with the right to maintain foreign currency accounts (anywhere) up to an amount equal to three months' turnover in foreign currencies with other currencies; also, administrative obligations were largely suppressed. These details show that the *indirect* effects of the safeguards-exchange controls (Art. 108, EEC) can damage intra-EC trade and have *de facto* protectionist effects also inside the EC. A complete separation of 'trade' and 'financial' aspects in exchange controls proved to be illusory in the years 1982–4. For convergence not to cause fragmentation of the Internal Market, it is necessary to put a Community 'ratchet' behind the unilateral relaxation of the safeguards controls, achieved over 1985–7.

Italy

MCAs

Italy adheres to the policy of eliminating (negative!) MCAs, as agreed in the Community in the early 1980s. For instance, the country maintained a negative MCA of 2.3 per cent (on average) on 1 January 1983, returned to zero one year later but had to incur another MCA of 2.3 per cent by 1 May 1985. Its problem clearly is that MCAs reappear with every realignment in the EMS. With 11 realignments in eight years, and Italy almost always changing by more than 1 per cent (the threshold for MCA to emerge), the removal of MCAs is a permanent phenomenon.

However, in recent years the EMS has achieved reasonable stability among those participating in the exchange-rate mechanism. Volatility shifted to the pound and the drachma, which – because of the ECU definition used for MCAs – caused a number of MCAs. Taking the pivotal case of MCAs for dairy products, Italy had no MCA on 1 June 1985, one of −1.5 per cent on 25 April 1986, one of −5.3 per cent on 1 May 1987, reduced to −3.8 per cent by 1 July 1987; the jump in 1987 is wholly due to the depreciation of the pound (Strijker 1986). Italy clearly has attempted to minimize the inimical effects of depreciation in the framework of the EMS on intra-EC agricultural trade.

VERs

Italy has not many VERs. There is only one known, *vis-à-vis* Pakistan for jute bags and for sunblinds and camping goods. Similar to France, the reasons lie in the extensive application of remaining national quotas. The most well-known but not the only example is the Italian car quota of 3,000 cars (!) from Japan obviating the 'need' for a VER in contrast to the French. Quotas focus heavily on Japan and a few NICs. For instance, the 1984–5 list of Italian quotas *vis à vis* Japanese exports contains 32 four-digit products and 47 instances of quotas. It is also interesting that Italy has the highest number of *non*-MFA six-digit NIMEXE products under surveillance (117) of all EC countries.

Furthermore it ought to be kept in mind that Italy may still have comparative advantages in a number of product markets, currently penetrated by NICs (certain textiles; segments of the clothing market; fashion shoes; fashion leather products; quality toys; etc.). Altogether, the issue of VERs in Italy is not a serious one.

The border case is the MFA. Despite Italy's remaining comparative advantage in up-market products, Italy is still a strong proponent of the MFA. Apart from enjoying the usual kind of rent seeking, it is, above all, trade diversion inside the common market that has benefited Italy enormously. According to the number of products under surveillance in 1985, Italy (like France) applied surveillance to all 159 six-digit NIMEXE most-sensitive products under MFA III, but (unlike France) only 24 out of 192 sensitive products and a mere 27 out of 400 less-sensitive products (Pelkmans 1987a). The relaxation of the application of Art. 115, EEC, interfering with intra-EC trade is therefore a problem for Italy, but it is a long-standing problem with seemingly no direct relation with the EMS and exchange-rate stability.

Public aid to industry
The widespread conviction that Italy has made extensive use of public aid to industry is based on fragmentary data, anecdotes and the fact that numerous laws were passed with substantial funds. However, appropriate statistical information is hardly available. Two important reasons are that a substantial share of aid takes forms which are hard to discover and even harder to evaluate in terms of their 'grant element' ('off-budget' items such as state participation in capital, various fiscal deductions, etc.) and that actual disbursement was either much later or lower than the funds originally allotted under the law. The latter phenomenon led, for instance, to carry-overs between (temporary) funds under different laws. The following must therefore be approximative. This chapter does not pretend to provide the accurate picture that even the EC Commission has thus far not been able to publish.

Probably the most complete statistical survey is by Artoni and Ravazzi (1986). They include:

- Aid to public enterprises, both direct subsidies of various kinds and participation in capital (to reduce or prevent the increase of debt burdens, hence, a form of loss coverage).
- Transfers via financial institutions, giving aid; especially regional facilities, export credit subsidies and technology.
- Export insurance subsidies.
- Off-budget transfers via special funds (for restructuring of sectors; for innovation; and separately, in addition, for steel and the electronic sectors).
- Industrial subsidies for the Mezzogiorno (additional).
- Other special arrangements, including fiscal (VAT) and pension facilities in the Mezzogiorno.

The total estimates by the authors show a rapid increase from 4,700 billion lire in 1978 and 3,700 billion lire in 1979, via 7,580 billion lire in 1980, 8,000 billion lire in 1981, 13,500 billion lire in 1982, to more than 19,000 billion lire in both 1983 and 1984. As a percentage of GNP a rise from 1.36 per cent in 1979 to 3.6 per cent in 1983 and 3.21 per cent in 1984 is observed.

It is clear from the literature that this rise can be explained by the gradual deterioration of certain sectors (above all, steel), by the desire of the respective Italian governments to turn public enterprises into 'employment machines' and by under-capitalization inherited from the 1970s. The employment aspect precedes the EMS (e.g. Fornengo 1986, esp. p. 51; Sandri 1987; Eisenhammer and Rhodes 1987; etc.) and was challenged more and more strongly in the course of the 1980s. Precisely when Italy began to take seriously the convergence commitment in the EMS (i.e. beginning in 1983), the axioms of not-closing-plants and restructuring without pain were relaxed considerably.

Certainly, the famous Law 675 of 1977 has not been effective. A major complaint was that the interest subsidies, as the key tool, were entirely offset by the restrictive effects of monetary policy! Moreover, procedural delays have been such that delays of disbursement went up to three to four years! It is highly doubtful that this policy has been an effective *response* to a restrictive policy mix, augmenting the distortions in the common market. The loss coverages are an exception, but, apparently, they were heavily concentrated in the crisis sectors.

Export credit and interest subsidies
A key difference between the French and the Italian export credit interest subsidy system is the ceiling the Italians apply. Although the ceiling varies over the years, it has clearly restricted the use of export credits in having avoided open-ended financing. The Medio-credito has an endowment fund of 1,364 billion lire, which is annually supplemented by money from the state budget. The constraints have caused problems in that eligibility does not guarantee a firm or bank that the financing can always be obtained. How the *de facto* rationing operates does not seem to be published.

Most important in Italy are buyer credits in foreign (convertible) currencies. For contracts in lire the lowest rate of (subsidized) credits are still above the OECD minimum rates (OECD 1987, p. 88). Contracts in foreign currencies are popular because the nominal interest rate is low, whilst, since 1979, the exchange risk can be covered via the official insurance agency SACE (the Societa per la' Assicurazione e il Credito all'Esportazione) for contracts beyond 18 months. The cover is complete in the sense that the difference between the official exchange rate at the day of signing the contract and the rate at which payments are made is insured. However, the amount may be limited and, in the event of depreciation of the lira, the exchange-rate profit is to be paid to SACE. Like France, Italy once had a 'cost escalation insurance' but dropped it in late 1974.

According to Artoni and Ravazzi (1986), export credit aid increased rapidly from 1978 (120 billion lire) via 300 billion lire (1980) and 960 billion lire (1982) to 1,274 billion lire (1983) and 1,712 billion lire (1984). The burden of insurance rose a little faster from 29 billion lire in 1978 and 24 billion lire in 1980 to 388 billion lire in 1983 and 775 billion lire in 1984.

Following Simonazzi (1985, p. 254) the share of export credit subsidies in industrial value-added rose from 0.226 per cent in 1978 via 0.311 per cent in 1980 and 0.534 per cent in 1982 to 0.58 per cent in 1983.

This increase has given rise to concerns about the costs of the instrument (see, e.g. Onida *et al.* 1987), culminating in a recent reform of the system. Nevertheless, there can be no doubt that the effects of convergence have been felt less by Italian exporters (to non-EC countries) thanks to these subsidies. Whether these measures were prompted or intensified by convergence seems doubtful as the increases were rampant already before 1983 and are probably linked to the debt crisis. With respect to the exchange-risk cover no separate data are available but there is no reason not to repeat the observation for France with regard to the dollar rise up to 1985.

Finally, one interesting difference between Italy and France seems to be the share of short-term export credits in the total. Whereas Banca Commerciale Italiana (1987, p. 2) claims that 80 per cent of all trade credits are short-term (and hence never eligible for any support whatever), Messerlin (1986, p. 388) quotes a share of 25 to 30 per cent for France.

Exchange controls
From the early 1970s Italy used exchange controls in varying ways and with various degrees of stringency up to 1985, when a gradual dismantling was initiated. There is little doubt that the controls have had restrictive effects on trade, at times possibly more restrictive than the French controls. The controls preceded the EMS and, when strict, were inevitable responses to exchange crises. The impact on trade has been greatest when safeguards Art. 108, EEC were invoked. The May 1974 introduction of an import-deposit scheme for importation of certain goods (imposing a six months' zero-interest deposit in lire equivalent to 50 per cent of the value) was an infringement of Community law, even under the safeguard clauses. Nevertheless, it was withdrawn only in May 1985. And in 1976 purchases of foreign exchange for settling a foreign transaction carried a three months' zero-interest deposit of 50 per cent, followed later by a tax (of 7 per cent) on currency purchases.

However, a continuously returning instrument is the variation of the terms of settlements of exports and imports and variations in restrictions of foreign trade financing of exports in arrears and of imports in advance. This leads-and-lags problem was controlled with a myriad of measures, and with dismantling and reintroductions over more than fifteen years. More generally, trade financing has proved to be crucial for Italian exchange controls because capital (and bank reserves) controls have already been strict for a considerable period. Yet, there is no economic assessment of the incidence of such strictness and volatility of controls on trade credits and settlements. Lacking this evaluation, there is no way of judging the application of the proposition. One can only acknowledge that exchange controls have been greatly relaxed after 1985, i.e. after inflation came into the one-digit range.

Giavazzi and Pagano (1985) show that exchange controls had the same effect as in France: they severed the link between interest rates on the Eurocurrency market and domestic interest rates in the period of great divergence of inflation rates. After some first adjustment, Italy is also shifting to the use of interest rates to maintain exchange-rates stability, with less reliance on exchange controls.

CONCLUSIONS

The question addressed in this chapter is whether the possible 'deflationary bias' in the EMS has prompted Member States to become more protectionist, hence undermining the common market and adding to protectionism in the world.

Nineteen instruments, which could all be called 'non-tariff barriers', have been scrutinized on the basis of three criteria, establishing whether they could possibly be relevant for the proposition. For five instruments these criteria were met, so that the *recent* increase in protection could perhaps be linked to or prompted by demand constraints (including an interest squeeze) having accompanied the consolidation of the EMS and the convergence at a low rate of inflation. These five tools are VERs, public aid to industry, export credit and insurance subsidies, MCAs and exchange controls. Although the German MCAs especially have the effect of limiting somewhat the market outlets for Italian and French farmers, they have decreased, not increased, under convergence.

With respect to the other instruments, the following conclusions can be drawn for France, Germany and Italy:

1. *VERs:* especially for France there was a clear upsurge in the early EMS period; if one includes the Multi-Fibre Agreement, one could argue that the lack of growth in general restrained even more the sectoral saturation of demand, and hence provoked a stricter MFA III and IV.
2. *Public aid to industry:* all three countries have stepped up public aid, probably France the most, Germany clearly too. In Italy policy data are the weakest but of course loss coverage and off-budget items did increase enormously for a while. In some sectors the common market has been seriously impaired (shipbuilding; steel; even cars and textiles/clothing to some extent).
3. *Export credit and insurance subsidies:* they only affect the internal market indirectly, yet they do amount to a considerable 'protection'

for exporters (for trade outside the EC). Data are approximative. The French case is well studied: it shows clearly that the 'fixed-rate' rule has led to an effective proportional increase of subsidies with the increase in interest rates. However, it hardly affects the EC as such directly, and it must be a transitory effect. Italian subsidies were similarly effective in that exchange risk was also covered (as in France), but total subsidy outlays were lower. Observe that the German commercial interest rates were most of the time *at or below* the OECD rates (issued since 1976), so that subsidies were small (their scope also being limited).

4. *Exchange controls:* France and Italy traditionally employed exchange controls and the EMS did not change that before convergence became accepted in the domestic politics of the two countries. The safeguard-controls particularly have had trade-impeding effects via restrictions on the terms of settlement and on leads and lags. With convergence, both countries substitute interest-rate variation for exchange controls as the central instrument to maintain exchange-rate variability in the EMS. This points to a *reduction* in protection prompted by convergence.

In short, this leaves VERs, public aid and export subsidies. However the first two have a strong sectoral application. In our view, it cannot be maintained that the deflationary bias is playing a dominant role in these 'crisis sectors'; at best, a more expansionary Germany might have caused some slight relief in demand. The sectoral adjustment problems in steel, cars and shipbuilding are the consequence of over-capacity, with roots in the 1970s. Moreover, technological progress (in steelmaking; robotics in cars) has accentuated these over-capacities. Furthermore, comparative disadvantages *vis-à-vis* NICs play a role, especially in shipbuilding and textiles and clothing. Finally, a degree of demand saturation, limiting sectoral growth, played a role (steel demand was partly subsituted by other materials; clothing; to some extent cars; ships).

The sectoral explanation is less relevant for export credits although the strong sectoral concentration in all three countries should not be dismissed too quickly as irrelevant. The Melitz/Messerlin (1987) explanation for high export credits under exchange-rate stability with a strong currency can be endorsed, although it applies to only a relatively small part of foreign trade. Moreover, with convergence continuing, the effects of this approach peter out.

The chapter also shows that no judgement can be passed without being fully aware of the protection *already* in place. This applies both to VERs and subsidies, but especially to the former since they have to be evaluated together with 'grandfathered' quotas which France and Italy still have. The protection already in place may have a more restrictive impact under convergence, not only because of some remaining discretionary elements at Member-State level, but also because demand growth may be 'assigned' fully to domestic producers.

Finally, in focusing on new protection and existing protection one might lose track of other initiatives which point exactly to the opposite. The EC Commission's White Paper is now ratified in the Single European Act. By the end of December 1987 one quarter of the announced measures had already been adopted. The sweeping character of the 1992 plans (Pelkmans and Robson, 1987) largely coincides with the forceful convergence witnessed since early 1985.

The proposition in the beginning of the chapter is thus likely to have very limited appliability in the EC and EMS of the 1980s. This is not to deny that there is a deflationary bias – the chapter does not purport to substantiate this – but, if so, it:

(a) led to little *additional* protection, attributable to convergence; the effects that were found are transitory or reduce with convergence;
(b) was accompanied by intiatives of market integration that overwhelm, indeed, eliminate any intra-EC protection of any conceivable variety.

APPENDIX 5.1

A search among 13 instruments

The following instruments will be discussed with a view to incorporating them in the section beginning on p. 113: administrative frontier formalities, monetary compensatory amounts, VERs, non-agricultural quotas, surveillance, technical barriers, public procurement, public aid to farmers, public aid to industry, industrial export subsidies, indirect taxes, minimum prices and exchange controls.

Administrative frontier formalities
The 1980s have seen a gradual tightening of the Community rules for customs procedures and frontier formalities. In other words, what was outside the EC realm (last column in Table 5.1) is brought in via the Single Act or via inter-governmental decisions with similar effects; omissions in the *acquis* are tackled step by step; implementation of EC directives becomes less of a problem as directives are replaced more and more by regulations; and in matters of execution the discretion of Member States will diminish due to the completion of the Internal Market and the (recent) introduction of the single customs document (with extremely detailed administrative instructions, down to multi-linguistic code words, etc.). The fact that customs officers remain at the inner borders until 1993, however, is a standing invitation to use them occasionally, particularly for

discretionary application of some of the other instruments in Table 5.1.

The first criterion is not met, except for one brief spell in the autumn of 1982 when France suddenly tightened administrative border controls (and was convicted later by the Court of Justice of the EC). Given two devaluations of the French franc in the EMS, following an expansionary policy of the Mitterrand government, and a second one held as probable, the impression was created that the second criterion was met: border measures were to slow down imports to improve the trade balance. Although there was irritation and protectionist incidents did take place, they hardly affected trade flows in a systematic way. If anything, the reputation of France as a loyal EC member was damaged and the measures were quickly withdrawn or brought into the negotiations about the single customs document, then taking place.

Even more conspicuous in that period was the French decision to proceed with the import formalities of (Japanese and EC!) videotape recorders in a small inland customs office in Poitiers. This blunt attempt to blackmail the EC Council and force it to formulate a set of joint VERs for Japan worked effectively as in February 1983 ten VERs were concluded. Nevertheless it would be false to consider this incident as the outcome of an unsustainable exchange rate or policies leading to convergence. The issues relate to Japan's targeted exports and are strictly sectoral. France has made it very clear that it is a strong proponent of the internal market programme which aims to exclude these practices.

Italy's complex system of import licensing (Grilli 1980) has some discretionary elements for imports from certain developing countries and Eastern Europe. However, the first criterion is almost certainly not met and the second does not apply. Recent simplification and stricter surveillance by the Commission make it unlikely that the third criterion is met. The FRG has no licensing system except in the framwork of EC decisions.

For all these reasons, this instrument has been eliminated from the discussion.

Monetary compensatory amounts
Commonly agreed agricultural prices in ECUs will diverge in intra-EC trade in terms of national currencies if a revaluation leads to positive MCAs (i.e. subsidies of green exports; taxes on green imports) and a devaluation to negative MCAs. They amount to an automatic shelter against exchange-rate realignments (criterion 2). The instrument was introduced long before 1978 and discrete manipulation is not possible at Member-State level, given EC decision-making. Here we have a clear instance of where a refusal to adjust (to exchange-rate changes) has made a mockery of the internal (agricultural) market. The problem for the proposition at the beginning of this chapter is that it is exchange-rate *instability* rather than stability that causes MCAs to become important.

The success of the EMS has reduced the problem of MCAs; typically, the UK, not participating in the exchange-rate mechanism, has the largest (negative) MCAs. Therefore, one could have excluded MCAs from discussion, were it not for the fact that it is especially the countries with appreciating currencies (Germany, less so the Netherlands) which resist the removal of positive MCAs (i.e. criterion 1 applies). MCAs is included in the section beginning on p. 113.

Voluntary export restraints (VERs)

These 'agreements' evade GATT rules in that, while constituting a quantitative restriction to trade, they take the legally innocuous form of self-restraint by the exporting country or its exporters as a group. VERs are legally and politically impossible within the EC. All VERs of EC countries are 'concluded' with third countries, mostly Japan and some NICs. A (major) border case is the Multi-Fibre Agreement whose quantitative protection takes the form of quotas (i.e. the import countries enforce, unlike a VER) but where the volumes and the MFA-framework are negotiated among importers and exporters. National VERs either infringe Community law or erode the *acquis* in trade policy. They infringe Community law if they are concluded between private business associations (because they form restrictive business practices forbidden in Art. 85.1, EEC). If Member State A concludes a VER in product x, competitive conditions in A's x market will likely differ from the rest of the Community's x market, although Art. 115, EEC, has not been invoked (hence, the distortion is unauthorized). Therefore, a VER for the US or Sweden is not quite the same as one 'obtained' by an EC Member State, as the latter affects the proper functioning of the common market.

In political practice, domestic pressures have apparently been such that the Commission has neither initiated infringement procedures under Art. 85, EEC, nor under Art. 115, EEC, but has preferred political solutions in the Council. One reason for this may well be the Commission's fear of double defiance: a court ruling might be openly defied – which would be damaging to the fragile Community – and the rising popularity of national VERs may be defiant of the exclusive trade policy powers of the Community. An inference of dubious merit is then that the Commission must pre-empt this national protection by evading GATT rules *Community-wide* so as to rescue the common trade policy. It is clear that this configuration amplifies the bargaining position of the four biggest Member States in cases of strong domestic political pressure for selective protection.

The first criterion is met as the utilization of national VERs markedly increased between 1978 and 1982. The second criterion does not apply as VERs are always highly specific in terms of products and the country of exports. The third criterion is also met since VERs are undoubtedly utilized to soften or lower the speed of adjustment. VERs therefore are included.

Non-agricultural quotas
One has to be extremely careful before casting a judgement on the current situation on quotas of EC Member States. It is correct to stress that the Community has exclusive powers with respect to quotas. It is equally correct to add that, in conformity with GATT rules, the Community has abolished non-agricultural quotas. On the other hand, one can point to a rather long list of Member States' quotas, discriminating specific third countries, that is still in existence in 1988! This list is formally a Community catalogue of 'authorized' exceptions, in view of the unwillingness of Member States to give them up. Observe that this list has survived alongside the increasing utilization of national VERs as well as the emergence of VER-based systems of volume protection in steel and textiles and clothing, sometimes at both levels of government.

Adding up the four-digit CCT-headings[4] subject to Member States quotas for each Member State (Benelux as one) of the EC – 10 for 1984, one finds 143 product sectors with restrictions for all six-digit products and another 55 product sectors with selective application at the six- (or higher) digit level (Pelkmans 1987b, Table 2.3). This counting excludes the Multi-Fibre Agreement. The import volume affected, as a percentage of extra-EC imports, amounted in 1984 to 2.2 per cent for FRG up to 6.1 per cent for France (not counting the energy sector) and 6.5 per cent for Italy. It is likely that the relevant import flows would be higher in the absence of quotas although the discriminatory nature of the quotas has probably caused so much trade diversion that the net impact of abolition on imports might well be small, with the exception of cars and a few other products. The quotas strongly discriminate against Japan and a few Asian NICs.

It is crucial to acknowledge, for the purposes of this chapter, that these quotas have shown virtually complete rigidity: no increase in restrictiveness has been permitted by (EC) policy-makers (although, of course, the economic incidence of a given quota will still change if demand varies). The first criterion is not met. They cannot serve as an instrument to respond to temporary (macroeconomic) pressures, so that the third criterion is not met either. Being quantitative restrictions, they do stem additional import competition induced by higher exchange rates (criterion 2) but only from some sources in a highly discriminatory way. There is no reason to expect that depreciation would itself be a motive to remove them (as the last one-and-a-half decades has already shown). No matter how protectionist some of these quotas are, they are irrelevant for the proposition of the first section.

Surveillance
Community surveillance of imports consists in the acceleration of the processing of statistical information on selected products (from selected countries) imported into the EC as a whole or a single Member State. The actual execution of this EC procedure is left to the Member States, or

by specific authorization to one Member State. In this respect, the row 'surveillance' in Table 5.1 has to be read in conjunction with the row 'administrative frontier formalities'. Some Member States require special import documents for this purpose, implying *a priori* monitoring (rather than *a posteriori*), in turn leading to less-flexible procedures and the possibility that the 'necessary' documents are (temporarily?) refused so as to exert pressure or deter importers. However, even when surveillance is *a posteriori*, it acts as a threat to exporters not to overstep certain limits or growth rates that may have been informally notified to them. Within the MFA framework, surveillance is essential for triggering certain safeguard options such as the 'surge mechanism', the 'basket exit' or mere consultations.[5] In other product markets where surveillance is applied, monitoring might be a compromise solution in bilateral negotiations, hence they may serve as a stepping-stone to a future VER. Finally, surveillance may serve to *prevent* a fragmentation of the internal market as long as the monitoring and the regular discussions in the Trade Council would suffice to obviate recourse to safeguards Art. 115, EEC. Thus, surveillance is in the interest of the Commission (it serves the commonness of trade policy, while preventing disparities in the internal market) but it also strengthens the hand of Member States with domestic protectionist pressures. No wonder that the practice of monitoring became rather popular in the late 1970s. The levelling-off in the 1980s might be explained by new VERs having substituted the import surveillance, by progress in adjustment, by the relative attraction of the US market for LDC's exports (at least up to 1986) and by the rising concern of Commission and Council that monitoring had lost its marginal and exceptional character and begun to look like neo-protectionism, which was to be resisted.

In recent studies[6] attempting to quantify non-tariff protection, the surveillance practices of EC countries are likely to contribute heavily to the observed increase in the frequency indices used. Although there is anecdotal evidence of some deterrent effect, it is hardly conceivable that the recent tightening of administrative customs procedures in the EC (as well as some EC case law) has left much room for systematic policy. To the extent criterion 1 would be met at all (which is difficult to establish), the application is extremely product-specific and applies to selected countries. The connection with convergence seems far-fetched. Surveillance is not carried over to the section beginning on p. 113.

Technical barriers
One has to appreciate the complexity of this category, with endless opportunities for tiny incidents of covert protection. The Community is unique in that case-law, Art. 30, EEC and a long drawn-out programme for technical harmonization have dramatically reduced the technical barriers in the common market. Going against the thrust of the proposition in the first

section is the fact that the Community greatly increased its ambition in the early 1980s, precisely when the EMS was kept together only with difficulty. Early in 1983 a far-reaching directive (83/189) was adopted, comprising standstill obligations for any *new* technical barrier. These (potential) barriers are discovered thanks to an exhaustive notification obligation, enforceable with infringement procedures. The Community decided in 1985 to accelerate the removal of technical barriers by means of a 'new approach' (see Pelkmans 1987a), implying references to standards in the law (rather than minute details), application of safety and health objectives to large product groups and greater emphasis on mutual recognition. The first directives have already been adopted without too many difficulties.

The Community's accomplishment in technical harmonization in the last five years, the 'new approach' and the strict judicial review of the Court, Art. 30, EEC (prohibiting all 'measures with equivalent effect' to quantitative restrictions) – especially after a landmark ruling in 1979[7] – render it almost impossible to utilize (new) technical barriers for national protection in the sense of this chapter. Whilst it is clear that criterion 2 is not met in the case of technical barriers, criteria 1 and 3 do not apply either.

Public procurement
Until 1986, the EC did not materially influence the undisputable national preference in public procurement. The approach was legalistic (cf. a general prohibition in 1969) and procedural (two basic directives in the 1970s). The economic incidence of the EC policy was practically nil.[8] Though formally superior to the GATT approach, the EC rules did not lead public buyers to alter their economic conduct.

The White Paper on the completion of the Internal Market promises to change this. A number of initiatives are currently (1988) being discussed, such as the tightening of procedures both for public supplies and public works, and the extension of the public supplies directive to key sectors for public procurement as public transport; water, gas and electricity; and telecom. Only armaments are left out in view of Art. 223, EEC, excluding defence matters.

Nevertheless public procurement is surely an instrument for 'national' protection, one that even in the EC is hard to detect and difficult to prevent. What is more doubtful, however, is whether this 'instrument' lends itself to well-co-ordinated planning in response to macroeconomic developments. National politicians will have incentives to opt for a few spectacular cases of national anti-cyclical procurement or prototype development (under supply contracts, with high-risk loans) but, in general, public procurement is badly co-ordinated inside national administrations (except, perhaps, in France). The bulk of important purchases depends on long-term supply relationships and on material needs which means that criterion 2 is not met except possibly for public works (but here the delays are great). Moreover, since the national preference is already very strong (nearly 100 per cent), it may only be further increased at very high costs, say, of incompatibility, technical inefficiency, lower service quality or late delivery. The only way out might be to tie sub-contractors also to national procurement or national value-added but, of course, local-content laws violate EC law (apart from augmenting inefficiency). Even buy-national campaigns have been outlawed by the Court of Justice of the EC. So the first criterion is not fulfilled either.

The third criterion is more problematic. Public procurement and public works are suited for selective anti-cyclical expenditure that does not leak abroad in the first stage. Unfortunately, useful data on public procurement are virtually absent. Nevertheless, the following arguments lead to exclusion of this instrument for the proposition. First, fiscal restraints accepted in the framework of 'convergence' reduce the scope for anti-cyclical preferential public procurement. Second, the proposition refers to an increase in protection and this is hardly possible with public procurement given the almost exhaustive preference granted to national supplies which fall under the EC directive; the sectors excluded until today are widely recognized as being preferentially supplied as well. Third, although the proper functioning of the common market is negatively affected, no doubt, there is nothing 'new' about it. There is no evidence that the current fragmentation should be attributed even in part to a deflationary bias in the EMS. If anything, the traditional rigidity of Member States with respect to telecom equipment procurement is loosening up and moves to combine industrial co-operation with joint procurement in armaments are being seriously considered.

Public aid to farmers
In contrast to the prohibition of public aid to industry, public aid to agriculture is not restricted by the general competition rules of the Treaty (cf. Art. 42, EEC), except when explicitly laid down in regulations under Art. 43, EEC. The result has been an almost total lack of co-ordination or harmonization of national aids to agriculture. A major study, done for the Commission (Didier and Assoc. 1984) shows that data are both incomplete and only partially comparable. With a great many caveats the study concludes that *national* aids together amounted to between 85 and 90 per cent of the disbursements of the *Community*'s Agricultural Fund for 1980.[9] It also shows that many Member States have a fragmented approach, in only one case really being a 'policy'. Items such as various forms of tax relief appear to be unclear, difficult to quantify and incomparable among Member States. The four main objectives of such aids are: improvement of production structure at the farm level, research and human capital investment in agriculture, expenditure 'upstream' of the farms (i.e. processing, etc.) and rural area development. The large disparities in absolute and relative

amounts for the four objectives among the Member States, as well as per capita, may have distortive effects in the Internal Agricultural Market. But it is not convincing to maintain that these aids provide great scope for Member States to respond to macroeconomic developments. Three categories of aid may be manipulated for such purposes: social security for farmers, tax relief for investments (particularly in times of high interest rates and high inflation, the real after-tax rate may even become negative) and rural aid (as a complement to regional policy which must comply with EC criteria). A flagrant abuse of the EC policy-void with respect to agricultural aids was of course President Giscard d'Estaing's decision to suddenly disburse extra income aid to French farmers in April 1981, in an attempt to win the farmers' votes one month later. This purely political gift was not motivated by employment or trade considerations, but it did reveal the tenuity of 'common' income support, even in the presence of automatic national adjustments via the MCAs.

Criterion 1 might apply if national aid had greatly increased after 1978. With the exception of (especially Dutch) investment aids, there are no clear indications of this. Criterion 2 does not apply. Criterion 3 is not met because most aid does not relate to current market shares and employment. One big exception ought to be mentioned in order to prevent any misunderstanding: Germany has substituted the removal of positive MCAs by equivalent reduction of VAT rates for farm products (after EC approval), beginning in 1984. This kind of national 'aid' is not dealt with here but under MCAs (see page 113 ff.).

Public aid to industry
Public aid to industry in the EC is forbidden apart from certain exceptions as well as exemptions based on the criteria mentioned in Art. 92.3, EEC. In the ECSC Treaty, Art. 4 prohibits public aid unconditionally. There is little doubt that Member States have responded to sectoral and even macroeconomic developments with public-aid programmes much more aggressively than with most other national instruments of protection. Yet, this assertion is exceptionally hard to substantiate quantitatively. Governments have found it difficult or impossible to come up with exhaustive reports or total figures on all direct and indirect public aid to industry. One may argue that it is not in the interest of the ruling coalition to reveal all details and the totals; even the opposition may feel inhibited for electoral reasons.

During the 1970s and in the first years of the 1980s, public aid to industry exploded and the Commission saw herself confronted with inward-looking Member States. It was obvious that she wished to obtain political backing from the Council (in order to improve notification and to prevent defiance of court rulings) and that the Council was sharply divided over some avenues of action and indecisive with respect to other ones. Domestic political pressures were simply too overwhelming in Member States for each one to offer self-restraint. The standard argument was that social and regional reasons motivated financial support but, in addition, some degree of 'matching' aid also had to be provided to offset the deleterious consequences of distortive aids elsewhere in the EC. Such non-co-operative games represent a mirror-image of tariff wars and are self-defeating. The questions are how early in the game 'learning' starts to transform non-co-operative conduct into co-operative conduct and how important a joint institution's role (backed by mutually agreed rules) can be.

It took six years before aids to the steel industry (although strictly forbidden in the ECSC Treaty) became subject to an Aid Codex (1981), regulating how to run down different kinds of subsidies until 1986 and which (social) subsidies were permitted thereafter. Having come to terms with these 'beggar-thy-neighbour' practices, capacity-reduction plans could be agreed so as to remove the underlying cause of the subsidy race. In textiles and clothing, glass and ceramics and a number of ad hoc cases as well as with instances of horizontal subsidy programmes and loss coverages of public enterprises, the EC Commission began to resume its role of the guardian of the Treaty with a much more active pursuit of infringements cases and early consultations on national subsidy programmes. The situation remained worrying in the car industry and outright non-co-operative in shipbuilding – the only sector where the EC has failed to make any impact and prices are solely determined by a combination of preferential public procurement, subsidized export credit and direct aid to the sector (given price tenders of competitors).

Figure 5.1 provides a rough idea of the Commission surveillance of state aids. It can be observed that from 1973 until 1982 the number of subsidy programmes increased, with a major leap in 1976. After 1982 there is a clear downward trend. This decrease may be attributed to a combination of factors such as budget constraints in the Member States, a change of social-political climate causing disenchantment with state aids, the achievement of some adjustments, the Aid Codex in steel (strictly limiting all steel subsidies, notified after 1983) and the growing realization that the Commission's course of action was justified and in everybody's interest. Indeed, Member States began to use EC surveillance and Court rulings to reinforce their stance on subsidies in domestic politics. The Commission also reports[10] an 'increasing trend for Member States to modify their initial proposals or to abandon them altogether after the infringement procedure is opened'.

The real problem in assessing state aids is their absolute magnitude (which Figure 5.1 does not indicate). The nature of the distortion can be discussed in economic terms but has little meaning if the amounts of subsidy per product, per firm, per major investment, per product development, etc., are not known. Also in a macroeconomic perspective, size considerations may provide indications of the net transfers to sectors or industry

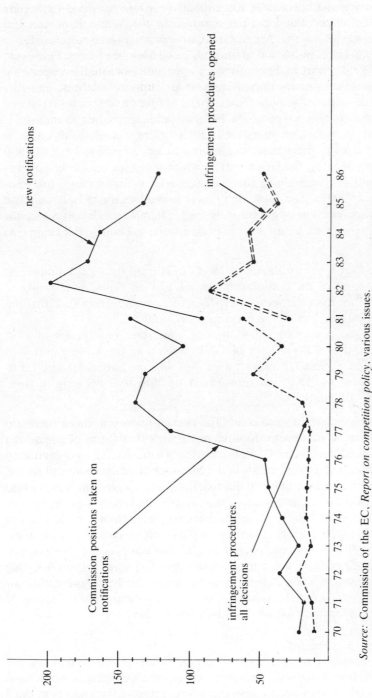

Source: Commission of the EC, Report on competition policy, various issues.
Notes: State aids, here, exclude agriculture, fisheries and transport. Observe that one notification may lead to more than one 'position' and one infringement procedure leads to two decisions, but not necessarily in the same year.

Figure 5.1 Commission surveillance of state aids to industry

at large, perhaps as substitutes for implicit transfers provided by border protection or undervalued exchange rates. In the White Paper on the Completion of the Internal Market the Commission promised to publish a report in 1986 on all public aid to industry in all Member States. However, by late 1988 no report had been issued, apparently because transparency and comparability are insufficient for an appropriate analysis, and disbursement practices of Member States have at times been confusing, if not messy. A recent official report on Belgian public subsidies to industry[11] showed that, over the five years 1981–5, the average *annual* subsidy total for steel (excluding fiscal relief) amounted to Bfr 35 billion (± ECU 800 million; current rate), the larger part of which was kept out of the government budget! For coalmining this was some ECU 200 million, for shipbuilding ECU 100 million (although this is a small sector in Belgium) and for textiles and clothing approximately ECU 90 million. The macroeconomic significance of these amounts may be illustrated by the following two indicators:

1. These four sectors obtained in 1984 direct (non-fiscal) aid totalling ± 35 per cent of the corporate taxes paid by all firms in Belgium; all firms other than the state enterprises received non-fiscal aid totalling nearly 80 per cent of the corporate tax total.
2. Fiscal and non-fiscal aid to private and state enterprises in 1985 amounted to 7.3 per cent of GNP; excluding the state enterprises (railways; regional transport; mail; housing and Sabena), some 2.5 to 3 per cent of GNP was transferred to industry operating in competitive EC markets.

Such figures *are* alarming and create the presumption that this kind of aid policy amounts to neo-protectionism, replacing other forms of protection that are not feasible. Since 1985 Belgian subsidy totals have hardly decreased (except in steel).

The first criterion is met given the sharp increase in state aids in the late 1970s. The second criterion may or may not be met, and requires further investigation. As is clear from the Belgian case, more than half of fiscal and non-fiscal aid together is spent in the non-tradeables sector. For tradeables, one way to verify whether exchange-rate effects are at issue is to see whether state aids respond with a lag to appreciation. The third criterion is also fulfilled. Therefore, state aids to industry appear to be a potentially important route to soften the impact of convergence and slow the speed of adjustment under deflationary or disinflationary policies.

Industrial export subsidies
Inside the common market there is no question of direct and indirect export subsidies. However, Member States have developed somewhat divergent credit and insurance instruments with respect to exports to third

countries (despite Arts. 112/113, EEC). Consultation and information procedures initiated in 1973 are supposed to solve problems of 'matching' among Member States' agencies as well as to provide rules for very large export contracts with sub-contractors in one or more Member States. It is especially in the latter case that the internal market has to remain without distortions.

Direct export subsidies are forbidden in GATT. Indirect subsidization via export credits and insurance may in theory be defended as a policy correcting market failure (privately uninsurable risk whether for solvency or political reasons or both). In practice it may degenerate into a mercantilist tool to outcompete others in the scramble for export markets. This danger has been recognized by the OECD, especially since in 1976 the arrangement on guidelines for officially supported export credits came into being. Since all EC countries are members of this agreement the potential for a mercantilist struggle is rather contained.

Nevertheless export-credit subsidies have a direct relation with 'convergence'. This has to do with the way criterion 2 is fulfilled. Since the EMS requires exchange-rate stability and since this will lead to disinflationary policies in weaker-currency countries, convergence will cause real-interest rates to increase in those countries during several years. If interest rates are subsidized down to a level close to that in, say, Germany, variations caused by convergence pressures will be offset. However, the general conclusions of Melitz and Messerlin (1987, p. 155) that 'export subsidies allow the economy to enjoy the benefits of high exchange rate without suffering undue costs in output or the current account' has only limited empirical value because of at least two reasons. First, export-credit interest subsidies vary with destination of exports, the subsidy being small or zero for exports to OECD countries. Therefore disinflationary policies will impose 'undue costs' on exports to EC countries and other OECD countries, at least to the extent foreign buyers are allowed to defer payment. Neither should it be forgotten that the bulk of export credits is short-run, and hence are rarely if ever subsidized in any EC country. Second, the point refers to disinflationary policies during an adjustment period. These policies and periods differ in severity and timing among Germany, France and Italy given their initial inflation rates in the early 1980s. Therefore, the given minimum interest rates in the OECD arrangement lead to different rates of subsidization, causing different burdens on the budget. Thus, Germany enjoyed the 'benefits of high exchange rates' without export-credit subsidies being large, whereas countries like France and Italy saw the costs appear on the budget. This point is strengthened by a practice of extending contracts (maximum duration permitted by the OECD Arrangement is 8.5 to 10 years) after termination on the original terms of the contract, which may make it possible to enjoy even lower interest rates than the OECD minima.

The first and the second criteria are clearly met. The third criterion is also met if the objective is defined as maintaining employment in the export sector or market shares in third countries under disinflationary circumstances.

Indirect taxes
Based especially on Arts. 95, EEC and 99, EEC, Commission, Council and Court have achieved almost complete neutrality of national indirect taxes in the Community. Remaining fiscal problems relate to the complete harmonization of the taxable product base and the approximation of VAT and excise rates, besides a number of technical aspects that bear no relation to potential protectionism. Strict judicial review on the structure of excises on alcoholic beverages, aiming to prevent 'indirect protection' (a term used in Art. 95, EEC) for a particular national liqueur or spirit, exemplifies the rigour of the Treaty. It has made it virtually impossible to exploit this instrument for purposes of protection, except in certain services (like road haulage). This chapter deals with product markets, however. Since none of the three criteria apply, it will not be dealt with in the section beginning on p. 113.

Minimum or prescribed prices
National price controls are still recognized by the EC for sectors such as energy, medicines and cigarettes. This may lead to considerable distortion of, say, energy inputs into tradeable goods, especially for intermediate products such as aluminium, steel and bulk chemicals. On the margin this may benefit domestic producers. Price controls for pharmaceutical products are derived from concerns of consumer protection and control of health expenditures. Minimum prices coupled to a *national* VER are not sustainable in the EC unless the entire EC industry would collude to raise prices in that national market. Otherwise 'parallel imports' would undermine the agreed price since a VER does not permit the use of Art. 115, EEC (on national safeguards). The two conspicuous cases where minimum prices have been coupled to VERs (videotape recorders and steel) were Community-wide. They served as fast-track substitutes for anti-dumping procedures (which are also Community-wide). The failure to meet any of the three criteria for *national* minimum prices removes this instrument as candidate for discussion.

Exchange controls for trade
Exchange controls in the EC are supposed not to hinder intra-EC trade. Generally, this has been accomplished although they do represent an extra barrier for engaging in such trade, particularly as administrative procedures

are known to be cumbersome and time-consuming (see, for example, Nême, 1986). Rather, it is the safeguards Arts. 108–9, EEC, which hang like a sword of Damocles above this untouched freedom of trade. Since the introduction of flexible exchange rates, the Commission and the Monetary Committee refrained from exercising any surveillance on the application of such safeguards until December 1984, except for direct trade restrictions.

Exchange controls in EC Member States have generally aimed at keeping financial capital from flowing *out*, except in Germany (and a brief spell in 1971 in the Netherlands) where restraints on inflows have been used. To the extent that outflow controls have kept the rate overvalued, imports of goods must have been stimulated and this cannot be termed protectionist. It is only when recourse is taken to safeguards that additional exchange controls may imply indirect restrictions on imports, especially the imports of products for which price considerations are dominant and those whereby the terms of a financial settlement is an important element of competitiveness. Exchange controls have frequently taken the form of curbing almost any deferral of payment for foreign importers.

Whenever safeguards are invoked, Art. 108, EEC, affecting intra-EC trade or making it more costly than before, a straightforward beggarthy-neighbour policy is combined with one slowing down the rate of depreciation. If problems of macroeconomic mismanagement are serious, this 'free ride' can be accepted for a while, but, if sustained, is likely to impair the functioning of the common market. The idea of safeguards is to win time in order to stabilize expectations in the money, capital and foreign exchange markets with respect to future macroeconomic policy so that 'undershooting', hence a vicious circle of depreciation and inflation, can be prevented, without too restrictive and too volatile an interest-rate policy. Precisely because trading partners have to carry part of the burden, this ought not to take more than the brief period before austerity measures begin to take effect. At the same time, the impact on intra-EC trade is mitigated by the (*ceteris paribus*) higher exchange rate, kept up via safe-guard restrictions.

Criterion 1 is fulfilled as higher demands with respect to exchange rate stability, that the EMS imposes, have been met to some extent by variations in exchange controls and safeguards. The second criterion is also met (in this case, not only the effects but the exchange rate changes themselves are mitigated). The third criterion does not apply. Hence, the section beginning on p. 113 discusses exchange controls, including safeguards.

Altogether this leaves *five instruments* that have been studied more closely (see pp. 113–30) for the FRG, France and Italy: monetary compensatory amounts, VERs, public aid to industry, non-agricultural export subsidies and exchange controls.

NOTES

1. See Brander and Spencer (1983); Dixit (1984); several essays in Kierzkowski (ed.) (1984), and in Krugman (ed.) (1986).
2. See Pelkmans (1984, ch. 8).
3. How prudent the court is became clear in the Tezicase (dealing with import permits, Art. 115, for textile products, already in free circulation in the common market). Ruling of 5 March 1986; case 242/84.
4. CCT: common customs tariff.
5. See van Dartel (1983) and Spinanger and Zietz (1985).
6. Notably Nougues Olechowski and Winters (1986) and Balassa and Balassa (1984).
7. The 'Cassis-de Dijon' case (no. 120/78); see Wyatt and Dashwood (1987, ch. 10).
8. See the report of the Commission 'Public supply contracts', COM(84)717 of 14 December 1984 (esp. Table IV).
9. The Community's Agricultural Fund disburses aid in the form of price support ('intervention purchases') as well as 'structural' subsidies. Price support extends to surpluses even when they are very large, although ceilings have been introduced in several important product markets; this price support absorbs more than 95 per cent of the fund's resources, amounting to around 65 per cent of the EC budget. If national (mostly structural) aid is nearly as high, distortions may well become substantial.
10. *Fifteenth Report on Competition Policy* (on the year 1985), p. 138 (Brussels/ Luxembourg 1986; EC).
11. Public aid to companies (in Dutch), *Tijdschrift van de Nationale Bank van België*, National Bank of Belgium, January 1987.

6 · EUROPEAN FINANCIAL INTEGRATION AND NATIONAL BANKING INTERESTS[1]

Benjamin J. Cohen

Why is the European Community unable to achieve formal financial integration? At a time of rapid innovation, deregulation, and structural change in global financial markets, the persistent refusal of such key EC members as France and Italy to fully liberalize capital flows on a regional basis seems curious, even anachronistic.[2] Here is a group of countries – ostensibly a 'Community' – whose very *raison d'être* is supposed to be creation of a Common Market. In 1985, the ambition of an 'area without frontiers' was solemnly reaffirmed when all twelve member-governments adopted a Single European Act, aiming for 'completion' of the so-called Internal Market by 1992. And in late 1986 this was followed by a formal agreement to remove controls on a wide variety of capital movements within the Community – the first such EC accord in nearly a quarter century.[3] Yet, in practice, resistance to the collective goal of full financial integration remains strong in individual European states. How can we explain this apparently anomalous behaviour?

The short answer, of course, is 'politics'. Elements of politics as well as economics are obviously entangled here. But what exactly do we mean by 'politics' in this context? That is the question to be addressed in this chapter, focusing on the main political factors that may help to explain continued resistance to the economic goal of financial integration in Europe. Although particular reference will be made to the three core continental countries of France, Germany and Italy, the scope of the chapter is purely conceptual. The aim is to aid in developing a possible research agenda for future empirical study.

Because of the tangle of economics and politics here, the question addressed in this chapter is best approached using formal analytical concepts and models drawn from the contemporary scholarly literature on International Political Economy (IPE). Methodologically, I shall argue below, financial integration may be understood as a kind of public good in scarce supply. That scarcity of supply, in turn, may be understood as the consequence of strategic interactions among key actors at two separate but interrelated levels of operation: at the Community level, where the actors are the member governments, each one pursuing its own national policy preferences within the web of regional economic interdependence; and at the national level, where actors include all domestic groups with actual or potential influence over those governmental policy preferences. The challenge for the analyst is to comprehend the dynamics of each of these two levels of operation as well as how they interact and evolve over time. The purpose is to gain insight not only into what it is that constrains the supply of the public good of financial integration in Europe but also how its supply might eventually be increased in the future.

MEANINGS OF FINANCIAL INTEGRATION

To begin, we must be clear about what we mean by financial integration. In common usage, the word 'integration' simply denotes the bringing together of constituent parts into a whole. In economics, however, the meaning of the term is not nearly so clear-cut. Three distinctions, in particular, have to be borne in mind.

First is a distinction between integration as a *process of change* and as a *state of being*. Regarded as a process, integration in economics encompasses measures designed to abolish permanently various forms of discrimination between actors belonging to different national states; viewed as a state of being, it can be represented by the permanent absence of such discrimination between national states. The process of integration takes place over the period of transition during which actors adjust to the abolition of discrimination. When these adjustments are completed, integration as a state of being comes into operation.

Second is a distinction between integration in a *negative* sense and in a *positive* sense. In a negative sense, integration simply means the removal of barriers at the frontier to economic intercourse between actors belonging to different national states; in a positive sense, it involves in addition standardization or harmonization of all relevant *domestic* policies, requirements and regulations. Integration in the negative sense is a necessary condition for the promotion of economic intercourse, but may not be sufficient. Integration in the positive sense may be sufficient but not necessary.

Third is a distinction between variations in the *scope* of integration, depending on the range of transactions involved. The scope of integration may be conceived narrowly or broadly, depending on the number of types or categories of operations encompassed by the abolition of discrimination.

Each of these three distinctions is important in defining the meaning of financial integration for the purposes of this chapter:

1. *Process of change versus state of being.* This distinction is important because it relates directly to the time profile of the benefits and costs of

financial integration. The benefits of financial integration, as we shall see, largely accrue only when integration operates as a state of being; the costs, by contrast, are largely associated with the transition period when adjustments are still required of many of the actors involved. As a result, a trade-off is generated between (fairly certain) costs in the short term and (rather less certain) benefits in the longer term, with the formal or informal comparison of the two affected by each actor's own effective discount rate for comparing present and estimated future values. Since such a calculus is undoubtedly a key factor in helping to explain the persistence of resistance to financial integration in Europe, it is clear that this chapter must take explicit account of *both* stages in defining the meaning of financial integration for analytical purposes.

2. *Negative versus positive.* This distinction is important because of the heavily regulated nature of the financial-services sector as an industry. In a negative sense, financial integration may be understood simply to be synonomous with free trade in financial assets (capital mobility); that is, with the elimination of all exchange controls on relevant transactions. But given the vast differences in domestic policies applied to financial activity in each country, affecting rights of establishment or operation, integration in this sense alone would be far from sufficient to remove all forms of discrimination between national states. Integration in a positive sense would be required as well, in the form of standardization or harmonization of all domestic requirements and regulations relating to rights of establishment and operation for financial enterprises, to truly achieve an 'area without frontiers'. This is the meaning that will be employed in this chapter. Financial integration will be understood to be synonomous not just with capital mobility but with mobility of institutions and institutional activity; that is, with the freedom to provide financial services anywhere in the Community – one genuine market.

3. *Scope.* This distinction is important because of the close functional links that exist between different types or categories of financial transactions. Commercial banking *per se*, stripped to its essence, consists simply of the business of taking deposits and making loans. But banks in practice also engage in a wide variety of other related market activities, from securities underwriting and trading to investment management or leasing, all overlapping in one way or another with other classes of financial intermediary (e.g. investment banks, brokerage houses, thrift institutions). And these activities, in turn, are closely related to and affected by the public policies and operations of a variety of relevant governmental agencies, including most importantly the central bank of each country. Where do we draw the line for analytical purposes?

For the purposes of this brief chapter, the line must certainly be drawn to exclude the policies and operations of central banks and other purely governmental (i.e. non-market) agencies. We must not confuse financial integration with other broader concepts such as monetary union or currency union. A monetary union involves the unification and joint management of the monetary policies of participating countries; a currency union (or exchange-rate union) involves the permanent fixing of exchange rates between participating countries. Neither one of these is a necessary prerequisite for the other: historical examples abound both of currency unions between countries with formally independent central banks (e.g., the Scandanavian Currency Union of the nineteenth century) as well as of monetary unions between countries with formally independent exchange rates (e.g., the Belgium–Luxembourg Economic Union of the twentieth century). Nor is either monetary or currency union a necessary prerequisite for full liberalization of non-governmental capital movements and activities (as, e.g., the old British-led sterling area well demonstrated in the years during and after World War Two). The definition of financial integration to be used here will thus assume the continued existence of both formally independent central banks and potentially variable exchange rates. Our focus will be on the integration of market operations alone.

Furthermore, within the broad range of market operations, our focus will be on commercial-banking operations alone, excluding the related activities of other classes of financial intermediary. The excuse here is purely one of convenience: concentrating on banks alone makes the problem a good deal more analytically tractable, albeit at some loss in terms of descriptive richness. Fortunately, the loss would not appear to be great, since, as we shall see, much of what can be said about banks (whether private or state-owned) may easily be extended to other market institutions as well. Once developed in the more narrow context of banking relations, this chapter's analytical approach can be readily applied to a much wider range of financial transactions and transactors.

In summary, then, financial integration is defined for the purposes of this chapter as a process of change as well as a state of being, encompassing all measures of liberalization or harmonization required to create a single market for commercial banking services anywhere in the European Community. The problem, once again, is to explain why this objective is so difficult to achieve.

BENEFITS OF FINANCIAL INTEGRATION

Resistance to the objective of financial integration in the Community would be relatively easy to understand if there were little or no potential benefit to be derived from the phenomenon. However, that does not seem to be the case. Quite the contrary, in fact. Conventional economic analysis suggests quite convincingly that, in practice, rather substantial gains could be expected to accrue to such a group of countries from the creation among them of a single market for commercial banking services. Economic welfare would be increased to the extent that opportunities for efficient financial intermediation are effectively enhanced (e.g. Llewellyn 1980).

Intermediation through banking operations contributes to economic welfare in at least five separate ways: (a) by providing mechanisms for the disposal of savings or financial surpluses and the financing of investments or financial deficits; (b) by helping to bridge the different portfolio preferences of surplus and deficit actors; (c) by allocating funds to the most efficient users; (d) by enabling risks to be diversified and transferred from ultimate savers, and (e) by allowing changes to be made in the structure of portfolios. These five effects have a positive impact on real resource efficiency, as compared with a world of no banking intermediation, by influencing not only the allocation of investible funds among competing claims but also the aggregate volume of saving and investment. Such gains accrue to each country separately from the operation of its own national banking system. By extension, an integration of national systems may confidently be assumed to add to such gains *in toto* by opening up new opportunities for savers or investors to take advantage of any cross-border differences in the price or non-price characteristics of available banking services, leading towards equalization of rates of return on comparable assets and liabilities and/or closer covariance of such rates. In effect, the economies of participating countries would be brought closer to the elusive ideal of Pareto-optimality in general-equilibrium terms.

Note, however, the two words 'general' and 'equilibrium'. The key to understanding the persistence of resistance to financial integration in Europe, despite its evident potential benefits, lies therein.

Consider first the word 'equilibrium', a central concept in conventional economic analysis, which following standard practice has been defined by one economist as synonomous with 'a constellation of selected interrelated variables so adjusted to one another that no tendency to change prevails' (Machlup 1964). This concept clearly implies a state of being rather than a process of change. That is, it focuses thought on conditions prevailing after all adjustments have been completed, rather than on the ease or difficulty of the adjustments themselves. Quite naturally, use of the equilibrium concept tends to distract attention from any burdens or losses that may be associated with the requisite period of transition. Or to put the point differently: it encourages thinking about comparative statics, contrasting before and after, rather than about the dynamics of adjustment, how we get from here to there. Benefits of final outcomes are stressed, rather than the costs of the process of change required to achieve them.

All of this is perfectly legitimate, of course, for the purposes of pure economic theory or model-building. But it can be seriously misleading when applied unquestioningly to practical problems of political economy such as the issue of financial integration in Europe. To understand why financial integration is resisted (its 'politics'), analysis must stress costs as well as benefits, the difficulties of transition as well as the allure of the final outcome – because that is surely what the key actors themselves are always doing! In any given actor's rational calculation of the attractiveness of a single market for banking services, the burden of adjustment is bound to figure prominently, particularly since costs must be borne 'up front' long before most benefits can be expected to accrue. Costs, moreover, being immediate, can be calculated with a higher degree of certainty than more remote potential gains. It would hardly be surprising, therefore, if quite a high discount rate were to be used by many of the most important actors involved when estimating the present value of future gains to be compared with losses in the short term. Resistance may result directly from this difference in the time profile of the benefits and costs of financial integration.

Related to this is the word 'general', another central concept in conventional economic analysis, which may be taken to be synonomous with effects for all actors together rather than for any one actor separately. As most commonly applied, this concept is allowed to imply an identity of interest between the particular and the whole. That is, if something is regarded as beneficial *in toto*, then it tends to be assumed to be beneficial *inter se* as well. Quite naturally, such usage serves to distract attention from any divergences that may exist between individual incentives and collective incentives. Or to put the point differently: it encourages thinking of all 'public' goods as if they were 'private' goods as well. Resistance to anything that can be expected to raise economic welfare in the aggregate, such as financial integration in Europe, may therefore be dismissed simply as myopic or irrational.

In reality, however, not all 'public' goods are 'private' goods too. Quite the contrary, in fact. Public goods are defined by two key characteristics: (a) non-rivalry (meaning that one individual's consumption or use of the good does not reduce its availability to anyone else); and (b) non-excludability (meaning that once the good is provided, it is available to all).

Private goods, by contrast, exist where one individual's consumption precludes use by others, and where providers can ensure that only those individuals who pay for the good may obtain it. In the case of private goods, obviously, market incentives exist for adequate overall supply by individual producers. In the case of public goods, on the other hand, as is well known, market production in the aggregate is bound to be sub-optimal because of the lack of such incentives. A divergence exists between individual interests and the collective interest, and 'free riding' is encouraged even where *general* benefit can be demonstrated. Why should potential providers be willing to bear any of the costs of production if supply must be more or less automatically available to all? Why should potential consumers be willing to pay any price if no one can be excluded from use? Resistance in such cases is by no means myopic or irrational.

European financial integration is arguably one such case. True, individual services to savers and investors are essentially private goods that would presumably continue to command a price even after creation of a single banking market in the Community. But there are also undeniable public-good elements in the broader externalities to be expected from the enhancement of opportunities for efficient financial intermediation – the anticipated positive impacts on the allocation of investable funds and the aggregate volume of savings and investment – that would be freely available for all. Insofar as this is true, financial integration may therefore be understood as a kind of public good in scarce supply. General welfare advantages notwithstanding, integration will be resisted to the extent that divergences exist between collective incentives and individual incentives, with such divergences in turn arising from differences in the gains and losses that can be anticipated by each actor separately. For the question addressed by this chapter – Why is European financial integration so difficult to achieve? – the answer most appropriately must be sought in these public-goods aspects of the problem. There, ultimately, is where we find the real meaning of 'politics' in this context.

SYSTEMIC ANALYSIS OF FINANCIAL INTEGRATION

Analysis of financial integration as a public good necessarily focuses attention on strategic interactions among the key actors involved. And foremost among these actors are of course the Community's several national governments, which as formally sovereign entities still retain ultimate political authority in Europe. A useful starting point for discussion, therefore, is to be found at the Community level, in the incentives that may exist for either co-operation or conflict among EC Member States on this sensitive issue of economic policy. As indicated, particular reference will be made here to the core continental countries of France, Germany and Italy.

Models for discussion at the Community level are provided by that branch of contemporary IPE literature that is devoted to so-called *systemic* analysis of the politics of international economic relations.[4] The basic unit of analysis in this type of literature is the 'state', ordinarily identified with each country's central governmental decision-makers. States are assumed to be unitary, rational, and egoistic actors. 'Unitary' means that the internal processes by which state policy preferences are determined may, in effect, be disregarded. 'Rational' means that policy preferences are consistent and ordered, and that states are capable of calculating the costs and benefits of alternative courses of action in order to maximize their utility in terms of those preferences. And 'egoistic' means that their utility functions are independent of one another, in the sense that no state actor gains or loses utility simply because of the gains or losses of others. (They are self-interested, not altruistic.) The methodological value of these assumptions is that they make state preferences constants rather than variables for purpose of analysis: conceptions of self-interest are given and invariant. Discussion is thus able to focus entirely on constraints and incentives for state behaviour that derive from the broader system of inter-state relations – hence the rubric 'systemic' analysis. Behaviour, in Kenneth Waltz's language, is studied from the 'outside-in'.[5]

Viewed from this perspective, the resistance of individual EC members to the collective goal of financial integration seems less anomalous than may have appeared at first glance. Certainly the broad economic benefits to be expected from creation of a single Community banking market would seem to accord with each government's rational conception of its own self-interest. Incentives clearly do exist for members to co-operate in pursuit of this objective – but only insofar as prospective gains to them individually may safely be assumed to exceed any future losses they might incur; that is, only insofar as the trade-off between the joint goal of financial integration and egoistic national policy preference appears on balance to remain favourable in each state's separate benefit–cost calculation. Otherwise, the public good will be perceived by at least some of them as a private 'bad'. Member governments may rationally resist increasing the supply of a public good if it threatens to conflict seriously with the achievement of other established objectives of national policy.

In practice, financial integration is indeed likely to threaten (or be thought to threaten) conflict with at least two established policy objectives of at least some EC members. Creation of a single banking market, as noted, would mean free movement of capital leading towards equalization and/or covariance of rates of return on comparable assets and liabilities. At the macroeconomic level, these effects obviously would make it more difficult, if not impossible, for governments individually to preserve autonomy of national monetary policy for domestic stabilization purposes. Likewise, at the microeconomic level, they would make it more difficult, if not impossible, for governments individually to influence the allocation of available financial resources among different industrial sectors or regions of the domestic economy. Independence of monetary policy and discretion in credit allocation are both highly valued 'nationalistic' goals in the utility functions of most EC states: the former, especially, in Germany and Italy; the latter, especially, in France. The risk of losses to any of these countries in terms of either of these goals would suffice to make a single banking market seem to them a private bad rather than a public good, creating divergences between collective incentives and individual incentives for promoting the integration objective.

The risk of losses might not in actual fact be very serious. The public good might not really be so bad. At the macroeconomic level, for instance, many economists assert that autonomy of national monetary policy is in practical terms illusory owing to the assumed absence of any long-run trade-off between inflation and unemployment in individual economies. The basic argument in favour of an independent monetary policy is that it can presumably be used to achieve and maintain a welfare-maximizing balance between inflation and unemployment; in technical language, to achieve and maintain some preferred point on the country's Phillips curve, which is assumed to be negatively sloped. In the long run, however, most economists agree, the Phillips curve is likely to be not negatively sloped but rather vertical, at the 'natural' rate of unemployment, owing to the inevitable impact of all attempts to alter the inflation–unemployment mix on inflationary expectations. In effect, the (negatively sloped) short-run Phillips curve merely shifts up or down along the (vertical) long-run Phillips curve, with only transitory effects on output or unemployment rates. And indeed, if the private sector's expectations are 'rational' in the sense used in economic theory today, not even transitory effects will occur: an independent monetary policy merely permits a government to choose its own inflation rate, but does nothing to achieve domestic stabilization in real terms. In that 'ideal' case, loss of monetary policy would threaten no true loss at all.

The world in which we live, however, is not so ideal. Expectations in reality normally are not 'rational' in this sense. Stickiness of wages and prices does make for a negatively sloped Phillips curve in the short run, which in turn means that an independent monetary policy is indeed capable of influencing the inflation–unemployment mix at least transitorily. The longer such transitory effects may be expected to persist, the greater will be a government's incentive to do all it can to preserve its own monetary autonomy; and this incentive will be greater still if, in practice, the authorities tend to employ an effectively high discount rate in comparing the benefit of such transitory effects (which would be immediately lost in the event of financial integration) with the present value of financial integration's potential future gains. The nationalistic goal of an independent monetary policy is by no means an illusion.

Likewise, at the microeconomic level, many economists assert that discretion in credit allocation is illusory owing to the fungibility of money in financial markets. If a government tries to use the banking system as an instrument of industrial planning or regional development, encouraging certain kinds or directions of lending at the expense of others, the markets will in this view simply make appropriate adjustments to ensure that available financial resources still go to sectors or regions where rates of return appear highest; and the more 'perfect' the markets, the swifter the adjustments. But, of course, in the real world markets are rarely as 'perfect' as that – certainly not in countries like France or Italy. In such countries, governments are indeed capable of effectively channelling credit allocation, at least to a degree; and the incentive to preserve that capability will obviously vary directly both with the degree of *de facto* control at present and with the effective discount rate applied to the potential gains of financial integration in the future. The nationalistic goal of discretion in credit allocation is no illusion either.

If neither goal is an illusion, then it is not at all surprising that individual EC members like France or Italy, behaving as rational egoistic actors, would persist in their resistance to the collective goal of financial integration despite the broad economic benefits to be expected. For at least some such countries, the public good does undoubtedly look like a private bad. That is, prospective costs in terms of their own established policy preferences undoubtedly do diminish incentives to co-operate on this Community issue, particularly if each separately can hope to free ride on any joint initiatives by others – in effect, enjoying the efficiency gains of a freer EC banking market without having to pay any of the price. In this respect, the situation is a prime example of the classic problem of collective action analyzed so cogently by Mancur Olson more than two decades ago (Olson 1965), and recently summarized by Robert Keohane as follows:

> In situations calling for collective action, cooperation is necessary to obtain a good that (insofar as it is produced at all) will be enjoyed by all members of a set of actors, whether they have contributed to its provision or not. When each member's contribution to the cost of the good is small as a proportion of its total cost, self-interested individuals are likely to calculate that they are better off by not contributing, since their contribution is costly to them but has an imperceptible effect on whether the good is produced. Thus ... the dominant strategy for an egoistic individualist is to defect, by not contributing to the production of the good. Generalizing this calculation yields the conclusion that the collective good will not be produced, or will be underproduced, despite the fact that its value to the group is greater than its cost.
>
> (Keohane 1984, p. 69)

The problem of collective action, in turn, may be efficiently analyzed using the intellectual tools of formal game theory. The observable tendency towards under-production of public (collective) goods is equivalent, in game–theoretic terms, to saying that any potential for joint gain through co-operation may well be destroyed by competition over relative shares. In a variable-sum game, by definition, players have interests that are neither completely irreconcilable nor entirely harmonious. Incentives exist, therefore, not only for co-operation but also for conflict (non-co-operation, defection), depending on how potential 'pay-offs' happen to be structured in any particular instance.

In principle, any number of 'pay-off structures' may be conceived where co-operation rather than conflict would be encouraged as the dominant strategy for all players. In practice, however, such games appear to be comparatively rare in relations among sovereign states. Much more common is a broad class of games where quite the contrary tends to hold true; that is, where despite the prospective benefits of co-operation, the pay-off structure is such that at least some state players can rationally hope to gain more by instead defecting to act on their own. That is where the parallel with public goods comes in. For if some or all states do try to act unilaterally rather than co-operatively, the outcome most likely will turn out to be inferior overall; that is, unrestrained competition over relative shares is likely to become so severe that it will end up reducing the size of the pie for all, eliminating all potential for joint gain. (The public good will be under-produced.) This class of games features such familiar names as Stag Hunt, Chicken, and of course the notorious Prisoners' Dilemma.[6] All are regarded by most IPE scholars as reasonably accurate facsimiles of strategic inter-actions among national governments, including EC governments, in the real world today.[7]

The common characteristic of such games is that co-operation in the collective interest is desirable but not automatic. Preconditions necessary to inhibit defection are lacking: co-operation must be *promoted* to be success-ful. The question is: Can the nature of such games be changed in ways that will enhance prospects for co-operation? In other words, can strategic choices be modified? Given established state preferences, are there any elements in the broader inter-state system that may be manipulated to favourably alter environmental constraints and incentives for national behaviour? Can the benefit–cost calculations of rational and egoistic state actors be so influenced as to make commitment to collective action appear significantly more attractive for any or all of them separately? This is the central challenge that has been taken up at the level of systemic analysis in the contemporary IPE literature. Applied to the subject of financial integration in Europe, that literature suggests a number of potentially important topics for future empirical study, which for the purposes of a possible research agenda may be grouped under a trio of headings cor-responding to the three component variables of any such rational calculus: (a) the *benefits* of co-operation; (b) the *costs*, and (c) the *discount rate* used in comparing them.

Benefits

It is a well-known insight of game theory that, in principle, incentives for co-operation in any given strategic interaction may be considerably en-hanced by supplementing the benefit side of a state's benefit–cost cal-culation with 'side-payments' (in plain language, bribes) of one kind or another. Side-payments may be either 'issue-specific' (i.e. offered within the specific game itself) or 'issue-linked' (i.e. offered in more or less closely related games). In the present context, one intriguing question for future study is whether, in practice, side-payments of either type could conceivably be developed on a scale sufficient to reduce individual state resistance to the collective goal of financial integration in Europe. Could recalcitrant governments, in brief, be bribed to co-operate?

Certainly the means for such bribery are available – if they are wanted. There are two reasons for this. First, financial integration is not a 'single-play' game, with pay-offs limited to the outcome of a single strategic choice. Rather, it is a continuing interaction, the equivalent of an iterated game where decisions must be repeated and hence where supplementary benefits over time can be offered to discourage defection – where the 'shadow of the future' looms large, to use Robert Axelrod's phrase (Axelrod 1984). Second, financial integration is not an isolated game, with pay-offs un-related to other areas of interaction among the players. Rather, it is quite obviously 'nested'[8] within a whole set of institutionalized relationships among EC governments, any or all of which could possibly be tapped to provide potentially attractive side-payments in return for desired national commitments. The setting is ripe for rewarding co-operative behaviour.

For example, if a country such as Italy resists financial integration be-cause of a perceived threat to its monetary autonomy, the Community's existing short-term and medium-term mutual credit facilities could be made specially available, possibly even at subsidized interest rates, to offset any destabilizing capital movements that might result – an illustration of a possible issue-specific side-payment. In similar fashion, if a country like France is resistant because of a perceived threat to its discretion in credit allocation, supplementary financial resources could be made available to it for planning or regional development purposes, again possibly at sub-sidized interest rates, through the European Investment Bank or parallel EC institutions. Or, alternatively, issue-linked concessions might be offered in a non-financial area such as agriculture, where the Community's common farm policy could conceivably be redirected to provide additional benefits as an incentive for co-operation in creating a single banking market. Given the dense and continuing network of relationships in existence within the EC, opportunities for bribery along these lines are clearly not in scarce supply.

The key question, then, is not supply but demand: Will the available means be wanted? Since side-payments of either type must be paid for, some actor or actors must be prepared to absorb their costs – which means that we are still caught in the classic collective-action dilemma of how to avoid underproduction of a public good. At least one state individually must be willing to pay disproportionately for the collective goal of financial integration. Is there any such state in the EC today?

The obvious candidate is Germany, which is already the dominant financial power on the European continent. With the possible exception of Great Britain, no other Community member would appear to have more to gain from creation of a single EC banking market. Germany's 'universal banks' seem well prepared, in terms of size, experience and expertise, to take full advantage of new rights of establishment and operation in other member-countries; Frankfurt might well find itself the continent's leading financial centre, ranking perhaps second only to London in the Community as a whole. And not even Britain can rival the Federal Republic of Germany in material resources at hand to invest in suitable side-payments to countries like France or Italy. If bribery is to be the route to financial integration in Europe, Germany would seem the only plausible paymaster.

Indeed, were Germany to play this role, it would be perfectly consistent with the so-called 'theory of hegemonic stability' as it has been developed in the IPE literature – the popular argument that provision of public goods like 'order' or 'openness' in international economic relations requires the presence of a single, strongly dominant actor (a hegemon) prepared to absorb the necessary costs (e.g. Kindleberger 1973; Krasner 1976; Gilpin 1981). Large actors, unlike small ones, cannot assume that they have imperceptible effects on whether a public good is produced; furthermore, being large, they presumably stand to lose more from under-production. Hence, it may be assumed that they have more of an incentive to take the lead in ensuring co-operation by all players, even should that mean bearing a disproportionate share of the cost. In the European context, this clearly means Germany.

But will the hegemon's incentive *suffice* to persuade Germany to play the role of paymaster on behalf of financial integration? As critics of hegemonic stability theory have contended, hegemonic leadership may not in fact be a sufficient condition for the emergence of co-operative relationships, nor even a necessary condition.[9] Co-operative relationships may develop in the absence of a strong, dominant power; they may fail to develop even in the presence of one. Yet not even the theory's critics question that hegemony can in practice help to *facilitate* co-operation in economic relations. This is because the asymmetry of incentives makes achievement of successful collective action more *probable* than it would otherwise be. The issue is whether the hegemon's incentive can somehow be translated into genuine action; that is, whether the leader can indeed be persuaded to lead. The availability of means for bribing other EC governments is not enough. Germany also has to want to use them.

Thus one topic for a future research agenda concerns the potential leadership role of Germany in underwriting possible side-payments through Community institutions to overcome individual state resistance to creation of single EC banking market. Until now, the hegemon's incentive has *not* sufficed to persuade Germany to play such a leadership role on this issue. Many explanations are possible. In the eyes of the German government, the incentive may simply not seem sizable enough to warrant the requisite commitment of resources; alternatively, having already served for so long as the biggest net contributor to the EC budget, Germany may be reluctant in an era of fiscal stringency to take on yet more financial responsiblities. Or it may reflect a broader and possibly growing disaffection with the Community in Germany, as reported in some recent polls of the German population (*The Economist* 11 Apr. 1987, p. 46). The need is to sort through these and other possible explanations for the correct answer. Does the Federal Republic in fact have a disproportionate incentive to ensure co-operation on the financial integration issue? And if so, why has it until now not shown more willingness to bear a disproportionate share of the cost? In short, why has Germany not led?

Costs

Another well-known insight of game theory is that 'sticks' as well as 'carrots' may be useful, in principle, to enhance incentives for co-operation in any given strategic interation. That is, it is possible not only to reward players via side-payments if they co-operate; it is also possible to punish them, via sanctions of one kind or another, if they refuse – in effect, working on the cost side rather than the benefit side of a state's benefit–cost calculation. Like side-payments, sanctions may be either issue-specific or issue-linked. Another intriguing question for future study, then, is whether, in practice, sanctions rather than side-payments might be developed on a sufficient scale to promote the objective of EC financial integration. In brief, if recalcitrant governments cannot be bribed to co-operate, could they be coerced into doing so?

The logic of sanctions is that they serve in effect to 'privatize' a public good, depriving non-co-operators of a free ride. As some IPE scholars have been careful to note (Conybeare 1984), the distinction between private goods and public goods – so neat in theory – is in reality more one of degree than of kind, particulary as concerns the characteristic of non-excludability. Even goods that are truly non-rival may nonetheless be excludable, in the sense that free riding could be penalized. Individual players might possibly be excluded directly from the benefits of collective action via issue-specific sanctions; or else they might be made to pay some price for those benefits, via issue-linked sanctions, insofar as they cannot be excluded directly. Either way, where such possibilities do exist, the principle of reciprocity can be invoked, establishing a direct connection between actors' present behaviour and anticipated future gains. Defection can be made a costly strategic option.

Financial integration is clearly one such case. As with side-payments, means for coercing recalcitrant governments are certainly available within the dense and continuing network of EC relationships, if they are wanted. The setting is as ripe for punishing defection as it is for rewarding co-operation. Instead of offering linked concessions through such programmes as the common farm policy, for example, benefits could conceivably be withheld from those who refuse to commit themselves to collective action on the financial-integration issue; instead of making more resources available through the Community's mutual credit facilities or the European Investment Bank, access to financing for such states could be partially or even wholly curtailed. Or, more directly, sanctions could be imposed within the specific context of financial integration itself, e.g. by denying Community-wide rights of establishment and operation to the banking institutions of non-co-operating members or by denying citizens of those members access to various services available in the newly created Community banking market. Opportunities along one or another of these lines are manifold. Sticks, like carrots, are not in scarce supply.

Thus the key question here too is not supply but demand: Will the available means be wanted? Sanctions do not occur spontaneously – certainly not if, as with side-payments, they must be paid for. Where costs are involved, the imposition of sanctions requires a positive decision on the part of co-operating states to effectively privatize the public good. (Even where the imposition of sanctions results automatically from activation of some trigger mechanism, creation of the mechanism itself requires a positive decision.) Hence we are still caught in the classic collective-action dilemma of how to gain the commitments needed to avoid under-production. As Joanne Gowa has written, 'costly exclusion is itself a public good,' (Gowa 1986a, p. 15). One free-riding problem (the risk of non-co-operation in the game as a whole) is replaced with another (the risk of non-co-operation in the imposition of sanctions within the game). States co-operating in the creation of a single banking market must also be willing to penalize other members for non-co-operation; that is, they must be prepared to genuinely commit themselves to a credible policy of reciprocity. Is there any such prospect in the EC today?

In some respects prospects appear good, owing precisely to the nesting of the financial-integration issue in a pre-existing Community. IPE scholars identify several possible inhibitions to a credible policy of reciprocity among states, including especially: (a) difficulties in monitoring behaviour; (b) difficulties in focusing sanctions on defectors, and (c) difficulties in apportioning responsibility for sanctions (e.g. Axelrod and Keohane 1985, pp. 234–8, 244–7; Keohane 1986, pp. 1–27). All three of these kinds of inhibitions, however, can be eased by the operation of established EC institutions, which both increase the 'transparency' of state actions and facilitate the swift and effective enforcement of rules. A policeman, if needed, is readily available in the European Commission; a judge, in the European Court of Justice. It is not necessary to persuade governments (e.g. Germany) to suffer the possible opprobrium of taking on either of these unpopular roles themselves.

In other respects, however, prospects ironically may be impeded by those very same institutions, insofar as they permit defectors to retaliate more easily against any sanctions imposed upon them. Penalty may be returned for penalty, stick for stick, in a pattern of 'echo effects' that could be repeated virtually ad infinitum, threatening mutually harmful policy conflict across a broad range of linked issue-areas. As Robert Axelrod has regretfully remarked, 'the trouble with [reciprocity] is that once a feud gets started, it can continue indefinitely' (Axelrod 1984, p. 138). The result may well be to leave all players far worse off than before, unless defences can be established to prevent an endless cycle of reprisals. And this in turn may lead back to a necessity for side-payments, to bribe defectors in the financial area to forego opportunities for retaliation that might otherwise be available to them through the network of EC relationships. Reciprocity, clearly, is a two-edged sword.

Thus another topic for a future research agenda concerns the potential for a credible policy of reciprocity to overcome individual state resistance to the joint goal of a single EC banking market. Can effective sanctions be designed that would not provoke mutually harmful echo effects? Or must penalties necessarily be packaged together with attractive rewards in order to ensure all players' commitments to collective action? In short, how far can the Community go in using coercion to achieve co-operation?

Discount rate

Finally, there is the discount rate that states effectively use in their benefit –cost calculations. In principle, this variable too may be modified to enhance prospects for co-operation in any given strategic interaction. In most games, as in the case of EC financial integration, potential gains tend to be both more remote and less certain than prospective losses. On the one hand, this means that most players can be expected to value future benefits at a considerable discount when comparing them with more immediate costs. (In technical terms, they implicitly have a positive rate of time preference or high discount rate.) On the other hand, it means that an opportunity exists for increasing incentives for co-operation – even apart from any possible side-payments or sanctions – insofar as players can be induced to place a higher value on future pay-offs. (In technical terms: insofar as their positive rate of time preference, or discount rate, can be reduced.) A third intriguing question for future study, then, in the present context, concerns whether this is an opportunity that could be successfully seized in practice. Could the resistance of individual governments to the EC's collective goal of financial integration conceivably be reduced, to any significant extent, by somehow persuading them to revise their customary rate of time preferences?

That rates of time preference can in principle be revised is without question, since the process of discounting is by definition subjective rather than objective in nature. That is, any value attached to the future is in the eye of the beholder, a matter more of cognition than fact. As Robert Axelrod and Robert Keohane have written: 'Perceptions define interests ... Decision making in ambiguous settings is heavily influenced by the ways in which the actors think about their problem.' (Axelrod and Keohane 1985, pp. 229, 247). It follows that if ways of thinking can be altered, incentives for behaviour will be changed as well, hence leading to a modification of strategic choices.

This is not to suggest that decision making, being grounded in perception, is therefore irrational in any meaningful sense. Rather, it means simply that rationality may be *bounded* significantly, owing to the ambiguity of the setting in which decisions have to be made. Governments' abilities to make calculations and compare alternatives may be constrained by limits imposed by uncertainty on their information-processing capacities. The concept of bounded rationality was first developed by Herbert Simon (e.g. Simon 1982). A key implication of the concept is that if uncertainty can be reduced by one means or another, constraints on rational benefit–cost calculations will be reduced as well, raising the value that actors attach to remote future pay-offs and thereby making commitment to collective action appear relatively more attractive in the short term. A key question, then, for the analytical purposes of this chapter, is whether any such means can be found in the EC today. Can member governments, in effect, be provided with a better understanding of the prospective benefits of a single banking market?

The question necessarily focuses attention on the European Commission, the body best placed to help provide that understanding. At the centre of the Community's institutionalized network of relationships the Commission has already established itself as a primary source of sound and reliable information relevant to all members; with its reputation for organizational impartiality and disinterested commitment to the collective good, it can be assumed in general to be trusted by individual governments. Thus a third topic for a future research agenda concerns the potential educative role of the Commission in promoting financial integration. Can the Commission successfully alter states' perceptions of their own interests on this issue? Can an information campaign be mounted that would substantially alter existing rates of time preference? In short, can EC governments be persuaded to change their customary ways of thinking?

UNIT LEVEL ANALYSIS OF FINANCIAL INTEGRATION

Until now, our discussion has focused on strategic interactions strictly at the *Community* level, with state behaviour studied exclusively from the 'outside-in'. Useful as such systemic analysis is, however, it is clearly not enough. States in the real world obviously are not purely unitary actors with invariant utility functions: conceptions of national self-interest do not simply materialize out of thin air. As numerous scholars have pointed out, full understanding of state behaviour in the international political economy demands analysis from the 'inside-out' as well; that is, at the national level too, encompassing strategic interactions among all *domestic* actors with actual or potential influence on state actions abroad (e.g. Gowa 1986b). In short, we must also investigate the domestic basis of foreign economic policy. The assumption that we may casually disregard the internal processes by which state policy preferences are determined is unrealistic and potentially misleading – helpful as a first approximation, but certainly not the last word. In methodological terms, the approach is parsimonious but partial. As Keohane has written:

> No systemic analysis can be complete. We have to look beyond the system toward accounts of state behavior that emphasize the effects of domestic institutions and leadership on patterns of state behavior. That is, we will have to introduce some unit-level analysis as well. We have to look from the inside-out as well as from the outside-in.
>
> (Keohane 1984, p. 26)

Models for discussion at the national level are provided by that branch of the IPE literature devoted to so-called *unit-level* analysis of the politics of international economic relations.[10] The basic unit of analysis in this type of literature is the 'domestic structure', variously identified with different social or economic forces capable of exercising some degree of influence on the country's central governmental decision-makers. Just which aspects of the domestic structure may matter most in any particular circumstance will differ, obviously, from country to country and from issue to issue, depending on the general substance of each problem as well as the specifics of each state's own internal organizational arrangements. It is not at all surprising, therefore, that in practice the number of models developed by scholars working at this level of analysis, for application in given instances, tends to be quite large. What distinguishes the many alternative models from one another are the specific elements of internal policy networks that are picked out in each case for special emphasis. What unites them is a common perception of domestic structure as a crucial intervening variable between the international system and individual national behaviour.

Precisely because the number of such models is so large, unit-level analysis has often been criticized for going too far in sacrificing parsimony for the sake of realism. Remarks Keohane, a sympathetic critic: 'Parsimonious theory, even as a partial "first cut", becomes impossible if one starts analysis here, amidst a confusing plethora of seemingly relevant facts' (Keohane 1984, p. 25). Adds Bruno Frey, a less sympathetic critic: 'The most important shortcoming is its non-analytical structure.... The approach is descriptive, historical and (sometimes) anecdotal' (Frey 1984). Even conceding these criticisms, however, unit-level analysis remains essential to highlight the role of internal characteristics of states in explaining external policy preferences. Systemic analysis can identify only the outer parameters (constraints and incentives) for state behaviour; it cannot explain what specific 'nationalistic' strategies and goals a government will actually choose within the context of any given issue. These choices, in each case, will depend as well on the nature of their purely domestic strategic interactions. As Frey himself admits: '[The approach] is useful in pointing out problems, to give general insights, and helping to grasp the particular forms of institutions and political processes relevant for international political economics' (Frey 1984).

In general, unit-level models can be grouped into two broad classes: *governmental* models, which focus on strategic interactions within the narrow organization of government itself; and *societal* models, which focus on strategic interactions within the broader economic and political structure of a nation. Most familiar among governmental models is the so-called bureaucratic-politics paradigm, stressing bargaining and negotiation specifically between the state's various central decision-makers. Government is seen not as homogeneous but rather as a conglomerate of institutional actors with differing perceptions of national (and personal) interests; policy preferences are seen as the product of a never-ending process of tugging and hauling among them. Most familiar among societal models is the so-called interest-group approach, stressing bargaining and negotiation on a broader scale, between central decision-makers on the one hand and other societal actors on the other. A distinction is drawn between the 'state', identified with the public sector (the apparatus of political authority), and 'society', identified with the private sector (various economic and political groups); and policy preferences are seen as the product of the interrelationships of the two sectors. The IPE literature abounds with studies comparing the explanatory power in individual countries of models drawn from each of these two classes.[11]

Does this mean that one of the two classes is necessarily preferable to the other? Not at all: the two are really complementary rather than competitive. They simply call attention to different sets of relevant actors. In the present context, both may potentially contribute to our understanding of the 'politics' of EC financial integration, though clearly it would be impossible within the limits of this brief chapter to use them to give more than a hint of all the complex forces and relationships actually involved. Unit-level analysis, as indicated, is by definition empirical, whereas this chapter is purely conceptual. The discussion in the following few paragraphs is therefore intended to be no more than illustrative of the various elements of internal policy networks that ought to be included in a future research agenda.

Governmental models, for example, point to the critical role that may be played by key bureaucratic entities whose institutional interests might seem threatened by creation of a single banking market. Incentives for individual actors in the public sector may diverge quite sharply from collective incentives on this issue. I have already mentioned the risk that financial integration poses for the autonomy of national monetary policy, for instance. For central banks, this would inevitably translate into losses of power, prestige, and privileges within the apparatus of political authority, implying an unfavourable benefit–cost trade-off as seen from their own point of view. Whatever net gains there may be for the nation as a whole, therefore, central banks themselves – or at least some officials of those institutions – might well persist in opposing any new Community initiatives in the banking area, hence exerting a crucial particularist influence on the shape of overall government policy. And the more powerful is the central bank's bargaining leverage in state councils, of course, the greater that influence is apt to be. In the EC today, the central banks of Germany and Italy are especially prominent in their respective national policy networks.

Similarly, the risk that financial integration poses for state discretion in credit allocation might well lead to opposition from other important governmental actors as well – in particular, from finance ministries (or at least from those offices or individuals in finance ministries with responsibilities in this area). Here too there are threatened losses of institutional power, prestige, and privileges. Hence here too there may be a crucial particularist influence on the shape of overall government policy. That would appear to be especially likely in the case of France, where there is a long history of state involvement in the channelling of available financial resources.[12]

In parallel fashion, societal models point to the critical role that may be played by key actors outside the public sector, where individual incentives could also diverge sharply from collective incentives. Here it is perhaps most useful to draw a distinction between the handful of leading commercial banks in each country, on the one hand, and the much greater number of smaller institutions on the other. Every EC member's banking system is characterized by a hierarchy of some sort. In Germany, below the few well known universal banks (including especially the Big Three: Deutsche, Dresdner, and Commerzbank) can be found a myriad of lesser known specialized and/or localized intermediaries, e.g. regional and savings banks and agricultural and commercial credit co-operatives. Likewise, in France a narrow circle of giant money-centre institutions (e.g., Banque Nationale de Paris, Credit Lyonnais, Société Generale) operates side-by-side with a much wider outer circle of smaller specialist establishments. And even in Italy, with the most fragmented banking system of the three countries, there are evident differences between the very largest financial intermediaries (e.g., Banca Nazionale del Lavoro, Banca Commerciale Italiana,

Credito Italiano) and other participants in Italian credit markets. The importance of these hierarchies, in the present context, stems from the typically far greater involvement of leading banks in international – as opposed to purely domestic – banking business. This comparative difference of international involvement is likely to mean that a rather deep cleavage exists between the attitudes of most big versus small institutions on the subject of a single banking market in Europe.

Europe's biggest banks, by and large, already earn a sizable portion of their profits from cross-border operations of one kind or another. Tested by competition on a global scale, they are apt to view a single regional market more as an opportunity than a threat. Just the opposite reaction, however, can probably be expected from many smaller banking intermediaries, for whom national restrictions on rights of establishment and operation are perceived virtually as a guarantee of continued commercial viability. Small local banks may well calculate that their own interests are not served by financial integration no matter how great net gains may be for the nation as a whole, and hence lobby accordingly – creating yet another particularist influence on the shape of overall government policy.

A similar distinction might be made between the suppliers of more or less closely related financial services, whose markets also tend typically to be characterized by hierarchy with varying degrees of international involvement. Bigger investment banks, brokerage houses and insurance companies, like bigger banks, are more apt to view financial integration as an opportunity; whereas smaller establishments, like most small banks, could probably be expected to lobby in opposition. And yet more elements could be added by looking at the various users of banking or related financial services and the role they play in internal policy networks. Bigger non-financial enterprises with established credit ratings would potentially be in a position to exploit new opportunities for borrowing outside their accustomed domestic markets; whereas smaller borrowers might legitimately worry about a decline of credit availability should integration cause a drainage of funds away from local intermediaries. In fact, the list of potential particularist influences that could be studied in each EC member is anything but short.

At this level of analysis, then, the practical challenge is to identify just which domestic forces are most influential on the specific issue of financial integration and to investigate just how their interaction in each EC member affects the determination of observed policy preferences over time. In addition to the strategic game played between states (international politics) is a game played within states (domestic politics), between supporters and opponents of a single banking market both inside and outside of government. And as at the level of international politics, so at the level of domestic politics, the question is whether the nature of the game can be changed in ways that will enhance prospects for inter-state co-operation on the issue. Can opponents be either bribed or coerced by supporters? Can resistance be reduced by altering the value integration's opponents attach to the future? Technically, can established conceptions of national self-interest be favourably altered by acting to modify the rational, egoistic benefit–cost calculations of individual domestic actors? That, in essence, is what 'inside-out' analysis is all about.

TWO-LEVEL INTERACTIONS

However, not even 'inside-out' analysis is the last word. Necessary as it is as a complement to systemic analysis, it is still not enough, as such, to complete our understanding of state behaviour on issues like EC financial integration. What unit-level analysis provides is insight into the domestic basis of foreign economic policy – the effect of the internal on the external. What it lacks is the reverse – the effect of the external on the internal. The relationship between the two levels of politics, domestic and international, clearly is two-way, not unidirectional. Domestic structure may have systemic consequences; but it may also be affected by systemic considerations. As a final stage of analysis, therefore, we must also explore how and to what extent the internal processes of states may be constrained or influenced by their external environment. In brief, the domestic and international games must be integrated in full. As Peter Gourevitch has written:

> The international system is not only a consequence of domestic poli-
> tics and structures but a cause of them. . . . International relations and
> domestic politics are therefore so interrelated that they should be
> analyzed similtaneously, as wholes.
>
> (Gourevitch 1978)

Regrettably, the task is easier said than done. While links between the domestic and international games are frequently acknowledged in the IPE literature (Axelrod and Keohane 1985, pp. 241–2), useful models for integrated two-level analysis – obviously a complex intellectual challenge – are only beginning to be developed by enterprising scholars (Putnam 1986). Hence here again, as in the previous section, it is possible to give no more than a hint of all that may actually be involved. By way of illustration, I shall concentrate on just one particular dimension of the two-level game – the opportunity created by external interdependencies to alter internal strategic interactions through formation of implicit or explicit transnational coalitions. Such opportunities ought to be plentiful within the EC's already dense network of institutionalized relationships.

Assuming state preferences to be the outcome of domestic politics, it follows that observed policies may be modified insofar as the balance of internal forces can be tipped by the addition of significant pressures from

influential external sectors; that is, insofar as effective transnational coalitions may be formed between key bureaucratic entities or interest groups
at home and like-minded counterparts elsewhere. Possibilities along
these lines are, in principle, manifold. Two examples from recent writings
should suffice to demonstrate the relevance of such coalitions in actual
practice.

One example is supplied by my own recent book, *In Whose Interest?*
International Banking and American Foreign Policy (Cohen 1986). The
subject of this book is the complex and often conflicting relationship
between the private banking system of the United States and the makers of
America's foreign policy in Washington. One finding of the book is that
when tensions do develop between these two sets of actors on specific
international issues, attempts are frequently made by either side to sway
the decisions of the other by forging alignments with influential third parties
outside the country (e.g., foreign governments or multilateral institutions).
Moreover, the evidence is clear that such *de facto* coalitions can indeed
lead to changes of official state policies.

A second example is supplied by Robert Putnam and Nicholas Bayne in
their 1984 study of the annual economic summits of the seven major industrial nations, *Hanging Together* (Putnam and Bayne 1984). As Putnam and
Bayne point out, divisions *within* governments are usually thought to
hamper, rather than promote, policy co-operation *between* them. But the
authors' careful analysis of the summit experience suggests otherwise:
internal divisions in some instances have actually served to facilitate inter-
state co-operation, insofar as opportunities were created for formation of
powerful alliances of like-minded officials in different countries. In effect,
external pressures worked to alter internal strategic interactions. In the
authors' own words:

> International pressures ... allowed policies to be 'sold' domestically
> that would not have been feasible otherwise.... Summits have fre-
> quently eased international tensions by strengthening the hands domes-
> tically of those within a government who favored an internationally
> desired policy.
>
> (Putnam and Bayne 1984)

These examples thus suggest one final topic for a future research agenda
on EC financial integration, concerning the potential for forming effective
transnational coalitions to help promote a single banking market. Could
supporters in practice put together effective alliances across national
frontiers? Would such efforts be aided or hindered by the EC's existing
network of relationships? And what role might the European Commission
play, perhaps as planner or catalyst? Attempts to answer these questions
would complete the integration of the domestic and international games on
this issue.

CONCLUSIONS

In summary, I have argued in this paper that the 'politics' of EC financial integration can best be understood as a problem of collective action, a 'game', involving two separate but interrelated levels of 'play': inter-state and intra-state. Financial integration itself is understood as a kind of public good in scarce supply, demanding direct and explicit co-operation among the Community's members to overcome inherent tendencies toward under-production. Since divergences exist between collective incentives and individual incentives, co-operation must be promoted to be successful. And since this in turn requires a modification of the strategic choices of at least some of the key governments involved, analysis must necessarily focus on the underlying benefit–cost calculations of both state and non-actors. At issue are national policy preferences: how these interact internationally (systemic analysis), how they are determined domestically (unit-level analysis), and what the connections are between the two levels of politics. Only by such analysis can we hope to gain the full insight needed to help improve prospects for the creation of a single banking market in Europe.

All this suggests a rather long research agenda. Individual topics for possible future empirical study have been highlighted at various points in the preceding discussion. I now conclude with a brief recapitulation of the main questions:

Systemic analysis

Here the issue is whether or how, given established state preferences, systemic constraints or incentives for state behaviour might be manipulated to enhance prospects for co-operation. The main questions are: Could side-payments be developed, most likely under the leadership of Germany, to add to the benefits of co-operation? Alternatively, could effective sanctions be imposed, making use of Community institutions, to make non-co-operation more costly? Or could governments' rates of time preference be successfully altered, perhaps through an information campaign by the European Commission?

Unit-level analysis

Here the issue is whether or how, given the broader system of inter-state relations, the 'domestic structures' of states might be manipulated to enhance prospects for co-operation? The main question is: Could established conceptions of national self-interest be favourably altered by acting to modify the benefit–cost calculations of individual domestic actors?

Two-level analysis

Here, finally, the issue is whether or how, given both the existing inter-state system and established state preferences, external interdependencies might be manipulated to alter internal policy processes. The main question is: Could implicit or explicit transnational coalitions be formed to tip the balance of domestic forces on this issue in individual EC states?

These are the questions. Can we find the answers?

NOTES

1. Helpful comments and suggestions on an earlier version of this chapter were received from Joanne Gowa, Paolo Guerrieri, Robert Keohane, and Pier Carlo Padoan. The research assistance of Thomas Kalil is also gratefully acknowledged.
2. The emphasis here is on the word 'fully'. Much financial liberalization, it must be acknowledged, has indeed occurred in recent years in the Community, even in France and Italy. On France, see e.g., *The Economist*, 29 Nov. 1986, pp. 75–6; on Italy, see e.g., the *International Herald Tribune*, 23 May 1987, p. 1. But it is also true that many barriers still remain in the EC to segment national banking markets, and much opposition obviously still remains to their removal.
3. See e.g., *The Economist*, 22 Nov. 1986, p. 84. The agreement effectively implemented a plan that had been proposed by the European Commission just six months earlier. See Commission of European Communities, *Programme for the Liberalization of Capital Movements in the Community* (Brussels, 23 May 1986).
4. For some particularly noteworthy examples of recent contributions to this literature, see e.g., Keohane (1984); and Oye (ed.) (1986).
5. Kenneth Waltz (1979), p. 63. 'Outside-in' or 'systemic' analysis corresponds to what in an earlier formulation Waltz had described as his 'third image' of international relations, locating the sources of state behaviour in attributes of the inter-state system. This was in contrast to his 'second' and 'first' images, which located the sources of state behaviour in, respectively, the structure of individual states and the nature of individual men. See Waltz (1959).
6. These as well as other games are each distinguished by a unique pay-off structure, understood to stand for the preference ordering of players among available alternative combinations of strategies. In an elementary two-player game, four such combinations are available from the point of view of each player separately: mutual co-operation (CC), mutual defection (DD), uni-lateral defection (DC), and unrequited co-operation (CD). In Stag Hunt, both players' preference ordering is: CC > DC > DD > CD. In Chicken: DC > CC > CD > DD. And in Prisoners' Dilemma: DC > CC > DD > CD. These are all *symmetrical* games. Games may also be *asymmetrical*, where the preference orderings of individual players differ. Two especially prominent examples of the latter are Bully and Called Bluff.
7. See especially the essays collected in Oye (ed.) (1986). But cf. Duncan Snidal (1985a).

8. The concept of 'nesting' is attributed to Vinod Aggarwal (1985). This book is based on a doctoral dissertation completed in 1981.
9. See e.g., Keohane, *After Hegemony*, ch. 3; and Duncan Snidal (1985).
10. For some particularly noteworthy contributions to this literature, see e.g. Katzenstein (ed.) (1978); and Krasner (1978).
11. See e.g. the following studies of United States foreign trade and monetary policies: Pastor (1980); Odell (1982); Baldwin (1985).
12. Although much liberalization has occurred in French credit markets in recent years, use of the banking system by the government to guide lending in desired directions is by no means a thing of the past. According to one estimate, as much as 30–40 per cent of loans now outstanding in France are the result of such public intervention. See *The Economist*, 29 Nov. 1986, p. 75. As one recent survey concluded: 'The most likely future for French banking . . . will be a continuation of the trend towards greater competition and flexibility, but with the state retaining ultimate control' (Marsh 1985, p. 95).

7 · MONETARY POLITICS IN FRANCE, ITALY, AND GERMANY: 1973–85[1]

John B. Goodman

The tension between political sovereignty and economic interdependence is a recurring theme in the world political economy. Governments, on the one hand, face strong domestic demands to achieve national economic objectives. On the other hand, due to the increasing links between national economies, the ability to achieve their goals is increasingly influenced by decisions made abroad. This problem is particularly acute in the area of monetary policy. The purpose of this chapter is to examine how three medium-sized European countries – France, Italy, and Germany – have navigated between the desires of their constituencies and the dictates of the international market.

The literature on the determinants of monetary policy tends to fall within two alternative perspectives. Each perspective starts from a different intellectual tradition, represents a different vantage point, and suggests different implications for policy. The first relies on the tools of economics, stressing the effect of increasing international financial integration on domestic monetary policy. Implicity, it adopts the vantage point of a small country with a highly open economy whose monetary policy is tightly constrained by exogenous international forces. For a small country, the cost of seeking to insulate its economy from external events is so high that its government generally sees no choice but to follow a policy of domestic adjustment.

The second perspective, by contrast, is grounded in concepts of political science: parties, elections, and interest groups. Implicitly, it adopts the perspective of a large country with a more closed economy. Due to its economic resources and overall power, a large country, like the United States, is able to exert a preponderant influence not only on the day-to-day conditions in world markets, but also, and more importantly, on the underlying rules, norms and procedures that govern the international financial system (Kindleberger 1973). As a result, it is able to preserve a significant degree of policy autonomy. Monetary policy in a large, more closed economy is therefore more likely to be responsive to domestic political factors (Beck 1984; Calleo 1982; Woolley 1983).

Each of the two viewpoints offers useful insights into the process of monetary policymaking, but neither alone provides an adequate basis for explaining monetary policy in medium-sized countries, such as France, Italy and Germany. These countries are neither so small that their monetary policies are determined by international economic pressures, nor are they so large that their policies primarily reflect domestic concerns. In medium-sized countries, monetary policy is more likely to reflect the tension between international economic factors and domestic political ones. The key to understanding the process of monetary policymaking in a medium-sized country, therefore, is to determine the logic of the interaction between these two different kinds of factors. That logic turns upon the role of institutions (Evans, Rueschemeyer and Skocpol 1985; Hall 1986; Zysman 1984; Black 1982, Woolley 1983). In the area of monetary policy, institutions structure the influence of both domestic political pressures and international economic conditions. For this reason, institutions – at both the international and domestic levels – are especially relevant to the study of monetary policymaking in medium-sized countries (North 1981).

Previous comparative studies of monetary policy, for the most part, have adopted a statistical approach, relying on the technique for reaction function analysis. Although these studies have been able to indicate the relative weights of domestic and international factors on monetary policy, they have had great difficulty disentangling the actual preferences of the monetary authorities from the economy constraints they faced.[2] For this reason, I have chosen, instead, to use a comparative case study approach. Specifically, I have attempted to reconstruct the major decision points in the monetary policies of three countries – France, Italy, and Germany. In conducting this analysis, I have relied both on the available secondary sources and over 150 interviews with key participants and informed observers of the monetary policymaking process in the three countries.[3]

France, Italy, and Germany have pursued very different monetary policies since the breakdown of the Bretton Woods system of fixed exchange rates in 1973. In the early years of floating exchange rates, all three countries behaved as if they faced no external constraints, and their monetary policies diverged sharply. German monetary policy became very restrictive. French and Italian monetary policy, by contrast, became more expansionary. By the early 1980s, however, the central banks of the three countries were all practising restrictive policies (Izzo and Spaventa 1981, pp. 73–136).

Monetary divergence in the early 1970s resulted from the differing impact of domestic political factors on monetary policy in the three countries, and this, in turn, was determined by the degree of central bank independence. As financial integration increased, however, it became more and more costly for countries to pursue monetary policies that diverged from the world trend. Recognition of this external constraint led to the creation of the European Monetary System (EMS) in 1979, which amplified the political costs of policy divergence, especially for weaker currency countries. As a result, the monetary policies of the three countries have progressively converged towards a more restrictive course.

INTERNATIONAL SOURCES OF MONETARY CHANGE

Economic interdependence among the advanced industrial countries has risen steadily in the post-war period. Due to technological advances in the financial industry and a reduction in the barriers to capital movements, the pace of this integration has been particularly rapid in the world's financial markets.[4] The ability of the monetary authorities in France, Germany and Italy to pursue independent monetary policies has been greatly reduced. In response to this, national strategies were followed to reduce the degree of interdependence. A fundamental step in this direction was the adoption of floating exchange rates (Friedman 1953; Johnson 1969; Gowa 1983). Yet floating did not provide the hoped-for panacea. Most countries were unwilling to accept the massive swings in exchange rates that resulted from policy divergence. Over time, countries have thus gradually faced an ever-increasing external constraint on monetary policy.

Adjustment represents the second response to this dilemma. The pressure to adjust to external constraints has weighed much heavier upon countries that face downward pressure on the exchange rate than on those that face upward pressure.

Germany has generally enjoyed greater room for manoeuvre than its neighbours due to its preference for a relatively more restrictive monetary policy. After the shift to flexible exchange rates in 1973, the Bundesbank instituted a number of restrictive monetary measures; considering the appreciation of the mark, this was an acceptable price to pay for its ability to tighten monetary policy (Emminger 1976). In the view of the central bank, wringing inflation out of the economy more than compensated for any negative effects a rising exchange rate would have on exports. As it turned out, the effects were quite small, since exporters found room to cut costs, and foreign demand for German exports proved to be relatively inelastic (Deutsche Bundesbank 1977, pp. 37–38).

The German authorities became more concerned about the movement of the exchange rate in 1977–8, when the loss of confidence in the dollar spurred a further appreciation of the mark.[5] The fact that the economy had still not fully recovered from the recession of the mid-1970s made the deflationary aspects of currency appreciation particularly unwelcome. The Bundesbank essentially had two choices. Either conduct a monetary policy consistent with its stated targets for monetary growth (8 per cent in 1977

Table 7.1 German monetary targets and results

	Percentage changes			
	Target		Result	
	year-on-year [2]	annual average	year-on-year [2]	annual average
1975 CBMS [1]	8	—	9.9	—
1976 CBMS	—	8	—	9.2
1977 CBMS	—	8	—	9.0
1978 CBMS	—	8	—	11.5
1979 CBMS	6–9	—	6.3	—
1980 CBMS	5–8	—	4.9	—
1981 CBMS	4–7	—	3.5	—
1982 CBMS	4–7	—	6.0	—
1983 CBMS	4–7	—	6.8	—
1984 CBMS	4–6	—	4.6	—
1985 CBMS	3–5	—	4.2	—

Source: Deutsche Bundesbank.
Notes
[1] Central bank money stock.
[2] Fourth quarter of previous year to fourth quarter of current year. For 1975: December 1974 to December 1975.

and 1978) and allow the exchange rate to appreciate, or loosen monetary policy to brake the rise of the mark and overshoot the monetary targets (see Table 7.1).

A majority of the Bundesbank's Central Bank Council (the principal decision-making board) favoured the latter course. As the council members saw it, conducting a monetary policy consistent with the stated monetary targets would have been very costly in light of the external pressures on the German economy. According to a subsequent internal central bank report: 'In order to keep the stricter monetary targets originally planned, it would have been necessary in 1977–8 to raise the lombard rate considerably (by an average of 1 percentage point in 1977 and 3.5 percentage points in 1978). With such a policy the D-Mark would have appreciated distinctly faster ... this would have resulted in a significant loss of growth.'[6] Moreover, the Central Bank Council did not believe that lowering interest rates was inconsistent with its domestic objectives. Since demand was low and inflation was falling, the Central Bank Council believed that monetary policy could be loosened without endangering price stability (interviews).

External factors played a more important role in the formation of German monetary policy in 1980–81, when the combination of rising American interest rates and a German trade deficit led to a rapid depreciation of the mark. Instead of allowing the depreciation of the mark to gradually increase exports and restore external equilibrium, the Bundesbank decided to raise interest rates to halt the drop in the mark and prevent its inflationary effects. As explained in the Bundesbank's report for 1979:

There is no reason to use the depreciation of the Deutsche Mark as an economic policy instrument for adjusting the balance of payments. To begin with, the depreciation primarily increases the importation of infla-tion, raises the costs of imports, and tends to reduce the foreign exchange revenue from exports. Only after some while can a reaction to the depre-ciation in the sense of a decline in imports and greater success in the export field be expected ... and the more the change is delayed, the more radical are the adjustment measures required.

(Deutsch Bundesbank 1980, p. 41)

Increasing financial integration heightened the external constraint on German monetary policy in the mid-1980s, even when its currency faced upward pressure in the exchange markets. A recent example occurred in the period late 1986 to early 1987. With a tumbling dollar, the Bundesbank decided that it had to lower interest rates in order to limit the appreciation of the mark.

The Bundesbank's orientation toward international institutions reflects the importance of stability in German monetary policy. It has not needed to obtain financial resources from other countries, but has been uncon-strained by their actions. The Bundesbank has been willing at times of its own choosing to provide assistance to other countries, but it has refused to accept binding commitments which might limit its own autonomy.

Due to its strong currency status and ability to influence the rules and operations of regimes such as the EMS, Germany has thus been able to pursue a relatively independent monetary policy, even if the costs of such a policy have risen over time. Policy autonomy has been much more costly for Italy and France, however, given their desire to practise expansionary monetary policies relative to world trends.

In 1973 such policies generated sharp downward pressure on the franc and lira and helped fuel current-account deficits in their respective econ-omies. Their responses to this exchange-rate pressure were quite similar. Both countries pulled out of the snake to free their monetary authorities from the obligation of drawing down reserves.[7] Yet neither country was willing to allow the value of its currency to be set solely in the market. Dur-ing the course of the year, the two central banks imposed capital controls and intervened heavily in the exchange markets. Funds were also sought on international markets, but as Italy found, its access to the Euromarkets was nearing its limits. As pressure on their currencies mounted and their reserve levels fell, both governments came to the conclusion that they could not avoid monetary restriction, which they instituted in 1974 (Spaventa 1983; Lauber 1983, pp. 81–9).

Yet the timing and the degree of monetary restriction were influenced by each country's ability to negotiate additional financial assistance from other countries, such as Germany and the United States, and from international institutions, such as the IMF and the EEC. Italy's negotiating position was especially strong because of foreign concern that its economic problems would lead to Communist participation in the government – an outcome, it was feared, which would lead to Italy's political withdrawal from the western alliance. As one German official put it: 'You can be sure Germany will not let Italy go down the drain and bring the Communists or Fascists to our doorstep' (quoted by Posner 1978, p. 253).

Thus, Italy was able to negotiate very favourable conditions when it turned to the IMF for a stand-by loan in 1974. The fund allowed Italy several years to eliminate its trade deficit so as not to 'require an intolerable degree of domestic deflation' and send the Italian economy into recession. (IMF 1984; Spaventa 1983, pp. 442–3). These conditions – relatively lax compared to the fund's usual standards – reflected the fact that Italy was the first advanced industrial country to seek fund assistance after the oil price rise and that its stand-by credit was the largest fund transaction since 1969. The IMF viewed the loan to Italy as a means to firmly 'establish the fund's role in the new situation of imbalance caused by the oil shock' (Spaventa 1983, pp. 448–9).

In addition to the IMF's Special Drawing Rights (SDR) 1 billion, Italy received during the course of 1974 $1,885 billion from the EEC, SDR 1.7 billion under the IMF oil facility, and $2 billion (against a gold guarantee) from the Bundesbank (Spaventa 1983, pp. 442–3). Without these funds, the Italian authorities would have been obliged to restrict monetary policy more rapidly and more severely. Italy's experience thus seemed to indicate that the greater a medium-sized country's domestic economic problems or its *political* importance to its economic partners, the stronger its external negotiating position.[8]

This sequence was repeated in 1975 and 1976, when France and Italy again adopted overly expansionary policies (compared to Germany and the United States), faced even greater external pressures, and were forced to tighten their monetary policies a second time (Goodman 1987, chaps. 3–4; Tasgian 1983; Delattre 1986). Again, Italy was able to negotiate financial assistance to ease the burden of domestic adjustment. This time, however, Germany, the United States and the IMF were not willing simply to bail Italy out and insisted upon domestic reforms which would bring Italy's policies more in line with world trends (*Financial Times*, 17 February, 27 February, 10 March 1976; Spaventa 1983).

A growing recognition of the severity of the external constraint led both countries to join the EMS in early 1979.[9] France and Italy hoped that tying their currencies to the mark would provide an external discipline to their monetary policies (Giavazzi and Pagano, 1986). Yet participation in the EMS alone did not guarantee that countries would not choose to adopt divergent policies. Whereas the Bundesbank conducted a restrictive monetary policy in the early 1980s (as did Italy), the newly-elected socialist government in France initiated a policy of monetary expansion (Fontaneau and Muet 1985). What the EMS did was to make such divergence more visible.

Between 1981 and 1983, the franc had to be devalued three times – events which the French considered a blow to their prestige. The third exchange-rate crisis in March 1983 represented a critical point for the socialist government's macroeconomic policy. A number of President François Mitterrand's senior advisors recommended leaving the EMS, allowing the lira to float, adopting import controls, and continuing a policy of monetary expansion. Mitterrand, however, decided against this protectionist alternative, apparently swayed by studies conducted by the Finance Ministry which showed that leaving the EMS would not solve France's economic problems. According to these reports, withdrawing from the EMS would immediately result in at least a 20 per cent depreciation of the franc. To prevent inflation from soaring and the balance of payments from deteriorating further, the government would have to impose a stringent deflationary programme (interviews). But, to soften the blow of the adjustment, Germany and the other countries agreed to provide France with a loan of 4 billion ECUs to finance its balance of payments deficit (Vesperini 1985, p. 205).

The March 1983 devaluation marked a watershed in the economic thinking of the socialist government. Although President Mitterrand may have hoped that a world recovery in 1984 might allow France to adopt a more expansionary policy, he acknowledged that France could not pursue a policy of domestic expansion in the midst of world recession. Priority had to be given to reducing inflation to the levels attained by France's major trading partners. As Prime Minister Mauroy explained:

A real left-wing policy can be applied in France only if the other European countries also follow policies of the left. . . . If the French resign themselves to living with an inflation of 12 per cent, they should know that, because of our economic interdependence with Germany, we will be led into a situation of imbalance. France must rid herself of this inflationary disease.

(*L'Express* 8 April 1983)

This new goal reflected the socialists' acceptance of the need to adjust to the constraints imposed on France as a result of its integration in the world economy. It was underscored by the government's decisions to modernize French financial markets – essentially increasing France's financial integration into the world economy and thereby making it more difficult to pursue a monetary policy that diverged from world trends (Lebegne 1985, p. 27).

Due to the growth of financial integration, governments and central banks in medium-sized countries such as France, Italy, and Germany have thus faced increasing external pressure on their monetary policies. The rise in financial integration did not mean that these countries were unable to adopt monetary policies which diverged from world trends. What it meant was that the price of such divergence became greater – i.e. the trade-offs they faced in terms of inflation, growth, and external balance became less tolerable. External pressures have been greater on countries running current-account deficits with weak currencies than on those running current account surpluses with strong currencies.

But domestic factors are not irrelevant to the degree of autonomy a country enjoys in the international financial system or to the process of adjustment to the external constraint. France, Italy, and Germany did not all face the same burden of adjustment. The weight of the burden depended upon whether they were facing upward or downward pressure on the exchange rate, and this pressure depended, at least in part, on the kind of monetary policy they chose to pursue. The explanation for these differences lies primarily at the domestic level. Similarly, it is at the domestic level that we can explain why countries facing similar exchange rate pressures, like Italy and France, adjusted to the external constraint at different speeds.

DOMESTIC SOURCES OF MONETARY POLICY

Monetary policy plays a crucial role in the macroeconomic management of advanced industrial countries. Not surprisingly, it can therefore be an important political issue. Understanding the different monetary strategies pursued by France, Italy, and Germany, as well as the speeds with which they adjusted to the external constraint, requires an analysis of the role of domestic politics. The critical difference between the three countries was the degree of central bank independence from the government. Where the central bank is independent, as in Germany and post-1981 Italy, monetary policy is relatively free from partisan and other political influences and will be more anti-inflationary. Where it is dependent, as in France and pre-1981 Italy, monetary policy will be more sensitive to political influences. The literature on economic policymaking focuses, in particular, on three political variables: elections, parties, and labour power.

Timing of elections

Monetary policy can be a useful tool for incumbent politicians who desire to influence economic conditions at election time. According to the political business-cycle hypothesis, governments will attempt to stimulate the economy before an election in order to increase income and reduce unemployment, even though such policies may put the economy on a worse footing in the long run. The premiss of this hypothesis is that economic conditions affect electoral outcomes. Voters are assumed to be myopic; that is, they base their electoral decisions only on current economic conditions and ignore, or at least undervalue, future events.[10]

Yet evidence that monetary policy was actually manipulated for this purpose varied significantly across the three countries and across the time-period examined in this study. Cross-nationally, the influence of electoral timing on monetary policy was very strong in France, less strong in Italy, and virtually non-existent in Germany. This variation did not reflect any significant cross-national differences in the willingness of politicians to alter monetary conditions. Indeed, politicians in all three countries often sought to lower interest rates or increase credit growth in pre-electoral periods. Rather, it reflected differences in the degree of central bank independence across the three countries. The degree of central bank independence determined whether or not a government could translate its monetary preferences into policy. Hence, monetary policy was more likely to be influenced by electoral pressures in countries with dependent central banks and less likely in countries with independent central banks.

In France, which has a dependent central bank, evidence of economic manipulation was found prior to both the presidential election of 1974 and the parliamentary election of 1978. The 1974 presidential election was provoked by the sudden death of Gaullist President Georges Pompidou. Prime Minister Messmer and Finance Minister Valery Giscard D'Estaing quite consciously decided not to tighten monetary policy to the extent necessary to halt the deterioration in the balance of payments and the decline in the franc. Their reluctance was prompted by the government's fears that the Socialist candidate, François Mitterrand, would win the election and by Giscard's own presidential aspirations. The common programme of the Left (negotiated between the socialists and the communists in 1972) promised greater growth and called for widespread nationalizations and a substantial redistribution of income in favour of wage earners.[11] Giscard realized that Mitterrand's promise of change tapped a public desire for social reform. His campaign therefore ignored the need for restrictive economic policy measures and called instead for social 'change without risk' (Charlot 1974, p. 80 and p. 99). A key strategist for Giscard later explained: 'We did not speak of the oil shock during the entire campaign. Why? Because the left denied that this was a crisis' (interview).

The advent of the 1978 parliamentary elections also played an important role in the government's decision in 1977 and early 1978 to expand credit, widely overshooting its own monetary target (See Table 7.2). As one senior aide to Prime Minister Barre explained:

The Left seemed likely to win the elections. They argued that deficit spending should be increased. Therefore we had to be careful to maintain an economic situation in the country which would not provoke social

Table 7.2 French monetary targets and results

	Percentage changes	
	Target	Result
Unpublished targets		
1973 M2	15	15.0
1974 M2	14[1]	15.9
1975 M2	13	18.2
1976 M2	13	12.8
Published targets		
1977 M2	12.5	14.0
1978 M2	12.0	12.1
1979 M2	11.0	14.4
1980 M2	11.0	9.8
1981 M2	10.0[2]	11.4
1982 M2	12.5–13.5	11.5
1983 M2	10 then 9	10.2
1984 M2R	5.5–6.5	7.6
1985 M2R	4–6	6.9

Source: OECD Economic Surveys, *France*, January 1987, p. 55.
Notes
R = Resident.
[1] Implictly raised to 15–16 per cent in the second half.
[2] Implictly raised to 12 per cent in the second half.

unrest. We would have been right in economic terms, but we would have lost the election.

(interview, Barre 1980)

In the immediate pre-electoral period, fears in the financial community of a leftist victory provoked an increase in capital outflows, to which policy-makers reacted by raising interest rates.[12] Giscard's government was none the less able to get political mileage from these outflows, which it cited as evidence that a victory of the left would lead to a collapse of the franc (*Le Monde*, 10 February 1978; *The Economist*, 11 February 1978).

The Barre government did not undertake any direct monetary expansion prior to the 1981 presidential election. In the two quarters preceding the election, the government used several fiscal measures to stimulate demand, which, according to one estimate, led to 0.4 per cent increase in GDP for 1981 (Fontaneau and Muet, pp. 93–5). Monetary policy did not play a direct role in this stimulus, but the money supply was increased as a consequence of the government's added financing needs.

The French government did not engage in any monetary expansion prior to either the 1983 municipal elections (which it considered a referendum on its own policies) or the 1986 parliamentary elections. Monetary concerns were not absent, however, from the socialist government's electoral considerations. President Mitterrand chose to postpone his decision on whether to devalue the franc or leave the EMS until after the March 1983 municipal elections. Either decision, the government feared, would be interpreted by the voters as a sign of economic mismanagement. Consequently, to protect the franc, the central bank raised interest rates to record levels (Bauchard 1986, pp. 128–130). By 1986, however, the government had decided that international pressures did not allow France any room for a significant expansion, or even a less restrictive monetary policy, but it again sought to postpone a necessary devaluation until after the parliamentary election.

Italian governments have also sought to use monetary policy as a means to improve their prospects for re-election. Yet, for two reasons, they have had more difficulty in doing so. First, the frequency of crisis elections has hindered the ability of Italian governments to manipulate monetary policy.[13] Second, the possibility of influencing monetary policy was drastically reduced by the shift towards greater central bank independence in 1981.

Italian monetary policy was most strongly influenced by electoral pressures prior to the 1976 election. The Christian Democratic party (DC) feared that it would lose its dominant position in the Italian political system to the Communist party (PCI). The DC's position was doubly precarious. First, it was presiding over the most serious recession since the Second World War. Second, its ability to govern hinged on the support of the Socialist party (PSI), which after its own success in the 1975 local elections, did not hide its own desire to precipitate early elections to improve its standing at the national level.[14]

Some stimulus to the Italian economy was both politically necessary and economically feasible. In practice, the government directed the central bank to create a special export facility under which the banks could automatically refinance up to 50 per cent of their export loans at a preferential rate – a measure which had the effect of flooding the economy with money (Micossi and Rebecchini 1984).

DC leaders did not anticipate that this policy would provoke a collapse of the lira in January 1976, forcing the government to abandon its expansionary economic policy altogether.

In contrast to the 1976 case, electoral pressures did not alter the course of monetary policy prior to the parliamentary elections in June 1979. The reason lay in the unexpected timing of the crisis election. A government of national unity was formed in late 1976, which the Communist party (PCI) first supported and later joined as a member of the parliamentary majority. The PCI hoped that its support for the government's programme of economic austerity would increase its own legitimacy among the Italian electorate. In January 1979, however, PCI leaders decided that they could not continue to support a policy that was costly to their core constituency without the political benefit of joining the cabinet. When their demand was rejected, PCI leaders provoked a government crisis and an early election. The suddenness of the crisis limited the government's ability to adopt a more expansionary monetary policy (interviews, Kogan 1983, pp. 311–320).

The June 1983 parliamentary election was also a crisis election, but the timing was not unanticipated. Many top government leaders favoured a looser monetary policy in 1983. They were unable to implement it because the Banca d'Italia had become more independent in 1981 and was able to resist government pressures to lower interest rates.

Compared to monetary policy in both France and Italy, the lack of evidence supporting the political business-cycle hypothesis in Germany is quite striking. German monetary policy was not manipulated for electoral purposes prior to the 1976, 1980, or 1983 federal elections. This finding does not reflect the absence of government interest in the setting of monetary policy. Indeed, the Chancellor and his ministers were quite conscious of the effects of monetary policy both on the economy and on their prospects for re-election. But their influence over the course of monetary policy was limited by the independent status of the German central bank (OECD 1977, p. 71).

Disagreements between the Federal government and the Bundesbank over pre-electoral monetary policy did not always arise. Prior to the October 1976 federal elections, both the government and the central bank agreed that an expansionary monetary policy was necessary to stimulate economic activity. For the Bundesbank, however, this policy was influenced more by the state of the economy, than the timing of the elections. So long as the rate of inflation continued to fall, the Bundesbank was willing to provide support to the economy which had fallen into recession in late 1974. Interest rates were steadily lowered throughout 1975. Hoping that the economy was at last on the road to recovery, the Bundesbank set a slightly more restrictive monetary target for 1976 but allowed this target to be overshot in the summer when economic activity appeared to be falling off. Bundesbank actions in the period leading up to the 1976 elections were thoroughly consistent with the government's policy preferences, but were not significantly different from what they would have been in the absence of elections.

The Bundesbank's ability to resist electoral pressures was displayed more clearly before the 1980 federal elections. The German central bank had set monetary policy on a restrictive course in 1979 to dampen inflation. This policy shift created an open conflict with the federal government. Finance Minister Hans Matthofer had been aware, of course, that the Bundesbank was leaning in favour of an increase in interest rates. Opposing this initiative, Matthofer sent Manfred Lahnstein, state secretary in the Finance Ministry, to the Central Bank Council meeting on 18 January at which the interest-rate increase was discussed. Lahnstein argued that the economic situation did not yet require any tightening of monetary policy and that higher interest rates would only make financing the government's deficit more difficult and jeopardize the economic upswing. The Central Bank Council was apparently not convinced, however, and voted nearly unanimously for the interest-rate increase. At the press conference after the meeting, Lahnstein publicly criticized the decision (*Frankfurter All-gemeine Zeitung*, 23 January 1979; and interview with Central Bank Council member). Lahnstein's comments may have done the Chancellor more harm than good, however, for their immediate effect was to generate public and political support for the central bank.[15]

The Bundesbank continued to conduct a restrictive monetary policy in 1980, even after the economy had again fallen into recession, in order to stimulate capital inflows with which to finance the growing trade deficit. Chancellor Schmidt feared that this policy would increase unemployment and thereby damage his government's electoral prospects. Although Schmidt did not disagree with the Bundesbank in public, he was highly critical of its monetary policy in private. On numerous occasions, he told Bundesbank President Karl Otto Pohl that the central bank should lower interest rates, but was unable to overcome the central bank's resistance (interviews, Dyson 1981, p. 48; Pohl 1985, pp. 222–6).

The Bundesbank's independence from electoral pressure was also demonstrated in 1983, when it refrained from loosening monetary policy prior to the March parliamentary election so as not even to give the impression of political influence. This forebearance was particularly striking, given that a majority of the members of the central bank favoured the conservative government (which had come to power in October 1982) and wanted to lower interest rates for economic reasons. As one Central Bank Council member put it: 'if we had [lowered interest rates] six weeks before the election in March, we would have been accused by all kinds of people' of helping the Christian Democrat–Free Democrat coalition (interview). The Bundesbank thus waited until one week after election (which gave a majority to the CDU–FDP coalition) and then adopted the postponed interest-rate reduction (Deutsche Bundesbank 1983, p. 20).

Comparing the experiences of the three countries thus supports and refines the political business-cycle hypothesis. In cases where the central bank is dependent, governments do seek to manipulate policy to enhance their prospects of re-election. But, as the French and Italian cases suggest, their willingness to do so seems to be declining across time. In Italy, the decision to enlarge the central bank's independence removed monetary policy from the realm of electoral politics. And in France, the government chose not to manipulate monetary policy, even in the absence of an independent central bank. This evidence, based on only a few cases, is not absolutely conclusive, but it does conform to our expectations of the effects of increased financial integration on the role of domestic politics in monetary policymaking.

Party control of government

Since 1973 changes in the party control of government have occurred in France, Germany, and Italy. According to the party control of government hypothesis, the political party that wins an election will favour economic policies that reflect the economic interests of its core constituency. Left-wing parties will practise policies which lower unemployment, whereas conservative parties will practise policies which produce less inflation (Hibbs 1977; Black 1982a; Woolley 1983).

Have these governmental changes in France, Italy, and Germany had an impact on the course of monetary policy? The answer, based on a comparison of the three national cases, is mixed. In all three countries, political parties do hold views on monetary policy that tend to reflect the macro-economic preferences of their supporters. In general, left-wing parties favour lower unemployment, whereas right-wing parties favour lower inflation. However, party preferences do not necessarily translate into monetary policy outcomes. When parties take control of the government, they may be limited in their ability to alter the course of monetary policy.

Of the three countries, the strongest evidence for the influence of party control of government was found in the case of France. From 1973 to 1981, France was governed by a right-wing coalition under the presidency first of Georges Pompidou and then of Valery Giscard D'Estaing. According to the party-control hypothesis, monetary policy should have been anti-inflationary in this period. But in fact, the degree of monetary restriction varied in this period. In the early 1970s, monetary policy was strongly influenced by labour power and therefore aimed more at preventing un-employment.[16] Later in the decade, under Prime Minister Barre, the effects of the party variable became more important, and inflation rose on the government's list of concerns.

The election of a socialist president and left-wing majority in the National Assembly in the spring of 1981 led to a sharp shift in the course of monetary policy. With respect to the policies that the conservative government had laid out for the year, the new Socialist government immediately eased credit ceilings and raised the target for the growth of the money supply (see Table 7.2) (interviews). The effect of the socialists' control of government was sufficiently strong to overwhelm, at least for a while, the external constraint. In 1983, these external pressures led the socialist party to reconsider its ability to conduct an independent monetary policy.

Monetary policy has continued to be set with an eye to the external constraint under the conservative government of Jacques Chirac, elected in 1986. This outcome is consistent with our expectations regarding the behaviour of a conservative party in power. However, given the fact that French governments, both left and right, have been pursuing this course since 1983, a better explanation is found in the secular increase in external pressure confronting all medium-sized countries in the 1980s.

The course of Italian monetary policy provides more ambiguous evidence about the importance of the party control variable. The ambiguity reflects in part the prevalence of coalition governments in Italy. As James E. Alt has explained, 'partners in a coalition can veto initiatives that might be in the electoral interest of one coalition member by threatening to break up the coalition' (Alt 1985, p. 1021). Hence, rather than looking only at the principal party in power, it is necessary to understand the composition and dynamics of the governing coalition.

Although there have been fifteen governments in Italy since 1973, only a few changes in the nature of the governing coalition have occurred.[17] In 1973, Italy was governed by a centre-right coalition. Contrary to the predicted outcome, however, this coalition practised an excessively expansionary policy under pressure from the Italian trade unions (Flanagan, Soskice and Ulman 1983, p. 534). From 1973 to 1976, Italy was ruled by centre-left governments, formed around a Christian Democrat (DC)-Socialist (PSI) coalition. Economic expansion – even when it created significant balance of payments problems – was the PSI's condition for participation in the government. The PSI's importance to the government coalition gave it a large say in economic policymaking (Flanagan, Soskice and Ulman 1983; Kogan 1983, p. 280).

If leftist parties in power conducted more expansionary monetary policies than conservative parties, then Italian monetary policy should have become more expansionary between 1976 and 1979 when the parliamentary majority (albeit not the cabinet) was widened to include the Communist party in a government of national unity. Yet PCI participation led to a monetary policy which was generally in line with world trends. This outcome is counter-intuitive. Had the PCI been strong enough to govern alone, it might have favoured a looser monetary policy. But the PCI's goal at this time was to show that it could be a responsible member of government and therefore appeal to more centrist groups. Only by enlarging its base of support, the PCI believed, could it hope to play a more central role in Italian political life (Hellman 1977, pp. 155–82).

Moreover, the PCI was able to gain support for this policy from the Italian unions who were willing to moderate their demands to ease the rate of inflation. Indeed, it was for this reason that the other parties sought to gain PCI participation in the governing majority. The creation of a government of national unity was therefore instrumental in the shift to a more restrictive monetary policy (See Table 7.3).

From 1979 to 1986, the government was again controlled by a centre-left coalition, with a socialist prime minister in the final three years. The composition of the governing coalition had little impact on monetary policy. In contrast to the expansionary policy pursued by the centre-left coalitions in the early 1970s, monetary policy in the 1980s was generally restrictive. This outcome did not reflect a change in the policy preferences of the governing coalition. The PSI, which was institutionally stronger than in the early 1970s, continued to favour more expansionary policies, yet was unable to translate its preferences into policy (Valentini 1986, pp. 30–1). This

Table 7.3 Italian monetary targets and results

	Target[1]	%	Result[1]	%
1974[3] TDC[2]	22,400	18.6	20,015	16.6
1975[4] TDC	24,700	17.6	35,633	25.4
1976 TDC	29,500	17.5	34,048	20.2
1977 TDC	30,600	15.1	35,703	17.6
1978 TDC	38,000	12.9	49,240	20.6
1979 TDC	53,000	18.4	53,252	18.5
1980 TDC	59,300	17.4	63,150	18.5
1981 TDC	64,500	16.0	72,771[5]	18.0
1982 TDC	73,000	15.2	100,479[5]	21.0
1983 TDC	105,000	4.5	119,700	20.6

Source: Banca d'Italia; and Cesare Caranza and Antonio Fazio, 'Methods of monetary control in Italy: 1974–1983', in *The political economy of monetary policy: national and international aspects,* (ed.) Donald R. Hodgman, Federal Reserve Bank of Boston, 1983, Boston, p. 78.
Notes
[1] Billions of lire.
[2] Total Domestic Credit.
[3] April 1974–March 1975.
[4] April 1975–March 1976.
[5] Corrected for the effect of non-interest bearing deposits on payments abroad.

outcome was consistent with the increasing pressure of the international financial system, but, as we will see, reflected important changes in the degree of central bank independence as well.

Finally, party control of government provided little, if any, information about the stance of German monetary policy. Disagreement over the course of monetary policy between the two major parties – the Social Democrats (SPD) and Christian Democrats (CDU) – has occurred in the past thirteen years. These disagreements were muted by the continuous participation of the smaller Free Democratic party (FDP) in both SPD and CDU governments, but they were certainly not eradicated.

From 1973 to 1982, the government was composed of an SPD-FDP coalition, under Chancellors Willy Brandt (1972–4) and Helmut Schmidt (1974–82). During its tenure in office, the SPD often argued for a more expansionary policy, but government demands had no direct influence on policy. The Bundesbank was able to resist government pressure.

A CDU-FDP coalition took office in 1982. Contrary to the predictions of the party control of government hypothesis, the change in government did not lead the central bank to pursue a more restrictive monetary policy. If anything, its effect was probably the opposite. Many members of the Central Bank Council had been troubled by what they saw as the lack of economic leadership under the SPD government in 1982 and had been reluctant to loosen monetary policy. The change in government increased the likelihood that the growth of indebtedness would be brought under control. A decline in the government's deficit would reduce its financing needs and hence its demand for funds from the capital markets. In the Bundesbank's view, this would make more funds available for productive investments – a development it considered necessary for Germany's adjustment to the second oil crisis (Deutsche Bundesbank 1981, p. 36; Handelsblatt 19 January 1982).

Between October 1982 and March 1983, the Bundesbank reduced its key rates by one percentage point on three occasions. The first decrease shortly followed the vote of confidence in the new CDU-FDP government headed by Chancellor Helmut Kohl. According to one Central Bank Council member:

> We could take into account that there was now more confidence in the markets, and we thought that a lowering of our interest rates would contribute to a further increase in confidence. I wouldn't go so far as to say that because we had a new government, the Central Bank Council reduced interest rates, but the fact there was a new government was quite important to the mood in economic circles.
>
> (interview).

Under both SPD and CDU governments, the Bundesbank simply did not acquiesce in the policy preferences of the ruling coalition.

Thus, the significance of the party control of government hinges on the degree of central bank independence. In Germany, changes in political parties had little effect on the conduct of monetary policy. Similar party changes were more important in France and Italy although they appeared to be overwhelmed in the early 1970s by other domestic factors, in particular the role of labour. And as expected, the effects of party control declined over time as policymakers recognized the increasing power of the external constraint.

The role of labour

To understand the cross-national differences between French, Italian, and German monetary policy, it is necessary to look, not only at the preferences of politicians, but also at the power of labour. Unlike politicians, workers generally do not influence monetary policy by applying direct pressure on central banks. Rather, they create an economic and social environment which affects and constrains the policymaking calculus of the monetary authorities. Yet these constraints are much greater in countries with dependent central banks than in countries with independent central banks.

The most important dimensions of labour power are the ability of workers to protect (or increase) real wages, to maintain job security, and to threaten social unrest. All three dimensions make the conduct of a restrictive monetary policy more difficult and less effective (Black 1982a; 1982b, pp. 279–300; Gordon 1975). First, if workers seek and are able to protect real wages, then (all other things being equal) monetary restriction will increase unemployment and reduce corporate profitability. Second, if workers are protected from lay-offs, then restrictive monetary policy will reduce corporate profitability, but will have little immediate impact on unemployment and wages. Third, if workers are convincingly able to threaten social unrest, then the monetary authorities may well hesitate before adopting a deflationary policy to reduce inflation.

Along these dimensions, labour has been more aggressive in Italy and France than in Germany, although the militancy of the working class in each country has changed over time. Not coincidentally, the general behaviour of workers in these countries is influenced by the organizational features of the three national trade union movements. In both Italy and France, organized labour is fragmented between confederations, which affiliate a multiplicity of unions. In Germany, one confederation dominates the trade-union movement and is comprised of only sixteen industry-based unions. As David Cameron has shown, nations in which there is a single labour confederation composed of relatively few, industry-based unions tend to experience lower levels of strike activity and unemployment and smaller increases in both nominal and real wages and prices than do nations where organized labour is fragmented. The more unified the trade union movement, the more able it is to ensure that its members agree 'to exchange wage militancy and, more generally, militancy in collective bargaining for employment' (Cameron 1978, p. 173).

The degree of worker militancy clearly influences the policy trade-offs facing the monetary authorities, but it does not unilaterally determine their response. The way in which monetary authorities react to worker militancy greatly depends on the degree of central bank independence. Worker militancy has a stronger impact on monetary policy in countries with dependent central banks than it does in countries with independent central banks. Independent central banks are more willing to accept higher unemployment and lower profitability in order to pursue anti-inflationary policy. Reflecting the political interests of their governments, dependent central banks are more likely to accommodate worker demands rather than run the risk of provoking social unrest or even alienating workers who lose their jobs and businessmen whose profits decline. Of course, neither worker militancy nor central bank independence are static variables. Both can and have changed over time.

Bargaining aggressiveness was quite high in all three countries in 1973 as workers sought to maintain real wages and transfer the burden of adjustment to the oil shock to other sectors of the economy. Were labour power the sole determinant of monetary policy, we would have expected to find all three countries pursuing expansionary monetary policies. Yet quite different monetary policies were practised.

In 1974, the German public service and metal industry unions entered wage negotiations, demanding wage increases of 15 to 20 per cent. Both the federal government and the Bundesbank appealed to the unions to keep their wage demands in line with the official single-digit forecasts for inflation (8–9 per cent). These appeals were largely ignored, however. The unions negotiated inflexibly and finally achieved wage gains of 12 to 15 per cent. Apparently, 'the trade unions were counting either on the failure of [the Bundesbank's] stabilization policy or on an early switch to an expansionary course' (Kloten, Ketterer, and Vollmer 1985, p. 388).

If so, they underestimated both the power of the independent Bundesbank and its determination to reduce inflation. Recognizing that a continuation of its restrictive monetary policy would lead to increased unemployment, the Bundesbank none the less concluded that monetary restriction was more necessary than ever in order to hold down inflation. As Bundesbank President Karl Klasen later explained: 'If the wage increases had followed the recommendation of the federal chancellor, I personally had hoped that the Bundesbank would have been able to loosen its previous policy and allow interest rates to fall' (*Die Zeit* 1 March 1974). But Klasen said, 'we had no choice but to refuse to finance this inflationary settlement' (*Die Zeit*, 14 March 1974).

In France and Italy, on the other hand, the dependent central banks largely accommodated wage increases. This was surprising since governments in both countries were controlled by conservative parties, normally more sensitive to inflation than unemployment. But labour was so powerful that it overwhelmed the effects of party control of government. Fearing that more restrictive monetary policies would increase unemployment and provoke social unrest, both governments adopted expansionary policies. One former French government minister recalled: 'We had 500,000 unemployed . . . everyone believed that there would be a social explosion if the number reached 600,000' (Interview; Flanagan, Soskice, and Ulman 1983, p. 534). In stimulating their economies and allowing their currencies to depreciate, these countries sought to reduce real wages and increase employment. However, the higher level of employment enabled workers to restore their real wages. The governments then were forced to accept a process of accelerating monetary growth and depreciation as the price of maintaining employment at the desired level (Flanagan, Soskice, and Ulman 1983, p. 655).

Even in countries with dependent central banks, worker militancy was not always decisive in the setting of monetary policy. As these countries' external positions deteriorated, pressures for more restrictive monetary policies came to outweigh the pressures for monetary expansion. But the duration of these stabilization policies remained limited without union acquiescence. Thus, the restrictive monetary policies which both France and Italy put into effect in 1974 were jettisoned in favour of excessively expansionary policies in 1975 – under pressure from the unions (as well as political parties running for re-election).

As the 1970s wore on, two factors contributed to a general decline in the bargaining position of labour. First, the rise in unemployment levels reduced labour's bargaining power. Second, continued external pressures tended to weaken governments' concern with maintaining full employment (Flanagan, Soskice and Ulman 1983, p. 689).

Labour power continued to weaken in the early 1980s, as unemployment remained high, union membership began to fall, and labour solidarity declined. Although these changes had little influence on the course of German monetary policy due to the Bundesbank's independence, they, along with renewed external pressures, hindered labour's ability to influence the course of monetary policy in both France and Italy. In France, as the Mitterrand programme demonstrated, monetary policy was at times still used to accommodate higher wages or to reduce unemployment. However, the adoption of this policy lay more in the change in political leadership, than in pressure from a powerful working class. When the Socialist government switched its economic policy in the face of the 1983 balance of payments crisis, labour did not constrain its actions (*International Herald Tribune*, 28 March 1983; Bauchard p. 162).

In Italy, the most vivid demonstration of the central bank's ability to resist labour pressure was the Fiat episode of 1980. In the spring of 1980, Giovanni Agnelli, the head of Fiat, came to the Banca d'Italia and told Governor Ciampi that a devaluation of the lira (in the EMS) was necessary to ensure the competitiveness of Italy's auto manufacturers. Ciampi rejected any change in the lira's central rate, arguing that Fiat should push ahead with its restructuring programme rather than rely on the temporary effects of a devaluation (interviews). With no devaluation in sight, Fiat realized that it had no alternative but to go ahead full speed with the restructuring plan it had been developing, which included provisions to automate production and lay off 14,469 workers. In September, the unions responded with a strike that turned into 'the single most serious industrial stoppage in post-war Italy' (*Financial Times*, 25 September and 24 October 1980). On 14 October, a massive counter-demonstration of Fiat workers demanding the right to work, known as the March of the 40,000, brought an end to the strike, thereby enabling Fiat to undertake its restructuring plans (Flanagan, Soskice and Ulman 1983, p. 559).

Fiat's resistance to the labour unrest was undoubtedly facilitated by the decline in the power of the trade unions during the late 1970s. But the decline in trade-union power was itself partly due to the central bank's policy of refusing to accommodate wage pressures, which contributed to the weakening of the unions' bargaining position. In the words of a senior

Banca d'Italia offical: 'If we had continued to tell Fiat, "we will devalue as much as you want, when you want"', the March of the 40,000 probably would not have taken place' (interview). After 1981, the grant of independence to the Banca d'Italia cemented the central bank's ability to assign a lower priority to employment as a goal of monetary policy.

Labour power and militancy thus helps account for variations in monetary policy across both nations and time. Countries with less-militant working classes are more able to conduct restrictive monetary policies than are countries with highly militant working classes. But even when labour is highly organized, central bank independence will make it possible to pursue restrictive monetary policies.

THE IMPORTANCE OF CENTRAL BANK INDEPENDENCE

Within the confines of the international system, the degree of central bank independence from the government plays a crucial role in the monetary policymaking process. It acts as an intermediate variable which determines whether or not monetary policy is influenced by domestic politics. Dependent central banks enable political parties, electoral pressures, and labour to influence policy. Independent central banks dampen the effect of those variables on the monetary policymaking process.

Measuring the degree of independence requires the examination of the laws governing the organization and the operations of the central bank. Five criteria are especially important: the legal ordering of authority, the proportion of central bank board members appointed by the government, their term of office, the limits on the direct financing of government deficits, and the regulations concerning central bank purchase of government bills (see Table 7.4).[18]

The first criterion – the legal ordering of authority – focuses on the relative powers of the government and the central bank in the formation and implementation of monetary policy.[19] In France, policymaking power is vested in the National Credit Council, which is chaired by and reflects the views of the Treasury minister. The Banque de France advises the government on policy issues and executes its decisions. In Italy, the central bank proposes policy changes, but they must be approved by the Treasury minister in order to take effect. By contrast, the German central bank is unambiguously in charge of monetary policy. Its principal function is to safeguard the currency; in so far as is consistent with this function, the Bundesbank is 'required to support the general economic policy of the Federal Government'.[20]

Government influence over the course of monetary policy can also be exercised through its powers of appointment and removal. Indicators for these powers are the proportion of the central bank board members

Table 7.4 Elements of central bank independence

	France	Germany	Italy
Final legal authority for monetary policy	government	central bank	government
Proportion of central bank policy board members appointed by government[1]	3 of 3	10 of 21	4 of 4
Terms of members	at discretion of government	8 years	at discretion of government
Limits on central bank direct financing of the government (% of 1982 expenditures)	1%	2.3%	14.0%
Regulations concerning central bank financing of government through purchases of government bills	Central bank does not purchase bills on primary market, but will purchase all Treasury bills presented for refinancing by the banking system	Central bank prohibited from purchasing bills on primary market	Until 1981, central bank obligated to purchase gov't debt at primary auction. After 1981, central bank freed from obligation.

Source: Hans Aufricht, *Central banking legislation*, vol. II: Europe, The International Monetary Fund, 1967; Robin Bade and Michael Parkin, 'Central bank laws and monetary policy', Department of Economics, University of Western Ontario, March 1978, (Mimeo.); Banca d'Italia, *Bolletino economico* October 1983, pp. 56–60.
Note
[1] For France and Italy, the relevant board is the Directorate. For Germany, it is the Central Bank Council.

directly appointed by the government and the tenure of those appointments. In both France and Italy, the government appoints, and can remove at will, all members of the central bank directorates.[21] In Germany, only ten of the 21 members of the central bank council can be nominated by federal government; the other 11 members consist of the presidents of the Länd central banks who are nominated by the Länder governments. Central bank council members serve for eight-year terms and can only be removed for cause.

Finally, the degree of central-bank independence is influenced by the extent to which the central bank must finance government deficits. Financing can occur either when the government draws upon a pre-established overdraft facility or when the central bank purchases Treasury bills at auction. In France, limits on the direct financing of the government through its overdraft account are determined twice a year, as a function of the changes in the value of foreign exchange reserves. In 1982, the limit equalled approximately 1 per cent of the government's total expenditures. The Banque de France does not purchase Treasury bills at auction. However since the central bank will purchase all Treasury bills presented to it by the banking sector, it effectively provides the government's desired level of financing. In Germany, the Bundesbank is allowed to provide up to DM 6 billion in credit to the government (equivalent to 2.3 per cent of the 1982 expenditures), but only for the purposes of covering temporary seasonal imbalances. The central bank is prohibited from purchasing Treasury bills on the primary market. In Italy, the Treasury is able to draw the equivalent of 14 per cent of its annual expenditures from its overdraft facility at the central bank. Prior to 1981, the Banca d'Italia was also obligated to purchase all Treasury bills that were not placed at auction; after what became known as the divorce between the Banca d'Italia and the Treasury in 1981, the central bank was freed from that obligation, in effect allowing the central bank greater influence over the process of monetary creation.

When all five criteria are compared, a clear distinction emerges between the central banks of France and Germany. The former is dependent, the latter independent. The Banca d'Italia bridged the gap between these two positions, shifting from clear dependence in the 1970s to somewhat greater independence after the divorce in 1981.

The importance of central bank independence arises because of the different policy preferences of governments and central banks. In contrast with government officials, central bankers tend to be more concerned with the risks of inflation than with the costs of unemployment. References to protecting the public from the evils of inflation abound in the speeches of senior central bankers. In the words of Jelle Zijlstra, the former president of the Netherlands' central bank: 'We central bankers should remain intent on what I see as our primary task – irrespective of the many differences in our statutory positions – to be the guardians of the integrity of money.'[22] What are the sources of this conservative ethos which pervades central banks?

Several explanations have been suggested. One focuses on the bureaucratic attributes and interests of central banks. According to this view, the principal goals of central banks are to increase its income and prestige. Lafay and Aubin, for example, have argued that a central bank, like any bureaucracy, 'will seek to maximize both its discretionary budget and, in the long term, the net value of its trust capital' (Aubin and Lafay p. 6). As they see it, conducting an anti-inflationary policy serves both purposes. First, higher interest rates increase the central bank's financial receipts and foreign balances. Second, the bank's trust capital, or prestige, rises with its ability to maintain price stability and orderly market conditions.

Neither strand of the bureaucratic argument is completely convincing, however. It is not clear that a central bank must pursue a restrictive monetary policy to increase its revenues. Since a central bank's income depends upon the interest it earns on government securities, it may also have an incentive to purchase government securities, which loosens monetary policy (Toma 1982; Shughart and Tollison 1983). But whatever the monetary policy a central bank needs to pursue to increase its income, there appears to be little gain in doing so: all central banks are required to pay their residual profits to their respective governments (Bade and Parkin 1978, p. 16). The second strand of the argument – which predicts that central bankers will seek to lower inflation without provoking financial instability – at least conforms to the stated policy preferences of central bankers. Yet it does not explain why central bank prestige depends on reducing inflation, rather than increasing growth or enhancing profitability.

This problem can be better understood by focusing on the central bank's long-standing ties to the financial community. As John Woolley has explained: 'Central banks were not created for the purpose of macroeconomic stabilization. On the contrary, in every Western setting central banks emerged as a response to needs for a central institution to serve other banks' (Woolley 1986, p. 319). Their principal task was to ensure the stability of the credit system (Ciocca 1983, p. 15). Not surprisingly, the views of central bankers closely mirrored the concerns of the financial community.

Commercial banks seem to hold two conflicting views on the role of monetary policy. On the one hand, bank profits decline in periods of unexpected inflation. Banks are typically net-creditors – that is, institutions whose monetary assets exceed their liabilities. During periods of unexpected inflation, the net value of their financial holdings falls. For this reason, bankers oppose inflation and support generally more restrictive monetary policies. On the other hand, bank profits can also be sharply affected by abrupt changes in monetary policy. A steep and unanticipated tightening of monetary policy, for example, may force banks to borrow money (either from the central bank or on the money market) at a higher rate than the one at which they loaned it. Therefore, Woolley explains, 'bankers may care relatively little about the ease or tightness of monetary policy so long as they are not caught by surprise by sudden shifts in policy' (Woolley 1986, pp. 71–72).

These two views reflect different time horizons. In the short term, bankers appear willing to accept inflation in order to maintain market stability. Indeed, through the process of financial innovation, bankers have found ways to increase profits in an inflationary environment. But in the long run, 'rising inflation can be a major threat to the stability of the financial system and the efficient operation of the economic system. Inflation induces a flight from nominal assets into ones which maintain their real value, causes large portfolio swings and hampers the efficient operation of the price mechanism' (Bingham 1985, pp. 48–9). Although banks may lose when monetary policy is abruptly tightened, their long-term interests depend upon the ability of central banks to control inflation and maintain stability in the financial system. In this sense, central banks can be seen (and indeed, see themselves) as providers of a public good which banks, on their own, are unable to supply (Kindleberger 1978, chap. 4).

Governments are not unaware of the importance of price stability, but, as we saw in earlier sections, they are less willing than central banks to sub-jugate growth and employment to the fight against inflation. This does not mean that the relationship between central banks and governments is al-ways conflicting. The interaction of fiscal and monetary policy creates a strong incentive for the two authorities to coordinate their actions. But conflicts do occur.

These conflicts tend to be incremental in nature. Most often, the disagree-ments between governments and central banks focus on the amount or the timing of a monetary-policy decision: Should monetary policy be loosened now or next month? Should interest rates be lowered by one point or one half a point? The stakes of any particular decision may seem small, but such disagreements, cumulatively, have a strong impact on the course of monetary policy.

Disagreements between governments and central banks are most likely to occur in three types of circumstances. The first relates to the phase of the business cycle. Woolley notes:

As a period of expansion lengthens and evidence accumulates that full employment is being reached or that inflation is accelerating, central bankers, who place greater stress on evidence of growing inflation pressure, would be ready to tighten more quickly and more firmly than would fiscal authorities. Similarly, after a downturn or in a recession, fiscal policymakers would be ready to reverse course and to begin stimulating the economy sooner than the central bankers who would prefer to continue to wring the inflationary pressures out.

(Woolley 1983, p. 330)

The second relates to currency depreciation. The value of a country's currency can fall for a number of reasons. Often, depreciation is necessary to restore the competitiveness of a country's goods in foreign markets. Yet, it also has a strong effect on domestic prices. As the value of a country's currency falls, the price of its imports – and its overall price level – rises. Central bankers would be more concerned than governments with this effect and, regardless of the phase of the business cycle, be inclined to tighten monetary policy more quickly to limit it.

Third, even in the absence of significant internal or external economic problems, conflicts between the government and central bank can be caused by the government's desire to use monetary policy to stimulate a boom prior to an election.

These kinds of conflicts arose in all three countries. How they were re-solved hinged largely upon the degree of central bank independence. On the whole, the dependent central banks conformed to the government's agenda. Even the Bank of Italy which appeared quite influential in the 1970s (prior to the divorce) could not supplant the government's policy preferences with its own. Independent central banks, on the other hand, succeeded in pursuing policies which differed from those preferred by the government (disproving the notion that independent central banks merely serve as scapegoats for unpopular policies).[23] After the divorce, for example, the Bank of Italy became able to raise interest rates above the levels desired by the government. The Bundesbank was also able to resist government pressures to loosen monetary policy.[24]

This conclusion leads to two more fundamental questions: why do central banks become independent, and why is their independence preserved?

There is no simple answer to the first question. Beyond noting that the domestic balance of power must tip in favour of those opposing inflation, the conditions under which central banks gain their independence appear to differ across countries. These differences were quite apparent in the experiences of the German and Italian central banks. In Germany, the independent status of the Bundesbank can be attributed to Germany's defeat in the Second World War. Believing that the earlier dependence of the Reichsbank had led to the disastrous developments in the German economy, the allied powers and Germany's post-war leaders considered it essential for the central bank to be independent of all political bodies, including the federal government.[25] In Italy, the government decided to enlarge the Banca d'Italia's independence in the hope that this would help reduce its deficit – a move that was facilitated by the development of financial markets which could absorb government debt (Goodman 1987, pp. 181–95).

Central bank independence is not, however, etched in stone. It is guaranteed only by law or by agreement. In light of the conflicts that arise between governments and central banks, one would expect that governments would at times be inclined to reduce their independence. That governments made no such legislative efforts during the period under study undoubtedly reflects the significant resources which central banks can bring to bear to resist government pressures and put their own policies into effect.

Central banks possess two important resources which strengthen their hands *vis-à-vis* the government: technical expertise and a powerful constituency (Woolley 1983, pp. 338–40). The central bank's technical expertise gives it the ability to provide authoritative analyses and interpretations of recent economic developments, which it then can use to defend, and gain public support for, its preferred policies. Indeed, central banks quite consciously seek to influence public opinion through the press. One German central banker explained: 'From 1948, we made a very deliberate policy of getting the public on our side.... We attempted through all our publications and our speeches to explain our policies to the public and to convince them. . . . By explaining everything and making a very deliberate effort, we never came to the situation where a major party has ever attempted to touch our autonomy' (interview).

A central bank's independence is also bolstered by the support of its strong, and natural constituency – the financial community. More than any other group, bankers oppose inflation and support the policies preferred by the central bank.[26] They enjoy a great deal of political influence which can be mobilized in case of conflict. But more important is their power in economic affairs. The appearance of pressure on the central bank to adopt an inflationary policy can generate a loss of confidence in the financial and foreign exchange markets.[27] The more developed the financial markets, the more significant the resulting financial crisis for the national economy. Since all governments are concerned with macroeconomic performance, the prospect of financial crisis acts as a potent deterrent to twisting the arm of the central bank. Although the support of the financial community, along with technical expertise, may not be sufficient to create an independent central bank, they nonetheless can help an already independent central bank to maintain its status.

But if governments have been inhibited from changing the rules or laws establishing central bank independence, they have nonetheless sought to influence central bank behaviour through the appointment process. In both Italy and Germany, for example, governments sought to appoint central bank governors and board members whom they thought would be especially sympathetic to the governments' views. Here, too, central banks have developed means to resist political encroachment. As the Italian government's failed attempt to nominate Ferdinando Ventriglia as governor of the Banca d'Italia in 1975 showed, central banks have been able to mobilize external support to prevent certain nominations (Goodman 1987, pp. 151–3). Internally, central banks have also developed operating procedures which quickly integrate new appointees and transfer their loyalties to the central bank. German governments, for example, have often been surprised by the rapidity of this transition. Karl Otto Pohl, the current president of the Bundesbank, is a case in point. Pohl had served as an assistant to Helmut Schmidt in the early 1970s. Many viewed his appointment as an attempt to moderate the Bundesbank's restrictive monetary policy. However, as president, Pohl quickly asserted his independence and resisted pressure from Bonn – a switch that one central bank council wryly referred to as 'the Beckett effect' (interview). Another central bank council member recalled that whenever an SPD government minister made a strong argument at a central bank council meeting, 'one could be pretty sure that there was a counter-reaction on the part of the central bank council so as not to let it appear as if they were under pressure. And even those members who were SPD party members – and there were always four or five who were members – they always voted against it [i.e. the government's view]' (interview, Goodman 1987, pp. 302–322).

This does not imply that independent central banks can isolate monetary policy completely from partisan politics. Central banks are aware that lengthy disputes with governments and extremely unpopular monetary policies can jeopardize their independence.[28] For this reason, they will on occasion decide to comply with government pressures. This suggests that an independent central bank's power is not unlimited. Yet, the resources which it possesses allows it significant freedom from short-term political pressures.[29]

Independent and dependent central banks therefore do differ in their ability to resist political pressures and to impose their own monetary policies. But what is the effect of this difference on the conduct of monetary policy? The answer depends upon the importance of the external constraint. In the absence of external pressures, independent central banks will tend to practice what might be called a thermostat approach to monetary policy. That is, the central bank tightens monetary policy when the economy heats up and loosens monetary policy when the economy cools down (and inflationary pressures abate). Of course, independence is not a guarantee that central banks will not make mistakes.[30] But the evidence presented in this chapter indicates that central bank independence does contribute to the pursuit of a more anti-inflationary monetary policy. Dependent central banks, on the other hand, show greater variance in the kind of monetary policy they pursue. Their divergence from the straight thermostat approach, depends upon the settings of the political variables which weigh upon it.[31] In general, these pressures will contribute to a more expansionary monetary policy. Yet as governments have come to recognize the importance of the external constraint, they have more frequently resisted pressures to adopt such policies. Still, until such time as world capital markets are completely integrated, the politics of monetary policy will continue to be determined by the degree of central bank independence.

NOTES

1. I am grateful to James E. Alt, Sherri L. Wasserman Goodman, Robert O. Keohane, Robert D. Putnam, and Ambrogio Rinaldi for comments on this chapter. I would also like to thank the many officials who spoke to me about the formation of monetary policy in their countries on the condition that their comments should not be attributed.
2. Reaction-function models assume that both the preferences of the policymakers and the structural constraints on policy remain constant over time. This assumption is necessary since each coefficient in the equation implicitly contains estimates about both preferences and constraints. If preferences and constraints

remain constant over time, this technique works well. However, if either changes, the equation becomes difficult to interpret, and these difficulties are even more significant in a cross-national comparison. On some of the problems associated with reaction-function analysis, see James E. Alt and K. Alec Chrystal, 1983, ch. 6.

3. The reasons for this methodological choice are discussed in greater detail in John B. Goodman, 'The politics of monetary policy in France, Italy, and Germany, 1973–1985', Ph.D. dissertation, Harvard University, 1987, pp. 44–9.

4. Richard Cooper distinguishes between integration which 'refers to a single product over space' and interdependence which 'refers to the high substitutability of many products over space. In practice, high integration of markets, one by one, is necessary for high interdependence, but does not assure it'. See Richard N. Cooper, *Economic interdependence and co-ordination of economic policies*, 1985, p. 1199.

5. Between January 1977 and March 1978, the D-Mark rose by nearly 19 per cent against the dollar, rising from DM 2.4/dollar to DM 1.99/dollar (Deutsche Bundesbank, *Report for the year 1977*, p. 43).

6. These conclusions, based upon a simulation carried out with the econometric model of the Bundesbank, are reported in the Bundesbank's background paper for the G-7 working group on exchange rates, entitled, 'Intervention policy, monetary management and the final goals of economic policy', p. 24. As expected, the monetary targets for 1977 and 1978 were overshot by 1 per cent and 3.5 per cent, respectively.

7. Italy withdrew from the snake in 1973. France withdrew in 1974, rejoined in 1975, and pulled out again in 1976. On the history of the snake, see Loukas Tsoukalis (1977).

8. This behaviour is very similar to what Thomas C. Schelling described as the power to bind one-self: 'The government that cannot control its balance of payments, or collect taxes, or muster the political unity to defend itself, may enjoy assistance that would be denied if it could control its own resources.' Thomas C. Schelling, *The strategy of conflict* London: Oxford University Press, 1960, p. 23.

9. Although Italy's decision to enter the EMS was probably due more to general foreign policy concerns than to the country's economic dependency, membership in the fixed exchange-rate system nonetheless institutionalized the growing recognition of the external constraint on domestic policy (see Spaventa 1980).

10. William Nordhaus (1975, pp. 169–90). For a useful review of the political business-cycle literature, see Alt and Chrystal, *Political economics*, chapter 6. Statistical studies on political business-cycle behaviour in European countries have reached conflicting results. Woolley in 'Political factors in monetary policy' found no evidence of political monetary cycles in France and Britain, and only weak evidence in Germany. In contrast, Christian Aubin and Jean-Dominique Lafay found that monetary policy in France *was* loosened prior to elections; see, 'Monetary targets and positive monetary policy: an empirical analysis on monthly French data (1974–1984)', Université de Poitiers Centre de Recherche et d'Analyse Politico-Economiques, December 1985 (mimeographed).

11. *Programme commun de gouvernement du Parti Communiste et du Parti Socialiste* Paris: Flammarion, 1973.

12. Aubin and Lafay conclude that the behaviour of private economic agents may overwhelm the government's desire to manipulate the economy in the election period. Christian Aubin and Jean-Dominique Lafay, 'The positive approach to monetary policy: an empirical study of the French case 1967–1981', Université

de Poitiers Institut de Recherche et d'Analyse Politico-Economique, Poitiers, France.

13. Between 1973 and 1985, the three parliamentary elections (1976, 1979, and 1983) were all called before the end of the Parliament's five-year tenure.

14. In the 1975 regional elections, the DC received 35.3 per cent of the vote, the PCI 33.4 per cent, and the PSI 12 per cent (compared to 38.8, 27.2, and 9.6 per cent respectively, in the 1972 parliamentary elections). As a result, control of a number of regional and local governments shifted to the PCI. See Norman Kogan, *A political history of Italy*, New York: Praeger, 1983, pp. 289–90.

15. See, for example, the comments in *Frankfurter Allgemeine Zeitung*, 19 Feb. 1979; *Borsen-Zeitung*, 20 Jan. 1979; *Die Welt*, 20 Jan. 1979; and *Handelsblatt*, 22 Jan. 1979.

16. Woolley has found, for example, that interest rates under both presidents were lower 'than would have been suggested by economic targets alone'. Woolley, *Political factors in monetary policy*, p. 189.

17. The number of governmental changes is deceptive, since in many of the changes, the prime minister succeeded himself, or the same governing coalition remained in power. A list of all governments can be found in Mark Kesselman, *et al., European politics in transition*, Lexington, Mass.: D.C. Heath and Co., 1987, pp. 378–9.

18. This list does not include other factors – such as the existence of external budget controls – which do not vary across the three countries in this study. For contrasting views on the effect of organizational characteristics on central bank independence, see Robin Bade and Michael Parkin, 'Central bank laws and monetary policy', Department of Economics, University of Western Ontario, March 1978 (mimeographed); and John T. Woolley, 'Central banks and inflation', in Leon N. Lindberg and Charles S. Maier (1984) pp. 318–48.

19. On the organization, procedures, and powers of the central banks of France, Italy, and Germany, see Hans Aufricht, *Central banking legislation*, vols I and II, Washington, D.C.: The International Monetary Fund, 1967; Banque de France, *La Banque de France et la monnaie*, Paris: Banque de France, 1983; Rolf Caesar, *Der Handlungsspielraum von Notenbanken*, Baden-Baden: Nomos Verlagsgesellschaft, 1981, chapters 4, 7, and 9; Deutsche Bundesbank, *The Deutsche Bundesbank: its monetary policy instruments and functions*, special series no. 7 Frankfurt a.M.: Deutsche Bundesbank, 1982; and Antonio Finocchiaro and Alberto M. Contessa, *La Banca d'Italia e i problemi del governo della moneta*, Rome: Banca d'Italia, 1984.

20. Article 12 of the Deutsche Bundesbank Act, translated in Deutsche Bundesbank, *The Deutsche Bundesbank: its monetary policy instruments and functions*, pp. 97–8.

21. The French Council of Ministers also appoints nine of the ten members of the central bank's General Council to serve for six-year terms, but this body plays little role in the monetary policymaking process. See Rolf Caesar, *Der Handlungsspielraum von Notenbanken*, p. 320.

22. Jelle Zijlstra, 'Central banking with the benefit of hindsight', the 1981 Per Jacobson Lecture, Washington, D.C.: Per Jacobson Foundation, 1981, p. 19.

23. The scapegoat hypothesis has been advanced by Edward J. Kane in 'Politics and Fed policymaking: the more things change, the more they remain the same', *Journal of monetary economics* 6, April 1980: 199–211; and in 'External pressures and the operations of the Fed', in *Political economy of international and domestic monetary relations*, (ed.) Raymond E. Lombra and Willard E. Witte, Ames: Iowa State University Press, 1982, pp. 211–32.

24. Similar findings for the United States are reported by Woolley in *Monetary politics: the federal reserve and the politics of monetary policy*, pp. 191–2. These conflicts call into question the Frey and Schneider model, which assumes that 'when the policies of the central bank and those of the government conflict ... the government will force the central bank to change its policy and to support the government's goal'. Bruno S. Frey and Friedrich Schneider, 'Central bank behavior: a positive empirical analysis', *Journal of monetary economics* 7, 1981: pp. 294.

25. Germany's previous experience with central bank independence also occurred as a result of foreign pressure. After the First World War, the allies became concerned that 'the German government was consciously destroying its currency to demonstrate its ability to pay the war reparations' and urged the Parliament to make the Reichsbank independent. Herbert Giersch and Harment Lehment, 'Monetary policy: does independence make a difference? – The German experience', Institut für Weltwirtschaft an der Universität Kiel, *Kiel Sonderdrucke*, 100, 1981, pp. 9–10.

26. This relationship is not necessarily a static one. Policies pursued by an independent central bank can create or shape the interests of bankers. For example, the Bundesbank long rejected the introduction of variable rate notes in Germany. This policy reduced the profit-making possibilities of banks in inflationary periods.

27. The collapse of the lira in early 1976 provided a telling example of this phenomenon.

28. As Frey and Schneider argue: 'In the long run the government has the means to overrule the central bank, these ranging from dismissal of the central bank's president and members of the governing board and their replacement with more compliant people, to the threat of completely taking over its functions': 'Central bank behaviour: a positive empirical analysis', pp. 294–5.

29. A similar argument is made by students of international regimes. The creation of international regimes, such as the GATT, reflects a particular international balance of power. But once created, regimes structure domestic interests, which enable them to continue to exist, even after that original balance of power has changed or shifted. See, for example, Robert O. Keohane, *After hegemony: cooperation and discord in the world political economy*, Princeton: Princeton University Press, 1984; and Judith Goldstein, 'The political economy of trade: institutions of protection', *American political science review* 80, March 1986, pp. 161–84.

30. Giersch and Lehment note, for example, that in 1922 the legally independent Reichsbank 'continued to finance government expenditures through the printing press .... There was an apparent incapability on the part of the Reichsbank to recognize the fact that monetary expansion was the main reason for the inflation'. See 'Monetary policy: does independence make a difference? – The German experience', p. 10. Monetarists argue that central banks are bound to make mistakes and therefore recommend the adoption of a strict monetary rule. For an overview of monetarist thought, see Thomas Mayer, (ed.), *The structure of monetarism*, New York: Norton, 1978.

31. As Alt and Chrystal note: 'The diverse inflation performances of the ... countries [with dependent central banks] reveal that there are limits to the explanatory power of the formal constitution of the central bank alone', *Political economics*, pp. 47–8.

8 · MACROECONOMIC POLICY PREFERENCES AND CO-ORDINATION: A VIEW FROM GERMANY

Elke Thiel

THE POLITICAL ECONOMY OF FOREIGN ECONOMIC POLICY OF THE FEDERAL REPUBLIC OF GERMANY

Introduction

The focus of this chapter is on German macroeconomic preferences and fundamental traits that have guided German macroeconomic policy. The analysis will first focus on German macroeconomic policy preferences in times of conflicting domestic and external economic objectives. Based on the findings of this first part the second part of the analysis will outline the main trends in German policy within the EMS. Conclusions will be confined to controversies concerning the means and ends of macroeconomic policy co-ordination as well as to some basic positions of the overall project regarding German policy within the EMS.

GERMAN MACROECONOMIC POLICY IN VIEW OF EXTERNAL DISEQUILIBRIUM

The German part in macroeconomic policy co-ordination has not always met expectations abroad. German economic policy has been considered to be too restrictive in view of sustained current-account surpluses and relatively low inflation. 'Over-sensitiveness' regarding inflation has been the main reason for German reluctance to indulge in a more expansionary macroeconomic policy co-ordination within the Group of Seven and within the EMS as well.

At the time of Bretton Woods, German exports largely benefited from periods of real D-Mark under-valuation. Although circumstances have changed considerably since the introduction of floating exchange rates, it is still suspected that German macroeconomic policy supports export-led growth. Strong German efforts to adjust the current-account deficit in 1979–81 and less concern to reduce current-account surpluses may have enforced this view. The emphasis of analysis is, however, not on the question of whether German policy could have done or could do better. The pre-eminent question is how German economic preferences correspond with co-operative endeavours abroad, i.e. on the part of Group of Seven countries, but primarily within the EMS community.

Price stability objectives

There is no way to speak about German macroeconomic policy without mentioning German sensitivity regarding inflation. Since Germany has experienced two periods of extensive inflation after World War One and World War Two, price stability has always been the dominant political priority. Price stability is considered as an indispensable means to secure a social consensus regarding income distribution, to protect private savings and to prevent creditors from deprivation. This objective has always been strongly supported by all domestic groups, including the trade unions.

The German Bundesbank is committed to defend price stability by constitution and its status of autonomy provides the political independence to enforce this goal. All German governments have been very cautious to avoid any open conflict with the Bundesbank on monetary policy issues. Moreover, governments have been strongly aware that increasing inflation will erode confidence in the ruling coalitions and may thus endanger re-election.

When Chancellor Ludwig Erhard left office in December 1966 because he had lost the political support of his own party, a temporary increase of the inflation rate to 4 per cent at the turn of 1965 to 1966 was one of the reasons. As Chancellor Helmut Schmidt was replaced by Helmut Kohl in 1982, the federal budget deficit was a main argument in the *Wende* and the subsequent election campaign. Budgetary consolidation and a by all historical standards low (zero) inflation rate were a major asset in Chancellor Kohl's campaign for re-election in January 1987.

Short-term trade-offs between inflation and employment objectives are considered as being intolerable by the German public. It is widely assumed that inflation will not reduce unemployment, but hamper economic growth in a medium-term perspective. As long as monetary policy did not raise inflationary expectations, wage settlements have been kept broadly in line with price-stability goals.

The view that price stability is a prerequisite to a smooth functioning of the domestic economy was enforced by experiences in 1973–4, when inflation reached a peak of 7 per cent. Trade unions responded with a more aggressive wage policy because they anticipated further price increases. Government and Bundesbank officials gave strong warnings that wage increases as postulated in the range of 15 to 20 per cent would endanger employment.

Illusions on the part of the trade unions that the government led by the Social Democratic Party would eventually indulge in a policy shift towards economic expansion were nourished by Chancellor Willy Brand's remarks that he was not prepared to accept major risks for employment (Kloten, Barth *et al*. 1980). The government and private employers finally granted wage settlements of about 13 per cent apparently because they expected to augment their own receipts via inflationary tax or price increases (Gutowski, Hartel, Scharrer 1981). Inflation thus triggered a conflict on income distribution which again fuelled inflation.

Shortly after a path-setting wage settlement of 12 to 15 per cent had been agreed on in the public sector, the Minister of Finance and the President of the German Bundesbank commonly declared their intention to keep the inflation rate below 10 per cent by means of monetary restriction. This view was fiercely supported by the major German economic research institutes urging new efforts to bring inflation down (Kloten, Barth *et al*. 1980, p. 68). As the economic boom and inflationary expectations finally broke down at the end of 1974 the trade unions had achieved real wage increases but 1.7 million employees lost their jobs (Gutowski, Hartel, Scharrer 1981). It is widely assumed that the process of labour substitution by increasingly capital-intensive ways of production in German enterprises and the relocations of labour-intensive productions to low wage countries would have been pursued less quickly if wage settlements had been more moderate.

The events of 1974 proved the firm commitment of the Bundesbank not to accommodate excessive wage settlements. It further revealed that inflation does not solve social conflicts but will even endanger social consensus. It strengthened the view that the government could not guarantee full employment but that the trade unions had to bear employment responsibility by moderate wage settlements as well. Most important, this lesson had been taught when the Social Democrats led the ruling coalition and may thus help to explain why macroeconomic policy perceptions do not really differ so much from one government to the other. The general conclusion for German economic policy, however, was that it has to follow a more steady and predicable path to which private economic decisions were to adjust (Kloten, Barth *et al*. 1980).

When the inflation rate stepped up again to a 6 per cent level in 1980, the German Bundesbank reacted timely to prevent a spread of inflationary mentality. Wage settlements are kept in a 7 per cent range, thus allowing only for a 1 per cent real-wage increase. Due to their 'painful' experiences with the stabilization crisis of 1973–4, all economic agents were obviously more prepared to adjust to monetary restriction. The announcement of monetary targets by the German Bundesbank, introduced in December

1974, was perceived and certainly helped to make monetary policy more predictable and thus to stabilize expectations.

The German policy dilemma: imported inflation

As all domestic economic agents have been generally prepared to adjust to the monetary path given by the German Bundesbank, price-stability goals have been pre-eminently endangered by imported inflation resulting from export surpluses and capital inflows since the mid 1950s. More than any other country, Germany has been faced with the policy dilemma of achieving price stability and exchange-rate stability simultaneously. Exchange-market interventions to keep the D-Mark pegged to the dollar poured hot money into the country so that the Bundesbank lost control over money supply. D-Mark appreciation offered an escape, but decisions to adjust parities were always taken too late to prevent inflationary pressures.

Why have decisions to appreciate the D-Mark been delayed despite strong inflationary pressures from abroad? Whereas the Bundesbank was obliged to intervene in the exchange market to keep the D-Mark pegged to the dollar, the final decision for parity adjustment was on the side of the German government. For obvious reasons, officials on both parts are generally very anxious not to give any hint that diverging views are held regarding such delicate questions as exchange-rate adjustments. Some further insights have been, however, revealed in a retrospect given by Otmar Emminger, former Vice-President and President of the German Bundesbank (Emminger 1976).

Strong market pressures on the D-Mark first occurred in 1956–7 and resurged in 1960. It is quite interesting to see that Ludwig Erhard, then Minister of Economics, was by far the main proponent of parity adjustment, strongly opposed by Chancellor Konrad Adenauer and a majority on the part of the Bundesbank. The main arguments against appreciation can be summarized as follows:

Trade surpluses were largely considered as a cyclical rather than a structural phenomenon; thus a D-Mark appreciation would be premature. This view was further supported by forthcoming German commitments to large international payments, such as foreign debt repayments, reparations and development aid. Trade surpluses therefore had to be achieved in order to finance deficits in other accounts. While the D-Mark was strong in comparison with other European currencies, the German balance-of-payments position was considered to be still rather fragile with respect to the dollar area in view of a pre-scheduled capital liberalization in 1956, aimed to achieve the full convertibility of the D-Mark, formally announced at the end of 1958.

In the course of events, support for D-Mark appreciation increased on the part of the Bundesbank because it turned out that accommodating inflation was the alternative. After all efforts to counter inflationary pressures by monetary restriction had failed, the Bundesbank gave way to a policy of internal adjustment by lowering interest rates in autumn 1960. Her obvious 'capitulation' finally raised serious concern in Bonn and thus helped to pave the way for a 5 per cent D-Mark appreciation in March 1961. 'This was one of the rare cases that a Bundesbank decision for monetary expansion was met by open resistance of the government' (Emminger 1976, p. 506). Appreciation came, however, too late to prevent domestic price increases.

While early reluctance to achieve the first D-Mark appreciation is quite understandable in view of prevailing uncertainties, the delayed decision to appreciate the D-Mark in October 1969 caused more suspicion that German interests in exports were the main reason for resistance. The second D-Mark appreciation of 9.3 per cent took place shortly after the German federal election when the social – liberal coalition came to government and the issue was most fiercely disputed domestically. In view of past experiences, the Bundesbank strongly emphasized a timely D-Mark appreciation as early as September 1968. This was, however, rejected by the Minister of Economics, Karl Schiller, who was then in charge of monetary affairs before this authority was transferred to the Ministry of Finance (Emminger 1976, p. 517).

As massive inflows of hot money urged for an immediate decision in the following month, the Great Coalition of the Christian Democrats and the Social Democrats was deeply divided on this issue. When Minister Schiller, a Social Democrat, turned to support a D-Mark appreciation for price stability goals the pros and cons became a dominant issue in the federal election campaign. The German academic community participated in this debate, submitting strong arguments for a D-Mark appreciation and for exchange-rate flexibility as well.

The German economy had experienced a recession in 1966 and had recovered in early 1967. The economic upswing was first supported by fiscal expansion and then pushed by strong export demand. Apparently, opponents to a D-Mark appreciation on the part of the German administration favoured an export-led boom in accordance with the export interests of German industries and commercial banks. If the D-Mark was not revalued, however, the Bundesbank would turn to monetary restriction to counter imported inflation. Efforts to resist market pressures for a D-Mark revaluation would benefit export industries, but the burden would be borne by the domestic sector of the economy. Private and public domestic investments would be hampered by a more restrictive monetary policy and by measures aimed to encourage capital outflows in compensation of trade surpluses.[1]

German trade surplus had increased to 3 per cent of GNP in 1967–8, compared with a trade surplus of 1 per cent to 1.5 per cent of GNP, set as a target for external equilibrium in the medium-term projection for economic policy given by the government.[2] In view of such large external imbalances, the Council of Economic Advisers recommended a 5 per cent D-Mark appreciation as being neutral to business-cycle performances. Declining exports would initially have to be compensated for by public investments. D-Mark appreciation would, however, enforce international competition and support price stability. This would help to keep wage settlements on a moderate path. More favourable conditions for domestic investments would then soon step up economic activities.[3]

Domestic controversies on parity adjustment lasted for several months and the German public became more aware of and informed on the issue. When the question of parity adjustment was first raised in the late 1950s, uncertainty prevailed regarding the implications of a D-Mark appreciation, partly because this was a very new situation. Strong efforts had been made to achieve export performance, which was considered most important for economic reconstruction and for German participation in an open world economic system. The argument that international competitiveness should not be endangered by a premature revaluation seemed to be very plausible. The process of looming inflation caused by a delayed parity adjustment was less obvious. The domestic debate on a D-Mark appreciation, accompanied by strong arguments for exchange-rate flexibility on the part of German economic think tanks (Kasper 1970) helped to broaden public understanding and thus to make future parity adjustments and the final suspension of fixed exchange rates more acceptable to the German public.

Resuming German policy under conditions of pegged exchange rates, the impact of sustained international divergencies in inflation rates and a comparatively restrictive German macroeconomic policy on export performances was broadly underestimated. The risks of a D-Mark appreciation were thus weighted higher than its opportunities. This bias in German macroeconomic policy turned out to collude with export industries' interests, whether it was intended or not.

Managed floating

In May 1971, large capital inflows from the dollar area triggered the German decision to let the D-Mark float upwards temporarily, just before President Nixon suspended the dollar–gold convertibility in August 1971. Exchange-rate flexibility was broadly favoured as an appropriate means to enhance German autonomy in achieving low-inflation goals by subsequent D-Mark revaluations. In view of American intentions to reduce the current-account deficits, a D-Mark revaluation would help to adjust international imbalances (Muller-Groeling 1971; Giersch 1971).

With the introduction of managed floating in early 1973, the German Bundesbank gained discretion to defend price-stability goals (Pohl 1985, pp. 73–82). D-Mark appreciations were promptly achieved by market forces and could thus no longer be delayed by domestic controversies. From the end of 1972 to the end of 1975, the D-Mark rose by 15 per cent on a trade-weighted average and experienced a further 15 per cent appreciation in the course of 1976. The current-account surplus was steadily reduced to 0.7 per cent of GNP in 1977 (Bundesbank 1978, p. 37). In the first years of floating, the German economy experienced a 'virtuous circle'. Despite an extensive D-Mark revaluation export competitiveness remained high because domestic costs and prices benefited from relatively low domestic inflation, supported by currency appreciation, to such an extent that detrimental effects of revaluation on international competitiveness were largely compensated for (Bundesbank 1977, p. 31).

The stabilizing impact of D-Mark appreciations on domestic prices has always been considered as an advantage on the part of the German Bundesbank. But even under conditions of floating, it has turned out that the fundamental dilemma facing German economic policy in the 1950s and 1960s has not been solved. Because the D-Mark is used as a reserve currency alternative to the dollar, exchange-rate fluctuations, pushed by large international capital flows, have been rather significant in certain periods. The Bundesbank lost monetary control by exchange-market interventions and tolerated an overshooting of monetary targets in order to stabilize the exchange rate.

German foreign trade amounts to a quarter of GNP. Rapid shifts in exchange rates, such as a D-Mark appreciation *vis-à-vis* the dollar of 30 per cent within one year in 1977–8, followed by a sharp D-Mark decline and a new rise of the D-Mark of more than 50 per cent in the course of two years from February 1985 to February 1987 therefore cause uncertainties for investments and high costs of adjustment for the domestic economy. German dependence on foreign trade is evidence of the close integration of the German economy in the international division of labour.

In view of a high specialization in modern production and comparatively small domestic markets, German firms have to rely on foreign markets to achieve economies of large scale. About one in five jobs depends on exports, and investment industries ship 40 per cent of their production abroad. D-Mark over-valuation thus threatens domestic economic activities and employment. A large portion of imports is confined to intra-industrial trade. German industries do thus have to compete with foreign industries in export and domestic markets as well.

German domestic production would, however, come to a halt, if it were not fuelled by imports of energy, raw materials and semi-finished products. A decline in the external value of the D-Mark therefore has an immediate effect on domestic inflation. This may help to explain recent remarks on the part of German economic officials that world economic growth is pre-eminently threatened by exchange-rate fluctuations and not by failures to achieve domestic expansion via macroeconomic policy coordination.[4]

Under conditions of floating, the Bundesbank has time and again been faced with the policy dilemma of defending price stability and calming down large exchange-rate fluctuations simultaneously. The strategy has been to keep both objectives in a delicate balance, but the dominant emphasis has been to prevent inflation.

The German commitment to economic expansion in 1978

The continuous decline of the dollar in 1977–8, accompanied by large German capital inflows from the dollar area, triggered a real D-Mark appreciation of 2.5 per cent in 1977 and another 2.5 per cent in 1978 on a trade weighted average (Bundesbank 1978, p. 20). After a 5 per cent growth in 1976, the German business-cycle slowed down in the course of 1977. Export demand weakened in 1977 in view of low economic growth abroad. The Bundesbank tolerated overshooting of monetary targets in 1977 and 1978 because of fears that a more restrictive monetary policy would hamper an upswing of the domestic economy and would push further D-Mark appreciations.[5] To stop the dollar decline, however, more decisive steps to reduce the inflation rate on the part of the US were considered indispensable.

At the international level, the ensuing debate on macroeconomic policy co-ordination focused on the locomotive approach, demanding more substantial measures to expand the domestic economy on the part of Germany and Japan to counter world economic recession. The locomotive concept was and is strongly opposed by a majority of the German economic research institutes[6] and by economic authorities as well. Objections primarily focus on the demand-side approach of the locomotive strategy and the underlying assumptions concerning the international transmission of expansionary effects as well.

With regard to the German economy it was further doubted whether a substantial switch from export demand to domestic demand was feasible at this time. In contrast to the 1960s, German trade surpluses were not caused by enduring D-Mark under-valuation but did occur despite a subsequent nominal and real revaluation of the D-Mark. The surplus of current account had already been reduced to 0.7 per cent of GNP in 1977, compared with 3 per cent of GNP in 1969. Although exports still played a decisive role in business-cycle performance, economic growth was more than in previous years supported by domestic demand in 1978 (Bundesbank 1978, p. 11). Given a high degree of specialization, export decline could not be easily compensated for by a management of domestic demand. As the Bundesbank pointed out in its annual report for 1977, further attempts to reduce the German export surplus would most probably slow down domestic economic activities and German imports as well (Bundesbank 1977, p. 37). This argument also holds for the current situation.

The German commitment to fiscal expansion amounting to about 1 per cent of GNP at the Bonn summit in July 1978 was widely criticized domestically. Due to social reforms and counter-cyclical fiscal expansion in previous years, the federal budget deficit had grown from a rather balanced federal budget in 1970 to DM 35 billion in 1975. The total public deficit[7] amounted to DM 58 billion in 1975 against a surplus of 1.4 billion in 1970. Public expenditure as a portion of GNP had steadily increased to more than 46 per cent in 1975 compared with 33 per cent in 1960. Starting in 1975, strong emphasis was therefore given to budgetary consolidation on the part of the federal government, the states and at the communities level.

With respect to the weak business cycle fiscal policy again switched to more expansionary measures in the course of 1977. As economic growth was still sluggish in spring 1978, it was speculated among the German public whether and by what means fiscal policy was to give a bolder push to economic expansion. The issue was highly controversial. Robert Putnam and Nicholas Bayne have argued that the support of the Bonn summit probably helped Chancellor Helmut Schmidt to achieve the more expansionary policy shift he favoured domestically (Putnam, Bayne 1984). German participants in the Bonn summit have emphasized that the Bonn package has to be considered as a whole. Their own commitment thus helped to bring about American commitment to deregulate oil prices, considered the most important part of the deal.

The German Council of Economic Advisers took a more critical view in its 1978–9 report. An additional fiscal expansion had been concluded although previous measures introduced in 1977 had not yet displayed their full expansionary impacts. Tax reliefs, being the main source of fiscal expansion committed in 1978, primarily pushed demand for consumption instead of improving the climate for private investments. A huge increase in public deficits was predictable.[8] Critics thus focused on the fact that fiscal expansion in pursuit of the German summit commitment was preeminently of a Keynesian type of demand management. The perception on the part of the majority of German economic think tanks, however, was that economic growth and employment had best to be supported by a supply-side oriented policy including a decreasing share of the public sector in the domestic economy.

The full effect of fiscal expansion was displayed in 1979. Budget deficits increased to 3 per cent of GNP when the German economy already boomed. This not only contributed to the turnaround of the balance of current account to a deficit in the same year but also reduced the room to manoeuvre for future fiscal expansion when economic growth turned out to be negative and unemployment increased in the following years.

Adjustment to current account deficits

In the course of 1979, the German balance of current account turned into a deficit in the wake of the second increase in oil prices. This was considered as a rather fundamental change in German external economic conditions to which the domestic economy had to adjust. The sharp decrease in export surpluses from DM 41 billion in 1978 to DM 9 billion in 1980 raised doubts about whether German firms had lost their international competitiveness and their capacity to adjust to structural change, especially with regard to strong challenges by Japanese firms in the domestic and international market.[9]

Faced with a continuous decline of the D-Mark *vis-à-vis* the dollar, adding to domestic inflation, the Bundesbank responded with monetary restriction. This course was further enforced by weak notations of the D-Mark within the EMS in 1980 and early 1981. When the D-Mark regained its strength in the EMS in the course of 1981, after a sharp rise in German interest rates, German monetary policy set the path for monetary policy of other EMS members. Although a surplus in the balance of current account was achieved in 1982, German interest rates were kept at relatively high levels in view of further declines of the D-Mark *vis-à-vis* the dollar and capital outflows triggered by high interest rates in the US and strong dollar expectations.

It is widely held that European monetary policy in response to the dollar rise has been too restrictive with respect to a severe unemployment within the European Community. In France, the newly elected government of President Mitterrand had shifted policy to expand domestic demand in mid-1981. When the French franc was subjected to exchange-market pressures and had to be depreciated a few months afterwards, it turned out that domestic expansion and lower interest rates were not to be achieved by France unilaterally. It was argued that a German reduction in interest rates should give the lead to a concerted interest-rate reduction within the EMS.

On the German part, a co-ordinated reduction of interest rates within the EMS was opposed primarily for the following reasons: given lower European interest rates, capital outflows to the dollar area would probably increase and European interest rates would then rise again as a result. Capital controls could be introduced to prevent capital outflows, but those suggestions were rejected for reasons of principle and because an effective control of international financial transactions by German authorities was not feasible. Moreover, capital regulations would erode confidence in the D-Mark as an international reserve currency (Thiel 1987, pp. 353–87).

The view that German monetary policy was too restrictive in 1980–1 was shared by German economic think tanks as well, although with a different political conclusion. Economic research institutes, the Council of

Economic Advisers and the Wissenschaftlicher Beirat, i.e. the advisory board of the German Ministry of Economics, pointed out that the Bundesbank's monetary targets were set too low to keep monetary volumes in accordance with real growth potentials.[10] It was thus recommended that monetary policy should be re-established on a potential-oriented path in line with supply-side strategies. This of course included the possibility of a still sharper D-Mark devalution in the short run. The assumption was, however, that expectations would soon turn to stabilize the external value of the D-Mark. The German inflation rate was still low compared with inflation abroad. Lower interest rates and moderate wage settlements would stimulate domestic investments. Capital outflows would come to a halt (Flic, Heinemann 1981, pp. 129–55). This strategy may, however, have required that the D-Mark had to quit the EMS at least temporarily.

The German Bundesbank followed a more a cautious path limiting monetary expansion to the extent this was to be achieved without endangering further D-Mark devaluations. In this view, the stabilization of the exchange rate was an essential part of the Bundesbank commitment to defend price stability. Import prices increased to 20 per cent in 1981 and pushed domestic inflation to 6.7 per cent. The Bundesbank was thus not prepared to take the risk of a sharper D-Mark decline, as was suggested by recommendations of a potential-oriented monetary policy. It was at least uncertain when and from what low level the D-Mark would finally catch up. In the meantime, inflation could increase considerably triggering further D-Mark declines and interest-rate increases as well (Emminger 1982).

At no time has depreciation been considered as a means to regain international competitiveness. The decline of the D-Mark in 1980 to 1985 had indicated a loss of confidence in the German economy as a place to invest. To get market support for a sustained reduction in interest rates and to encourage private investment prospects, economic growth had to be supported by domestic stability, i.e. lower inflation and budgetary consolidation.[11]

Restrictive monetary policy in adjustment to exchange market pressures may have been considered the more important than a large increase in public deficits. Although the federal government, the states and the communities had agreed to keep net expenditures at the same level as in 1980, i.e. DM 59 billion, to contribute to the adjustment of the current-account deficit and to give room for private investments, public deficits were estimated to explode to DM 80 billion or 5 per cent of GNP in 1981. Moreover, expenditures were primarily increased for consumptive purposes while public investments were severely reduced by budgetary cuts.[12] Inflation increased to 5.4 per cent in 1980 and 6.7 percent in 1981 and it was feared that monetary expansion and a sharper decline of the D-Mark would trigger trade-union demand for more substantial wage increases in compensation for inflation. Monetary policy thus had to bear the whole burden of adjustment.

Budgetary consolidation

Although it was agreed in principle that fiscal policy had to adjust to current-account deficits as well, this task was only to be achieved against strong political pressures. Economic growth was negative in 1981 and 1982 and the rate of unemployment doubled from 3.3 per cent in 1979–80 to 6.7 per cent in 1982. The trade unions pressed for employment programmes while the ruling social–liberal coalition became more and more divided on the issue of how to achieve budgetary consolidation in the course of 1982. The CDU–CSU opposition threatened a complaint to the constitutional court, claiming that the 1981 federal budget had violated article 115 of the German basic law. Under the provision of article 115, net federal debt increases are not permitted to exceed federal expenditures for public investments. The opposition thus exploited the fact that the federal budget for 1981 only accounted for public investments of DM 30.5 billion while debt increases amounted to DM 37.4 billion.[13]

In July 1982, the social–liberal coalition reached a compromise on the federal budget for 1983. Total expenditures were scheduled to increase by only 2 per cent to DM 250.5 billion, which was the lowest rate of increase ever achieved for all federal budgets in the Federal Republic. The federal budget deficit was forecast at DM 28.5 billion, just below the DM 34.5 billion deficit estimated for 1982. The general intention was to reduce expenditures for consumptive purposes and to encourage investments.

Chancellor Helmut Schmidt had to assure support of his own party for cuts in social benefits. In an essay published in *Vorwarts*, a periodical edited by the SPD, he pointed out that total payments for social transfers had increased from 25.7 per cent of GNP in 1970 to 31 per cent of GNP in 1981. The German social net had become too expensive. The share of public investments in total public expenditures decreased from 12 to 7.5 per cent at the same time. On the other hand, taxes and other duties charged on labour incomes already accounted for 30.4 per cent of the total amount of wages and salaries in 1981, compared with 22.7 per cent in 1970 (Schmidt 1982).

Budget proposals for 1983 included cuts in social payments and tax privileges while an additional DM 1.3 billion were confined to measures supporting employment. Public reaction was rather negative on both sides of the political spectrum. The trade unions proclaimed that the squeeze of expenditures primarily hurt the poor, the sick and the unemployed, and public health insurance announced protest demonstrations on behalf of their 32 million members. German business federations doubted whether budget schedules based on a 3 per cent economic growth forecast were to be achieved. The German Association of Saving Banks pointed out that total public indebtedness would soon surpass DM 600 billion. Annual interest services would then amount to DM 50 billion, i.e. 40 per cent of net private savings.[14]

Controversies regarding fiscal policy peaked in September 1982 in the wake of the parliamentary budget debate. Chancellor Helmut Schmidt had to resist party pressures for a more substantial employment programme. The Federation of German Industries demanded a decisive shift in fiscal policy, i.e. bolder cuts in social expenditures and in subsidies, tax reliefs to step up private investment and a more steady path of public investment.[15] A few days later, the liberal Minister of Economics, Graf Lambsdorff, submitted a proposal of how to achieve this turnaround,[16] widely applauded by German business circles and strongly objected to by the trade unions.[17] Divergencies regarding fiscal policy within the social-liberal coalition were a dominant reason for the *Wende* in the German government shortly afterwards.

The new government put strong efforts into budgetary consolidation. The total budget deficit was reduced from DM 65.2 billion in 1982 to DM 36 billion in 1986, i.e. 1.8 per cent of GNP, primarily by cuts in public expenditures including a slow-down in public investments. The rate of total public expenditures in GNP declined from 47.5 per cent in 1981–2 to 45.3 per cent in 1985. Lower demand for public credits helped to improve the financial conditions for private credit demands. Budgetary consolidation was furthermore considered an achievement, because it paved the way for the German tax reform without triggering a new blow-up of public deficits (Bundesbank 1984, p. 1).

The current debate on domestic expansion

German medium-term economic growth is estimated at 2 to 2.5 per cent and this will be too low to achieve a substantial reduction in the present rate of unemployment of about 8 per cent. The unemployed receive financial support by the Bundesanstalt für Arbeit, but it is a matter of serious concern in the Federal Republic that enduring individual unemployment will threaten social integration and is rather frustrating and demotivating for young people.

It is generally agreed, however, that unemployment problems cannot be solved by short-sighted employment programmes.[18] Different views are held concerning the adequate strategy to increase employment by means of structural change in a medium-term perspective. The majority of economic think tanks including the Council of Economic Advisers have recommended a market-oriented approach to achieve more sufficient economic growth: deregulation and economic openness, tax relief to encourage investments, the reduction of all kind of subsidies and more flexibility in the labour market.

The Social Democratic opposition and the trade unions have given more emphasis to working-hours reduction and to the means of achieving public investments in accordance with future social requirements, such as environmental protection, energy saving and public services.[19] Wage settlements allowed for moderate wage increases in recent years but included provisions to reduce the working time, e.g. part-time employment, pre-scheduled retirements and lower working hours. The trade unions strive for a reduction of working hours from 40 or 38 to 35 hours a week and the expectation is that this will help to create new jobs. Economic think tanks have given strong warnings, however, that the unit costs of production should not be increased by lower working hours, because this would erode international competitiveness.[20]

The dominant issue in the German domestic debate on economic policy is the tax reform to be implemented in 1990. Income tax was reduced in 1986 and a second reduction was approved in 1988. Tax reliefs will total DM 44 billion up to 1990, and DM 13.5 billion in 1988, including the DM 5 billion committed as the German part of the Louvre Accord. Tax reform includes a drop in corporate tax from 56 to 50 per cent and a cut in the top marginal rate for personal incomes from 56 to 53 per cent, a decrease of the minimum tax rate from 22 to 19 per cent, a rise in basic personal tax allowances and some reliefs for investments.

Out of the total DM 44 billion, net tax reliefs are targeted to be DM 25 billion to be financed by public credits. A residual amount of DM 19 billion is supposed to be financed either by cuts in subsidies or by other tax increases, primarily on the part of consumer taxes. When tax reform was announced in February 1987, the government did not say how it would be financed, primarily because it was anxious not to scare off voters in the forthcoming state elections. This has enforced controversies regarding the final implementation of tax reform in the German republic.

The Social Democratic opposition has taken every opportunity to exploit the fact that tax reform will endanger budgetary consolidation (*Handelsblatt*, 22 Sept. 1987, p. 4). It is argued, however, that the deficit may rise more substantially given lower economic growth and increased German financial contributions to the European Community. From its point of view, tax reliefs primarily benefit medium and high incomes.[21] Although the Minister of Finance has declared that he will not increase value-added tax to finance tax reform for the time being, it is suspected that the forthcoming harmonization of tax rates within the European Community may work out in that direction. The negative impact tax reform already has on income distribution will then turn out to become even worse.

On the other hand, it is argued that tax reform is too eager to achieve a balanced distribution of tax reliefs instead of giving bolder incentives to investment activities (Boss 1987, pp. 46–60). On the part of the economic research institutes and the Council of Economic Advisers, critics have focused on the fact that tax reform has to be supplemented by more decisive steps to reduce subsidies in accordance with a supply-side strategy.[22] Total subsidies are estimated to be DM 120 billion a year. To reinforce market mechanisms, liberal-minded German economists have figured out DM 33 billion for subsidy cuts, that could immediately be achieved in all parts of the economy.

A substantial reduction of subsidies has been most strongly supported by the Liberal Democrats. The government will, however, not risk a further increase in unemployment by substantial cuts of subsidies granted to special industries. The German states are differently affected by structural change. Some of the *Länder* have a strong regional concentration of declining industries, i.e. agriculture in Bavaria, coal and steel in North-Rhine-Westphalia and the Saarland and shipbuilding in Bremen, Hamburg and Kiel. They therefore will firmly resist any plans to reduce subsidies in this area.

Tax reform has been strongly opposed on the part of the *Länder* and communities,[23] even by those ruled by the CDU–CSU.[24] The states' and communities' budgets have to bear a large burden of tax reliefs. If economic growth slows down to 1.5 per cent instead of 2.5 per cent the fall-off in tax receipts will become even more severe and their already tight financial situation will change for the worse. In view of a rather gloomy economic outlook, the federal government may be faced with strong demands to stretch the final implementation of tax reform beyond 1990. The CDU–CSU holds the majority in the German Bundesrat. Nevertheless, the government may have to offer financial compensation to the states and the communities to get Bundesrat approval for the final implementation of tax reform in view of broad criticism throughout its ranks.

German tax reform is intended to stimulate private economic activities in accordance with supply-side strategies. Although it is accepted that public deficits will temporarily grow as a result, the general emphasis is to reduce the share of the public sector in domestic economic activities. Public deficits have, however, increased in 1987 more than anticipated and will, furthermore, widen in 1988. Faced with strong domestic opposition regarding tax reform on both ends of the political spectrum the German government may not see much room to manoeuvre to further accelerate tax relief beyond the commitment of the Louvre Accord or to expand domestic demand by other means of fiscal expansion for the time being. But fiscal expansion will probably be stronger than intended in view of widening budget deficits.

GERMAN POLICY WITHIN THE EMS

German preferences in macroeconomic policy outlined above do of course have a decisive impact on German policy within the EMS as well. As will be pointed out in this chapter, German self-perception of EMS leadership does not always coincide with other EMS members' demands for a German leading role. German policy will probably not compromise on domestic expansion in return for internal market achievements. This is, however, not to say that German policy is not sensitive to the implementation of the EMS. Divergencies primarily confine themselves to different views regarding the appropriate strategies in achieving this goal rather than conern the goal itself.

EMS achievements: German critique and approval

Prevailing uncertainties regarding dollar fluctuations, as is well known, triggered the decision to establish the European Monetary System in July 1978, just a few weeks before the Bonn summit took place. The EMS was seen as an opportunity to limit detrimental effects of dollar disturbances on the European economies and to give new momentum to European integration as well. Its predecessor, the European 'snake', had evolved as a D-Mark block, including only the smaller European currencies, as France had left the system while Great Britain, Ireland and Italy did not take part from the beginning.

The EMS was and is considered an important element in German–French relations. Launched on the initiative of President Giscard d'Estaing and Chancellor Helmut Schmidt, the EMS was framed to make the participation of the larger members of the European Community more acceptable, especially with respect to France.

The decision to launch the EMS raised strong German domestic opposition. It was broadly held that the German government had approved the EMS primarily for political reasons, i.e. to bring France back into the system, and the EMS was not considered an advantage for German economic policy. In view of the German policy dilemma at the time of Bretton Woods, strong preference was given to floating exchange rates as a means to enhance monetary autonomy. EMS commitments for exchange market interventions on the part of the German Bundesbank would again expose the German economy to strong inflationary pressures from abroad. Monetary autonomy, gained by exchange-rate flexibility, would thus be forgone.

Since the European 'snake' had evolved as a D-Mark block, the influence of German macroeconomic policy had become rather strong. All members of the 'snake' broadly shared German perceptions of economic stability. Bundesbank commitment to a system of pegged exchange rates did therefore not really infringe on its capability to check inflation. The EMS was to include other principal Common Market economies and it was therefore less certain whether economic policies would always converge to achieve price-stability goals.

The EMS would not have been established if it had been supported by strong concerns on the part of all participants to regain price stability after years of high inflation. Stable exchange rates within the EMS were considered to further this goal. In view of still large divergencies in domestic inflation and in past economic policy preferences as well, German critics gave strong warnings, however, that EMS membership might sooner or later conflict with German economic priorities. Given large credit facilities, weak-currency countries would make less effort to adjust domestically towards low inflation goals.

It is widely suspected on the part of the German academic economic community that the average rate of inflation tends to increase within an area of pegged exchange rates. German economists and politicians have therefore always emphasized that economic convergence within the EMS must be achieved in the direction of price stability (Schluter 1984). The German public has always paid close attention to whether the EMS will perform to this end.

The European Monetary System has functioned in a more favourable way than suspected by earlier German opponents and has thus gained *ex post* approval even by those critics. Inflation rates have decreased substantially in all member states and monetary policy has become more convergent. The EMS so far has not interfered with German priorities for price stability. The influence of German macroeconomic policy turned out to be more dominant than had been expected, primarily because the common understanding on price stability goals, that had supported the EMS at the beginning, turned out to be rather persistent. This was the case when the French franc was subjected to pressures within the EMS in 1981 to 1983 as a result of a more expansionary policy shift under President Mitterrand. France did not leave the EMS as it did the snake in previous years, but instead adjusted its policy towards a more stabilizing path.

Neverthless, the German public is still highly sensitive to the fact that German EMS membership may eventually expose the domestic economy to imported inflation. Every German debate on the EMS has primarily centred on this point. Moves concerning the EMS that might indirectly reduce German control over inflation or that might even infringe upon the status of autonomy of the German Bundesbank have met with cautious reluctance on the side of German officials and have evoked strong warnings on the part of economic think tanks and the more informed public.

Close German attention has always been paid to the question of whether economic convergence achieved within the EMS is solid enough, so that the system may become more coherent. Although monetary policies have converged, fiscal policies have not. Budget deficits are considered a main source of future instabilities. Capital controls rather than converging economic fundamentals have been given as a reason for past exchange-rate stability.

Critics of the EMS within the German public moreover have focused on the fact that parity realignments were often decided too late and failed to adjust exchange rates to the extent required by diverging economic fundamentals. The EMS has thus caused a tendency of real D-Mark undervaluation. German exports have benefited from delayed realignment. This has been detrimental to other Common Market members' competitiveness and has thus given rise to protectionism in those countries (Scharrer 1983, pp. 175–213).

Regarding the statement that protectionism is largely a result of conflicting macroeconomic policy objectives, which have prevented economic expansion, the emphasis of German criticism is, however, on delayed realignments, and not on overly restrictive German policy. The conclusion thus is that parities should be adjusted not too late whenever this is needed and not that German macroeconomic policy should be less restrictive.

A common policy *vis-à-vis* the dollar

The EMS was launched at a time when the German economy was strongly affected by international monetary disturbances. Large capital inflows from the dollar area exposed the D-Mark to strong exchange-market pressures in 1977–8 and D-Mark overvaluation became a major concern. With the reduction of the US current-account deficit in mind, officials in the Carter administration temporarily 'talked the dollar further down'. Prior to November 1978, all calls that the US should make a decisive step to fight inflation in order to stop the dollar decline had been faced with an attitude of 'benign neglect'. The German government was pressured to expand the domestic economy instead.

Those experiences may have promoted the decision to launch the EMS on the part of the German government, but the Bundesbank and the German economic think tanks held a different view. It was doubted whether the EMS could absorb exchange-market pressures from the dollar area at all. Inflation was high in some of its member countries and it was feared that the EMS would soon break down if a further dollar decline forced a new D-Mark revaluation. It was thus advantageous to the early performance of the EMS that the Carter administration shifted policy later in 1978 and 1979 to stabilize the dollar and that the D-Mark entered a phase of weakness with the advent of a strong Reagan-dollar in the following years.

The dollar rate of the D-Mark has always been a serious concern in German economic policymaking. Dollar fluctuation does have a decisive impact on German import prices for oil and other raw materials. As the D-Mark has become a reserve currency alternative to the dollar, German monetary policy has been more exposed to international capital flows than that of other countries. The effect of US interest-rate levels on German interest rates is rather strong. German monetary policy has been most cautious to keep interest-rate differentials within a range that will not induce large capital shifts from one country to the other.

Bilateral monetary co-ordination between the US Federal Reserve System and the German Bundesbank, already established in the 1960s to defend the dollar–gold standard, was rather close at certain times, but German monetary policy was also adjusted unilaterally, as the US followed an attitude of benign neglect. Since the introduction of the European Monetary System in 1979, the management of the dollar–D-Mark relationship has more or less determined dollar relations with all EMS currencies as well.

Within the EMS, co-ordination with regard to the dollar has been achieved, mainly by intra-marginal exchange market interventions. Although the D-Mark has been subjected to dollar fluctuations more than other EMS currencies, Germany has not encouraged further moves towards a concerted dollar policy within the EMS, as recommended by some economic experts and the European Commission.[25] Proposals to agree on dollar rate targets and to assign common credit facilities to finance dollar interventions have not received German support.[26]

The issue of a concerted dollar policy became most acute in 1981–2 in view of calls for a co-ordinated reduction of European interest rates independent of levels in the US (Thiel 1987). As already outlined, German policy was aimed at halting the D-Mark decline *vis-à-vis* the dollar by means of monetary restriction at this time. A common strategy with regard to the dollar was thus primarily prevented by different domestic economic-policy objectives. Even those who generally recommended a German monetary expansion and a temporary downward floating of the D-Mark as a consequence, thought that the D-Mark would rebound sooner if it were not tied in the EMS.

A common policy *vis-à-vis* the dollar has, however, been objected to on grounds of principle as well. Since the introduction of the EMS, central bank co-ordination in the dollar exchange market has increased, although it has been achieved by discretion and not by more binding rules. More definite obligations to defend a common target for the dollar rate may indirectly reduce monetary autonomy on the part of the German Bundesbank, to an extent not intended at this stage of the EMS. Massive exchange-market interventions may be unavoidable in order to keep all EMS currencies in line with a common dollar target. A concerted dollar policy may therefore indirectly interfere with domestic monetary-policy objectives.

Macroeconomic policy co-ordination

The EMS has performed rather well to the extent that monetary and price stability has increased, but no policy co-ordination has been achieved so far to counter rising levels of unemployment. It has been argued that the EMS community has followed an over-restrictive economic course as all other members have adjusted macroeconomic policies to keep their currencies in line with the D-Mark. German leadership within the EMS has performed well with respect to price-stability objectives but with those of faster economic growth and high employment. As inflation has already been reduced to low levels, more decisive steps to increase employment are judged overdue.

The EMS may therefore need closer macroeconomic policy co-ordination to fight unemployment instead of the more indirect policy co-ordination via pegged exchange-rate mechanisms pursued in the past (Franzmeyer 1983). Potentials for economic growth that both a large Common Market and a closer macroeconomic policy co-ordination may offer have not yet been fully exploited. The European Commission has submitted comprehensive strategies for domestic policy to promote economic growth (EC Commission Economic Report 1984–5). The implementation of the internal market by 1992 is a strong element in this strategy, but it implies a closer co-ordination of macro and microeconomic policies as well.

Given low, near-zero German inflation, budgetary consolidation, current account surpluses and a strong D-Mark but disappointing economic growth, Germany is considered an ideal candidate for domestic expansion. Other EMS members will have to remain more cautious to not put domestic economic stability at risk. Those calls coincide with even stronger pressures for German domestic expansion on the part of the United States. German commitment to accelerate tax reform was part of the Louvre Accord in February 1987, which aimed at preventing further slides of the dollar and reducing current-account imbalances, i.e. primarily a US deficit and German and Japanese surpluses.

As it has already been pointed out in the first part, German tax reform is a controversial domestic issue and has sparked strong criticism throughout the political spectrum. It remains open to what extent tax relief will encourage investments, and budget deficits may widen beyond what is anticipated. German economic growth most likely will reach no more than 2 per cent in the near future, too low to reduce domestic unemployment by much and too weak to fuel economic growth within the EMS community. German monetary policy may tighten if fiscal deficits expand and inflation increases.

Complaints on the part of the EMS community that German macroeconomic policy has been too restrictive in view of low inflation but high rates of unemployment in all EMS countries have received a favourable response in circles close to the Social Democrats, matching demands there for domestic expansion. The German Social Democratic members of the European Parliament actually called for domestic expansion instead of a D-Mark appreciation within the EMS in January 1987 (VWD Europe, Jan. 1987). According to this view, the EMS does need a closer co-ordination of macroeconomic policies. Social Democratic governments may, however, take a more cautious view on this issue and on fiscal expansion as well recalling past experiences when budget deficits became uncontrollable after fiscal expansion in 1978.

On the part of the German economic think tanks, the Deutsche Institut für Wirtschaftsforschung has placed more emphasis on European macro-economic co-ordination than the others, fully in line with its overall recommendations for fiscal expansion. The dominant view among economic experts is, however, that economic growth growth must primarily be achieved by supply-side strategies. Criticism therefore has centred on slow progress achieved in deregulation including a firmer stance by the German government in favour of a quick implementation of the European internal market. But a faster economic growth should not be achieved at the costs of inflation and the risks of budgetary consolidation.

The implementation of the EMS

The original schedule was to implement the institutional framework of the EMS within two years, i.e. by 1981. This would have included a certain delegation of monetary authority from the national level to the European Monetary Fund. It goes without saying that this step has not yet been achieved and will be most sensitive.

The pre-eminent obstacle is that national monetary constitutions differ to the extent that the central bank is part of the government in some EMS member states and enjoys a status of autonomy in others. From a German point of view, any implementation of the institutional framework of the EMS has to preserve the political autonomy of EMS monetary authority (Schluter 1984) but this may be considered quite differently on the part of other EMS members. The Single European Act, approved in February 1986, therefore subjects the institutional implementation of the EMS to Article 236, requiring ratification by the national parliaments.

The German government and the Bundesbank have supported EMS to the extent that this does not dilute control to check domestic inflation. This path has been completely in accordance with the prevailing mood within the German public on the question of EMS implementation. German involvement in the EMS has even been extended just beyond the line of what some more concerned domestic critics would have liked to concede.

Instead of a premature institutional implementation of the EMS, emphasis by German political authorities as well as the public has been given to the internal market approach, including capital liberalization. Germany has long removed capital controls. As the D-Mark is used as a currency of reserve, German policy has to be more cautious than others not to trigger capital outflows by means that may erode confidence in the D-Mark as an investment currency. It is generally agreed that restrictions of international capital flows do just that. Capital liberalization is favoured by the German business community. It is claimed, however, that liberalization should not be confined to Common Market transactions, but should be applied *erga omnes* with respect to third countries.

As a *quid pro quo* for capital liberalization on the part of other EMS members, the Bundesbank gave final approval for the private use of the ECU in June 1987.[27] This step had been resisted for years, primarily because the ECU is a currency index and German law does not allow application of indices in business contrasts. Although this move has been largely approved by the German banking community, it is still doubted whether the ECU will be more extensively used in private domestic transactions by the German public.

It is widely held that advantages offered by a private use of the ECU primarily apply to weak-currency countries, because it is considered a means to reduce the risk of inflation in private contracts. The ECU may eventually gain a broader acceptance in international transactions by the German business community. The private use of the ECU, however, is not considered as a step that will really improve the functioning of the EMS and promote its final implementation.

It has long been criticized by Germans that EMS performance in exchange-rate stability has partly been achieved through mechanisms of capital controls. Recent moves towards capital liberalization will probably add pressures for domestic and parity adjustment. The EMS then will have to meet a decisive test. Calls for closer macroeconomic policy coordination within the EMS have thus become more acute lately.

Proposals to step up monetary policy co-ordination within the regular consultations of the European Monetary Committee, as recommended by the Padoa-Schioppa report (1987), have met with resistance from the German public.[28] Because this Committee is dominated by the Ministers of Finance, monetary policy may lose its independence. If tensions within the EMS increase as a result of capital liberalization, German economic advisers will probably give more support to an increase of the margins set for exchange-rate fluctuations as they have already recommended. At the Ministers of Finance meeting at Nyborg in early September 1987, steps to strengthen the EMS mechanisms were approved, primarily via an extension of credit facilities in support of intra-marginal interventions. The provision is, however, that central banks have to agree if their currency is used in exchange-market interventions and that official balances can only be settled in ECU with the approval of the creditor bank.[29] The Bundesbank thus stepped up its commitment to defend the EMS, but did not give up its discretion to keep domestic inflation under control.

CONCLUSIONS

German economic policy exhibits a pattern of continuity and prevailing economic priorities, such as price stability and budgetary consolidation, have moreover been sharpened by past economic experiences. Domestic economic priorities have time and again conflicted with external economic objectives in view of external disequilibrium. German economic policy preferences can therefore be best illustrated by its course of adjustment at these specific times.

The domestic base

The Federal Republic of Germany is one of those countries thinking that inflation is quite costly. Economic policy has been most cautious, not to raise inflationary expectations, because this will trigger social conflicts on income distribution. Short-term trade-offs between inflation and jobs are not considered tolerable. The German Bundesbank is committed to price-stability objectives by constitution and its status of autonomy provides political independence in pursuing this goal. Fiscal policy has become more prudent in view of past experiences that fiscal expansion did not sub-stantially reduce unemployment but that public deficits, blown-up in the following years, became less manageable.

Given price stability as a strong domestic priority, the policy dilemma caused by external disequilibrium has time and again been imported in-flation and the burden of adjustment fell mainly on monetary policy. At the time of Bretton Woods, parity adjustment had to be decided by the government and decisions were taken too late to prevent inflation.

With the introduction of managed floating, the German Bundesbank won discretion to defend price stability goals and the stabilizing impact of D-Mark appreciations on domestic prices has always been considered an advantage. In view of currency overshooting, however, the Bundesbank has again been faced with the policy dilemma of defending price stability and of mitigating large exchange-rate fluctuations simultaneously.

German adjustment to external imbalances has, however, followed dif-ferent paths, depending on whether the objective was to reduce a current account deficit as in 1979–81, or to prevent further D-Mark appreciations as in 1977–8 and more recently. As a decline of the D-Mark triggered domestic inflation, the Bundesbank responded by tightening monetary policy. The pre-eminent emphasis was to balance the current account and to re-strengthen the D-Mark.

At times of a D-Mark appreciation, the Bundesbank has tolerated over-shooting of monetary targets but has been most cautious to check inflation as well. D-Mark revaluation infringed upon exports, but low inflation and gains in terms of trade assisted German international competitiveness. German exports furthermore benefited from increasing demand abroad, either on the part of the US, OPEC or within the Common Market. Trade surpluses turned out to be rather persistant.

The conclusion is that German policy of adjustment has been biased to the extent that it has tolerated a D-Mark revaluation more than a D-Mark decline, primarily for price stability goals and that for the same reasons monetary policy has been more concerned with reducing the current-account deficits than with limiting sustained current account surpluses.

Nevertheless, the question remains why adjustment was not achieved by fiscal policy. German fiscal expansion, agreed to at the Bonn summit in 1978, displayed its full effect in 1979, when the economy already boomed and the balance of current account turned into a deficit. Public deficits ran out of control in the following years and fiscal policy lost its room to manoeuvre. Monetary policy may have been less restrictive in 1981–3 if fiscal policy had not failed to achieve budgetary consolidation. Furthermore, already huge budget deficits ruled out fiscal policy as an instrument to stimulate domestic demand in view of rising unemployment. When Chancellor Helmut Schmidt was replaced by Helmut Kohl in 1982, the new government made strong efforts to balance the budget as a precondition to tax reform, starting in 1986.

Tax reform scheduled for 1988 and 1990 is aimed to stimulate private economic activities and investments. The general intention is to reduce the share of the public sector in GNP and to not put budgetary consolidation at risk. As budget deficits have already largely increased in 1987, this goal may, however, not be met and fiscal policy will became more expansionary than anticipated.

The issue of tax reform has raised strong domestic opposition throughout the ranks. Criticism has centred on its impact on income distribution as well as on its squeezing effect on the already tight budgets of the German states and communities. Financial compensations are demanded from the government and calls to step up local public investments, long favoured by the parliamentary opposition, have gained support by communities' representations.

German authorities see less room for faster non-inflationary domestic economic growth in the short run than is assumed abroad, and have therefore resisted calls for means to further accelerate domestic demand. The economic growth forecast in the range of 2 per cent in 1988 will, however, be too weak to reduce high levels of unemployment. The central question therefore is whether or not medium-term economic growth can be shifted towards a higher path. German officials and a majority of German economic think tanks hold that tax reform and deregulation including the implementation of the European internal market are an appropriate means to improve conditions for future economic growth. The domestic opposition has placed more emphasis on immediate measures to enhance public investment. All would agree, however, that price stability is most important.

Macroeconomic policy co-ordination

German preferences in international economic policy co-ordination strongly reflect domestic economic priorities. If policy co-ordination is to provide a public good, the objective is to achieve both – monetary and price stability and co-operation should not compromise between inflation and economic expansion. Cautiousness is furthermore supported by past experiences that inflation may increase to high levels before governments react and that it will be rather costly to bring inflation down again.

In view of economic openness and German dependence on both exports and imports the external value of the D-Mark has always been a strong German concern. The German Bundesbank has time and again tolerated an overshooting of monetary targets to stabilize the exchange rate *vis-à-vis* the dollar and within the EMS as well. In both arenas, the Bundesbank has been confronted with the policy dilemma to achieve price stability and to stabilize the exchange rate at the same time, but discretion has helped to keep both objectives in a delicate balance.

In order to achieve a closer co-ordination of macroeconomic policies, the Group of Seven countries agreed at the Tokyo Summit in 1986 to apply economic indicators to a regular surveillance of economic policies in co-operation with the International Monetary Fund. Exchange-rate targets have furthermore been suggested as a means to bring more continuity in macroeconomic policy co-ordination, thus combining the merits of rules and discretion. Neither of these strategies, however, provide a common standard of monetary and price stability to which macroeconomic policy co-ordination has to be strictly confined. Diverging views may be held concerning the right set of exchange-rate targets and different policy conclusions may be drawn from economic indicators. Individual countries may thus be faced with strong majority pressures to adjust their policy in the direction favoured abroad.[30]

From a German standpoint it is therefore most important to sustain the discretion in international macroeconomic policy co-ordination that provides the means to eventually defend domestic economic priorities if objectives in macroeconomic policy co-ordination diverge substantially.[31] Although more American emphasis has recently been given to economic co-ordination, all past experiences suggest that strong preference is given to discretion on the part of the US as well whenever international co-operation will interfere with domestic economic autonomy. The Group of Seven countries re-confirmed their commitment to co-ordinate policies in view of the sudden crash in stock markets at the end of October 1987. All efforts should be made to improve the functioning of the international monetary system, but sustained monetary stability may not always be re-achieved in international monetary relations, due to economic divergencies and different perceptions in macroeconomic policy as well.

The European Monetary System

The European Monetary System probably provides a more reliable basis for monetary stability and macroeconomic policy co-ordination and has already proved its coherence in view of wide dollar fluctuations. Priorities for price stability are largely shared by all members and economic policies have become more congruent. The EMS is complementary to the implementation of the internal market in 1992 and both are integral parts of the overall process of European integration.

It is widely assumed that Germany has profited most from the European Monetary System: 'namely stable exchange rates, free capital movement and an independent monetary policy' (Tsoukalis 1987, p. 18). The latter results from the dominance of the D-Mark within the EMS. The framework of the EMS, however, does not prejudice the dominant role of a national currency within the system. As the D-Mark has gained such a position this has primarily been because adjustment to the D-Mark has been supportive of low-inflation goals on the part of other EMS members. Priorities for price stability have commonly been shared by all EMS members from the beginning and it was by this criterion that the EMS had gained the approval of the German public. Monetary policy was moreover less independent, as frequent interventions by the German Bundesbank in EMS–exchange markets and in the dollar market as well interfered with domestic monetary targets.

Monetary policies will be linked even more closely by measures supporting intramarginal exchange market interventions, approved at the Ministers of Finance meeting at Nyborg in September 1987. It is therefore doubted whether German leadership can safeguard price stability, if this goal is not furthermore strongly supported by other principal members of the EMS as well. German officials have for instance favoured a British participation within the system for this reason and have strongly emphasized that leadership should be shared with other EMS members to insure price stability in the future.

German sensitivity regarding inflation is comparatively high and German economic policy therefore tends to display a deflationary bias, at least if it is weighted by other countries' economic preferences. Although unemployment is high-priority, policymaking within the EMS has paid most attention to price-stability objectives and has rather neglected employment goals. While Germany is looking for partisans to keep the EMS in line with its own strict domestic priorities for price stability, the EMS community does expect a leading German role towards domestic expansion and a German push for the final implementation of the institutional framework of the EMS.

German authorities hold that a further step up of domestic demand can not be achieved without inflation. The Common Market area may, however, offer larger capacities for non-inflationary growth. German officials have favoured the implementation of the internal market for this reason, but not a closer co-ordination of domestic expansion within the EMS. This is primarily through fear that inflation could become less controllable if

German leadership in domestic expansion induced other members to step up domestic demand as well and to adopt a more relaxed stand on inflation.

If the final goal is the implementation of the EMS replacing German leadership in price stability by a leading German role in economic expansion this is not a real alternative from a German point of view. The more informed German public is quite sensitive to the fact that macroeconomic policy co-ordination within the EMS may eventually compromise on inflation, and will not support policy steps in that direction. Given the dominant view that economic growth is best achieved via price stability, German policy within the EMS is to strongly support this goal (Kloten 1987).

A more appropriate approach to the promotion of policy co-ordination would be to start discussion on how to ensure independence of monetary authorities within the institutional framework of the EMS. Although this may be looked at as a typical German position, steps in this direction may strengthen confidence that monetary policy will not accommodate inflation if fiscal policy becomes more expansionary.

There is a hypothesis that protectionism is largely a result of conflicting macroeconomic policy objectives, which have prevented economic expansion. German exports have admittedly profited by late realignments and D-Mark undervaluation at least temporarily. A German conclusion is that protectionism within the common market area partly results from parities kept on 'non-competitive' levels. The emphasis of criticism therefore is on delayed realignments, and not on overly restrictive German policy. It is true that EMS membership offers a potential increase of bargaining power in international monetary relations, but early moves towards a common policy vis-à-vis the dollar are not considered an appropriate means to this end from a German point of view. The risks of a concerted dollar policy have been weighted higher than its benefits so far. The German position therefore is that a common policy vis-à-vis the dollar- and the yen-area must first be based solidly on a more sustained convergence within the EMS in economic fundamentals.

As the EMS performs to this end, European economic policy will become more independent of the United States. The international monetary system may then evolve on a dollar-yen-ECU basis, as envisioned by President Mitterrand. In that event international monetary relations, so far dominated by the US, will be established on more equal terms. In view of the weak performance of the international monetary system, the European Monetary System offers an option for a more independent European role in international monetary relations in the future. The more immediate purpose, however, is to further strengthen economic coherence within the EMS first.

Capital liberalization and the implementation of the internal market do require a closer co-ordination of monetary policies. The German government, and even more so the Bundesbank, have supported the EMS more strongly than some domestic critics would have liked, but will not give up their discretion to check inflation. We may therefore not expect any more spectacular steps to implement the institutional framework of the EMS on the German part, as long as autonomy of monetary institutions is not ensured. German involvement in the EMS may, however, increase by discretion and economic policy co-ordination may gradually be adapted to internal market requirements in the process of learning and understanding.

NOTES

1. 'Sachverständigenrat zur Begutachtung der gesamtwirtschaftlichen Entwicklung, Alternativen aubenwirtschaftlicher Anpassung', *Jahresgutachten 1968–9*, Stuttgart, 1968, p. 58.
2. Ibid. p. 58.
3. Ibid. pp. 71–4.
4. For example, Tietmeyer, quoted from *VWD Europa*, 10 March 1987.
5. *Geschäftsbericht der deutschen Bundesbank für das Jahr 1977*, p. 19f and 1978, p. 27.
6. For example, Enno Langfeldt, Norbert Walter, 'Weltkonjunktur: Belebung bei deutlicher Differenzierung', in: *Die Weltwirtschaft*, no. 1, 1978, pp. 1–12 (12); Otmar Issing, 'Falsche und richtige Wege aus der Dollarkrise', in: *Wirtschaftsdienst*, no. 4, 1978, pp. 168–72; Dietmar Gebert, Joachim Scheide, 'Die Lokomotiven-Strategie als wirtschaftspolitisches Konzept', Kiel 1980 (Institut für Weltwirtschaft).
7. Including the federal, the states' and the communities' budget and social securities.
8. 'Sachverständigenrat zur Begutachtung der gesamtwirtschaftlichen Entwicklung, Wachstum und Währung', *Jahresgutachten 1978–9*, Stuttgart 1978, pp. 172–5.
9. 'Sachverständigenrat zur Begutachtung der gesamtwirtschaftlichen Entwicklung, Unter Anpassungszwang', *Jahresgutachten 1980–81*, Stuttgart 1980, p. 91.
10. 'Die Lage der Weltwirtschaft und der westdeutschen Wirtschaft im Herbst 1980', in: DIW (Deutsches Institut für Wirtschaftsforschung), Wochenbericht, vol. 47, no. 44–5 (1980), pp. 453–72 (468); 'Sachverständigenrat zur Begutachtung der gesamtwirtschaftlichen Entwicklung, Unter Anpassungszwang', *Jahresgutachten 1980–81*, Stuttgart 1980, p. 206; 'Wirtschaftspolitik bei defizitärer Leistungsbilanz, Gutachten des wissenschaftlichen Beirats beim Bundesministerium für Wirtschaft', 23 Feb. 1981, BMWI, Studienreihe 31; Wolfgang Filc, 'Dollarkursorientierung: eine erfolglose Konzeption der Bundesbank', in: *Wirtschaftsdienst*, vol. 64, no. 6 (Sept. 1984), pp. 442–7.
11. The German Council of Economic Advisers took a similar view in its 1981–2 annual report, Sachverständigenrat zur Begutachtung der gesamtwirtschaftlichen Entwicklung, Investieren für mehr Beschäftigung, *Jahresgutachten 1981–2*, p. 402.
12. *Geschäftsbericht der Deutschen Bundesbank für der Jahr 1981*, pp. 33f.
13. Deutsche Bundesbank, *Auszüge aus Presseartikeln*, No. 57, Frankfurt 24 June 1982, p. 8.
14. Deutsche Bundesbank, *Auszüge aus Presseartikeln*, no. 60, Frankfurt 5 July 1982, pp. 1–5.

15. Deutsche Bundesbank, *Auszüge aus Presseartikeln*, no. 79, Frankfurt, 10 Sept. 1982, pp. 2f.
16. Deutsche Bundesbank, *Auszüge aus Presseartikeln*, no. 80, Frankfurt, 13 Sept. 1982, pp. 14f.
17. Deutsche Bundesbank, *Auszüge aus Presseartikeln*, no. 82, Frankfurt, 16 Sept. 1982, p. 4.
18. 'Besteht Spielraum für eine aktivere Konjunktur und Wachstumspolitik? Zeitgespräch mit Otto Schlecht, Hans-Jürgen Krupp, Armin Gutowski', in: *Wirtschaftsdienst*, no. 11, 1986, pp. 539–48.
19. *Die Wirtschaft ökologisch und sozial Erneuern, Entwurf der Kommission Wirtschafts- und Finanzpolitik beim Parteivorstand der SPD*, Bonn, November 1985; Johann Welsch, 'Ansätze der Strukturpolitik als Beschäftigungspolitik – "Mehr Markt" oder beschäftigungsorientierte Strukturpolitik?' in: WSI-Mitteilungen, *Zeitschrift des Wirtschafts- und Sozialwissenschaftlichen Instituts des deutschen Gewerkschaftsbundes*, vol. 38, no. 5 (May 1985), pp. 263–74.
20. For example, '*Jahresgutachten 1986–7* des Sachverständigenrates zur Begutachtung der gesamtwirtschaftlichen Entwicklung', Deutscher Bundestag, 10. Wahlperiode, Drucksache 10/6562, 11 Nov 1986, p. 149.
21. For example, Hans-Georg Petersen, 'Ein Dokument der Mut- und Kraftlosigkeit', in: *Wirtschaftsdienst*, vol. 67, no. 4 (April 1987), pp 174–80.
22. '*Jahresgutachten 1985–86* des Sachverständigenrates zur Begutachtung der gesamtwirtschaftlichen Entwicklung', Deutscher Bundestag, 10. Wahlperiode, Drucksache 10/4295, 22 Nov 1985, p. 135.
23. 'SPD-regierte Länder verstärken Widerstand gegen die geplante Steuerreform', *Süddeutsche Zeitung*, 29 Sept 1987, p. 1.
24. '"Wir müssen die Steuerreform neu überlegen"', interview with the Minister-president of Baden-Württemberg, Lothar Späth, *Der Spiegel*, 8 June 1987, pp. 21–4.
25. Jacques van Ypersele, 'Zur pragmatischen Weiterentwicklung des EWS-Ein machbares wie wünschenswertes Programm', in: Scharrer, H./Wessels, W. (ed.), *Das europäische Währungssystem*, Bonn 1983, pp. 123–146; EC-Commission, *Economic Report 1980–81*, p. 95.
26. Elke Thiel, 'Das EWS im internationalen Währungssystem: Eine Herausforderung für die USA? Äußere Profilierung und innere Konvergenz', in: Scharrer, H./Wessels, W. (ed), *Das europäische Währungssystem*, Bonn, 1983, pp. 355–81.
27. 'Die Märkte der Privaten ECU', *Monatsberichte der Deutsche Bundesbank*, vol. 39, no. 8 (August, 1987), pp. 32–40.
28. EG-Studie zur 'Entthronung der DM', *VWD-Europa*, 30 June 1987, pp. 5f; Frankfurter Geldpolitik schon unter brüsseler Einfluß? VWD-Europa, 21 Sept. 1987, pp. 8f.
29. Pöhl: Bundesbank-Autonomie nicht gefährdet, *VWD-Europa*, 15 Sept. 1987, pp. 3f.
30. For example, '*Jahresgutachten 1986–7* des Sachverständigenrates zur Begutachtung der gesamtwirtschaftlichen Entwicklung', Deutscher Bundestag, 10. Wahlperiode, Drucksache 10/6562, 1986, pp. 130–4.
31. For example, Helmut Schlesinger, 'Finanz und Geldpolitik – Elemente internationaler wirtschaftlicher Kooperation', Deutsche Bundesbank, *Auszüge aus Presseartikeln*, no. 63, 2 Sept. 1987, pp. 1–6.

9 · EXPANSIONARY POLICIES IN A RESTRICTIVE WORLD: THE CASE OF FRANCE

Pascal Petit

The poor achievements of the French economy in the 1980s raise two questions of economic policy. The first one refers to experience of re-flation policy in a world economy dominated by restrictive policies. Does a medium-sized economy have any room for manoeuvre left to escape the general pattern of stagnation? The second question, though closely related, concerns more specifically France as an economy which in the 1960s worked out an efficient expansion policy – a kind of modern capitalism – of which 'indicative planning' was the major characteristic. How come, then, that the economy in the OECD major which experienced the highest growth rate after Japan during the 1960s now lags behind its trading partners in the 1980s? The fact that France launched a rather mild reflation in 1981–2 at the worse time of all, as it coincided with a low in the world economic cycle, provides only a minor part of the answer. It underlines that the room for manoeuvre has considerably narrowed, even if it could have been more ample during an upward phase of the cycle. Such an explanation thus draws attention to recent changes in the role which the external constraint plays on the making of economic policy.

Therefore if France's past economic policy has turned into a relative failure, one has to question the conditions in which the most important change since the 1960s occurred, i.e. the greater integration into the world economy (the ratio of exports to GDP rose from 15 per cent in 1960 to 25 per cent in 1980; similar figures for imports are respectively 12.9 and 25.2 per cent). This raises the issue whether there were or appeared to be factors which limited the ability of the French economy to adjust to external changes more than in other similar (let us say, European) countries. In other words, has the external constraint been more binding on France and why? We shall try to address this issue from an economic-policy perspective, in some kind of follow-up to the debate opened in the 1960s on France's success. This is not to say that structural specifics have no part in the explanation. France in the 1970s was an industrialized, relatively rich economy, which had developed its own version of 'fordism' (combining enlargement of markets, high productivity gains and expansion of final demand), where some differences from other countries remained regarding the relative weights of economic activities or the use of modern techniques. Greater integration into the world economy unbalances such a fordist growth model, which is forced to secure its trade links. The drive towards competitiveness is building up and it concerns all aspects of economic policy. We shall not discuss the basic components of this competitiveness which would help to answer our first question on growth regime adjustment in medium-sized economies, but will focus on the set of institutions and policies organizing the external relations of the economy. This concern for broadly defined foreign policy issues therefore mainly addresses the question of the relative performance of France among similar economies.

External constraint is a pure policy issue in that it does not directly involve firms, which are faced with competition regardless of its internal or external aspect, but central government's action. Nevertheless, what is feasible depends strictly on the nature of each nation-state and the ways in which it handles its external relations. Foreign policy should be seen very comprehensively as including more or less separate issues on defence, exchange and trade. Therefore, a long-term perspective will, at some point, be needed to account for the combination of these different issues.

We shall proceed in our investigation in four steps. To begin with, we shall quickly assess economic achievements in the late 1970s and early 1980s as compared to the OECD average. This will give some idea of the magnitude of the relative failure of the French economy in the recent period. It will prove useful to extend the comparison over a longer term, e.g. over the whole period of economic interdependence.

The second step will expand on the rationale for external constraint. It will recall, in a long-term view of France's history, the issues involved and their combination when we consider the management of a country's international relations. It will question why the hierarchy in policy objectives may differ among countries in rather similar positions, such as France, the UK or West Germany.

A third section will then account more precisely for the expansionary economic policies of the 1980s. Facts will be analysed within the conceptual framework previously developed, to point out what hindered successful adjustments to changes in the external constraint.

The fourth part will conclude on the perspectives open to reflation policy and on features of growth regimes for medium size economies in a largely integrated world economy.

FRANCE'S COUNTER-PERFORMANCES DURING THE PRESENT STAGNATION

We have already mentioned France's counter-performances in the present stagnation; they must now be precisely assessed and set into their long-

Table 9.1 Real gross domestic product in recent decades (average % changes)

Periods	1960–68	1968–73	1973–9	1979–84
France	5.4	5.9	3.1	1.1
7 major OECD	5.1	4.6	2.7	1.9
EC	4.6	4.9	2.4	1.0

term historical context before we proceed to investigate the external relations issue.

To begin with, let us consider the average growth rate of GDP over the recent business cycles. As synchronization of these cycles has increased in the 1970s, we shall simply compare France's achievements with the average of the seven major OECD countries (as given by OECD Historical Statistics, Paris 1986). The last two cycles – namely from peak 1973–9 and 1979–84 – correspond to times of generalized slow growth, if compared with the 1950s and the 1960s. During the last cycle, 1979–84, France's economic growth rate is below the OECD average (1.1 per cent versus 1.9 per cent) (see Table 9.1). Similar features are observed at the sectoral level of manufacturing and services. Only in agriculture do we see a reverse trend with a 2.2 per cent growth rate versus 1.3 per cent on average, which is all the more noticeable since agriculture grew at a lower, slightly below average pace in times of general expansion. Apart from agricultural activities, it thus seems that France's growth performance in the post-war period came to an end in the early 1980s.

In a long-term perspective, one is reminded of France's relatively poor performances in the 1918–39 inter-war period (see Table 9.2), where French economic growth was weaker than that of its trade partners. This retrospective view also reminds us that in the modern history of industrialized economies what we now call slow growth was formerly the rule and post-war expansion an exception. This might suggest that the French economy could be back on some long-term growth course (in Janossy's sense), less successful that those displayed in other countries. Thus post-war performances would only have been a parenthesis, favoured by some interruptions during the war. Such a hypothesis would be in accordance with the fact that modern French capitalism in the 1950s and 1960s was clearly linked to definite historical conditions of the time and not to some secular Colbertian or Napoleonic tradition (Petit 1984, 1987). But this thesis of some long-term deficiency in France's capacity to develop is strongly opposed by historians as recalled by Bouvier (1987), who rightly stresses that France's development sustained long-term cycles of acceleration and deceleration like other industrialized countries, and that during these up and down swings, indicators like GDP per head displayed similar dynamics. In that respect, Table 9.2 is misleading in that it does not use proper indicators and proper cycles. If anything, Bouvier (1987) would stress that long-term

Table 9.2 Real domestic product in an historical perspective (average yearly % change)

	1820–70	1870–1913	1913–50	1950–73	1973–84
France	1.7	1.7	1.0	5.1	2.2
OECD	2.6	2.6	1.8	5.5	2.3
EC	2.2	2.0	1.4	4.8	1.8

Source: Maddison, 1981, 1987, OECD Historical Statistics.
Notes
[1] For EEC average before 1973, countries included are: Germany, UK, Netherlands, Belgium, France, Italy (except for 1820–1870).
[2] For OECD 7 majors average, Italy, Japan and Canada are not included before 1870.

upswings and downswings are more marked in France than in other countries. Historians attribute the reasons for such Kondratiev cycles to a multiplicity of causes and the specificities of national history. Therefore, we can tell only a part of the story by looking at the foreign relations of only one nation state. Such an external perspective will be linked all the more relevantly with macroeconomic performances in these times of economic interdependence.

We should thus restrict our analysis to periods of economic interdependence, e.g. when one country has to significantly adjust its own internal economic policies to disturbances in some partner's economy – in accordance with Cooper's definition (1985). This economic approach of interdependency does not, however, precisely establish the beginning of interdependence. Cooper (1968) advocates that it started only after the First World War when reductions in transaction costs facilitated trade flows and affected more widespread national activities. Yet, a number of authors (see Mistral 1985; Ashworth 1952) tend to date interdependence as far back as 1860, when the Anglo-French Treaty helped to launch an era of free trade. If only symbolically, we shall retain this dating, as it is also the benchmark of what we shall call an autonomous or self-centred French trade policy.

Following these remarks, we are left to question the specificity of France's management of its external relations and how it can contribute in explaining her achievements, either worse or better than other countries', over the last century's cycles. We have also hypothesized that this foreign-relations issue has gained importance in the last decade and will focus on it.

First, though, three more points should be made to stress the non-conjunctural and specific nature of current counter-performances, that are neither due to maladjustments and delays, nor worsened by erroneous socialist policies.

Yearly economic growth rates show that relatively poor performances can be traced back to the mid 1970s and have continued up to 1987 (see

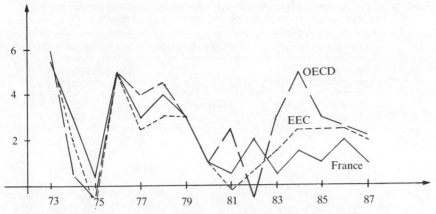

Figure 9.1 Real gross domestic products (yearly % changes)

Fig. 9.1). France's poor achievements in the late 1970s and early 1980s are, therefore, not tied to more conjunctural factors, nor merely a part of a wider European sclerosis nor attributed to the choice of economic indicators.

We can now proceed to question the causes for this set-back, or more precisely, the part which may have been played in it by the external constraint. It is not that simple to assess directly how binding the external constraint is or has been. To test such an external-constraint hypothesis on strictly economic terms, one can take a set of sound hypotheses on the links between economic growth and a more or less autonomous external demand and estimate a potential growth rate to be compared with the actual growth rate. This test does give some valuable information on the effectiveness of the external constraint – provided the growth model is relevant. The Harrod simple-growth model constitutes the crudest form of such a test.

Following Thirlwall (1979), such a crude growth model can be estimated using recent evaluations of export and import income elasticities (see Table 9.3). These figures, which display a potentially larger-than-average effect of world demand on the growth of France's economy, are in accordance with her relative performance over the period (1964–81). In other words, the external constraint does not seem specially binding for France, when only income effects are considered.

But the main shortcoming of this first approach to the external constraints is that it does not account for price effects. When both price and income effects are accounted for, estimations of price effects are, on the whole, rather uncertain (see Table 9.3); the reaction of France's export price changes is thus imprecise while imports seem to react more strongly to price changes than in other countries. The underlying determinants of

Table 9.3 External constraints measured by elasticities of export and import (annual estimates over the period 1964–81; ( ) student t

	Income and price export elasticities of export[2]		Ratios of income elasticities[1]		Income and price import elasticities of import[2]	
	World demand	Price	Manufact.	Total	GDP	Price
France	1.18 (33.8)	0.12* (0.2)	1.03	1.21	2.21 (30.4)	−0.55 (−2.5)
Germany	1.07 (16.5)	−0.48 (−1.7)	0.76	1.00	2.50 (61.0)	−0.00* (−0.1)
Italy	1.11 (22.2)	−2.05 (−5.5)	1.15	1.28	2.08 (14.8)	0.03* (0.4)
UK	0.8 (33.0)	−0.17* (−1.7)	0.51	0.78	2.99 (19.4)	−0.30 (−2.0)
US	0.99 (5.4)	−0.74 (−2.6)	0.64	0.88	3.13 (11.5)	−0.65 (−3.8)
Japan	1.55 (22.9)	−0.42* (−1.0)	2.43	2.35	1.22 (15.6)	−0.33* (−1.0)

Source: 'European economy', n. 16, July 1983, p. 137 140.
Notes
* Estimation not significantly different from zero.
[1] Income elasticities of export and import (respectively to world demand and GDP) are directly estimated, their ratio estimates some elasticity of GDP to world demand.
[2] Income and price elasticities of export (resp. import) are here simultaneously estimated.

these elasticities must, therefore, be worked out to assess any recent drift in growth differentials.

First, one must be directly convinced of the importance recently given to the external-policy issue. Working on the priority actually given to different policy objectives in the mid 1980s, Oudiz (1985) has shown that French policy largely favoured improvement of the current-account ratio over output growth or inflation, while Germany gave higher ranking to this last objective. Table 9.4 shows the revealed different trade-offs for France, Germany, the United Kingdom and Italy. Despite this priority in policy objectives, the trade balance did show some specific difficulty in recovering from external price shocks and remained mainly, though decreasingly, negative, over the whole cycle (see Table 9.5 and Fig. 9.2). Recovery in other European economies was always quicker. Surplus on current transactions points to similar lags in adjustments. Large lasting deficits raise the question of the limits to indebtedness. If worries over persistent large trade deficits dominated the change from the Chirac to the Barre government in 1976, the debt issue only became central in 1983 under the socialist government. More recently, a deficit in the trade of manufactured goods, in the first semester of 1987, has been seen as another sign of alarm at the French

Table 9.4 Revealed preferences in policy objectives in the mid 1980s
(trade-offs in %)

Country	Output u1	Inflation	Current account ratio u2
Germany	1	−5.6	.3
France	1	−1.9	3.4
United Kingdom	1	−.9	.9
Italy	1	−1.2	1.4

Notes: These estimations have been done by Oudiz (1985) in comparing actual and potential growth paths of European economies.

Table 9.5 Trade balance as a percentage of GDP (average % changes)

Periods	1960−67	1968−73	1974−9	1980−4
France	0.8	0.4	−0.2	−1.3
7 major OECD	0.6	0.5	0.0	−0.3
EC	0.2	0.7	0.0	0.1

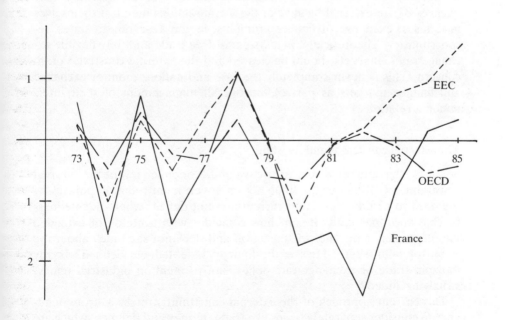

Figure 9.2 Yearly % changes 1973−87

economy's incapacity to accommodate its external exchanges. This deterioration seems to follow directly from France's trade structure and especially from the importance of its exports in OPEC countries, which experienced sharp income reductions.

The question is, therefore, whether such structures can be changed. The shortcomings of French entrepreneurs are often blamed for the difficulty in adjusting to the evolution of world trade. Examples of such criticism were recently given by two successive Trade Ministers, Mrs Cresson, blaming 'the traditional neglect for industry of capital owners' and Mr Noir pointing to 'the lack of business spirit'.[1] This criticism is similar to the charges which were addressed in the past against the capitalists during the inter-war period. This convergence does not mean that the diagnosis is correct, nor that we are back in the 1930s; but it clearly suggests that some revision is called for in the management of the external constraint.

THE RATIONALE FOR THE EXTERNAL CONSTRAINT

It seems paradoxical that the slackening of the external constraint should depend on firms' greater dynamism. The external constraint does not exist, *per se*, at firm level. Firms face competition in markets, whether internal or external, in which they are willing to expand, taking into consideration transaction costs. Only at the macroeconomic level do the specific consequences of the external balance of these transactions manifest themselves in terms of exchange or finance problems, largely resorting to states' responsibilities. Theoretically, in a system of free trade and fully flexible exchange rates, markets should be cleared and the external constraint of no concern. This is never completely the case and nations monitor exchange and finance markets as part of the overall management of their international relations.

The external constraint and the state

So far, we have taken a very restrictive and economic view of the external constraint, pointing out the limits set on government reflation policies by the need to avoid a persistent current-account deficit, when indebtedness reaches an upper limit. It somehow coincides with a notion of extended interdependence in times of stagnation and does not say much about the room for manoeuvre. How is the limit to indebtedness defined? Is any move in trade or exchange-rate policy, not to mention industrial policy, strictly excluded?

This current approach of the external constraint stresses a strong tendency to consider separately issues like trade, money and defence, which are all part of the state's monitoring of a national economy's external relations.

We choose instead to focus on three central issues in foreign affairs namely defence, money and trade. In a historical perspective, these three issues successively acquired a reality of their own. Through time, the weight of each issue varies and we have reached a stage in the last decades where the trade issue has gained great importance (as recalled in Cooper 1973), giving full economic meaning to interdependence, as referred to previously. We assume that this historical process may shape some of the national characteristics influencing the ways in which national governments presently deal with external relations.

But the main benefit we see in a short survey of the past is the broadening of our scope regarding how defence, exchange and trade issues can be combined in varying weights. We shall try to assess these influences in addressing the three foreign-policy issues of defence, money and trade. Let us recall, to begin with, the different stages which led foreign policy issues in France to extend to these three dimensions.

Defence necessities strictly oriented all other issues until late in the eighteenth century, as illustrated by Adam Smith's comment on the Act of Navigation: 'As defence is of much more importance than opulence, the Act of Navigation is perhaps the wisest of all the commercial regulations of England.' The history of modern nation states (which excludes the merchant-cities) witnessed, from the sixteenth century onwards, the progressive rise of money and trade as specific foreign-policy issues. The states, whose legitimacy was initially founded uniquely on defence, first gained progressive control over money and then linked the trade issue with control over new production techniques. In France, these developments came about through a series of impressive failures.

Public monopoly over mintage was only achieved in France in the mid sixteenth century. The power and the room for manoeuvre it brought the state remained limited, however. A real turning point was reached in the seventeenth century with the approach, defended by the mercantilists, which emphasized that gold was precious because it was money and not the other way round. But this recognition was not enough. Two things were still needed to give monetary policy some room for manoeuvre as distinct from defence or budget policy: a banking system and the development of paper money.

France experienced two failures while entering this 'modern phase of government'. First, Law's system, an ambitious experiment in the early eighteenth century combining two innovations, paper money and bank credit, collapsed for lack of confidence. Second the 'paper money' issued in the late eighteenth century by the French Revolution (although close, in principle, to the old asset-pawning practice – church and aristocrats' properties being the assets) was not accepted and led to radical enforcement (price taxation and capital punishment). This situation was blamed on Pitt's manoeuvrings to depreciate the new French currency (Einzig 1962).

The abolition of enforcement led to hyperinflation. The experiment came to an end in 1797 with an official return to silver money. The Banque de France, which was created three years later under Napoleon, was to be remarkably cautious in the years to come. The franc, introduced in 1803, was given a metal parity, which was to remain unchanged for 125 years (not withstanding short periods of non-convertibility, c.f. Einzig 1962, ch. 16).

The rise of the trade issue is more difficult to trace. It has always been obvious (and clearly expounded by the mercantilists) that government should favour the expansion of trade, if only for fiscal reasons. Trade controls and direct intervention were the means for pursuing such an objective. Strategic concerns could motivate specific state interventions, as demonstrated by Colbert's policies in favour of shipyards. Tariffs, quotas and trade restrictions also varied according to military alliances. The monetary issue took the upper hand over commercial 'policies', when they aimed at favouring the entry of gold or silver.

The real change took place in 1860, with the Anglo-French Treaty of Free Trade, which was based mainly on 'modern' economic motives (following an entrepreneurial logic as opposed to the more speculative simple trader logic). A new drive for liberalization ensued from the drive towards industrialization and mechanization. To catch up with the changes taking place in the technical system, especially in the United Kingdom, was a general concern for all countries at the time. Whereas agricultural products and textiles had constituted the bulk of world trade until then, commerce in machinery increased very rapidly. The 1860 Anglo-French Treaty of Commerce, by which France abolished all prohibitions on the import of British goods and lowered many duties (while Britain lowered import duties on French wines and silk goods!) included a most-favoured nation clause which subsequently helped to promote a general reduction of protectionism in Europe. It ushered in a twenty-year period of 'laissez-faire', and initiated fully-fledged modern external constraint of international relations. In this sense, modern external constraint can be dated as far back as the mid nineteenth century.[2]

To conclude let us add, in accordance with Mistral (1985), that this period of free-trade policy was deceitful: external accounts deteriorated, industrial production slowed down, while foreign competition inflicted a major blow to a poorly efficient agriculture. Thus the successive experiences through which a comprehensive 'foreign policy' matured were rather negative. Some recurring features, shaping contemporary external constraints, follow from this early past.

Modern external constraint: past regimes and crises

To examine the extent and the nature of these influences from the distant past, we shall first take a closer look at the main foreign-policy options which followed the laissez-faire period up to the present crisis. Our break-down of time will roughly distinguish the first half of the century from the thirty years of post-World War Two expansion, thus encompassing two relatively deceitful periods: the 1930s and a successful era in the 1950s and 1960s.

The first period does not correspond to any real steady set of options which can be qualified as a regime monitoring the country's international relations (especially when two wars and a worldwide economic recession constituted major crises). Nevertheless, it maintained some characteristics throughout, reducing foreign dependence and developing colonial links. The handling of international relations during the period may appear both as the reaction to the deceitful experiments of the nineteenth century and as the cumulative consequence of troubled times and protectionist pressures all over the world.

Let us review the main lines of the three foreign-policy issues. The defence issue was largely oriented by the antagonism with Germany and the drive to develop, geographically and then economically, a colonial empire. This did not keep France from being concerned with its influence and role on the world stage, a strategy of 'grandeur' which was to be a constant through both periods.

As for exchange policy, the First World War put an end to the laissez-faire period (under the gold standard adopted in 1878). The inter-war period was rather chaotic with repeated devaluations and high speculative pressure which nearly went out of control as in 1924 and 1928, and again in 1937, in defiance of Blum's government. Speculation and capital flight due to lack of political confidence were new on many grounds. First, they contrasted widely with the long-term stability through wars and revolutions of the previous century. Old fears for convertibility and stability of laws or the experience of assignats died hard, especially among countryfolk (see Sauvy 1984, vol. I, ch. 1). An important shift also occurred in part: while speculative moves had always been attributed to manoeuvres from foreigners, capital flight in the mid 1920s during the left government (Cartel des Gauches) took on political overtones (defiance from the wealthy, *le mur d'argent*). This evolution was largely confirmed in 1937, when the debate about devaluation and capital flight prefigured that of the early 1980s. This open crisis in exchange policy during the inter-war period was not really circumvented by either exchange-control measures or through alliances such as the Cold Bloc or the Tripartite Agreement.

The trade issue was marked by a return to protectionism, especially in favour of agriculture which had been affected by the previous laissez-faire period at least up to the 1930s, when international and climatic conditions combined to cause an agricultural crisis as severe as the one experienced in late nineteenth century. One should notice that the period under review covers decades of relative acceleration followed by a decade of relative deceleration in comparison with France's main partners. One can thus distinguish a first period up to the crisis of the 1930s, in which moderate protectionism allowed for the development of new modern industries, from a second period, during the 1930s, in which increased protection worldwide and erratic exchange rates led traditional industries to take advantage of colonial markets, which, however, were detrimental to modern industries. Such was the context which accentuated the backwardness and malthusianist aspect of industrial firms of the times.

On the whole, this phase appears as a period of reaction, in which the management of international relations led to an about-turn in defence, exchange and trade policy. The international environment was only partly responsible for it. Failure of the nineteenth-century national experiences also played its part in this account, with regard to the evolution of agriculture, to relations between modern and traditional industries/enterprises and to the attitude towards national currency. Developments in this last issue, with increased sensitivity of capital flight and speculation to political situations, announced one of the forms the external constraint was to actively take in the following period.

After the chaotic development of the 1930s, the post-Second World War period constituted a real break with the emergence of a specific form of 'modern capitalism' as Shonfield (1965) called it. But this new balance between public and private power, which launched the 'thirty glorious years', has been constantly challenged by the driving forces of international trade. The new developmentist spirit was largely channelled through public institutions or firms linked with the public sector. Such a mixed economy tended to bolster national independence all the more. Paradoxically, the French economy's strong dependence on US loans and Marshall aid during the reconstruction period was a major factor in enlarging the role of the state as the only source of finance in the economic recovery. This paradox is demonstrative of the whole period, in which France's comeback as a major power was closely linked to US hegemony. The same may be said of a large number of Western economies, but the peculiarity comes from the contradiction between a national system aimed at planning (even if only indicatively) and US hegemony which relied on the expansion of world trade as a counterpart to its worldwide defence role.

In this sense (of a developing contradiction which resulted in the progressive decay of French planning after the mid-1960s) the regime of external relations which goes from the early post-war period to the mid-1970s can be qualified as a 'forced transition' to free trade and foreign exchange. This transition should not be seen as the result of direct pressure from institutions like the OECD or the GATT. Rather, the need to progress towards freer exchanges was calculated step by step to either solve internal problems (like the modernization of agriculture, excess capacities in coal and steel) or to face new balances of power at world level (decolonization,

Suez and Middle East supply). Commitments to free trade in the UK or Germany were more spontaneous and restrictions considered as transitory, while France adjusted when pressed by obvious necessities.

Illustrations are numerous. Let us start with the intensification of trade, bound to become a rising issue in a world where the US hegemony largely took care of the two other issues in foreign affairs. We shall not dwell on minor points of restrictive practices and invisible barriers, which might lie behind free-trade agreements. It is not at all obvious that unfair play was involved in setting up agreements like the ECSC (European Coal and Steel Community) and then the Common Market.

The latter offered a sphere of expansion, protected from overseas competitors, to an agriculture which had doubled its production per man during the 1950s, thanks to mechanization and the use of fertilizers. Guaranteed prices helped to progressively reduce non-competitive units and to settle chronic peasant unrest, which dated as far back as the nineteenth century. The prospect of a common market was a real challenge for traditional industries, which had to adjust to the loss of colonial markets. Such were the necessities. Modern industries were thought to be able to resist foreign competition. In many cases they did even better and these successes on export markets were 'unplanned'. A symbolic example is the car manufacturer Renault, which in the early 1960s wanted to export more and, therefore, did not respect its centrally advised production level. Growing integration in the world economy offered more autonomy to the firms and loosened the ties of indicative planning. By the end of the 1960s, the planning system reverted mainly to financing large and more or less successful programmes in aeronautics, nuclear energy, computers etc.

It was also in the nature of the French system that these industries, working mainly on state programmes, for the administrations (telephone, defence) or for large public firms (utilities, transport) contributed positively to the trade balance. This was not genuine, in the sense that these exports to foreign states partly relied on direct government negotiations. Big contracts and barter exchanges with oil-producing countries which took place after the first oil price shock, when the external constraint became severely binding, illustrate these situations *a posteriori*.

The arms trade is certainly the major sector of this kind. In 1980 the arms trade surplus represented half of the total manufactured goods surplus (F 16.3 billion for a total surplus of F 34.7 billion). The importance of these arms exports contrasts with the relative decline in military expenditures which occurred between the 1950s and the 1970s (from 7 per cent of GDP to less than 4 per cent). This shift is symbolic of the new balance between defence and trade issues which progressively developed during the thirty years of post-war expansion in which France was given many occasions to measure her military power: from the Suez expedition to the decolonization wars. In this perspective, the choice for national nuclear armament was coherent with the strategy of 'grandeur' and the nationally based growth project. The kind of medium-sized warfare economy which France developed also opened up possibilities for civil and military trade. The sale to Iraq of a nuclear plant in 1976 thus constitutes another example of the connection between existing public programmes and exports promoted by government in a situation of active external constraint.

Let us now turn to the money and exchange issue. In the kind of package deal, which at the time represented the international regime under US hegemony, the part concerning money and exchange was clearly the most difficult to accommodate in the economy. From the start it explicitly required free convertibility of the franc within a system of fixed exchange rates. It took over ten years, i.e. until 1958, despite American aid in the late 1940s, to adjust to these recommendations. The main reason for this difficulty came from highly inflationary domestic pressures. Price inflation was a lax way to solve conflicting issues over distribution (especially between wage earners and non-wage earners), which were not taken into account in the new management of the economy. Successive competitive devaluations were used to adjust these internal pressures and to support the development of industry (see Mistral 1975). The successful 20 per cent devaluation in 1958 and the founding of the Fifth Republic marked a truce but not an end to instability and internal mistrust of the franc. In 1968 political defiance led again to capital flights, devaluations and exchange controls.

Restrictions were enforced on foreign investments over the whole period. Exchange policy remained a vulnerable issue. Therefore, the collapse of the Bretton Woods system in the 1970s left the franc more exposed to speculation, all else being equal, than similar currencies. This was quickly demonstrated after the first oil shock, the impact of which was aggravated by an increased inflation in 1973.

The mid 1970s ended what we may call a period of 'forced integration' to account for the relative antagonism between the free trade option of the hegemonic system and the new form of dirigism at work in France. French planning was reduced to a more standard form of interventionism under the heads of the different ministries. Meanwhile, integration acquired momentum. The Common Market was a reality (with 50 per cent of France's exports and 69 per cent of imports in manufactured products in 1979) which kept a dual structure with agricultural and industrial issues being dealt with separately. Therefore, the policy debate which developed in the late 1970s was not so much on free trade versus protectionism, as on whether industry could follow the general drive for competitiveness (the industrial imperative) or whether the level of interdependence should be reduced. To avoid a disorderly and crisis-ridden approach, this last option required international bargaining and co-operation (c.f. Hoffman 1978), which was not on the agenda. The first option, to strengthen competitiveness, had to take into account the scattering of the weak and strong points of France's involvement in world trade. But there was no common ground between the length and the uncertain effectiveness of any policy to facilitate structural adjustments and the rapidity and the magnitude of the crises that could take place in finance.

In effect, the real blow to old French foreign policy was not so much to have a high level of intertrade, as to be in a highly volatile international money system. Since the 1930s, the money issue was left unresolved, in the sense that it mixed opposition against the franc and inflationary solutions to internal social conflicts with its functional role as a means of transaction. In a world of fixed and organized exchanged rates, where periodic devaluations and exchange controls could be set up, viable if not satisfying arrangements could be made. The breaking up of the Bretton Woods agreements and the dollar crisis greatly increased the influence of capital markets over exchange rates and conditioned what could be done in trade.

The MacCracken report in 1977 made this new level of interdependency clear when it recommended giving priority to reducing inflation. Internal price inflation was, thus, becoming more of a foreign-policy issue at precisely the time when a flexible exchange-rate system should have ended this linkage. Such a bias was all the more binding in countries like France, more prone to inflation and capital flight.

THE EXTERNAL CONSTRAINT ON
MITTERRAND'S REFLATION POLICY

The overall strategy

The difficulties encountered by the Barre government, which peaked in 1980 when a point of GDP growth above the low EEC average of 0.5 per cent was accompanied by a sharp increase in the trade deficit (see Table 9.1, Table 9.4), made the binding nature of French integration in the world economy quite clear. Therefore, when Mitterrand won the presidential election in May 1981, his strategy was strictly bound to balancing what could be done economically and politically in the short run with what could be placed in a longer-term perspective. The challenge was to set up new institutions and linkages that would progressively restore some room for manoeuvre to resume economic growth and reduce unemployment. These reorganizations were to increase competitiveness and develop some synergy between national activities so as to reduce the external dependence of France's economy, without resorting to open protectionism. Large consistent institutional changes were to take place rapidly to benefit from the impetus of an electoral victory under a presidential regime which offered the new government unprecedented power. Meanwhile, mild reflation was to soften social acceptance of these institutional changes and delays in full recovery. Stringent political conditions are required to extend on a long-term basis full employment policies which were only perceived in a short- or medium-term perspective (Petit 1986). An alliance with the Communist party, the revival of concerted planning, as well as the renewal of labour laws and plans for decentralization were all thought to facilitate the accept-ance of long-term policy objectives.

To balance this comprehensive internal restructuring, the strategy in foreign relations was surprisingly conservative. Defence and diplomacy were planned to very strictly follow an Atlantic perspective so as to reassure the Western bloc. Commitments to trade agreements within the GATT and the EEC were to be respected, given France's large integration into the world economy and to avoid retaliation. On the exchange issue, the European experiment of the EMS, which offered protection against the fluctuations of the dollar, was to be pursued.

In such a context the failure of the reflation policy and the 1983 U-turn can be attributed either to exaggerated oversized reflation which had detri-mental effects on the set of feasible policies or to an underestimation of the constraint put on reflation by adverse trends in competitiveness.

In this section we shall stress that the latter explanation is the more likely.

A moderate and brief reflation policy

The reflation policy in 1981 and 1982 was, by current standards, brief and moderate, as acknowledged by Fontaneau, Muet (1985) and Sachs, Wyplosz (1986). This reflation policy relied on both budgetary and non budgetary measures. The former were rather balanced; the budget deficit in 1981, an election year, was only pushed up to 1.5 per cent of GDP (against 1 per cent as planned by Barre in his 1981 budget) as compared with the EEC average of 5 per cent (see Table 9.6). This feature effectively doubled in 1982 rising to 3 per cent, although an obvious slowdown in all attempts at reflation occurred as soon as mid 1982. Raising the minimum wage was the main non-budgetary reflation measure. In real terms the minimum wage went up by 5.8 per cent in 1981 and by 4.2 per cent in 1982. But once again the effect of these measures on the wage bill was softened by reductions in social security taxes. Nevertheless, this cautious attitude was accompanied by rises in household consumption of 1.7 per cent in 1981 and 2.7 per cent in 1982 which exceeded the corresponding growth rates of GDP (respec-tively 0.2 per cent and 1.9 per cent). But these discrepancies were brought about much more by changes in wage formation than by economic-policy measures.[3]

The rise in wages (3.1 per cent in real terms in 1982) was certainly boosted by the rise in minimum wages and by the reduction of the working week, from 40 to 39 hours, a measure which the government only advised.

Table 9.6 Outlays and net lending of government (as a % of GDP)

Years		Average 68–73	Average 74–79	80	81	82	83	84	85
France	O	39.0	43.7	46.4	49.1	51.1	52.0	52.7	52.4
	L	0.6	−0.9	0.2	−1.8	−2.7	−3.1	−2.9	−2.6
EC	O	37.9	44.0	46.4	49.1	50.3	50.8	51.0	52.5
	L	−0.5	−3.2	−3.1	−4.8	−5.0	−4.8	−4.8	−4.6
OECD	O	32.4	37.1	39.5	40.1	41.6	41.7	40.7	40.6
	L	−0.2	−2.3	−2.5	−2.8	−4.2	−4.6	−3.8	−3.7

Source: OECD historical statistics.
Note: O: Outlays; L: Lending.

But more decisive and somewhat unexpected in the absence of large social movements, was the fact that wage rises have been buttressed by a change in the balance of power between employers and workers.

Otherwise, levels of government outlays remained quite in pace with what was done in other European countries (see Table 9.6), while net lending of government was kept at a, comparatively, very low level. This celebrated (but moderate) reflation policy was solemnly put to an end in March 1983 (solemnly to curb expectations which had fuelled increases in consumption, in Delors' own words). The distinct move towards restrictive policies which accompanied the 8 per cent devaluation of March 1983 was blamed on the binding nature of the external constraint.

Was the binding nature of the external constraint the outcome of a policy error or of a slowdown in the world economy?

Fontaneau and Muet (1986) have estimated the macroeconomic impact of the whole set of policy measures taken over the years 1981–3. Table 9.7 presents these estimates, as deviations from the initial reference growth path. The overall effects were modest: +1.7 per cent for GDP over the whole period, while unemployment was reduced by 171,000 and employment increased by 323,000. As noticed, the boost given to consumption (+2.3 per cent over the three years) overtook the global effect on GDP, but still the effect on investment was much bigger (+4.8 per cent). These features of consumption and investment growth implied a noticeable increase in the trade deficit: 23 billion francs in 1982, 36 billion francs in 1983. The rise in consumption contributed largely to this deficit, as the trade deficit in household equipment (cars excepted) and consumer goods doubled between 1980 and 1982 (from −9.4 billion francs in 1980 to −20.8 billion francs in 1982), while the surplus in the automobile industry was reduced by 6.6 billion francs. But investments also played a large part in this deterioration as their import content is twice as big.

Table 9.7 The reflation policy of 1981 and 1982 (deviations from reference path)

	1981	1982	1983
	Real terms in annual growth rates		
GDP	0.3	0.9	0.5
Household consumption	0.5	1.2	0.6
Investment	0.6	2.5	1.7
	Levels in thousands		
Employment	36	225	323
Unemployment	−19	−117	−171
	Levels in billions		
Trade deficit	−4.5	−23	−36
Net lending of government *ex post*	−9.8	−43	−35

Source: Fonteneau, Muet (1986, p. 129).

These increases in deficits thus represented respectively 0.6 per cent and 0.9 per cent of GDP. By comparison Fontaneau and Muet (1986) have estimated that the 1975 reflation under the first Chirac government led to a decrease in trade balance of 0.8 per cent of GDP. Therefore, the policy was not really oversized and, if judging only from the features mentioned, there was no need for a drastic change in tone. The policy could have been scaled down progressively or selectively.

Another factor, which worsened the situation, was the depression of world demand in 1982. While the French government, along with OECD experts, anticipated a reflation of world demand after the 1980–81 trough of the second oil shock, the depression deepened. French policy was therefore out of phase. France's external markets were stagnating while her internal market was one of the few opportunities left for internal business expansion. At the time France kept her market share of world trade (if compared with the eight OECD majors), but this resulted in a stagnation of the volume of exports and a rise in the volume of imports. In such a perspective, the policy would seem to have failed because it was 'anti-cyclical' (in contrast with 1975). If so, the policy had to be postponed rather than reversed, as soon as it became clear that no propitious momentum would be given by the external markets.

In our opinion the picture is more worrying. Long-term weaknesses of the manufacturing industries were becoming apparent (some of them a concern for most old industrialized countries) which could only be cured in the long term. Financial markets and speculations against the franc were exerting continuous pressures, to which no devaluation could any longer easily put a stop.

ADVERSE TRENDS IN FOREIGN RELATIONS

The trade issue: from a Common Market venture to the embarrassment of worldwide free trade

In the early 1980s, association with the Common Market had become an insuperable fact and to pull out was no longer a policy issue. The deep integration of the European economies clearly seemed to forbid any radical break from a, by then, one-generation-old trade agreement.

The Common Market had, by the early 1980s, reached its maturity. It had also appeared as a very rigid structure whenever confronted with any kind of challenge, like the collapse of the international monetary system or the energy crisis in the 1970s. No real efficient common stand, policy or institution could be set up at the time at European level. The Common Market retained, rather strikingly, the sectoral duality of its beginning between agriculture and industry issues. While internal arrangements which were rather protectionist against the rest of the world were con-stantly discussed in agricultural trade, industrial trade kept pace with the general liberalization trend spurred by the GATT worldwide negotiations. On new matters like energy and services, no real common position could be attained at the European level. The room for manoeuvre of any European country was therefore reduced, being committed by intra-European agree-ments on agricultural and industrial issues and without strong common stands on others.

The trade-policy issue was thus clearly limited in the early 1980s, once the option to pull out of the Common Market was discarded.[4] Therefore, in case of a deficit in the trade balance or in the balance of payments, if the devaluation option is also ruled out (which we shall see in the next section), only structural or industrial policies remain to ease the external constraint. Although such structural sectoral policies are not active in the short term, they are decided at a national level (leaving some room for direct govern-ment action) and eventually are efficient in the longer run.

The actions taken in the energy sector in the mid 1970s showed such efficiency. After the first oil price shock, France, like most European coun-tries, tried to increase its independence ratio (production/consumption of energy) through substitutions and more efficient uses. A large pro-gramme to develop nuclear energy, initiated in the 1970s, brought this ratio from 22.5 per cent in 1973 to 34.5 per cent in 1982 and 46.2 per cent in 1986 (as compared to the EEC average of 42.2 per cent in 1982 (UK excepted).

Despite this policy, the cost of net energy imports could not be met by surpluses in agricultural and industrial products (see Tables 9.8 and 9.9). The surplus in the trade of agricultural products, which is largely the

Table 9.8 Balance of payments: structure and changes

Balances	Billions of FF						
	1980	1981	1982	1983	1984	1985	1986
Goods	−87.6	−87.1	−136.4	−88.4	−69.3	−69.4	−33.1
of which industry	35.1	55.4	29.7	60.2	97.1	83.0	32.7
of which energy	−133.5	−162.6	−179.6	−168.9	−190.5	−181.9	−91.4
Services	53.2	56.6	67.2	81.7	97.9	97.4	85.7
of which tourism	9.2	7.7	11.7	21.8	28.6	30.1	21.8
Goods and Services	−34.4	−30.5	−69.2	−6.7	28.6	28.0	52.6
Transfers	15.7	2.7	−10.7	−28.3	−32.5	−26.7	−23.7
National financing capacity	−18.7	−27.8	−79.9	−35.0	−3.9	1.3	28.9
% of GDP	−0.7	−0.9	−2.2	−0.9	−0.1	0.03	0.6
Balance FOB/FOB	−62.0	−59.4	−93.5	−43.3	−21.9	−24.9	0.4
Balance CIF/FOB including military equipment	−84.8	−83.6	−131.4	−83.3	−61.0	−61.3	−27.8

Source: National accounts.

outcome of the Common Agricultural Policy, displayed an increasing but unsteady trend which averaged 10 per cent of the energy bill during 1980–85. Ups and downs remained (especially in 1982, see Table 9.9), due to changes in the dollar rate or weather conditions.

Deficit in trade of manufactured goods was more than double the agricultural trade surplus (during 1980–85, see Table 9.9), leaving a huge trade deficit. Moreover, the free trade orientation of the Common Market in manufactured goods resulted in large deficits in France's intra-European trade (see Table 9.9). It demanded an improvement in the surplus in manufactured goods, too small and ill-oriented when compared to the average or medium-to-large industrial economies.

An active industrial policy to boost competitiveness

In the above perspective, Mitterrand's long-term industrial strategy intended to reorganize activities so as to reduce the interdependence of the French economy[5] while enhancing its competitiveness.

Two kinds of measures were taken. The first enlarged the nationalized-industry sector, with firms taking up medium-term contracts to pursue objectives in line with planning. The second set of measures operated through sectoral plans, organizing access to product markets and co-ordinating improvements in production processes. This new co-ordination was meant to reduce the import content and to boost exports. Difficulties came from the following:

Table 9.9 Trade balances: deficits in manufacture trade with EC countries are larger than surpluses in agriculture (in billions of francs)

	1980	1981	1982	1983	1984	1985	1986
Agricultural products	11.3	20.7	14.2	20.9	24.6	30.1	26.2
Manufactured products[1]							
intra EEC	−33.2	−41.4	−69.2	−56.7	−50.1	−54.8	−73.3
OECD non EEC	−21.5	−21.3	−30.7	−25.8	−12.8	−10.2	−18.5
non OECD	73.2	96.6	109.3	121.4	128.6	117.6	90.4
Total	18.5	33.9	9.4	38.7	65.7	52.6	−1.4
Military equipment	16.2	21.2	20.1	21.5	31.6	30.4	34.1

[1] Military equipment excluded.

- The weakness of new nationalized firms requiring intense restructuring.
- The heavy financial requirements to accommodate the decline of old industries (coal, steel, shipbuilding).
- The limits set to sectoral plans by the Common Market regulations and by their dispersed structure (as in the machine-tools industry).
- The lack of industrial models defined in practical terms so as to co-ordinate the strategy of modern industries.

As no real central co-ordination was set up, this industrial strategy somehow extended the interventionism of public sponsored programmes which immediately followed upon the decay of indicative planning. Zysman (1978) has underlined that, while it may succeed in some 'technically stable, heavy investment, production-oriented industries', it generates problems in 'technically unstable, market-oriented industries'. Therefore, the main benefit of these industrial policies was to give a new start on the international market to industries (either old or new) which were in difficulty at the beginning of the 1980s. This implied reshuffling management, restructuring the firm's production range and helping with the modernization of equipment.

The new opportunities given to industrial activities were nevertheless largely hampered by: (a) the length of the reorganization process; (b) the instability on exchange and finance markets, and (c) the initial disadvantages in price and quality competitiveness, which gave large momentum to the penetration ratios.

Weaknesses of the trade structure

The weak and strong points of French industries were well assessed by the end of the 1970s. The distribution of income elasticities of exports and imports at a sectoral level (see Table 9.10) helps to illustrate the gap in trade-balance dynamics. Most sectors display high import elasticities to GDP and a positive trend. Only in 'armaments, shipbuilding and aero-nautics', do we see export elasticities to world trade greater than one, combined with a positive trend. Furthermore, high-import elasticity in the sector, which is also the best exporter, stresses a strong link between imports and exports (especially clear with the arms trade). Studies at a more detailed sectoral level (55 industrial sectors) outline that performing and non-performing activities are scattered throughout all types of activities, modern or traditional, equipment or consumer products (Delattre 1986). Even at this detailed level, the trade balance still very often displays a deficit with industrial countries and a surplus with developing countries. This dispersion and this triangular trade are considered major weaknesses of France's integration in world trade.

Discrepancies in income elasticities account largely for the continued deterioration of penetration ratios for manufactured products in the 1980s: they increased by one-fifth between 1980 and 1986.[6] But this overall figure is not at all peculiar to the French economy. The overall penetration ratio of the French economy (share of the national market supplied by imports) averaged 25 per cent over the period 1981–5, which is less than in the UK (27 per cent), West Germany (27 per cent) or Italy (28 per cent). This ratio increased in France by two points between 1981–5, as it did in the EEC average. It can thus be argued that France's integration in world trade is following the general pattern of all developed industrial economies (see Hazart and Khong 1987).

The characteristic of the structure of French trade has to be looked for at the more disaggregated level mentioned above. This specificity appears in the particularly high ratio of intra-branch trade which, according to Lassudrie-Duchene and Mucchielli (1979), averaged, in 1974, 81 per cent in France versus 77 per cent in the UK, 61 per cent in Italy, 58 per cent in W. Germany, 54 per cent in the U.S. and 44 per cent in Japan. Lafay (1985) also underlined this noticeable intra–branch specialization, as he found only five agricultural products with large surpluses in France. Such a tightly-knit network of trade could have advantages of its own. International trade theory explains this intra-sectoral trade mainly through product differentiation and market integration, which seems to oppose the specialization process of the comparative-advantages thesis. It could effectively correspond to an intra individual sector specialization towards high-quality or innovative products. According to Debonneuil and Delattre (1987), the higher prices of exports, when compared with imports, in each individual branch suggest that such is the case. But this feature has to be combined with the two others given by the directions of trade flow (triangular trade) and by the widespread trade deficit of most individual sectors.

These widespread trade deficits in individual sectors and with developed

Table 9.10 Elasticities of imports and exports

Column groups: (1)–(3) Internal market; (4)–(9) Imports [(4)–(6) Relative prices, (7) Others, (8)–(9) Imports]; (10)–(12) World demand; (13)–(18) Exports [(13)–(15) Relative prices, (16) Others, (17)–(18) Exports].

Sector	(1) TCAM	(2) ELAS	(3) CONT	(4) TCAM	(5) ELAS	(6) CONT	(7) Others	(8) TCAM	(9) ELAS	(10) TCAM	(11) ELAS	(12) CONT	(13) TCAM	(14) ELAS	(15) CONT	(16) Others	(17) TCAM	(18) ELAS
Iron and steel	1.0	1.3	1.3	-0.1	-0.6	0.0	0.7	2.0	1.9	4.3	0.9	3.8	-0.5	-1.1	0.6	-3.2	1.2	0.3
Non ferrous metals	2.5	0.9	2.2	-1.4	0.0	0.0	0.2	2.4	1.0	5.1	1.6	8.1	2.1	-1.1	2.4	-3.4	2.3	0.4
Construction materials	2.6	0.9	2.3	-1.0	-0.4	0.4	1.6	4.3	1.6	2.3	0.9	2.1	-0.2	-1.1	0.2	-0.6	1.7	0.7
Glass	3.0	1.2	3.7	-2.0	-0.8	1.5	1.7	6.8	2.3	5.9	1.0	5.8	0.8	-1.1	-0.9	-0.7	4.2	0.7
Basic chemicals	1.6	1.1	1.7	-1.1	0.0	0.0	3.7	5.4	3.4	8.3	0.8	6.4	0.5	-1.1	-0.6	-0.4	5.4	0.7
Paper	2.4	1.6	3.7	-0.7	-1.1	0.7	-0.5	3.9	1.7	4.4	1.2	5.5	1.4	-1.1	-1.6	-1.0	2.9	0.7
Plastic material	1.6	1.1	1.7	-0.4	-0.4	0.1	1.7	3.5	2.2	4.9	1.4	6.8	0.2	-1.1	-0.2	-1.7	4.9	1.0
Mechanical construction	3.2	1.4	4.4	-0.3	0.0	0.0	3.2	7.6	2.4	7.4	0.8	6.2	1.0	-1.1	-1.1	0.4	5.5	0.7
Electrical equipment	4.1	1.1	4.4	-0.5	-0.7	0.3	0.1	4.8	1.2	4.4	0.9	4.1	1.7	-1.1	-1.8	0.5	2.8	0.5
Investment machines	8.4	1.1	9.4	-1.6	-0.6	1.0	1.3	11.7	1.4	6.4	0.7	4.2	0.3	-1.1	-0.3	4.7	8.6	1.3
Automobiles	5.2	1.1	5.5	0.1	-0.7	-0.1	0.4	5.8	1.1	9.0	0.8	7.6	-0.1	-1.1	0.1	-3.1	4.6	0.5
Aeronautics, shipbuilding, armaments	4.3	1.2	5.3	-0.4	-1.4	0.6	-1.1	4.8	1.1	7.0	1.2	8.1	0.6	-1.1	-0.7	-4.7	2.7	0.4
Pharmaceuticals	3.0	1.3	3.8	0.2	0.0	0.0	1.7	5.5	1.9	3.3	1.4	4.7	-0.7	-0.8	0.6	-1.3	6.4	2.0
Textiles	3.6	1.4	4.8	-1.8	0.0	0.0	1.6	6.4	1.8	5.6	1.1	6.1	-0.3	-0.8	0.2	0.8	4.9	0.9
Leather	1.7	2.0	3.3	-1.5	-1.0	1.5	-0.6	4.2	2.5	6.5	0.5	3.4	1.3	-0.8	-1.0	-0.7	4.4	0.7
Wood	1.2	1.6	2.0	-0.8	-1.3	1.1	2.0	5.1	4.1	6.5	0.4	2.6	2.5	-0.8	-2.0	-0.4	0.9	0.1
Printing	3.3	1.2	3.9	-1.0	0.0	0.0	1.8	5.7	1.7	6.3	0.7	4.3	-0.5	-0.8	0.4	-1.2	1.9	0.3
	1.1	0.8	0.8	-0.3	-0.7	0.2	2.2	3.2	2.9	5.1	1.0	5.0					4.2	0.8

Notes
1 Growth rate of internal market.
2 Income elasticity of imports.
3 (3) = (1) × (2).
4 Growth rate of relative prices.
5 Price elasticity of imports.
6 (6) = (4) × (5).
7 Trend in imports.
8 Growth rate of imports.
9 Overall apparent elasticity of import to internal demand.
10 Growth rate of world demand.
11 Income elasticity of exports.
12 (12) = (10) × (11).
13 Growth rate of relative prices.
14 Price elasticity of exports.
15 (15) = (13) × (14).
16 Trend in exports.
17 Growth rate of exports.
18 Overall apparent elasticity of export to world demand.

These data are used in a detailed macroeconomic model Propage linked with the DMS macro model of INSEE.

countries could be blamed on some adverse trends in price competitiveness, due to high labour costs. The overall figure of a 16 per cent rise in the terms of industrial trade (prices of exports/prices of imports in national currency) between 1974 and 1984 strongly supports such thesis. But in contrast with this overall figure, Debonneuil and Delattre (1987) show that the effect of shifts in elementary terms of trade was felt mainly for a short period in the mid 1970s and that the bulk of the overall shift was due to structural effects of growth differentials among sectors. In other words, at the product level, devaluation and changes in production costs helped more or less to keep the terms of trade constant; but, on the whole, trade with higher terms of trade has been growing faster, inducing an overall shift in terms of trade. Therefore, a decline in price competitiveness cannot be blamed for the loss of market shares in the 1980s.

It follows that the decrease in market shares of manufactured products (from 74 per cent of the internal market in 1974 to 60 per cent in 1985, and from 11.2 per cent in 1979 to 9.9 per cent in 1986 of the exports of the main OECD countries) is tied to structural handicaps (lack of strong competitive points, triangular orientation of trade flows etc.). France's more non-OECD-oriented export markets for manufactured products have thus been affected in the 1980s by the slower growth of oil-producing countries and of over-indebted LDCs. Between 1980 and 1985, France's export markets grew at 2.9 per cent a year on average, while OECD total export markets grew at 3.9 per cent.

Power and defence

What we have called a defence and power issue is a dimension of foreign relations which underwent a great change during the US hegemony regime of international relations, in some kind of implicit partial trade-off between trade and power issues ('trade-off' fully exemplified in Germany and Japan). In the 1980s, the lowering in status of this power issue is obvious, whatever initiatives are taken. According to most outside observers, Mitterrand's policy of grandeur had stronger Gaullian characteristics than his predecessors. But, as noticed by Hoffman (1986), the basis for such peculiarities tended to narrow as France integrated more fully into the world economy and no longer presented any strong originality. The high personalization of this 'politique de grandeur' did not add to its credibility. The will to affirm, on one side, support to the Atlantic Alliance and to show, on the other side, independence in relations with third world countries might even have led to confusion or aroused hostility (in the case of Libya and Iran, for instance).

But too strong a deterioration of the image of this policy of 'grandeur' could, in turn, have affected markets involving government negotiations. It would have been all the more damaging in that the rise of the dollar and the income reduction of oil-producing countries, after 1981, sharply curtailed these markets. The arms trade illustrates these dangers, the surplus of trade in military equipment (after a pause, in 1982, in which some ethical reluctance may have played its part) has continued to rise from 21.1 million francs in 1981 to 34.1 million francs in 1986 (see Table 9.9). These figures of arms-trade surpluses are impressive when compared with the trade surplus in other manufactured goods which fluctuates highly. 1986 offers an extreme example with the highest arms trade surplus (34.1 million francs) as compared to a deficit of 1.4 billion in other manufactured trade. Nevertheless, these arms-trade benefits are no safe way to secure a long-standing positive balance of trade. If only in strict economic terms, these arms markets are politically and financially risky. They are concentrated mainly in Third World countries and are hazardous, as exemplified by the Iraq case. Between 1977 and 1982, arms sales to Iraq totalled 50 million francs (more than half the surplus on total arms trade). As the war exhausted Iraq's financial possibilities, arms sales started to drop off after 1982 to 3.4 million francs in 1986, while the debt towards France amounted to 3 billion dollars in early 1987.

This dangerous specialization in arms helps to explain why France's overall trade structure is more oriented towards the third world than in other main OECD countries. The surplus it thus gains in manufactures could help to balance its oil imports, but the instability of both exchanges prevents any reliable trade-off. Furthermore, the deficit in manufactured trade towards major OECD countries[7] may well be enlarged by the import contents of sophisticated weapons.

A comprehensive balance-sheet of this arsenal strategy (third biggest arms exporter with 11.5 per cent of world arms exports in 1983) remains to be drawn up (see Salomon 1986). The size of the surplus in arms trade, once its import contents are accounted for, will, very likely, be of a much smaller magnitude than displayed in Table 9.9. More fundamentally, the arms-trade surplus is directly threatened by three adverse trends. These are as follows:

1. A widening credibility gap in the policy of grandeur, which affects the arms clientele it brought with it.
2. A financial gap due to high levels of indebtedness and the past unpaid bills of potential buyers.
3. Strengthened competition due to the entry of new arms producers on stagnant markets.

Other trade in aeronautics, electronics or the nuclear field may benefit from the efficiency of government negotiations within international programmes or through export credits, and may thus benefit from the efficiency of government initiatives. The airbus international programme is a good example and its effect should not be underestimated: at times it can represent up to one-quarter of France's manufactured exports. Although such programmes offer a promising perspective in the European context, they strictly depend on long-term government initiatives and their extension presents the same inertia as the elaboration of the EEC common trade policy.

ON THE FINANCE AND MONEY ISSUE

It is certainly in the fields of money, finance and exchange-rate policy that the main challenges in the last decade have taken place. Three big issues were raised in the 1980s, concerning the advantages of a large devaluation, the burden of external debt and the necessity for the integration of financial markets.

All these issues were largely constrained by major characteristics of France's integration in the world economy. The devaluation potential was squeezed between the need to protect the franc from the vicissitudes of the dollar and its dependence on dollar billed trade. The load of external debt stemmed mainly from the high propensity to capital flights. The deregulation of France's medium-sized financial markets was largely forced by new competitive pressure on the big foreign financial markets.

To devalue or not

The first question faced by the socialist government, when coming into office, was whether to devalue, significantly, or not. The answer, like Blum's in 1936, was no. As usual for such an issue, there was no real debate *ex ante*, but an ongoing one *ex post*. It saw those who wanted to resume the policy of competitive devaluations of the 1950s and 1960s (which took place within a fixed exchange-rate regime), opposing those who wanted to preserve the two-year old stabilizing scheme (against the fluctuations of the dollar) provided by the EMS. Devaluation within the EMS required a bargaining with European partners and chiefly Germany. Such 'bilateral' negotiation differed completely from the multilateral Bretton Woods System, where France decided, on her own, competitive devaluations under the pressure of her internal conflicts. In this respect no advantage was taken of May 1981, either because the circumstances were less dramatic than in 1958 or because the international scene had changed and the economies had become more interdependent. Once a large competitive devaluation had been ruled out, the timing of small devaluations, which aimed at correcting the price inflation differential, was another matter which involved the need to avoid speculative moves (as well as Gaullian considerations for a policy of 'grandeur').

To appreciate what could have been the effect of a strong devaluation in the early 1980s is a central issue. There was some fear that changes in the overall structure of trade might have completely cancelled the benefits of any devaluation. Recent simulations with a macroeconomic model (see Catinat *et al.* 1985) show that the classic J curve (which expresses the successive decline and rise in the trade balance after a devaluation) remains, but with new characteristics. The initial decline is first accentuated, the delay in restoring the trade balance to its initial level is longer (three years) and the rise afterwards is greater.

Thus one has to wait five years to fully benefit from the devaluation. The risk of speculative moves, in the downward period, or of further cost increase in the meantime, postponing the outcome, tends to be dissuasive. Secondly, it was outlined that, if the J curve is maintained, it combines the highly positive and rapid effects of devaluation towards the D-Mark with the much more dubious effects of a devaluation against the dollar (in which oil and raw materials imports are labelled). Therefore, whether or not it is possible to devalue against the D-Mark but not against the dollar was a key issue. The exponents of a daring attitude towards devaluation assume that such bargaining with Germany could have been achieved (see Lipietz 1984).

The old question of the relationship between Germany and France thus reentered the scene. The two countries had devised the European Monetary System (EMS) precisely to counter competitive devaluations or revaluations among European currencies, provoked by rapid changes in the dollar rate. The option whether or not to pull out of the EMS divided the government over the whole period. Those (like Delors) in favour of pursuing the pro-European strategy of Schuman and Monnet won the case. The alternative, i.e. to quit the EMS, was unclear as to how to separate devaluations against the dollar from the D-Mark outside the EMS and this uncertainty increased as external indebtedness rose.

But to remain within the EMS was also very uncertain *a priori*. If France was inflation-prone then the EMS would require continuous technical parity adjustments to compensate for differences in inflation. This would both chronically damage France's competitiveness and pave the way for permanent speculative runs. The condition to be met was that the inflation differential with Germany could be reduced. Changes in labour relations in the early 1970s towards more collective bargaining, reductions in social conflicts in the late 1970s, as well as the price and wage freeze policy implemented by Barre, all encouraged exponents of the EMS to think that this condition could be met.

In effect under the socialist government increases in real wages rather kept pace with German rates if only for 1982 (see Table 9.11). Nevertheless, the price differential with Germany averaged 5 per cent yearly over 1979–85. One can see in Table 9.11 that the price differential in exports, unexplained by real wage differentials, even increased between 1973–9

Table 9.11 Prices and wages rate differentials between France and West Germany (in %)

		1973–9	1979	1980	1981	1982	1983	1984	1985
Real hourly wage rates in	G (a)	2.5	1.1	0.5	−0.8	−0.7	0.0	0.3	2.9
manufacturing	F (b)	3.7	2.1	1.3	0.9	3.1	1.4	0.3	−0.1
	b–a	−1.2	1.0	0.8	1.7	3.8	1.4	0.0	−3.0
Exports of goods implicit	G (c)	5.1	4.8	6.2	5.6	4.0	1.8	3.4	2.7
price index	F (d)	9.9	10.0	12.4	13.5	14.1	8.5	8.6	4.2
	d–c	−4.8	5.2	6.2	7.9	10.1	6.7	5.2	1.5
Differential in price index unexplained by wage rate differential	(e)	−3.6	4.2	5.4	6.2	6.3	5.3	5.2	4.3

Notes
e = (d–c) – (b–a)
F = France
G = West Germany

and 1979–85 from 3.6 per cent to 5.3 per cent. This suggested that the price differential with Germany was not so much induced by wage pressure as by increases in interest rates and profit margins (see Aglietta, Coudert, Mendelek 1987). It resulted in successive parity adjustments within the EMS which unleashed speculative moves, in turn fuelling new inflationary pressures. Devaluations which were close to 5 per cent against the D-Mark were carried out in October 1981, June 1982 and March 1983. The price competitiveness towards EMS countries was thus maintained at its 1980 level, at least up to 1984.

This exchange policy of mere adjustments is also sign of a partial failure of the EMS. While it could have helped to set up some co-operation between governments to co-ordinate economic policies, the successive weak devaluations of the franc and the absence of the pound sterling tended to turn it into a hierarchical system under the domination of the D-Mark (see Aglietta 1985).

The load of the external debt

From the start of the socialist government, a certain lack of confidence, which in our view is deeply rooted in history, generated large capital outflows: over the two years 1981 and 1982 it more than doubled the deficit in current accounts and increased the external borrowing requirements all the more. In May 1981, capital flight took largely the form of acquisitions of foreign securities and bonds (see Fontaneau and Muet 1985). On the whole, capital outflows in 1981 amounted to 79 billion francs which, added to the 26 billion francs of deficit in the current account, total a net figure of 105 billion francs to be financed essentially by borrowing from the private and banking sector (33 billion francs) and variations in official reserves (29 billion francs). This borrowing requirement rose to 124 billion francs in 1982. The integration of financial markets largely facilitated these exits of capital, despite a strengthening of exchange controls.

The combined pressure of current balance deficits and exits of capital led to an external debt which in francs had increased four times between 1980 (123 billion francs) and 1983 (451 billion francs) (but only doubled in dollar terms from 27 billion dollars in 1980 to 54 billion dollars in 1983). Political debate arose in early 1984 which showed that the corresponding burden of annuities remained moderate (6 per cent of exports) if external borrowing were not to go on at the same level. The turn to a restrictive policy in March 1983 invalidated this question by reducing five times the deficit in current accounts (see Table 9.8).

External indebtedness which had risen from 3.8 per cent of GDP in 1979 to 11.3 per cent in 1983 and 12.1 per cent in 1984 started to decline to 9.9 per cent in 1985 and 7.9 per cent in 1986. Change in economic policy and higher interest rates on the financial market thus seemed to alleviate the question of rising external indebtedness. But the confidence brought by the new policy and the economic incentive of interest rates differentials had a high cost: a lower level of activity than in other European countries (see Fig. 9.1).

Challenge on financial markets

The French financial system, until its reform in 1984, had been widely characterized as segmented and highly regulated.

Among the noticed peculiarities of the French financial system was the determination of the short-term interest rate by the central bank in relation to its reserves in gold and foreign currencies, while in other countries the rate of interest seemed to be linked more directly with the internal rate of inflation.

Therefore the French interest rate was prone to react to speculative pressures on the franc. In turn, high real rates of interest increased costs of borrowing which had a deflationary effect on the activity in an economy where the banks assumed the main part in financing investment and consumption. This role of the banks due to the segmentation of the financial system and to the narrowness of the stock and bond markets shaped a kind of debt economy, as was underlined at the end of the 1970s, when financial issues gained importance in stagnating industrialized economies (see Levy-Garboua, and Maarek 1985). In times of fixed exchanges rates, this more direct link between short-term interest rate and central bank reserves was not of permanent concern. In the more unsteady world of floating exchange rates, where speculative moves of capital on these monetary markets increased largely, it became much more binding.

The first policy would have been to strengthen the regulations limiting the mobility of capitals. But such a move would have run against a general trend of deregulation and financial innovations, largely brought about by the new information technology, after decades of trade expansion and cross-investments. It was therefore difficult to enforce and would have been, at some point, in opposition with EC or GATT agreements (especially on investment rights).

The alternative policy chosen by the socialist government in 1984 was to liberalize and to restructure the financial market, thus following numerous attempts at liberalization, specially in the late 1970s. The reform authorized new financial instruments and looked for a decompartmentalization of various capital markets, which included opening to foreign participants. It culminated in February 1986 with the opening of the Paris financial futures market (Matif). The move towards disintermediation and securitization was thought to change France from a debt economy to a more directly financed economy (see Artus 1987). But such transformation takes time, all the more since the Paris stock market was relatively small. Furthermore disintermediation, financial innovation and abolition of exchange controls agitate the demand for money and therefore the monetary policy, as experienced in other countries starting with a less-specific financial system. Therefore it follows that the outcome of such a policy is uncertain, on how deeply it will change the system and what its effects will be on the exchange policy. It certainly boosted capitalization, which rose to 25 per cent in 1986. It also favoured the success of the privatizations launched afterwards by the conservative government.

TOWARDS A NEW DEAL IN FOREIGN RELATIONS

We can now come back to the initial question: is the external constraint more binding in France than in similar developed economies? Is it structural or does it result from some policy error in managing foreign relations?

We started with a comprehensive view of the management of foreign relations, which included three dimensions: (a) power–defence strategy; (b) trade policy, and (c) finance money issue.

We then underlined that the ways in which these three issues are combined vary with time but remain influenced by some significant historical experiences. Thus some negative experiences with regard to money (lack of confidence, aversion for fiduciary money, attraction for gold, etc.) or trade (failures of laissez-faire attempts, propensity to call for protectionism or *dirigisme*) and even the power issue (with the continuous decline in 'grandeur' after World War Two) did convey to French foreign relations some of their specificity.

At some stage these characteristics buttressed the growth of the French economy. This seems to have been the case in the three decades of sustained economic growth which followed World War Two. The political environment allowed, when needed, competitive devaluation to take place in an international regime characterized by a fixed exchange-rate system under American hegemony. Trade followed the general expansion in world trade flows; it took advantage of both the old colonial network and the development of a Common European market. These specificities may not have been the major factors which explain that the French economy was going faster than its main trade partners. Internal capacities to mobilize resources (such as indicative planning) are more suitable candidates to account for this extra growth.

In the last decade of widespread slow economic growth, foreign relations may appear as more direct determinants in accounting for growth differentials. The world economy is by then much more integrated and this interdependence has been sharply increased by the two oil price shocks, which forced upwards the level of trade. Meanwhile the breakdown of the fixed exchange-rate system left more room for market mechanisms to shape foreign relations.

What could be seen as advantages in the management of foreign relations were turned into rigidities. The poor results of French economic growth, even compared with her European partners, could thus be related to her scattered trade performances, her 'indirect financing' system and the decline of status in her strategy of 'grandeur'.

France was engaged in triangular trades in which exports markets in the 1980s grew less than average. Efforts to keep down the trade deficit led to downward pressures on economic activity aimed at slowing down imports. Arms trade did help to alleviate the oil bill, although its net contribution, once import contents and financial risks are accounted for, is more questionable. Moreover the relative deterioration of French status in her strategy of power threatens these arms markets as competition increases. Yet the more constraining issue remained essentially financial with capital flights, rise of the external debt, upward pressure on interest rates, and increased mobility of capitals. The current balance of payments deficit therefore did not directly cause the external pressure. The sensitivity of the interest rate to external pressure together with the floating of exchange rates fuelled speculative moves. Devaluations were all the more risky, and furthermore the effects of across-the-board devaluations lagged behind and were minor.

All these adverse trends, eroding the basis of the system of foreign relations, could very well explain the particularly binding nature of the external constraint in the mid 1980s. It does not follow that nothing can be done to restore France's room for manoeuvre in the future.

First of all a lot of internal issues regarding distribution, work organization, or industrial policy remain open which can modify the trade basis in the long run. It is less a standard matter of price competitiveness and reduction in unit-labour costs than a matter of setting up new productions and networks towards new markets. This challenge is rather general and concerns most European countries. The threat of 'European sclerosis' cannot be addressed with the kind of short-term macroeconomic policies which nation states developed after the Keynesian revolution. States are now confronted with setting up long-term policies in a more interdependent world. International co-operation is highly desirable but due to conflicting interests it also has to be seen in a long-term perspective, as exemplified by the progressive evolution of the European institutions or the difficulty in setting up a new international monetary order.

A real test for European co-operation will be given by the capacity of European countries to act (and not only react) in the setting up of a new international monetary regime. It has been underlined that in a floating exchange-rate system, speculative pressure could hamper any proper adjustment of real exchange rates to true levels of competitiveness (see Effer 1986). Monetary co-ordination cannot take place without some harmonization of financial systems, which implies similar regulations to stabilize and to control financial markets. This goal is somehow a prerequisite to overcoming the barriers to European growth. If such a goal was achieved, organizing a new base for trade and development would become central, as the true level on which to compete.

The roots of competitiveness are to be found in a combination of existing dominant positions and national specificities. Restoration cannot thus be directly assessed. National specificities also include a specific mix of market and state. In times of economic crisis, balance sheets on these national heritages need to be drawn up to give a better idea of what can be changed, adjusted or preserved. In this perspective, we have stressed the close links between defence, money and trade issues in France's management of foreign relations. It is too restrictive a view to point to French business culture as a handicap to trade. Within a global project problems of formation can be overcome. Indicative planning was after all largely set-up by managers who participated in the productivity missions to the US in the 1940s and 1950s. Since then training in management has more or less followed the international standards. It is difficult to develop a comparative advantage at this level which will ensure a specific competitiveness to the French economy among the developed economies. It might thus be more appropriate to search for an original combination of state and market which would take advantage of the *dirigiste* heritage. The challenge will then be to take advantage of this specific experience without much help from state controls over finance and money. In a more interdependent world economy with co-operation, economic policies will definitely have a more limited scope. In that sense, a higher level of external constraint will remain. Policies could still rely on long-term projects of industrial structuring for which it is hard to get political legitimacy but where France has gained some experience. In this perspective active participation in macro-industrial projects in aeronautics, energy, biology, telecommunications, electronics, etc., at the European level is certainly a trump card.

NOTES

1. See Cresson 'Echec à la balance des efforts' in *Le Monde* 18 Aug. 1987; Noir 'Malheur aux élèves moyens' in *Le Monde*, 11 Aug. 1987.
2. To match our previous illustration of an historic combination of trade, defence and money issues, let us recall Bismarck's remark that the tribute paid by France after her defeat in 1870, had a surprisingly stimulating effect on her economy.
3. According to official estimates only 0.4 per cent of the 2.1 per cent increase in disposable income was the specific result of economic policy (c.f. *Comptes de la nation*, 1982, vol. 1, p. 60)
4. It does not follow that nothing was on the agenda of trade policy. Important matters, such as entries of new members, common stands in GATT, trade arrangements with eastern, far eastern or southern countries were continuously negotiated, but did not directly serve the short- or medium-term interests of member countries.
5. In Mitterrand's election platform, the share of external trade in GDP (23 per cent in 1980) was supposed to be brought below 20 per cent by 1990.
6. According to the 1986 National Account (new basis 1988) it reached 122 in 1986 from 100 in 1980.
7. Since the mid-1960s the exports/imports ratio of manufactured goods exchanged with the 10 OECD majors averages 0.8.

10 · THE POLITICS OF ECONOMIC POLICY CHOICE IN THE POST-WAR ERA

Peter A. Gourevitch

Economic policy turns on political choices. Only the most ardent positivist could believe that economic theory has the clarity to prescribe policy so obviously necessary no reasonable (or unreasonable person) could disagree. The creation of a Nobel prize in economics may indicate the development of an intellectual discipline but it certainly does not put economic policy beyond the realm of dispute.

The prescriptions of economic policy are therefore doctrines. As such, the doctrines have influence over policy-making. But the choice of policy must be analyzed in political terms. For a policy to prevail it must acquire power – it must have the support of critical decision-makers, it must win the formal support of those who have formal authority and to become reality, it must obtain the compliance of those who really act in the economy.

In the post-war period the industrialized market democracies have experienced a long-ranging debate over economic policy. We may identify three periods of argument:

1. The post-war settlement (1945–50): the struggle to shape the aftermath of war, involving conflicting interpretations of the pre-war depression, the war itself, and the issues of US–Soviet rivalry. This struggle led to the historical compromise, the formation of an accommodation among divergent groups and opinions around a mixed economy combining market and state regulation.
2. Keynesian hegemony (1950–71): the high period of the historical compromise, marking the strengthening of the accommodation, and the dimunition of disagreements around economic policy.
3. The new debate (1971-present): the erosion of the historical compromise, at least in its original form, and the reopening or resumption of the debate.

The dating of these periods is certainly open to question. The countries of Europe and North America have not gone through these cycles at the same time. The dates for one country don't work for another. In France and Italy for example, the disruption of the historical compromise is usually dated at 1968 and 1969; in Sweden, the compromise is formed in the 1930s, and so on. But the utility of the categories is the crucial point, for it provides the framework of comparison across national boundaries.

To explore the politics of the post-war economic policy debate across these three periods, we need two sets of analytic tools: first, a typology of policy alternatives around which the debate took place; second, a typology of political factors or explanations, the causal variables which shaped choices from among these policy alternatives.

POLICY ALTERNATIVES AND POLITICAL CAUSES

Countries 'chose' a policy or a sequence of policies. They do so from a set of alternatives. This is surely too simple a way of looking at it – countries are not individuals (what does 'chose' mean?) and the alternatives can never be clearly defined (as say between chocolate versus vanilla ice cream). But again, the logic of comparison requires that we make some simplifying assumptions – that a set of policy packages can at least be inferred from historical policy debates (if not deduced from logical alternatives) and that political processes lead to the selection of one among these.[1]

The policy alternatives may be defined as five options.

Option one: laissez-faire

Classical liberalism holds that the untrammeled free market yields the greatest output. The greatest efficiency comes from private calculations, from decentralized decision-making in response to the incentive for private gain. Hence, the task of the government is to leave the market alone. In good times or bad, the classical or neo-classical policy position is to allow the market to re-allocate resources, whatever the immediate cost in unemployment or business failure.

Option two: socialization and planning

The classical socialist alternative to the classical liberal position proposes to replace private control of investment by public control and to replace the market by planning. The socialists reject laissez-faire on two grounds: suboptimal economic outcomes and non-economic costs.

Option three: protectionism

The 'classical' capitalist deviation from laissez faire in times of trouble has been protectionism: tariff barriers against foreign imports. As a mode of state intervention, it involves the least departure from the classical position, in that it entails the least penetration of state action into the management of the firm: the tariff is a tax applied to a market.

Option four: demand stimulus

Demand stimulus consists of deficit spending by the government in order to prime the pump of a stagnating economy. Laissez-faire could result in a sub-optimal equilibrium. Deficit spending could pull the economy out of that trap.

Option five: neo-mercantilism

An old as well as new form of state intervention involves state action on behalf of specific industries or even companies through a variety of non-tariff techniques (credits, purchases, regulations, etc).

These then are the major families of policy around which debate has swirled in the post-war years. These policy alternatives as well as the politics surrounding them pre-date the war.

Political variables

The theories of economic policy choice are as varied as the theories of politics. To be workable, these too require simplification. Several political variables seem important. Each of these are dimensions along which countries may differ:

1. *The preferences of societal actors occupying important functions in the economy:* societal actors have leverage over policy because of their control over vital social activities: workers, investors, managers. These actors can apply pressure by offering or withholding their services, by working or striking. Their policy preferences in turn derive from their location in the economy, from the configuration of international and domestic market forces on their interests.
2. *Intermediate associations:* between societal actors and governments lie organizations which perform critical linkage functions of representation and mediation. Political parties organize elections, define policies and undertake other critical activities. Interest associations similarly carry out vital tasks which provide leverage in policy debate.
3. *State structure:* societal actors and intermediate associations work through formalized institutions. The formal organization of the state (the decision-making rules) and the bureaucracies which implement policy have themselves a considerable effect in mediating the activity of societal actors and intermediate associations.

4. *Economic ideology:* policy is shaped by an understanding of reality. Reality is often ambiguous. Reasonable individuals are likely to interpret circumstances differently, leading therefore to different predictions and prescriptions.
5. International state system: countries are constrained and influenced by their place in the international system of power rivalry and interstate competition. War, security issues, military procurement and other elements of the state system shape economic decision-making.

The debate over economic policy has occurred in political circumstances affected by these factors. Each has some bearing on the struggle about which policies prevail. Countries differ in these respects, in ways which contribute to an understanding of policy.

THE STRUGGLE OVER THE POST-WAR SETTLEMENT

The rebuilding of the post-war world involved the intermingling of factors of the moment (occupying armies, physical destruction, hunger) with influences of the past (the depression of the 1930s, the war-time years (the war itself, occupation, and resistance), earlier economic crises and conflicts, political traditions, and so on). Economic policy was one of a number of issues at stake. Others include the formation of political institutions and foreign policy.[2]

At the precise end of the war in 1945, the situation in countries varied widely. Sweden had escaped direct involvement in the war. Germany was devastated and dismembered. The experiences of Italy and France, of the United States and the United Kingdom, ranged to varying degrees between these endpoints.

The experiences of the pre-war period were also extremely varied: in Germany, constitutional democracy fell victim to the most virulent of the fascisms of that period. In Sweden, the UK and the US constitutional democracy held. Economic policy-making varied widely in these years as well. Sweden and the US experimented with demand management and regulation in a constitutionalist framework of free trade unions, while Germany experimented with demand management, state ownership and regulation in an authoritarian framework of controlled labour markets.

By contrast with these sharp divergences, the post-war years of Western Europe and North America saw a relative convergence around a historical compromise. The pattern of that compromise can be seen in the Swedish experience of the 1930s. While Hitler was coming to power in Germany, the Swedish Social Democrats worked out an alliance with the Agrarian Party – the so-called 'cow trade'. Each side reversed a traditional policy in exchange for support for another objective. The Social Democrats abandoned opposition to agricultural subsidies while the Agrarians abandoned opposition to worker unemployment compensation. At first employer organizations and conservative parties opposed this arrangement. When it proved electorally quite strong in the election of 1936, the accommodation was generalized, in more explicit fashion than anywhere else. Representatives of business, farmers and workers met together at Saltsjobaden in 1938 and worked out another deal: the socialists would accept private control of management and investment, in exchange for full recognition of union rights, high wages, welfare benefits, full employment; business would accept these policies, in exchange for control of economic enterprise and the avoidance of strikes; agriculture accepted these concessions to labour and business in exchange for continued agricultural support.

Thus by internal constitutional processes, shaped certainly by external events, but certainly worked out by independent groups, Sweden worked out the 'compromesso storico' before the war. The United States took some partial steps in that direction. Other countries reached this path only after the war and only because of it.

Germany

The war changed all societies quite strongly. The greatest change was obviously in Germany. The Allied victory permitted the destruction of the Nazi regime, opening the way to constitutional government, at least in West Germany. Allied intervention neutralized the authoritarian right, and in West Germany, the communist left. Post-war territorial arrangements wiped out the Junkers, and removed large areas of industrial Protestant Germany where the communists had been strong. Allied policies favoured centrist political elements, such as Konrad Adenauer and the Christian Democrats.

Adenauer and the Economics Minister, Erhard, rejected the planning approach advocated by the Social Democrats. Economic controls were lifted, and the economic miracle took off, aided by the Cold War and military spending. Unions were given strong organizational rights, even seats on boards. And a strong welfare net shielded people from the pressures of the business cycle.

United Kingdom

The election of 1945 produced the first non-minority Labour government in British history. After some brief experimentation, the planning/nationalization ideas of the Labour left were abandoned. Market mechanisms came back into play, only now in the context of an extensive welfare state, an expanded public sector, and a commitment to use demand management to sustain full employment. The contradictory impulses of the pound and the commonwealth started to cause problems in UK demand management (the stop/go problem) earlier than elsewhere, but Britain like the other countries of Europe experienced a great boom.

United States

The American picture remained more confused than the European. Where European countries saw some considerable expansion of programmes conceived in the 1930s, the US saw limits and curtailment: the Taft Hartly Act regulating labour unions is the clearest example; the failure of further expansion of welfare measures such as in health is another. But roughly speaking, the accommodation of the 1930s was consolidated in the post-war years. The Eisenhower Republicans blocked any major efforts to roll back the New Deal. Demand management gained ground both intellectually and politically.

France

The post-war accommodation was weakest in France and Italy. Conflict was sharpest in those countries, the outcome more uncertain. Severe labour conflicts occurred, the variance of debate was far wider, the compromise quite weak. In France, opposition by left and right drove other forces together into 'third force' governments. These linked Socialists, Christian Democrats and moderates but they faced strong opposition from a large Communist party and a strongly disaffected Gaullist group. With a rough political balance, came a rough balance of economic policy. After a round of nationalization and regulation, policy experimentation slowed. The French state remained more involved in the economy than the German, but by the 1950s it was clearly a capitalist economy operating within certain frameworks of regulation.

Italy

The political and policy battles in post-war Italy were also quite deep. France had the scars of political conflict in the 1930s and the occupation/resistance of the war years. Italy had the traumas of twenty years of fascism, ending in war, defeat, occupation and resistance. The political struggles were acute. Domestic disagreements about economic, social and political order took place in the context of the rapid emergence of the Cold War. The US and the USSR intervened in various ways, as did the Church. The Christian Democrats won, but there was certainly no consensus. In policy terms, the victory of the Christian Democrats led to the mixed capitalism being worked out in other places as well.

CONSOLIDATION OF THE COMPROMISE

Thus, all the countries in the decade after World War Two moved towards a social compromise. The political formulas have different labels and each their own individuality: Christian Democratic, Social Democratic, Labour, and so on. But roughly the formula involves compromise on the hard positions of pre-war years. The left accepted the market and property rights. The capitalists accepted trade unions and collective bargaining in a constitutionalist political framework, and the welfare state. Both groups supported agricultural programmes while the agricultural sector accepted support of industrial goals. All groups supported relatively open access to the international economy. All groups accepted some measures of government intervention and regulation. Demand management is a policy framework to be used to sustain full employment.[3]

These policies worked relatively well. Or, at least, they coincided with a prosperity whose roots are surely more complex than any one set of policies or decisions. The post-war decades experienced a great boom. Europe and North America entered a period of tremendous growth. Prosperity spread across class boundaries, allowing the development of mass consumption and involvement in the economy. Income disparities, unemployment dislocations and other social ills certainly remained, but the influence of prosperity was important. Social tensions eased. The compromises seemed far stronger than anyone had imagined possible in the days after the war.

Prosperity reinforced the economic policies thought to have caused it. The mixed economy and demand management coincided with prosperity. Public debate attributed causality to the linkage. The centre of gravity of policy debate moved away from fundamentals like nationalization, workers' democracy, market principles, protectionism, and the like, towards 'management' – what trade-offs in incomes policy and the Phillips curve? Prosperity reinforced this tendency strengthening the analytic approach to a demand-managed economy. The strengthening of the approach allowed widening and deepening of it. The European countries felt able to form the Coal and Steel Communities, then the Common Market. GATT, formed at the end of the war, was supported and extended.

The spread of the mixed economy marked a strong convergence in economic policy approaches. In sharp contrast to the inter-war years, the policy space of debate and of policy narrowed in the 1950s and 1960s. The European left felt obligated to moderate its policy tone – several socialist parties dropped their traditional commitments to nationalization and other features of marxist orthodoxy. In several communist parties, the seeds of 'Eurocommunism' were growing. Conservatives parties accepted the welfare state and the Keynesian approach to full employment. The parties of the far right withered.

EROSION OF THE HISTORICAL COMPROMISE

The very success of the post-war boom sowed the seeds of subsequent difficulties – we cannot say 'destruction' because the historical compromise has by no means been destroyed. It is nonetheless under considerable strain. That strain derives in large measure from changes in the international economy engendered by the post-war boom itself. As the economies of Europe and North America grew, and that of Japan as well, the world market grew too. As trade expanded rapidly, the international division of labour intensified. Other countries entered the production system. Competition led to rapid changes in the location of market leadership. New products and processes spread round the world.

These changes meant new costs and new opportunities. Economic changes altered the pay-offs of various policy and political arrangements. In each country, stiff foreign competition puts pressure on costs. To be competitive, costs must be cut – but who will bear that cost? Each group seeks to shift the blame and the burden on another. The politics of accommodation shifts to the politics of blame. The historical compromise of the post-war years was possible because recent experiences provided the framework for compromise; in the current situation the need for compromise seems less obvious – each group is tempted instead to make others pay costs.

The shift is sharpest in changing attitudes towards labour. The historical compromise turned vitally on a major change in the relationship of labour to other social categories. Before the 1930s, labour was, by and large, excluded as a coalitional ally to most other social groups. Farmers and business groups alike with rare exceptions avoided political coalitions where labour had a major voice. Labour was used in *de facto* policy coalitions, such as those which turned on protectionism and free trade, but except for certain crisis moments such as war time, alliance with labour unions and labour leaders was anathema.

The crisis of the 1930s, as we have seen, changed this dramatically. Labour led coalitions in some cases, such as Sweden, while being smashed in Germany. The war increased labour's role, and in post-war reconstructions especially in Europe, the institutionalization of labour into industrial relation and political life was a major shift. Both agrarian and business groups were willing to ally with labour, to make political and policy alliances, to provide benefits to labour in exchange for support in other areas. The willingness of these groups to play that role turned on some conflicts within each over strategy and the analysis of benefits.

Business alliance strategies

In business, as in agriculture, there have always been divisions about the right attitude towards labour, divisions connected to different positions on a variety of issues. Business groups, and agrarian ones, have had different 'marginal propensities' towards 'progressive' or 'conservative' alignment. Progressive alignments link business to labour and agriculture around programmes of better wages and working conditions, institutionalized industrial relations, social insurance systems, and constitutional government involving some sharing of power. Conservative alignments link these groups around programmes that favour investment-led growth, limited wages, weak unions, limited social insurance, and, in some instances, the use of state power to control labour.

For business conservatives, labour is a commodity, a factor of production for which they seek the lowest possible cost. Like a commodity, labour cannot be seen as having rights, or any claims to power. It must take what the market offers. Unions, from this viewpoint, are obstacles to the market, illegitimate attempts to use state power to obtain leverage, and so for conservatives, the preferred source of market stabilization is not high wages and social programmes to assure labour demand, but government purchases and cartels. Business-dominated corporatism, not tripartite bargaining, is what they prefer. Some conservatives have supported elements of social welfare, but this has been a controversial point. For business progressives, on the other hand, labour is not only an input to production but a major source of demand and a component of society with legitimate claims for resources and power. Progressives see benefits accruing to business from strong and stable labour demand, from an institutionalized system of labour relations, and from general conditions of good health, education, and living arrangements.

The emergence of progressive attitudes marked an important shift in the history of industrial societies. As long as workers made products that they could not afford to buy, labour–capital relations revolved around the price of the wage commodity. When mass purchasing power became fundamental to business prosperity, however, the possibilities of a collective game grew. Businesses began to think more broadly about the relationship between the situation of their particular firm and general conditions in the economy. Moreover, health workers, well-educated and respectfully treated and well-paid, contributed more to productivity than sick, harshly treated, poor ones. Unions could play an important role in the management of labour markets: stabilizing, organizing, disciplining, and recruiting. In politics some progressive property owners had come to see incorporation of the masses through democracy as a strategy superior to repression; some businessmen came to see that the same principle could be applied in economic life.

'Progressive' and 'conservative' are ideological categories. Their social location has varied over time their shifting relationships to the international economy. In the late nineteenth century the salient issue was trade, and conflicts over tariffs divided industrial elites. The internationalists became the progressives, looking for labour's help to achieve an open trading system. Progressive business seems to have been characterized by high technology, an export orientation, and the manufacture of finished consumption goods; and it also included shipping and international commercial banking. Electrical goods, chemicals, and household goods are particularly clear examples. Conversely, anti-labour views seem to have prevailed among companies with labour-intensive manufacture, high geographical concentration of the labour force, less flexibility in shifting resources, and high debt burdens. Iron and steel producers and mining companies appear to have been conservative nearly everywhere.

When the international trading system collapsed in the 1930s, these relationships shifted. Faced with stiff competition and collapsing world markets, the progressives stepped back from collaboration with labour. Their need to cut costs meant cutting wages and taxes, and hence conflict with labour. At the same time inward-oriented companies sought allies of their own. Despite their traditional enmity, they and labour were both more desperate for help than the international groups, and in the worst days of the Depression each became willing to support similar policies and politics. Out of the tangle of conflicting goals emerged a consensus in favour of stabilization and the management of demand, but the political formula varied widely from country to country.

When the world economy revived in the mid-1930s, relationships among groups changed again. The internationalists re-formed their partnership with labour, though with one very important addition: they accepted the goal of stabilization. Industries seeking this kind of market included those with high levels of investment debt, such as airlines and oil, and producers of consumer goods of many kinds. The post-war bargain would turn on this convergence of the old 'anti-corn-law' tradition of progressive labour relations with a newer compromise on 'stabilization'. The two coincided after the war around a mixture of Keynes and free trade which endured for a quarter century.

International economic conditions in the 1970s and 1980s undermined those understandings. The internationalization of production and consumption has severed the link between domestic stability and economic advantage, and the logic of the international market now applies pressure to drive down the costs to business of wages and taxes. No longer is it possible through the deployment of high technology to pass on the costs of highly paid domestic labour, for international competition is too strong. No longer is it possible for business to be assured of stabilized demand, for no country can provide that much security in its own markets or has the ability to impose arrangements on international markets. With greater uncertainty and stronger competition, all companies seek lower costs from labour, more freedom to manoeuvre in shifting around labour and other resources. High-technology producers and consumer-goods producers all seek to produce at the world's lowest cost, whatever the price to domestic labour.

Labour has thus lost its business allies. In Europe and North America business elites see labour as living above its and their means. And the economies of all of these countries have evolved in ways that diminish the number of blue-collar workers and the chances that solidarity will develop around union conceptions of worker welfare. Such groups as 'yuppies', and cadres of the emerging industrial economy, white-collar workers, and blue-collar workers in the new industries have little attachment to the concerns of the rustbelt unions.

Agricultural alliances strategies

The relationship between labour and agriculture has also involved massive shifts. In the nineteenth century, labour and agriculture were at loggerheads: the city wanted cheap food, the countryside cheap industrial goods. Other factors certainly hindered co-operation also, but my general point is that these two groups had a very difficult time collaborating against business forces. The crisis of the late nineteenth century split agriculture between growers of commodity crops for world markets and producers of high-quality foodstuffs for nearby urban-industrial markets. The latter, users of grains and other commodities produced by the former, were available as a potential ally for industry oriented towards free trade. Commodity crop growers were available for a protectionist alliance (in the United States, however, the positions were reversed; as efficient producers, commodity crop growers were free traders, while growers of high-quality food identified with the interests of protectionist manufacturing, their major market). Both groupings directed their negotiations at business, not to labour, and the populist alliances of the period failed.

The great crash of 1929 changed that pattern profoundly. Although farming continued to be internally complex, the universality of an agricultural distress that began in the 1920s and became acute in the early 1930s made all of its factions available for new politics and new policies. In several countries labour was willing to make a deal but business was not, and farmers were desperate enough to make the switch. Where farmer–labour alignments occurred, they were strong enough to attract some elements of business. The progressives, with their own policy goals, split off to accept pieces of the labour–agriculture programmes and this formed the historical compromise analyzed above.

Labour's success in forming alliances with agriculture did not last. Agriculture stayed with labour when times were bad but moved away when things got better. Extensive state programmes stabilized agricultural markets, providing a floor for farmers' incomes. Improved industrial performance strengthened urban markets for farm goods and generated jobs for the marginal agricultural population. Business overcame its antipathy for intervention in markets and became quite willing to offer agriculture the same arrangements as labour had or better. With population falling in the countryside, agriculture was becoming an interest group, able to offer its support to the highest bidder. Its leverage as a swing group was already quite clear in the 1930s, when it imposed limits on the reformism of the New Deal, the Swedish Social Democrats, and the French Popular Front.

In the 1970s and 1980s labour lost agricultural support. The smaller rural population and the continuation of farming subsidies have made agriculture less available as an ally. That loss is significant, not only in numbers of votes but in political ideology, particularly in arguments about the role of the state in capitalist democracies. Farmers, as owners of property, have bestowed on state intervention in the market a legitimacy that labour has always had difficulty sustaining by itself. Populist revolts based on the grievances of small capitalists against the market have extended the strength of the sellers of labour power when both groups are able to make common cause.

In the current period, however, the agricultural sources of such support have waned, and the current sources of populism (shopkeepers, small entrepreneurs, white-collar workers, professionals) appear to provide no such opportunities for alliance. On the contrary, their complaints seem directed particularly at labour. They link the economy's ills to unions and work rigidities, and to the expenses of the welfare state. Labour demands thus appear to have less legitimacy than those of other groups in the capitalist system.

Labour alliance strategies

Within the category of labour itself, two groups can be differentiated – unionized and non-unionized. The direction of and tendency for alliances seems quite different for the two. Union workers have been far more willing to follow their leaders within the labour-allied parties and the trade unions themselves than have non-union workers. The latter instead have been available for mobilization around other principles of solidarity (such as nationalism, religion, race and ethnicity) and other economic programmes. As a result, the tracing of political and policy coalitions involves following the behaviour both of leaders of the labour-union movement and of the non-unionized 'masses'.

In the late nineteenth century unions everywhere had a difficult time in finding allies. Most businesses hoped to prevent union growth: most of agriculture feared union radicalism. Labour did have an influence on policy and politics, but its role tended to be passive – though labour provided votes and other kinds of support, the movement's leaders did not share power. It took World War One and the depression to end that exclusion.

In Europe, labour entered the system during the Great War, lost ground in the 1920s, and re-entered more fully in the 1930s. In Germany the unionized groups held firm against Nazi appeals, but the radical right could claim the legitimacy of mass strength by tapping, among other groups, the non-unionized work force. In Sweden, the United States and France, labour union and labour party leaders became major participants in coalitional politics.

Part of the post-war compromise has been the institutionalization in the various countries of the rights and powers of labour unions. Industrial relations, plant management, social programmes and government adminis-tration all developed a large role for labour. In the 1970s and 1980s this position has come under attack, albeit to different degrees in different countries. Labour unions have become the central target of criticism by other groups of whatever is wrong with the economy. At the same time, various factors have weakened labour solidarity. The growing complexity of the economy, new industries, and prosperity have all made the tasks of collective mobilization more difficult. As long as other groups are able to contain their internal differences and direct criticism against 'labour, welfare, and the state' unions and organized labour movements will con-tinue to face problems. Labour parties may maintain themselves in office but they will do so only by modifying their policies, not with the labour-defensive policies they supported for many decades.

The state and societal actors

As the relationships among societal actors has changed over time, so has the relationship of the state to society in ways which shape policy outcomes.

One important change has been in the political location of state action. In the crisis of the late nineteenth century, the free market was blamed and protectionism plus some regulation was the response. In the depression of the 1930s, the market was blamed again, only this time much more exten-sively. In both of these crises the state and public policy were seen as instruments of capitalism and plutocracy. The task of political mobilization was to use the state to help groups in addition to business. With increased state action in the 1930s, state structure grew. The state became linked to a variety of social groups, including labour and agriculture. The regulatory state was involved with many groups.

When the crisis of the 1970s began, therefore, the political meaning of state action had changed. Activism was the incumbent philosophy, and the catchall state had replaced the night-watchman state. The state had never stopped helping capitalists, but now it was harder to portray it as serving capitalists alone. When economic troubles emerged, it became possible to argue that the problem was located deep in the incumbent model of state society relations, in an active state that gave a strong voice to workers and the poor, along with weak businesses. The state and its progressive allies could themselves become the objects of attack.

With the shift in the ideological location of state action have come important changes in the relationship of intermediate associations and state institutions in mediating the relationship between social pressures and policy outputs.

As the state has become more active, more able to intervene, the mechanisms which link the state to society have grown in importance as well. The more active state is both more powerful and more constrained. Its interventions frequently require the complicity of forces it seeks to regulate or direct. State action is frequently corporatistic – state and groups borrow from each other the authority to do what they cannot do alone.

In earlier periods of conflict about public policy towards the economy, intermediate associations were relatively weak while primary social groups were strong. Functional interests worked directly on politics and policy debate in a relatively unmediated way, and outcomes could be inferred fairly directly from the struggles of societal actors. Organizations shifted policy positions rapidly as their members' preferences shifted with new economic situations – the changes in Germany during the 1870s were the most spectacular example of this, as Junkers and manufacturers abandoned long-standing free-trade policy postures in favour of tariffs.

The struggle over policy content itself rewards organization. The late nineteenth century was a period of considerable development in mass politics. The rewards to organization were large and the process correspondingly rapid. The organizational space was relatively open, amenable to varying 'solutions', but by the end of the century the organizational vacuum was filled in and the space pre-empted. Parties and interest groups structured the political landscape in Europe and North America, and subsequent issues and groups would henceforth have to deal with them. These groups now mediated relations between society and the state quite strongly.

With the policy struggle of the 1929 depression the role of parties and interest groups loomed much larger than it had in earlier debates. In the United Kingdom one has to note the fight within the Labour party, the manoeuvring of Lloyd George and Keynes within the Liberal party to find allies. In Germany, one observes the efforts by Hitler to raid parties and interest groups, especially farmers, but also other social categories, and the complex interaction between the Social Democratic Party and its union affiliates over policy and political tactics. In Sweden, farmer–business–labour relations were shaped by leadership choices among the Agrarians and the Swedish Social Democrats, and by direct trilaterial bargaining at

Saltsjobaden. The Communist party switched tactics between the Germany of 1932 and the France of 1936. Union organizations, farm and industrial producer associations were crucial in the United States.

The list could continue but the message is clear: party and interest group associations interacted in complex ways with societal actors to produce policy and political results. Strategic choices by key organizations helped or hindered the adoption of demand stimulus policy at crucial moments in the political process of policy debate.

State capacity

Current discussions of policy formation have paid particular attention to the concept of state capacity – does the state have the organizational resources to carry out a particular policy task? This is an important element of policy debate. But it is one which is not uniform for all policy measures. Laissez faire quite obviously requires a lesser capacity than interventionist measures. Among state interventions, there is also a considerable variation. Socialization and planning clearly require considerable state capability. So does mercantilism. Protectionism requires less, and demand stimulus even less. This is important: the skill required for demand stimulus is informational – the knowledge of relationships needed to calibrate fine tuning. But it requires relatively few instruments of actual intervention.

Conversely, the politics of demand management may require a relatively high level of institutionalized capability in social accommodation. As demand management leads to consideration of who gets what, incomes policy becomes part of the agenda of economic policy. And incomes policy in turn is considerably affected by organizational relationships within social groups and between groups and the state – in short, corporatism. Highly corporatist organizational forms may enable demand stimulus, while poorly articulated forms may hinder it.

Thus Sweden and Austria are able to manage demand stimulus for full employment by using a variety of instruments and bargaining to contain inflationary pressures. The US and the UK may have a harder time doing so, since corporatist mechanisms are much weaker there. At the same time, the US and UK are more likely to chose demand stimulus (and protectionism) over mercantilist policies precisely because they lack the institutional and corporatist machinery for selective intervention in industrial policy.

International system

Debates over Keynesian policies, as with any economic policy, have been strongly influenced by political-military influences of security or aggrandisement. All countries are part of an international system of interstate rivalries.

These rivalries produce constraints and provide incentives for policies with important economic requirements and effects.

The importance of international pressures on national policy-making has often given rise to efforts at deriving policy choice from international system. 'Britain pursued free trade because of her navy, while Germany was protectionist because her position on the European landmass made her vulnerable to attack.' This is the most well-known formulation of this reasoning. It has some bearing on the demand stimulus debate.

Economic nationalism is a policy most available to large countries with large domestic demand. Smaller countries can only improve living standards by specialization in an intensifying international division of labour. Thus the economic nationalism which sustained interventions of the early 1930s could be explored by the US and Germany, but not by Sweden. No surprise that Sweden made the most rapid shift to linking demand stimulus to internationalist policy postures.

But the international environment can only be a loose framework shaping policy debate. The international environment is ambiguous enough that within each country there will be divergent interpretations of its meaning for national policy. Was Germany vulnerable to attack, or did her policies breed defensive hostility? There were many Germans from the 1870s onward who wished to insert Germany in a peaceful international trading regime. Their defeat has to do with domestic politics, of the complex kind we have already examined. Thus international rivalries, political or military, require the same disaggregated analysis as 'domestic' issues do. Security or strategic conceptions, like economic ideas, have no stronger claim to independence from political processes than any other goal or set of ideas.

This is true of military issues as well as economic ones. The difference lies only in politics, not in character. Military spending frequently is easier to sell politically than spending for social services or equality. More precisely, the political effect of such arguments varies over time and country. Demand stimulus concepts are neutral as the type of spending – public works, guns, or simply higher consumer income – and any will do. When military issues have strong political weight, demand management becomes military Keynesianism. Early examples of this include German navy building in the late nineteenth century. Hitler is another.

THE PARTICULAR WITHIN THE GENERAL

The broad changes analyzed in the preceding paragraphs – in cleavages around economic issues among social actors, in the institutions of intermediate associations, political parties and the state, in economic ideology, and in international factors – have altered the political context of economic

policy debates in Western Europe and North America. The issues which
defined the post-war settlement and the policy cleavages of the period of
high Keynesianism have been altered. The specific manifestation of these
general points alters from country to country.

The US and the UK

In both countries splits in the centre and left have permitted a strong
resurgence of conservative neo-classical analysis. Thatcher and Reagan
both led attacks upon the post-war settlement, attacking not only the
opposition party, but the accommodationism of the 'wets' within their own
party (Churchill, Eden, Macmillan; Eisenhower and Rockefeller) who had
led business acceptance of the historical compromise.

In the United States, the erosion of New Deal policy approaches preceded Reagan's election in 1980. Nixon's moves from 1971–4 marked
important shifts in the post-war economic order, involving protectionism
and the end of fixed exchange rates. An interest in deregulation quickened
under Carter. Important segments of the Democratic party were becoming
more critical of government 'entitlement' programmes, and less interested
in unions and union views of policy. Reagan succeeded in putting state
action and spending on the political defensive. At the same time, Reagan
does not appear to have consolidated either a political or policy approach:
the tremendous budget deficits, international debt, and trade deficits leave
the issue space very controversial.

In the United Kingdom, the Thatcher administration has successfully
taken advantage of strong splits in the opposition to win effective governing
power despite minority victories in the electorate. She has privatized many
sectors of the economy, and put considerable pressure on unions and welfare spending. Neither Thatcher nor Reagan has led any major rollback of
the welfare state – a definition of the limits of the neo-classical attack on
the post-war compromise. And neither has made any serious effort to slash
supports for agriculture, allowing, if anything, increases – another mark of
limits. Defence spending among other factors has supported increases in
state size, not a contraction.

Sweden

The successes of the Social Democrats in Sweden express a sharp contrast
to the US and UK pattern. There is fragmentation on the centre and right
which permits the continuation of these long records of political hegemony.
The Social Democrats have used their power to neutralize the pounding
pressures of international competition on their system of values. Market
signals are used to force economic readjustment, but various forms of
intervention are used to distribute the costs of adjustment (and the benefits)

more evenly across the population. Investment remains largely in private hands, while taxation pours large funds through to redistributive programmes. Labour market policies contain unemployment. The strength of the post-war settlement can be seen in the rather restrained nature of the changes wrought by the centre-right policies during its term in office.

Germany

Changes in relations among social groups have had parallels with changes in party coalitions. The highwater point of the post-war accommodation came with the entry of the Social Democrats into the Grand Coalition of the mid-1960s, then the SPD-led coalition with the Free Democrats. With the growth of economic difficulties in the 1970s, tensions between SPD and FDP grew. Just what price would the latter pay for alliance with the former? Free marketeers in the FDP prevailed, and the alliance crumbled. The different strands of German conservatism linked together in the Christian Democrats-FDP coalition.

France

French post-war history has been marked by a series of shocks whose relationship to social alignments has been very complex, and strongly affected by other issues (Algeria, the Constitution, foreign policy). While de Gaulle replaced the Fourth Republic and disposed of Algeria, he led a programme of economic modernization. Economic and political tensions exploded into the May-June revolts of 1968. Labour won a series of major economic concessions there, but not party-political ones. The political right and centre cohered throughout the 1970s to contain direct labour participation in governing. By the 1980s, overconfidence bred conflicts on the centre-right, and allowed a left victory.

But the effects of international economic change in post-war Europe are quite clear in what happened after the Socialists' victory: in the first year, Mitterrand tilted France strongly left, carrying out an extensive programme of nationalization, and of employment-oriented fiscal stimulus. Within a year, the government was forced sharply back toward centrist policies, and before long the actual behaviour of the French socialist government was not conspicuously different from that of more conservative counterparts in France and elsewhere in Europe.

Italy

There are some rough parallels with France in the Italian experience, with the Gaullist experience being the most conspicuous difference. The hot autumn ('autunno caldo') during the period 1968–9 marked a strong resurgence of labour market militance and consciousness. Eurocommunism seemed to set the stage for an important political shift in the country whose theoreticians invented the phrase 'historical compromise'. But the breakthrough in partisan terms has not happened. The Christian Democrats have retained power, and policy in Italy has remained roughly similar to the cautious mixtures of its continental counterparts.

CONCLUSION

The political economy of Europe and North America has become open and uncertain. The cleavage lines and institutions which anchored policy and politics have weakened. Economic change is one of the major causes of these shifts. An intensification of the international division of labour puts elements of labour, capital and agriculture into situations of conflict that disrupt earlier relationships. New issues of production, technology and economic organization cut through society in ways which are not captured by left-right conceptualizations and organizational forms. At the same time, new issues – involving economy, women, foreign workers, nuclear power and foreign policy – cut across parties and interest groups.[4]

The effect is to make politics and policy more plastic. The number of possible coalitions among social groups widens. This makes the behaviour of intermediate associations more important, as well as the behaviour of leaders. Creativity and luck matter more. Political victory goes to the well-organized and the unified. Fluid conditions may favour as well those who are less anchored in the past, more alert to new ways of conceptualizing issues and arguments. In the pre-war years, some of the more imaginative leaders were demons whose genius was evil. Other imaginative leaders strengthened democracy, constitutionalism and economic well-being. The 'crisis' of the present period is not likely to be as sharp as that of the pre-war years. As a result, the opportunities for striking leadership, for good or evil, are not as likely to be as great. But opportunities do exist. We can analyze some of the parameters which shape it, but partly, we can only hope.

NOTES

1. A fuller account of the policy options and explanatory variables may be found in Peter Gourevitch (1986). The book uses these tools to compare the crises of 1873–96, 1929–49, and 1971–3 to the present.
2. Particularly useful on the post-war settlement are: Andrew Shonfield (1965), Samuel Beer, *British politics in the collectivist age*; Leo Panitch, *Social democracy*; Mancur Olson, *The rise and decline of nations*; George Ross, *et al.*, *Unions change and crisis*; and Peter Gourevitch *et al.*, *Unions and economic crisis*. A more

complete statement of bibliographical sources for this article can be found as footnote references to the case studies of Gourevitch (1986).
3. On economic policy making see: John Goldthorpe (1984), especially the article by Fritz Sharpf, and a forthcoming book in German by Sharpf elaborating the themes of that article; Peter Hall, *Governing the economy*; Peter Katzenstein (1985); John Zysman (1984); Andrea Boltho (1982); Leon Lindberg and Charles Maier, (eds.), (1984); Suzanne Berger, (ed.), (1981).
4. An interesting analysis of current trends in the organization of production which has considerable implications for political cleavages is Michael Piore and Charles Sabel (1986).

REFERENCES

Aggarwal, V. (1985) *Liberal protectionism: the international politics of organized textile trade*, University of California Press, Berkeley, CA.

Aglietta, M. (1985) 'Europe: la décennie de tous les dangers', *Document de travail*, CEPII n. 85–05, September.

Aglietta, M. (1986) *L'ECU et la vieille dame*, Economica, Paris.

Aglietta, M., Coudert, V. and Mendelek, N. (1987) 'Politiques nationales et évolution du systèm monétaire européen', *Document de travail*, CEPII, June.

Aglietta, M., Orlean, A. and Oudiz, G. (1981) 'Des adaptations différenciées aux contraintes internationales', *Revue economique*, July.

Alt, J. (1985) 'Political parties, world demand and unemployment: domestic and international issues of economic activity', *American political science review*, vol. 79.

Alt, J. and Chrystal, K.A. (1983) *Political economics*, Wheatsheaf Books, Brighton, Sussex.

Artoni, R. and Ravazzi, P. (1986) 'I trasferimenti statali all'industria', in R. Artoni, and E. Pontarollo, (eds) *Trasferimenti, domanda pubblica e sistema industriale*, Il Mulino, Bologna.

Artus, P. (1987) 'La politique monétaire en France', *Revue Française d'Economie*, vol. II, 3, summer.

Ashworth, W. (1952) *A short history of the international economy since 1850*, Macmillan, London.

Aubin, C. and Lafay, J.D. (1985) 'Monetary targets and positive monetary policy: an empirical analysis on monthly French data (1974–1984)', Université de Poitiers, Centre de Recherche et d'Analyse Politico-Economiques, December, mimeo.

Aubin, C. and Lafay, J.D. (1986) 'The positive approach to monetary policy: an empirical study of the French case 1967–1981', Université de Poitiers, Centre de Recherche et d'Analyse Politico-Economiques.

Aufricht, H. (1967) *Central banking legislation*, International Monetary Fund, Washington.

Axelrod, R. (1984) *The evolution of co-operation*, Basic Books, New York.

Axelrod, R. and Keohane, R. (1985) 'Achieving co-operation under anarchy: strategies and institutions' in Oye (ed.), *Cooperation under anarchy*, Princeton University Press, Princeton.

Bade, R. and Parkin, M. (1978) *Central bank laws and monetary policy*,

Department of Economics, University of Western Ontário, mimeo.

Balassa, B. (1962) *The theory of international integration*, George Allen & Unwin, London.

Balassa, B. and Balassa, C. (1984) 'Industrial protection in the developed countries', *The world economy*, vol. 7, 4, December.

Baldwin, D.A. (1985) *Economic statecraft*, Princeton University Press, Princeton.

Baldwin, R. (1982) 'The political economy of protectionism' in J.N. Bhagwati, (ed.) *Import competition and response*, Cambridge University Press, Chicago.

Baldwin, R. (1985) *The political economy of US import policy*, MIT Press, Cambridge, MA.

Balladur, E. (1987) 'The EMS: advance or retreat', *Financial Times*, 17 July.

Banca Commerciale Italiana (1987) 'Trade credits in Italy: foreign exchange controls and the structure of foreign trade', *Selected issues*, Econ. Research Dept, Milan.

Banca d'Italia (1987) 'Contributi alla ricerca economica', special issue, Rome.

Bank for International Settlements, BIS (1987) *Annual report for the year 1986*, Basel.

Banque de France (1983) *La Banque de France et la monnaie*, Banque de France, Paris.

Basevi, G. (1987) 'Liberalization of capital movements in the European Community, a proposal, with special reference to the case of Italy, a Report to the EC Commission', Bologna, mimeo.

Bauchard, P. (1986) *La guerre des deux roses*, Spasset, Paris.

Beck, N. (1984) 'Domestic political sources of American monetary policy: 1955–82', *Journal of Politics*, vol. 46.

Beer, S. (1965) *British politics in the collectivist age*, Random House, New York.

Berger, S. (1981) *Organizing interests in Western Europe*, Cambridge University Press, New York.

Bergsten, C.F. and Cline, W. (1987) 'Promoting world recovery: a statement on global economic strategy by twenty-six economists from fourteen countries', Washington DC, Institute for International Economics, December.

Bergsten, F. and Williamson, J. (1983) 'Exchange rates and trade policy', in W. Cline, (ed.) *Trade policy in the 1980s*, MIT Press, Cambridge.

Bergsten, C.F. (1986) 'America's unilateralism', in C.F. Bergsten, E. Davignon and J. Miyazaki, *Conditions for partnerships in international economic management*, Report to the Trilateral Commission, n. 32.

Bernholz, P. (1987) 'The political economy of revaluation-induced protectionism under discretionary monetary regimes with flexible exchange rates', in H. Giersch, ed., *Free Trade in the World Economy*, Tübingen, Mohr.

Bhaduri, A. and Steindl, J, (1985) 'The rise of monetarism as a social doctrine' in P. Arestis and T. Skouras, *Post Keynesian Economic Theory*, Wheatsheaf Books, Brighton, Sussex.

Biasco, S. (1986) 'Currency cycles and the international economy', Banca Nazionale del Lavoro, *Quarterly review*, December.

Bingham, J. (1985) *Banking and monetary policies*, OECD, Paris.

Bini-Smaghi and Vona, L. S. (1987) 'Economic growth and exchange rates in the EMS: their trade effects in the changing external environment', presented to the EMS Conference, Perugia, to appear in F. Giavazzi, S. Micossi, M. Miller (1988) *The European Monetary System*, Oxford University Press, Oxford.

Black, S. (1982a) 'Politics versus markets: international differences in macroeconomic policies', American Enterprise Institute Studies.

Black, S. (1982b) 'Strategic aspects of the political assignment problem', in R. Lombra, W. Witte (eds) *Political economy of international and domestic monetary relations*, Iowa University Press.

Blanchard, O., Dornbusch, R., Dreze, J., Giersch, R. Layard, R. and Monti, M. (1985) 'Employment and growth in Europe: a two-handed approach', CEPS Papers n. 21, Brussels.

Blanchard, O., Dornbusch, R. and Layard, R. (eds) (1986) *Restoring Europe's prosperity*, MIT.

BMWI (1987) *Ausfuhrgarantien und Ausfuhrburgschaften der Bundesrepublik Deutschland*, Report of the year 1986, Ministry of Economic Affairs, Documentation Series n. 280, Bonn.

Boltho, A. (1982) *The European economy: growth and crisis*, Oxford University Press, Oxford.

Boss, A. (1987) 'Zur Steuerreform in der Bundesrepublik Deutschland', *Die Weltwirtschaft*, n. 1.

Bourguinat, H. (1985) *L'économie à decouvert*, Calman Levy, Paris.

Bouvier, J. (1987) 'L'amont de notre incertain avenir: les longue durées', *Le Débat*, September.

Brander, J.A. and Spencer, B.J. (1983) 'International R&D rivalry and industrial strategy', *Review of economic studies*, vol. 50.

Brander, J.A. and Spencer, B.J. (1984a) 'Tariff protection and imperfect competition', in H. Kierzkowski (ed.) (1984) *Monopolistic competition and international trade*, Oxford University Press, Oxford.

Brander, J.A. and Spencer, B.J. (1984b) 'Trade warfare: tariffs and cartels', in *Journal of international economics*, vol. 16.

Branson, W. (1979) 'Introduction to stock-adjustment dynamics' in *Macroeconomic theory and policy*, 2nd edition.

Branson, W. (1985) 'Causes of appreciation and volatility of the dollar', NBER working paper n. 1777.

Branson, W. and Rotemberg, R. (1980) 'International adjustment with wage rigidity', *European economic review*, vol. 13.

Branson, W., Fraga, A. and Johnson, R.A. (1986) 'Expected fiscal policy and the recession of 1982', in M.H. Peston and R.E. Quandt, *Prices, competition and equilibrium*, essays in Honour of W. Baumol, Phillip Allan.

Breton, A. (1981) 'Representative governments and the formation of national and international policies', *Revue Economique*, n. 2.

BRI (1987) Yearly report for 1986, Basel.

Brock, W. and Magee, S. (1978) 'The economics of special interest politics: the case of a tariff', *American Economic Review*, 68.

Bruni, F. (1986) 'L'evoluzione del mercato internazionale dei capitali e il sistema bancario italiano', in *Note economiche*, n. 3/4.

Bruni, F. and Monti, M. (1986) 'Protezionismo valutario e integrazione internazionale', in *Rivista internazionale di scienze economiche e commerciali*, n. 9.

Bruno, M. (1985) 'Aggregate supply and demand factors in OECD unemployment: an update', NBER working paper n. 1969.

Bruno, M. and Sachs, J. (1985) *Economics of worldwide stagflation*, Harvard University Press.

Bryant, R. (1980) *Money and monetary policy in interdependent nations*, Brookings, Washington.

Buiter, W.H. and Marston, R.C. (eds) (1985) *International economic policy co-ordination*, Cambridge University Press, Cambridge.

Caesar, R. (1981) *Der Handlungsspierlaum von Notenbanken*, Nomos Verlagsgesellschaft, Baden Baden.

Calleo, D. (1982) *The imperious economy*, Harvard University Press, Cambridge.

Cameron, D. (1978) 'The expansion of the public economy: a comparative analysis', *American political science review*, vol. 72.

Cane, E. (1980) 'Politics of Fed policymaking: the more things change, the more they remain the same', *Journal of monetary economics*, no. 6, pp. 199–211.

Cantoni, G. (1985) 'Nuovi strumenti agevolativi del mediocredito centrale nel campo del credito all'esportazione', *Banca impresa società*, vol. 4, 1.

Catinat, M., Pisani Ferry, J. and Schubert, K. (1985) 'Les incidences d'une dévaluation du franc ont-elles varié depuis vingt ans?', *Economie et statistique*, n. 3.

Cerny, P.G. (1987) 'The little big bang in Paris: financial market deregulation in a dirigiste system', workshop on deregulation in Western Europe, Amsterdam, April.

Charlot, J (1974) 'The end of gaullism?' in H. Perminon (ed.) *The presidential election of 1984*, American Enterprise Institute, New York.

Chesnais, F. (1986) 'Science, technology and competitiveness', in *OCSe STI Review*, n. 1.

Ciampi, C.A. (1987) 'Audizione dinanzi alla IV commissione permanente della camera dei deputati, indagine conoscitiva sul sistema e sull'ordinamento bancario e finanziario', in *Banca d'Italia bollettino economico*, February.

Ciocca, P. (1983) *La moneta e l'economia. Il ruolo delle banche centrali*, Il Mulino, Bologna.

Cohen, B. (1986) *In whose interest? International banking and American foreign policy*, Yale University Press, New Haven, CT.

Colander, D. and Koford, K. (1985) 'Externalities and macroeconomic policy', in S. Maital and I. Lipnowsky (eds) *Macroeconomic conflict and social institutions*, Ballinger, Cambridge, Mass.

Commission of European Communities (1985) *Completing the internal market*, COM(85)310 of 14 June 1985 (White Paper).

Commission of European Communities (1987) *Efficiency, stability and equity*, Padoa-Schioppa report, Brussels, April.

Commission of European Communities, *European economy*, Annual Economic Report 1986–1987, 30 November 1986.

Commission of European Communities, *Programme for the Liberalization of Capital Movements in the Community*, Brussels, 23 May 1986.

Conybeare, J. (1984) 'Public goods, prisoners' dilemmas and the international political economy', in *International Studies Quarterly*, vol. 28, n. 1, pp. 5–22.

Cooper, C.A. and Massel, B.F. (1965) 'Towards a general theory of customs unions in developing countries', in *Journal of political economy*, vol. LXXIII.

Cooper, R. (1968) *The economics of interdependence*, MacGraw-Hill, New York.

Cooper, R. (1973) 'Trade policy is foreign policy', *Foreign policy*, vol. 5.

Cooper, R. (1977) 'World-wide vs regional integration: is there an optimal size of the integrated area?', in F. Machlup (ed.), *Economic integration: worldwide, regional, sectoral*, Halstead, New York.

Cooper, R. (1985) 'Economic interdependence and coordination of economic policies', in R. Jones and P. Kenen, *Handbook of international economics*, vol. II, North Holland, Amsterdam.

Cornwall, J. (1977) *Modern capitalism, its growth and transformation*, Martin Robertson, London.

Corrigan, E. (1987) 'Coping with globally integrated financial markets', *Federal Reserve Bank of New York quarterly review*, n. 4.

Dasgupta, P. (1987) 'The economic theory of technology policy', in P. Dasgupta and P. Stoneman (eds) *Economic policy and technological performance*, Cambridge University Press, Cambridge.

Dauderstadt, M. (1987) Free markets versus political consensus, the international competitiveness of societies, *Intereconomics*, January/February.

Dean, J.K. (1984) 'Interest groups and political inefficiency', *European journal of political research*, vol. 12, pp. 191–212.

Debonneuil, M. and Delattre, M. (1987) 'Les pertes de parts de marché: la "compétitivité en cause"', *Economie et statistique*, n. 203.

De Brunhoff, S. (1978) *The state capital and economic policy*, Pluto Press, London.

De Cecco. M. (ed.) (1983) *International economic adjustment: small countries and the European Monetary System*, Blackwell, Oxford.

De Cecco, M. (1987) 'Le relazioni finanziarie tra internazionalizzazione e trasnazionalismo', in *Il Dollaro e l'economia italiana*, in A. Graziani (ed.) Il Mulino, Bologna.

De Grauwe, P. (1987) 'International trade and economic growth in the European Monetary System', *European economic review*, n. 31.

De Grauwe, P. and Fratianni, M. (1984) *The political economy of international lending*, International economics research paper n. 42, Centrum voor Economische Studien, Leuven.

Delattre, M. (1986) 'Forces et faiblesses des secteurs industriels: 1979–1984', Collections INSEE, Série E, n. 512.

Delorme, R. and Andre, C. (1983) *Etat et economie*, Le Seuil, Paris.

Deutsche Bundesbank (1982) *The Deutsche Bundesbank: its monetary policy instruments and functions*, Deutsche Bundesbank, Frankfurt.

Deutsche Bundesbank, *Monthly report*, various issues.

Didier, J. and Associates (1984) *Public Expenditure on Agriculture, Community Report*, study paper n. 229, EC Commission, DG VI, Brussels.

Dini, L. (1986) 'Per un mercato finanziario europeo integrato', Banca d'Italia, mimeo.

Dixit, A. (1984) 'International trade policy for oligopolistic industries', *Economic journal*, supplement.

Dornbusch, R. and Frankel, J. (1987) 'Macroeconomics and protection', in R. Stern, (ed.), *US trade policies in a changing world economy*, MIT Press, Cambridge.

Drèze, J. et al. (1987) 'The two-handed growth strategy for Europe: autonomy through flexible co-operation', Commission of the European Communities, *Economic papers*, n. 60.

Durupty, M. (1985) 'La place du nouveau secteur public dans l'économie nationale', *Annals of Public and Co-operative Economy*, September.

Dutailly, J.C. (1984) 'Aides aux entreprises: 134 milliards de francs en 1982', *Economie et statistiques*, n. 169.

Dyson, K.F. (1981) 'The politics of economic management in West Germany', *West European politics*, May.

Easton, S., Grubel, H. (1982) 'The costs and benefits of protection in a growing world', *Kyklos*, vol. 36, n. 2.

Effer, P. (1986) 'Europe in the world economy', report to the Commissariat au Plan, Paris.

Eingiz, P. (1962) *The history of foreign exchange*, Macmillan, London.

Eisenhammer, J. and Rhodes, M. (1987) 'The politics of public sector steel in Italy: from the economic miracle to the crisis of the eighties', in Y. Meny and V. Wright, (eds) *The politics of steel: Western Europe and the steel industry in the crisis years: 1974–1984*, Walther de Gruyter, Berlin/New York.

El-Agraa, A.M. (1984) *Trade theory and policy: some topical issues*, Macmillan, London.

El-Agraa, A.M. (1987) 'International economic integration', in D. Greenaway (ed.) *Current issues in international trade*, Macmillan, London.

Emerson, M. (ed.) (1985) *Europe's stagflation*, Oxford University Press, Oxford.

Emminger, O. (1976) 'Deutsche Geld und Wahrungspolitik im Spannungsfeld zwischen innerrem und ausserem Gleichgewicht 1948–1975', in Deutsche Bundesbank (ed.) *Wahrung und Wirtschaft in Deutschland 1876–1975*, II edn.

Emminger, O. (1982) 'Deutsche Geldpolitik im Zeichen des Monetarismus Deutsche Bundesbank', *Auszuge aus Presseartikeln*, n. 73, Frankfurt.

Epstein, G.A. and Schor J.B. (1985) 'The determinants of central bank policy in open economies', mimeo, University of Harvard.

Evans, P., Rueschemeyer, D. and Skockpol, J. (eds) (1985), *Bringing the state back in*, Cambridge University Press, Cambridge.

Fagerber, J. (1985), 'A post-Keynesian approach to the theory of international competitiveness', Norwegian Institute of International Affairs, Oslo, mimeo.

Federal Reserve Bank of New York, *1986 annual report*.

Federal Trust for Education and Research (1984) *The time is ripe – the European Monetary System, the ECU, and British policy*, November, London.

Finocchiaro, A., Contessa, A.M. (1984) *La Banca d'Italia e i problemi del governo della moneta*, Banca d'Italia, Rome.

Fischer, S. (1987) 'British monetary policy', in R. Dornbusch and R. Layard, *The British economy*, Oxford University Press, Oxford.

Flanagan, R., Soskice, D. and Ulman, L. (1983) *Unionism, economic stabilization and income policies: European experience*, Brookings Institution, Washington.

Flic, W. and Heinemann, H.J. (1981) 'Leistungsbilanzdefizite in der Bundesrepublik Deutschland: ein Problem der Anpassung oder der Finanzierung?', in *Konjunkturpolitik*, vol. 17, n. 3.

Fontaneau, A. and Muet, P.A. (1985) *La gauche face à la crise*, PUF, Paris.

Fornengo, G.P. (1986) 'Le politiche di ristrutturazione e salvataggio', in F. Momigliano, (ed.) *Le leggi della politica industriale in Italia*, Il Mulino, Bologna.

Francke, H.H. and Hudson, M. (1984) *Banking and finance in W. Germany*, St. Martin's Press, London.

Frankel, J. (1986) 'The sources of disagreement among the international macro models and implications for policy co-ordination', NBER, working paper n. 1985.

Franzmeyer, F. (1983) 'Die Abstimmung der Wirtschaftspolitik im EWS', in H. Scharrer and W. Wessels, (ed.) *das Europaische Wahrungssystem*, Bonn.

Freeman, C. (1981) *The economics of industrial innovation*, Frances Pinter, London.

Frey, B. (1978) *Modern political economy*, Martin Robertson, Oxford.

Frey, B. (1984) *International political economics*, Basil Blackwell, Oxford.

Frey, B. and Schneider, F. (1978) 'An empirical study of political economic interaction in the United States', *Review of economics and statistics*, vol. 60.

Frey, B. and Schneider, F. (1981) 'Central bank behaviour: a positive empirical analysis', *Journal of monetary economics*, vol. 7.

Friedman, M. (1953) 'The case for flexible exchange rates' in *Essays in positive economics*, Chicago University Press, Chicago.

Gandolfo, G. (1986) *Economia internazionale: vol. 1. La teoria Pura del Commercio Internazionale*, UTET, Turin.

Garret, G. and Lange, P. (1985) 'The politics of growth: strategic interaction and economic performance in the advanced industrial democracies 1974–1980', *Journal of politics*, vol. 47, n. 3.

Garret, G. and Lange, P. (1986) 'Economic growth in capitalist democracies 1974–1982', *World politics*, vol. 38, n. 4.

Giavazzi F. and Giovannini, A. (1986) 'The EMS and the dollar', *Economic policy*, n. 2.

Giavazzi, F. and Giovannini, A. (1987) 'Models of the EMS: is Europe a greater deutsche-mark area?', CEPS, Brussels.

Giavazzi, F. and Pagano, M. (1985) 'Capital controls and the EMS', in *Capital controls and foreign exchange legislation*, Euromobiliare Occasional Paper, Milan.

Giavazzi, F. and Pagano, M. (1986) 'The advantage of tying one's hands: EMS discipline and central bank credibility', DEPR Discussion Paper n. 135, London.

Giersch, H. (1971) *Thesen zur Sogennaten Währungskrise*, Kiel.

Giersch, H. and Lehment, A. (1981) 'Monetary policy: does independence make a difference? – the German experience', Institut für Weltwirtschaft an der Universität Kiel, *Kiel sonderdrucke*, n. 100.

Gilpin, R. (1981) *War and change in world politics*, Cambridge University Press, New York.

Goldstein, J. (1986) 'The political economy of trade: institutions of protection', *American political science review*, n. 80, pp. 161–84, March.

Goldthorpe, J. (1984) (ed.) *Order and conflict in contemporary capitalism*, Oxford University Press, Oxford.

Goodman, J. (1987) 'The politics of monetary policy in France, Italy and Germany: 1973–1983', unpublished PhD dissertation, Harvard University.

Gordon, R. (1975) 'The demand for and the supply of inflation', *Journal of law and economics*, vol. 18.

Gourevitch, P. (1978) 'The second image reversed: the international sources of domestic politics', in *International organization*, vol. 32, n. 4, pp. 881–912.

Gourevitch, P. (1986) *Politics in hard times: comparative responses to international economic crises*, Cornell University Press, Ithaca.

Gowa, J. (1983) *Closing the gold window*, Cornell University Press, Ithaca.

Gowa, J. (1986a) 'Ships that pass in the night? Neo-classical trade theory in a balance-of-power world', prepared for a conference on 'Political and economic analysis of international trade policies', mimeo, National Bureau of Economic Research, Gennaio.

Gowa, J. (1986b) 'Anarchy, egoism, and third images: the evolution of cooperation and international relations', *International organization*, vol. 40, n. 1, pp. 179–85.

Grilli, E. (1980) 'Italian commercial policies in the 1970s', *World bank staff working paper*, n. 428.

Gros, D. (1986) 'The effectiveness of capital controls in the presence of incomplete market separation', CEPS, Brussels.

Gualandri, E. (1987) 'Evoluzione dei sistemi finanziari e delle normative di vigilanza: Gran Bretagna, Francia e Italia', mimeo.

Guerrieri, P. and Padoan, P.C. (1986) 'Neomercantilism and international economic stability', *International organization*, vol. 41.

Guerrieri, P. and Padoan, P.C. (eds) (1988a) *The political economy of international cooperation*, Croom Helm, London.

Guerrieri, P. and Padoan, P.C. (1988b) *Libero scambio, protezionismo e concorrenza internazionale*, Il Mulino, Bologna.

Gutowski, A., Hartel, H.H. and Scharrer, H.E. (1981) 'From shock therapy to gradualism: anti-inflationary policy in Germany from 1973 to 1979', *Intereconomics*, vol. 16, n. 2.

Haggard, S. and Simmons, B. (1987) 'Theories of international regimes, *International organization*, vol. 41, n. 3 estate, pp. 491–517.

Hall, P. (1988) *Governing the economy*, Cambridge University Press, Cambridge.

Hamada, Koichi, (1977) 'On the political economy of monetary integration: a public economics approach', in R.Z. Aliber, *The Political Economy of Monetary Reform*, Macmillan, London.

Hamaui, R. and Pasinelli, M. (1987) 'Main measures of foreign exchange policy: 1972–1987', Banca Commerciale Italiana, Economic Research Dept, Milan.

Hardin, R. (1982) *Collective action*, Johns Hopkins University Press, Baltimore.

Haute Conseil (1984) *Rapport 1984*, vol. 1, *L'extension du secteur public: les objectifs et les realisations*, La documentation francaise for the Haute Conseil du Secteur Public, Paris.

Hayek, F. von (1976) *Denationalization of money*, Institute for Economic Affairs, Hobart Special Papers, n. 70, London.

Hayward, J. (1987) 'The nemesis of industrial patriotism: the French response to the steel crisis', in Y. Meny and V. Wright, (ed.) *The politics of steel: Western Europe and the steel industry in the crisis years: 1974–1984*, Walther de Gruyter, Berlin/New York.

Hazart, P. and Khong, V. (1987) 'Les importations françaises: une analyse statistique', Revue de l'IPECODE, n. 17.

Hellman, S. (1977) 'The longest campaign: communist party strategy and the election of 1976', in H. Penniman (ed.) *Italy at the polls: the parliamentary election of 1976*, American Enterprise Institute, New York.

Helpman, E. and Krugman, P. (1985) *Market structure and foreign trade: increasing returns, imperfect competition, and the international economy*, MIT Press, Cambridge.

Hibbs, D. (1977) 'Political parties and macroeconomic policy', *American political science review*, vol. 71.

Hicks, J. (1969) *A theory of economic history*, Clarendon Press, Oxford.

Hirschman, A.O. (1945–1980) *National power and the structure of foreign trade*, University of California Press, Berkeley.

Hoffman, S. (1978) 'Domestic politics and interdependence', in OECD *From Marshall to global interdependence*.

Hoffman, S. (1986) 'La France face à son image', *Politique etrangère* n. 1, 1986.

Holtham, G., Keating, G. and Spencer, P. (1987) *EMS, advance or face retreat*, CSFB Economics, London.

Ikenberry, J. (1986) 'The state and strategies of international adjustment', *World politics*, vol. 39.

IMF (1984) 'Exchange rate volatility and world trade', *IMF occasional paper n. 28*, July.

Izzo, L. and Spaventa, L. (1981) 'Macroeconomic policies in western European countries: 1973–1977' in H. Giersch (ed.) *Macroeconomic policies for growth and stability: a European perspective*, J. B. Mohr, Tübingen.

Jacquemin, A. and Sapir, A. (1987) 'Inter-EC trade: sectoral analysis', Centre for European Policy Studies, Brussels.

Jeantin, M. (1985) 'La nuova legge bancaria francese', in *Banca impresa e società*, n. 2.

Jervis, R. (1978) 'Cooperation under the security dilemma', in *World politics*, vol. 30, n. 2.

Johansen, L. (1982) 'A note on the possibility of an international equilibrium with low levels of activity', *Journal of international economics*, vol. 13, pp. 257–65.

Johnson, H. (1969) 'The case for flexible exchange rates', in G. Halm (ed.) *Approaches to greater flexibility of exchange rates*, Princeton University Press, Princeton.

Johnson, H.G. (1962) 'The economic theory of custom unions', *Pakistan economic journal*, vol. 10, pp. 14–32.

Johnson, H.G. (1965) 'An economic theory of protectionism, tariff bargaining and the formation of custom unions', *Journal of political economy*, vol. LXXIII.

Juettemeier, K.H. (1987) 'Subsidizing the federal German economy, figures and facts 1973–1984', *Kiel working paper*, n. 279, February.

Kaldor, N. (1981) 'The role of increasing returns, technical progress and cumulative causation in the theory of international trade and economic growth', *Economic appliquée*, n. 34.

Kaldor, N. (1985) *Economics without equilibrium*, University College Cardiff Press, Cardiff.

Kane, E. (1980) 'Politics and Fed policy making: the more things change, the more they remain the same', *Journal of monetary economics*, vol. 6, pp. 199–211.

Kane, E. (1982) 'External pressures and the operations of the Fed', in Lombra, Witte (1982).

Kasper, W. (1970) 'Zur Frage großerer Wechselkursflexibilitat', Tübingen, Kieler studien, n. 113.

Katseli, L. (1985) 'The prospects for international economic policy co-ordination: a panel discussion', in W.H. Buiter and R.C. Marston, *op. cit.*, pp. 376–9.

Katzenstein, P. (ed.) (1978) *Between power and plenty: foreign economic policies of advanced industrial countries*, University of Wisconsin Press, Madison, WI, 1978.

Katzenstein, P. (1985) *Small states in world markets*, Cornell University Press, Ithaca.

Keohane, R.O. and Nye, J.S. (1971) 'Transnational relations and world Politics', in R.O. Keohane and J.S. Nye, *Transational relations and world politics*, Harvard University Press.

Keohane, R.O. and Nye, J.S. (1977) *Power and interdependence*, Little Brown and Co., Boston.

Keohane, R. (1984) *After hegemony*, Princeton University Press, Princeton, NJ.

Keohane, R. (1986) 'Reciprocity in international relations', in *International organization*, vol. 40, n. 1, pp. 1–27.

Kesselman, M. et. al. (1987) *European politics in transition*, Heath and Co., Lexington, Mass.

Kierzkowski, H. (ed.) (1984) *Monopolistic competition and international trade*, Oxford University Press, Oxford.

Kindleberger, C. (1973) *The world in depression, 1929–1939*, University of California Press, Berkeley, CA.

Kindleberger, C. (1978) 'Government and international trade', Princeton University, *Essays in international finance*, n. 129.

Kindleberger, C. (1983) 'International banks as leaders and followers of international business', *Journal of banking and finance*, vol. 7, pp. 583–95.

Kindleberger, C. (1986) 'International public goods without international government', *The American economic review*, March.

Kloten, N. (1987) 'Paradigmswechsel in der Geldpolitik?', Deutsche Bundesbank, *Auszuge aus Presseartikeln*, n. 67.

Kloten, N., Barth, H.J. et al. (1980) 'Zur Entwicklung des Geldwertes in Deutschland', Tübingen, *Wirtschaft und Gesellschaft*, n. 5.

Kloten, N., Ketterer, K.H. and Vollmer, R. (1985) 'West Germany's stabilization performance' in L. Lindberg, C. Meier (eds) *The politics of inflation and economic stagnation*, Brookings Institution, Washington.

Kogan, N. (1983) *A political history of Italy*, Praeger, New York.

Krasner, S. (1976) 'State power and the structure of international trade', in *World politics*, vol. 28, n. 3, pp. 317–47.

Krasner, S. (1978) *Defending the national interest*, Princeton University Press, Princeton, NJ.

Krasner, S. (ed.) (1983) *International regimes*, Cornell University Press, Ithaca and London.

Krauss, M.B. (1972) 'Recent developments in customs union theory: an interpretative survey', *Journal of economic literature*, vol. 10.

Krugman, P. (ed.) (1986) *Strategic trade policy and the new international economics*, MIT Press, Cambridge.

Krugman, P. (1987) 'L'integrazione economica in Europa: questioni concettuali' in Padoa-Schioppa T. (ed.), *Efficienza, stabilità ed equità*, Il Mulino, Bologna.

Lafay, G. (1985) 'La spécialisation francaise: des handicaps structurels', *Revue d'economique politique*, n. 5.

Lake, D. (1984) 'Beneath the commerce of nations', *International Studies Quarterly*, n. 1.

Lamfalussy, A. (1986) 'Worldwide competition in financial markets: issues for banking supervisors', address delivered to the Amsterdam conference of banking supervisors, Amsterdam, October, mimeo.

Lanciotti, G. (1986) 'L'internazionalizzazione del sistema bancario italiano', Banca d'Italia, *Temi di discussione*, n. 77.

Langlois, L.N. (1986) *Economics as a process*, Cambridge University Press, Cambridge.

Lassudrie-Duchene, B. and Mucchielli, J.L. (1979) 'Les échanges intrabranche et la hiérarchisation des avantages comparés dans le commerce international', *Revue economique*, March.

Lassudrie-Duchene, B., Berthelemy, J.C. and Bonnefoy, I. (1987) 'L'importation et la production en France', *Economie prospective internationale*, n. 29.

Lauber, V. (1983) *The political economy of France*, Praeger, New York.

Layard *et al.* (1984) 'Europe: the case for unsustainable growth', Report of the CEPS Macroeconomic Policy Group, Centre for European Policy Studies Papers, 8/9.

Lebegne, D. (1985) 'Modernizing the French capital market', *The banker*, December.

Lefevre, T. (1985) *L'ECU: un nouveau marché*, PUF, Paris.

Lehoucq, J. and Strauss, J.P. (1988) 'Les industries françaises de haute technologie', *Economie et statistique*, n. 207.

LEI-Agricultural Economic Institute, The Hague, n. 338.

Levy-Garboua, V. and Maarek, G. (1985) *La dette, le boom, la crise*, Economica, Paris.

Lindberg, L. and Maier C. (eds) (1984) *The politics of inflation and recession*, Brookings Institution, Washington.

Lindblom, C.E. (1977) *Politics and markets: the world's political-economic systems*, Basic Books, New York.

Lipietz, A. (1984) *L'audace ou l'enlisement*, Editions la Découverte, Paris.

Llewellyn, D. (1980) *International financial integration*, John Wiley and Sons, New York.

Locatelli, R. (1986) 'La nuova legge bancaria tedesca: alcuni spunti di riflessione', *Banca impresa società*, n. 1.

Lombra, R. and Witte, W. (eds) (1982) *Political economy of international and domestic monetary relations*, Iowa State University Press.

Ludlow, P. (1982) *The making of the EMS*, Frances Pinter, London.

Machlup, F. (1964) *International payments, debts, and gold*, Scribner's, New York.

Maddison, A. (1964) *Economic growth in the West*, Norton, New York.

Maddison, A. (1981) *Les phases du développement capitaliste*, Economica, Paris.

Maddison, A. (1987) 'Growth and slowdown in advanced capitalist economies: techniques of quantitative assessment', *Journal of economic literature*, vol. XXV, pp. 649–98.

Maitland, I. (1985) 'Interest groups and economic growth rates', *Journal of politics*, vol. 47, n. 1.

Marsh, D. (1985) 'French banking and finance: winds of change', in *The Banker*, April.

Masera, R. (1987a) *An increasing role for ECU*, Princeton Essays in

International Finance, June.

Masera R.S. (1987b) *L'unificazione monetaria e lo SME*, Il Mulino, Bologna.

Mayer, T. (ed.) (1978) *The structure of monetarism*, Norton, New York.

Mayer, T. and Young, P. (1986) 'The European monetary system: recent developments', *IMF Occasional Paper* n. 48, Washington.

McCulloch, R. (1983) 'Unexpected real consequences of floating exchange rates', *Princeton essays in international finance*, n. 153.

McMahon, C. (1986) 'Stamp memorial lecture delivered at the university of London', 20 November, Bank for International Settlements.

Melitz, J. (1987) 'Germany, discipline and co-operation in the EMS', Perugia, mimeo.

Melitz, J. and Messerlin, P. (1987) 'Export credit subsidies', *Economic policy*, n. 4.

Messerlin, P.A. (1981) 'The political economy of protectionism: the bureaucratic case', *Weltwirtschafliches Archiv*, 177, 469–96.

Messerlin, P. (1986) 'Export-credit mercantilism à la française', *The world economy*, n. 4.

Micossi, S. and Rebecchini, S. (1984) 'A case study on the effectiveness of foreign exchange market intervention: the Italian lira', *Journal of Banking and Finance*, vol. 8.

Micossi, S. (1985) 'The intervention and financial mechanism of the EMS and the role of the ECU', *Banca Nazionale del Lavoro Quarterly Review*, December.

Minervini, G. (1986) 'Attuazione della Direttiva CEE 77/80 e libertà di concorrenza', *Note economiche*, n. 3–4.

Mistral, J. (1983) *Competitiveness of the Productive System and International Specialization*, OECD, Paris.

Mistral, J. (1985) '125 ans de contrainte extèrieure, Cahiers de l'ISMEA', Hors séries, n. 29.

Mistral, J. (1985) 'Vingt ans de redéploiement du commerce extérieur', *Economie et statistique*, n. 70.

Moon, B. (1982) 'Exchange rate system, policy distortion and the maintenance of trade dependence', *International organization*, n. 4.

Morishima, M. (1982) *Why has Japan succeeded?*, Cambridge University Press, Cambridge.

Mueller, D. (ed.) (1983) *The political economy of growth*, Yale University Press, Yale.

Mueller, D. (1987) 'The growth of government: a public choice perspective', *IMF Staff Papers*, vol. 34, n. 1, pp. 115–49.

Muller, D. and Groeling, H. (1971) 'Beitrage und Stellungnahmen zu Problemen der Währungspolitik', *Kiel discussion papers*, No. 10, June.

Mundell, R. (1962) 'The appropriate use of monetary and fiscal policy under fixed exchange rates', *IMF staff papers*, 9, pp. 70–77.

Nardozzi, G. (1983) *Tre sistemi creditizi*, Il Mulino, Bologna.

Nardozzi, G. (1987) 'Rapporto conclusivo della ricerca su "Aspetti strutturali e tendenze evolutive dei sistemi creditizi Francese, Tedesco, Inglese e Americano"', April.

National Bank of Belgium (1987) 'Public aid to corporations', (in Dutch), *Tijdschrift van de Nationale Bank van Belqië*, vol. 62, 1.

Neme, C. (1986) 'Les possibilités d'abolition du controle des changes français, in M. Vanheukelen and J. Pelkmans, (eds) *European integration of financial markets*, European Institute of Public Administration, Maastricht.

Nordhaus, W. (1975) 'The political business cycle', *Review of economic studies*, n. 42 pp. 169–90.

North, D. (1981) *Structure and change in economic history*, W.W. Norton, New York.

Nougues, J., Olechowski, A. and Winters, A. (1986) 'The extent of non-tariff barriers to industrial countries' imports', *World Bank staff working papers*, n. 789.

Odell, J. (1982) *US International Monetary Policy*, Princeton University Press, Princeton, NJ.

OECD (1986) *Historical statistics*, OECD, Paris.

OECD (1987) *The export credit financing systems in OECD Member countries*, 3rd edition, Paris.

Olson, M. (1965) *The logic of collective action: public goods and the theory of groups*, Harvard University Press, Cambridge, Mass.

Olson, M. (1982) *The rise and decline of nations*, Yale University Press, Yale.

Olson, M. and Zeckhauser, R. (1986) 'An economic theory of alliances', in *Review of economics and statistics*, 48, pp. 266–79.

Onado, M. (1986) 'Banche e istituti speciali: specializzazione o concorrenza?', in *Note economiche*, n. 3–4.

Onida, F. *et al.* (1987) 'Credito agevolato all'esportazione', (report), Istituto per la Ricerca Sociale, Milan.

ONU, (1983) *Transnational corporation in world development*, United Nations, New York.

Orlean, A. (1986) 'L'insertion dans les échanges internationaux: comparaison de cinq grands pays développés', *Economie et statistique*, n. 134, January.

Oudiz, G. (1985) 'European policy co-ordination: an evaluation', *Recherches Economiques de Louvain*, vol. 51, n. 3–4.

Oudiz, G. and Sachs, J. (1984) 'Macroeconomic policy coordination among the industrial economies', *Brookings papers on economic activity*, n. 1.

Oye, K. (1985) 'Explaining co-operation under anarchy', *World Politics*, 38, n. 1.

Oye, K. (ed.) (1986) *Co-operation under anarchy*, Princeton University Press, Princeton, NJ.

Padoan, P.C. (1985), 'Il ciclo politico-economico: alcune considerazioni', *Note economiche*, n. 5/6.

Padoan, P.C. (1986) *The political economy of international financial instability*, Croom Helm, Beckenham, Kent.

Padoan P.C. (1988) 'Sistema monetario europeo e politiche nazionali' in *Politiche monetarie e politiche di bilancio nella Comunità Europea*, Il Mulino, Bologna.

Padoa-Schioppa, T. (1985) 'Policy co-operation and the EMS experience', in W.H. Buiter, R.C. Marston, (eds) *International Economic Policy Coordination*, pp. 331–53.

Padoa-Schioppa, T., chairman (1987) *Stability, equity and efficiency*, Report for the Commission of the European Communities, Brussels.

Padoa-Schioppa, T. and Papadia, F. (1984) 'Competing currencies and monetary stability', in R. Masera and R. Triffin (eds), *Europe's Money*, Clarendon Press, London.

Panitch, L. (1976) *Social democracy and industrial militancy: the Labour Party, the trade unions and income policy, 1945–1974*, Cambridge University Press, Cambridge.

Pastor, R. (1980) *Congress and the politics of US foreign economic policy*, University of California Press, Berkeley, CA.

Pavitt, K. and Soete, L. (1982) 'International differences in economic growth and the international location of innovation', in H. Giersch (ed.), *Emerging technologies, economic growth, structural change and employment*, Mohr, Tübingen.

Pavitt, K. (1984) 'Patterns of technical change: towards a taxonomy and theory', SPRU, mimeo.

Pelkmans, J. (1984) *Market integration in the EC*, Martinus Nijhoff, Boston/The Hague.

Pelkmans, J. (1986a) 'Is protection due to financial instability? A sceptical view', published in P. Guerrieri and P.C. Padoan, 1988a.

Pelkmans, J. (1986b) 'The institutional economics of European integration', in M. Cappelletti, M. Seccombe and J. Weiler, (eds), *Integration through law, Europe and the American federal experience*, vol. I, Book 1, Walther de Gruyter, Berlin/New York.

Pelkmans, J. (1987a) 'The new approach to technical harmonization and standardization', *Journal of Common Market Studies*, vol. 25, March.

Pelkmans, J. (1987b) 'The European Community's trade policy towards developing countries', in C. Stevens and J. Verloren van Themaat, (ed.) *Europe and the international division of labour*, EEC and the Third World, a survey, n. 6, Hodder & Stoughton, London.

Pelkmans, J. and Robson, P. (1987) 'The aspiration of the White Paper', *Journal of Common Market studies*, vol. 25.

Petit, P. (1984) 'The origins of French planning: a reappraisal', *Contributions to political economy*, n. 3, pp. 65–84.

Petit, P. (1986) 'Full-employment policies in stagnation: France in the 1980s', *Cambridge journal of economics*, n. 10, pp. 393–406.

Petit, P. (1987) 'The economy and modernisation: an overview', in Gaffney J. (ed.) *France modernization*, Gower, Aldershot.

Pfisterer, H. and Regling, K. (1983) 'Die Rolle der ECU im privaten Bereich-Geringe ökonomische Anreize', in H.E. Scharrer and W. Wessels (eds) *Das Europaische Währungssystem*, Bonn.

Piore, M. and Sabel, C. (1986) *The second industrial divide*, Basic Books, New York.

Pohl, K.O. (1985) 'Deutsche Währungspolitik im Spannungsfeld der internationalen Währungsentwicklung', in *List-Forum*, vol. 13, n. 2.

Porta, A. (1986) 'Evoluzione delle strutture finanziarie e problemi di regolamentazione: recenti tendenze internazionali ed alcune considerazioni sul caso italiano', *Note economiche*, n. 3/4.

Posner, A. (1978) *Italy: dependence and political fragmentation*, in P. Katzenstein (1978).

Posner, M.V. (1961) 'International trade and technical change', *Oxford economic papers*, vol. 13, pp. 323–41.

Putnam, R. (1986) 'Domestic politics, international economics, and Western summitry', 1975–1986, or international co-operation and the logic of "Two-Level Games"', paper prepared for the 1986 meeting of the American Political Science Association.

Putnam, R. and Bayne, N. (1984) *Hanging together: the seven-power summits*, Harvard University Press, Cambridge, Mass.

Randall Henning, C. (1987) *Macroeconomic diplomacy in the 1980s*, Atlantic Institute of International Affairs, Atlantic Paper n. 65.

Robson, P. (1984) *The economics of international integration*, George Allen & Unwin, 2nd edition, London.

Ross, G. (1982) *Unions change and crisis: French and Italian union strategy and the political economy, 1945–80*, George Allen & Unwin, London.

Rotschild, K. (1986) 'Left and right in federal Europe', *Kyklos*, vol. 39, n. 3.

Russo, M. (1986) 'Why the time is ripe', lecture delivered to the Bow Group, House of Commons, London 19 May.

Sachs, J. (1986) 'High unemployment in Europe: diagnosis and policy implications', NBER working paper n. 1830.

Sachs, J. and Wyplosz, C. (1986) 'The economic consequences of President Mitterrand' *Economic Policy*, n. 2.

Salomon, J.J. (1986) *Le gaulois, le cow-boy et le samouraï*, Economica, Paris.

Sandri, S. (1987) 'Financing the partecipazioni statali system in Italy', *Annals of public and cooperative economy*, June.

Sarcinelli, M. (1986) 'The EMS and the international monetary system: towards greater stability', *Banca Nazionale del Lavoro quarterly review*, March.

Sauvy, A. (1984) *Histoire économique de la France entre les deux guerres*, Economica, Paris.

Scharrer, H.E. (1983) 'Der Wechselkurs und Interventiosmechanismus im EWS', in H.E. Scharrer and W. Wessels (eds) *Das Europaische Währungssystem*, Bonn.

Schelling, T. (1960) *The strategy of conflict*, Oxford University Press, London.

Scherer, P.M. (1982) 'Inter-industry technology flows and productivity growth', *Review of economics and statistics*, vol. II.

Schluter, P.W. (1980) 'Der europaische Währungsfonds – ein Modell fur ein stabilitatsorientiertes organ', in H.E. Scharrer and W. Wessels (eds), *Das europaische Währungssystem*, Bonn.

Schluter, P.W. (1984) 'Das wahrungspolitik zusammenarbeit – risiken und chancen für die Geldwert-Stabilität', in R. Hrbek and W. Wessels (eds) *EG-Mitgliedschaft: ein vitales Interesse der Bundesrepublik Deutschland?*, Bonn.

Schmidt, H. Bundeskanzler (1982) 'Beitrage zu einer zwischenbilanz 1982', Deutsche Bundesbank, Auszuge aus Presseartikeln, n. 34, Frankfurt.

Scott, A. (1986) 'Britain and the EMS: an appraisal of the report of the Treasury and the civil service committee', *Journal of Common Market Studies*, March.

Shonfield, A. (1965) *Modern capitalism*, Oxford University Press, London.

Simon, M. (1982) *Models of bounded rationality* MIT Press, Cambridge, Mass.

Simonazzi, A. (1985) 'Crediti all'esportazione e concorrenza internazionale', *Politica economica*, vol. 1, 2.

Snidal, D. (1985a) 'Co-ordination versus prisoners' dilemma: implications for international co-operation and regimes', *American political science review*, vol. 79, n. 4, December.

Snidal, D. (1985b) 'The limits of hegemonic stability theory', *International organization*, vol. 39, n. 4, Autumn, pp. 579–614.

Soete, L. (1981) 'A general test of technology gap trade theory', *Weltwirtschaftliches Archivy*.

Spaventa, L. (1980) 'Italy joins the EMS – a political history', Johns Hopkins University, Bologna Centre, *Occasional paper*, n. 32.

Spaventa, L. (1983) 'Two letters of intent: external crises and stabilization policies: Italy 1973–1977' in J. Williamson (ed.) *IMF conditionality*, Institute for International Economics, Washington.

Spinanger, D. and Zietz, J. (1985) 'Managing trade but mangling the consumer: reflections on the EEC's and West Germany's experience with the MFA', *Kiel working paper*, n. 245, November.

Steinherr, A. (1987) 'The macroeconomics of the ECU: the ECU and the working of the EMS', University of Leuven, mimeo.

Strange, S. (1982) 'Still an extraordinary power: America's role in a global monetary system', in Lombra, Witte (eds) 1982.

Strijker, D. (1986) 'Monetaire compenserende bedragen', LEI-Agricultural Economic Institute, The Hague, n. 338.

Tasgian, A. (1983) *L'imposta e il deposito previo sugli acquisti di valuta e la crisi della lira del 1976*, mimeo.

Tesauro, M. (1986) 'Exchange controls in Italy and possibile reform', in M. Van-heukelen and J. Pelkmans (eds) *European integration of financial markets*, European Institute of Public Administration, Maastricht.

Tharakan, P.K.M. (1985) 'Empirical analysis of the commodity composition of trade', in D. Greenway (ed.) *Current Issues in International Trade*, Macmillan, London.

Thiel, E. (1983) 'Das EWS im internationalen Wahrungssystem-Eine Herausforderung fur die USA?' Aussere Profilierung und innere Konvergenz, in H.E. Scharrer and W. Wessels (eds) *Das europaische Wahrungssystem*, Bonn.

Thiel, E. (1987) 'Europaische Koordinierung und internationale Interdependence – Eine vom Dollar unabhangige europaische Wirtschaftspolitik?', in H.E. Scharrer and W. Wessels (eds *Stabilität durch das EMS? Koordinierung und Konvergenz im europaischen Wahrungssystem*, Bonn.

Thirlwall, A. (1979) 'The balance of payments constraint as an explanation of international growth rate differences', *Quarterly review, Banca Nazionale del Lavoro*, n. 32.

Thirlwall, A. (1983) *Balance of payments theory*, Macmillan, London.

Thompson, W. and Zuk, G. (1983) 'American elections and the international electoral–economic cycle: a test of the hypothesis', *American journal of political science*, n. 3.

Thygesen, N. (1979) 'The emerging EMS, precursors, first steps and policy options', in *EMS*, di R. Triffin, (ed.) Banque National de Belgique.

Thygesen, N. (1979) *Exchange rate experiences and policies of small countries: some European examples of the 1970s*, Princeton Essays in International Finance, n. 136.

Thygesen, N. (1987) *The ECU market*, Lexington Books, Oxford.

Thygesen, N. and Gros, D. (1987) 'The EMS as a framework for European political co-operation: retrospective and prospective', CEPS, Brussels.

Tobin, J. (1987) 'A proposal for international monetary reform', in *Eastern economic journal*, n. 4.

Toma, M. (1982) 'Inflation bias in the Federal Reserve System: a bureaucratic interpretation', *Journal of monetary economics*, vol. 10.

Triffin, R. (1984) 'How to end the world's infession: crisis management or fundamental reforms?', in R. Masera and R. Triffin (eds) *Europe's money*, Oxford University Press, Oxford.

Tsoukalis, L. (1977) *The politics and economics of European monetary integration*, Allen & Unwin, London.

Tsoukalis, L. (1987) 'The political economy of the European monetary system', conference paper prepared for the Interdisciplinary conference on 'The political economy of international macroeconomic policy co-ordination', Andover, Mass.

Ungerer, H., Evans, O., Mayer, T. and Young, P. (1986) *The European Monetary System: recent developments*, International Monetary Fund, Occasional Paper, n. 48, Washington.

Valentini, M. (1986) 'Ciampi scontato', *Mondo economico*, 20 January.

Van Dartel, R. (1983) 'The conduct of the EEC's textile trade policy and the application of Art. 115, EEC', in E. Völker, *Protectionism and the European Community*, Kluwer, Deventer.

Van der Broucke, F. (1985) 'Conflicts in international economic policy and the world recession, a theoretical analysis', *Cambridge journal of economics*, vol. 9, pp. 15–42.

van Ypersele, J. (1983) 'Zur pragmatischen Weiterentwicklung des EWS-ein machbares wie wunschenswertes Programm', in H.E. Scharrer and W. Wessels (eds) *Das europaische Wahrungssystem*, Bonn.

van Ypersele, J. and Koeune, J.C. (1984) *The European Monetary System*, European Perspective, Brussels.

Vernon, R. (1979) 'The product cycle hypothesis in the new international environment', *Oxford bulletin of economics and statistics*, vol. 41.

Vernon, R. (1966) 'International investment and international trade in the product cycle', *Quarterly journal of economics*, vol. 80, pp. 190–207.

Vesperini, J.P. (1985) *L'economie de la France*, Economica, Paris.

Vilar, P. (1974) *Or et monnaie dans l'histoire*, Flammarion, Paris.

Visentini, G. (1985) 'Notes on Italian foreign exchange legislation', in *Capital controls and foreign exchange legislation*, Euromobiliare Occasional Paper, Milan, June.

Wallace, M. (1983) 'Economic stabilization as a public good. What does it mean?', *Journal of post-Keynesian economics*, Winter, pp. 295–302.

Wallich, H.C. (1983) *US Monetary policy in an interdependent world*, University of Princeton, Essays in International Finance, n. 157.

Waltz, K. (1959) *Man, the state and war*, Columbia University Press, New York.

Waltz, K. (1979) *Theory of World Politics*, Addison-Wesley, Reading, Mass.

Whiteley, S. (1983) 'The political economy of economic growth, *European journal of political research*, vol. 11, n. 2.

Woolley, J.T., (1983) 'Political factors in monetary policy', in D. Hodgman, (ed.) *Political economy of monetary policy: domestic and international aspects*, Federal Reserve Bank of Boston.

Woolley, J.T. (1986) in *Monetary politics: the federal reserve and the politics of monetary policy*, Basic Books, New York.

Wyatt, D. and Dashwood, A. (1987) *The substantive law of the EEC*, 2nd edition, Sweet & Maxwell, London.

Zihilstra, J. (1981) 'Central banking with the benefits of hindsight', *The 1981 Per Jacobson Lecture*, Per Jacobson Foundation, Washington.

Zysman, J. (1978) 'The French state in the international economy', in P.J. Katzenstein (ed.) *Between power and plenty*, University of Wisconsin Press.

Zysman, J. (1984) *Government, markets and growth*, Cornell University Press, Ithaca.

INDEX